VOLKSKAPITALISME

*Class, capital and ideology in the development of
Afrikaner nationalism, 1934–1948*

AFRICAN STUDIES SERIES   34

D1427642

BOOKS IN THIS SERIES

VOLKSKAPITALISME

Class, capital and ideology in the development of Afrikaner nationalism, 1934–1948

DAN O'MEARA

Professor Auxiliar, Centro de Estudos Africanos
Universidade Eduardo Mondlane, Maputo

CAMBRIDGE UNIVERSITY PRESS

CAMBRIDGE
LONDON   NEW YORK   NEW ROCHELLE
MELBOURNE   SYDNEY

CAMBRIDGE UNIVERSITY PRESS
Cambridge, New York, Melbourne, Madrid, Cape Town, Singapore, São Paulo, Delhi

Cambridge University Press
The Edinburgh Building, Cambridge CB2 8RU, UK

Published in the United States of America by Cambridge University Press, New York

www.cambridge.org
Information on this title: www.cambridge.org/9780521104678

© Cambridge University Press 1983

First published 1983
This digitally printed version 2009

A catalogue record for this publication is available from the British Library

Library of Congress Catalogue Card Number: 82–9504

ISBN 978-0-521-24285-1 hardback
ISBN 978-0-521-10467-8 paperback

Contents

Contents

Tables

Acknowledgements

The rewriting of an earlier draft was partially funded by a grant to the Southern African Research Program, Yale University, from the National Endowment for the Humanities.

The preparation of this book was eased by the assistance, advice and friendship of a number of people. Tim and Audrey O'Meara were a constant source of support. Kathryn O'Meara gave warmly and unstintingly.

My main intellectual debt lies with a unique group of scholars. Dunbar Moodie first aroused my interest in the Afrikaner economic movement. Despite differences in our approach, his consistent generosity with his time and his own research material has been a rare model of scholarly commitment. Geoff Lamb was an early source of encouragement and advice. I learned a great deal in extended discussions and collective writing with Rob Davies, David Kaplan, Mike Morris and, particularly, Duncan Innes. Stanley Trapido and Charles van Onselen shared with me their knowledge of early Transvaal politics. I am grateful to Martin Legassick and especially Harold Wolpe for many discussions on theoretical and other aspects of this study. Jacques Depelchin's theoretical prodding forced me to refine much of the argument. It will be obvious to the reader that I have drawn heavily on the work of each of these scholars.

Drafts of some chapters were presented at seminars at the University of Dar es Salaam, and the Southern African Research Program, Yale University. I am grateful to the discussants and participants for comments. For detailed comments on an earlier draft, my thanks to Richard Brown, Bill Freund, Philip Corrigan, Peter Gibbon, and again, David Kaplan, Dunbar Moodie and Harold Wolpe.

Finally, without Linzi Manicom's comments and criticisms, editorial eye, assumption of an inordinate share of domestic labour and child care, and, above all, constant support and comradeship, I should never have completed this book.

To them all, my deepest thanks.

DAN O'MEARA

Abbreviations

AB	Afrikaner Broederbond
AHI	Afrikaanse Handelsinstituut (Afrikaans Commercial Institute)
ANC	African National Congress
ANS	Afrikaans-Nasionaal Studentebond (Afrikaans-National Students' Union)
AP	Afrikaner Party
Asokor	Afrikaanse Sake-Ondernemings Korporasie (Afrikaans Business Undertakings Corporation)
Assocom	Associated Chambers of Commerce
AVBOB	Afrikaner Verbond Begrafnis Ondernemings Beperk (Afrikaner League Burial Undertakings Ltd)
Bond	Afrikaner Broederbond (Afrikaner Brotherhood)
Bonuskor	Bonus Beleggings Korporasie (Bonus Investments Corporation)
BOSS	Bureau of State Security
BWBB	Blankewerkers se Beskermingsbond (White Workers' Protection League)
CP	Communist Party (of South Africa)
CNETU	Council of non-European Trade Unions
EI	Ekonomiese Instituut (Economic Institute of the FAK, q.v.)
FAK	Federasie van Afrikaanse Kultuurverenigings (Federation of Afrikaans Cultural Associations)
FCI	Federated Chambers of Industry
fonds	Reddingsdaadfonds (Rescue Action Fund)
FVB	Federale Volksbeleggings (Federal Volks' Investments)
GK	Gereformeerde Kerk (Reformed Church)
G/NP	Gesuiwerde Nasionale Party (Purified Nationalist Party–see note 10, chapter 2)
GPC	Gold Producers' Committee
GWU	Garment Workers' Union
Hervormers	Hervormers organisasie binne die Mynewerkersunie (MWU reform organisation)

HNP	Herenigde Nasionale of Volksparty (Re-united Nationalist or People's Party)
ICU	Industrial and Commercial Workers' Union of Africa
KWV	Ko-operatiewe Wynbouers-Vereniging (Cooperative Viticulturalists' Association)
MP	Member of Parliament
MWU	Mine Workers' Union
NGK	Nederduits Gereformeerde Kerk (Dutch Reformed Church)
NHK	Nederduitsch Hervormde Kerk (Dutch Reformed Church – a separate church from the NGK)
NO	Nuwe Order (New Order)
NP	Nasionale Party (Nationalist Party-see note on translation)
NRT	Nasionale Raad van Trustees (National Council of Trustees)
NURAHS	National Union of Railway and Harbour Servants
OB	Ossewa Brandwag (Oxwagon Sentinels)
OFS	Orange Free State
RARO	Reddingsdaadbond-Amateurolprentorganisasie (RDB Amateur Film Organisation)
RDB	Reddingsdaadbond (Rescue Action Society)
SAAU	South African Agricultural Union
SABRA	Suid-Afrikaanse Buro vir Rasse Aangeleenthede (South African Bureau for Racial Affairs)
Safim	South African Farm Implements Manufacturers (Pty) Ltd.
SALP	South African Labour Party
Sanlam	Suid-Afrikaanse Lewensassuransie Maatskappy (South African National Life Assurance Co.)
Santam	Suid-Afrikaanse Nasionale Trust Maatskappy (South African National Trust Co.)
SAP	South African Party
Sasbank	Suid-Afrikaanse Spaar- en Voorskot Bank (South African Savings and Loan Bank)
TIB	Tegniese en Industriele Beleggings (Technical and Industrial Investments)
TLC	(South African) Trades and Labour Council
TO	Transvaalse Onderwysersvereniging (Transvaal Teachers' Association)
UIF	Unemployment Insurance fund
UP	United South African National Party
VVM	Voorrade Inkopers en Verspreidings Maatskappy (Supplies Purchasing and Distribution Co.)

Glossary

Liberal use is made throughout of Afrikaans terms. A glossary is thus included to assist the reader.

Aandeel Buro: Share Bureau (of the Reddingsdaadbond)
Afrikaans-Nasionaal Studentebond: Afrikaans-National Students' League
Afrikaanse Handelsinstituut: Afrikaans Commercial Institute
Afrikaanse Nasionale Kultuurraad: Afrikaans National Cultural Council
Afrikaans Taal-en Kultuurvereniging: Afrikaans Language and Cultural Association
Afrikaanse Vrouevereniging: Afrikaans Women's Union
Afrikaner Broederbond: Afrikaner Brotherhood
Arbeidsfront: Labour Front (of the Ossewa Brandwag)
bewusmaking: making (economically) conscious
Blanke Werkers se Beskermingsbond: White Workers' Protection League
boer: farmer (a term sometimes also used to describe Afrikaners)
boeredogters: daughters of boers
boereparty: farmers' party
Breë Kerklike Komitee: Broad Ecclesiastical Committee
broedertwis: division between brothers
broer: brother (term of address between Afrikaner Broederbond members)
bywoner: squatter
'Die Burger': The Citizen (daily organ of the Cape Nationalist Party)
Die Doktor: the Doctor (D.F. Malan)
diens: service
'Die Kruithoring': The Powder Flask (organ of the Federal Council of the Herenigde Nasionale of Volksparty)
'Die Transvaler': The Transvaler (daily organ of the Transvaal Nationalist Party)
'Die Vaderland': The Fatherland (Hertzogist daily newspaper)
'Die Volksblad': The People's Paper (organ of the Orange Free State Nationalist Party)
Eeufees: centenary (of the Great Trek)
eie: own, private
Ekonomiese Instituut: Economic Institute (of the Federasie van Afrikaanse Kultuurverenigings)

xii

Ekonomiese Volkskongres: Economic Congress of the Volk

Federasie van Afrikaanse Kultuurverenigings: Federation of Afrikaans Cultural Associations

Federale Volksbeleggings: Federal Volks Investments

fonds: the reddingsdaad fund (q.v.)

geldmag: financial power

Gereformeerde Kerk: Reformed Church

gesuiwerde: purified

Gesuiwerde Nasionale Party: Purified Nationalist Party (see note 10, chapter 2)

handhawing: promotion/assertion/defence (see note 4, chapter 4)

helpmekaar: mutual aid

Helpmekaarsvereniging: Mutual Aid Association

Herenigde Nasionale Party: Re-united Nationalist Party

hereniging: re-union

Herstigte Nasionale Party: Reconstituted Nationalist Party

hervormer: reformer (member of the Hervormingsorganisasie)

Hervormingsorganisasie binne die Mynwerkers Unie: reform organisation within the Mine Workers' Union

Het Volk: The People (an early political party)

hoofleier: leader-in-chief

'Inspan': Span in (journal of the Federasie van Afrikaanse Kultuurverenigings and Reddingsdaadbond)

Kapitaalkragtig: see note 4, chapter 8

Keeromstraat: Keerom Street (location of *Die Burger* office)

kerk: church

Kleinsake Finansieringsmaatskappy: Small Business Finance Company

'Koers': Directions (a journal)

Kommandant-General: Commandant General

kongres: congress

koppie: hill

kultuur: culture

kultuurpolitiek: cultural politics

Nasionale Party: Nationalist Party (see note on translation, p. xv)

Nasionale Pers: National Press

Nasionale Raad van Trustees: National Council of Trustees

Nederduits Gereformeerde Kerk: Dutch Reformed Church

Nederduitsch Hervormde Kerk: Dutch Reformed Church (but separate from the Nederduits Gereformeerde Kerk)

Noodhulpliga: First-aid League

Nuwe Orde: New Order

ons: we/us

oorheesing: domination

oorstrooming: inundation

Oranje Unie: Orange [Free State] Union (an early political party)

Glossary

Ossewa Brandwag: Oxwagon Sentinels
partypolitiek: party politics
platteland: rural areas
Rebellie: the Rebellion of 1914–15
red: see note 1, chapter 8
reddingsdaad: act of rescue
reddingsdaadbeweging: movement for the act of rescue (also used
    synonymously with 'the economic movement')
Reddingsdaadbond: Rescue Action Society
Reddingsdaadfonds: Rescue Action Fund
Republikeinsebond: Republican League
Saambou: Build Together (a building society)
Sakekamer: Chamber of Commerce
samesmelting: fusion
Sappe: members of the South African Party
smelters: fusionists
sowereiniteit-in-eie-kring: (theological doctrine of Divine) sovereignty in
    each sphere
Spoorbond: Railway League
Spoorbondkas: a savings bank established by Spoorbond
Stormjaers: Storm troopers (of the Ossewa Brandwag)
suiwering: purification
Uniewinkels: Union shops
verarming: impoverishment
vereniging: union
verklaring: declaration
volk: see note on translation (p. xv)
volkseenheid: unity of the volk
volksekonomie: volk's economy
volksfront: a front of the volk (national front)
'Volkshandel': Volk's Commerce (journal of the Afrikaanse
    Handelsinstituut)
volkskapitalisme: people's capitalism
volkskongres: congress of the volk
volksleier: leader (in chief) of the volk
Volksparty: People's Party
volksredding: the rescuing of the volk
volksverarming: impoverishment of the volk
Voorrade Inkopers en Verspreidings Maatskappy: Supplies Purchasing
    and Distribution Company
Voortrekker Pers: Voortrekker press
Vryetydsafdeling: Free-time section (of the Reddingsdaadbond)
'Wapenskou': Review of Arms (journal of the Afrikaanse-Nasionaal
    Studentebond)
wins: profit

Note on translation

Unless otherwise stipulated, all translations in the study are mine. The translation of some terms posed problems. The word *volk*, for example, has no direct equivalent in English, and is usually translated as either 'people' or 'nation'. Not only does it imply both these meanings, but, as employed in the nationalist lexicon, the term came to connote both an ethnicity and organic unity not conveyed in either of these paler English terms. Thus except for a few instances where the context indicates that either of the terms 'nation' or 'people' is more appropriate, I have retained the word volk untranslated, to convey the wider meaning.

Other Afrikaans terms encountered in the literature have no direct English equivalent. These are indicated in notes (e.g. n. 4, chapter 4; n. 1 and 4, chapter 8).

Strictly speaking, the Afrikaans *Nasionale Party* should be translated 'National Party'. However, common South African English usage refers to the National*ist* Party, which rendering I have retained.

It is ordained that we [Afrikaners],
insignificant as we are, should be amongst
the first people to begin the struggle
against the new world tyranny of Capitalism.

Jan Christian Smuts, *A Century of Wrong*

The landlady was a mean woman from the Midlands.
I don't mean that coming from the Midlands caused
her meanness. You'll get good people from there,
or from any airt or part of the world. But if
Cockneys or a Siamese are mean or decent, they'll
be mean or decent in a Cockney or Siamese way.

Brendan Behan, *Borstal Boy*

Introduction

> Whilst in everyday life every shopkeeper is well able to distinguish between what somebody professes to be and what he really is, our historians have not yet won this trivial insight. They take every epoch at its word and believe that everything it says or imagines about itself is true.
>
> Karl Marx, *The German Ideology*

The student uprising and general strikes in South Africa in 1976 dramatically focused attention on the growing mass struggles against the apartheid state. Since 1976, these struggles have taken an increasingly anti-capitalist form, and have been supplemented by a slowly escalating guerilla war waged by the military wing of the banned African National Congress. In the midst of the worst recession in the country's history, a new South African Prime Minister came into office in September 1978 claiming that the state confronted a 'total onslaught'.

The simultaneous economic crisis and intensified struggles of the 1970s posed as a central political question the requisite state policies to ensure renewed capitalist prosperity and stability. The ability of the ruling Nationalist Party to effect the necessary reforms became a pressing issue. Much attention was focused on Afrikaner nationalism as a result (e.g. Adam & Giliomee 1979). It is a central contention of this study, however, that the terms of many of the arguments have been miscast, and, in the process, the specific relationship between Afrikaner nationalism and the capitalist state has been misconceived.

The present Nationalist Party (NP) government has been in office since 1948. It regards itself as, and is almost universally acknowledged as, the political representative of the 'Afrikaner volk'. Its explicit ideology is that of Afrikaner nationalism. Its programme is apartheid, or the euphemism currently in use.[1] The capture of office by the NP in 1948 has generally been explained as the victory of the rigid, reactionary and racist ideals of a monolithic 'Afrikanerdom' over the modernising and integrative imperatives of economic development – as the triumph of ideology over the countervailing forces of production and the market economy. This is then extended into a

1

view of the post-1948 Nationalist government as the agent of an 'ethnic revolution' (Adam & Giliomee 1979: 36). Its apartheid policies are seen as external to, but productive of distortions within the otherwise rational and colour-blind operation of market forces, leading both to strains within the economy and acute social dislocation and racial conflict.[2]

This supposed antagonism between apartheid and capitalism has led to a widespread explanation of currently escalating social conflict in South Africa as the product of Afrikaner nationalism. The peculiar vices of Afrikaners – or, in the title of a recent BBC television programme, 'The White Tribe' – are held responsible for the present situation. On Afrikaners alone lies the onus to change. As a recent book put it: 'The great problem for South Africa... is essentially a problem for the Afrikaners, since they hold the power in everything that matters' (de St Jorre 1977:4).

In the face of the gathering political storms of the mid-1970s, and despite widespread demands for reform from powerful sections of the white population – most notably businessmen – the NP government appeared to intensify political repression and harden its apartheid policies. This response was widely seen as evidence of the intransigence of Afrikaner nationalism, retreating in the face of international censure and pressure for change into a narrow, but formidably defended laager, ready to fight to the finish to preserve white supremacy. 'No cracks in the Afrikaner monolith' and 'Afrikanerdom heads for the laager' were typical headlines of the mid-1970s (de St Jorre 1977). They reflected the widespread belief in a monolithic party controlled by the 'super Afrikaners' of the secret Afrikaner Broederbond (hereafter Bond), able to unite the volk behind its implacable position (Wilkins & Strydom 1978).

The open infighting in the NP since the 'Muldergate' imbroglio and the intense conflicts over policy changes introduced by P.W. Botha (O'Meara 1980) somewhat weakened this conventional view of monolithic Afrikaner nationalism. The erosion of support for the NP in the April 1981 general election has undermined it even further.[3] Yet the belief in a system of 'ethnic mobilisation' whose 'secret appeal' lies in providing 'psychological security rather than material benefits' (Adam & Giliomee 1979: 52 and 61), dominates the literature on Afrikaner nationalism.

In recent years, stimulated by the social struggles of the 1970s, a growing body of Marxist literature has challenged such interpretations. This is not the place to detail the now well-known thrust of these critiques, but suffice it to say that they reject the liberal notion of a fundamental contradiction between the racist apartheid policies of Afrikaner nationalism on the one hand and a supposedly inherently colour-blind capitalist economy on the other. On the contrary, despite sometimes deep differences, the various authors have all sought to situate the analysis of the South African social formation squarely within the context of the processes of capital accumulation and the class struggles through which it takes place. In analysing the apartheid phenomenon, much work has been done on the specific material conditions and class struggles of the late 1940s. Yet there remains a gap in this literature. Existing writings have extensively analysed aspects of the process of capital accumulation and the contradictions between class forces which established the material preconditions for the development of the apartheid state after 1948. Yet the existence of such contradictions does not automatically dictate the specific form of their attempted resolution in state policy. It is both mechanistic and undialectical to make a leap from the identification of particular class contradictions to the implementation of apartheid state policies. To do so ignores the vital concrete elements through which the struggle between classes is fought out: organisation and ideology.

The struggle between the exploited and exploiting classes is never simply a question of contending homogenous armies ranged against each other in a battle for supremacy. Rather, it rages at all levels and interstices of society and takes many forms, both spontaneous and organised. However, as Lenin pointed out time and again, the specific forms of organisation (and Gramsci would add, ideology) of various class forces are a vital element in the determination of the manner in which the temporary resolution of class contradictions takes place. Any analysis of the state and state policy must necessarily pose for itself the question of organisation and ideology – of the particular organisational and ideological forms of the collective harnessing of the forces of this or that class or alliance of classes.

For all the recent advances made in the analysis of the South African social formation, it remains to be explained how and why it was the Herenigde Nationalist Party (HNP), under the banner of Afrikaner nationalist ideology, which was able to mobilise and organise specific class forces in a form which temporarily resolved the crisis of the late 1940s on the basis of new state policies. To do so requires coming to terms with the particular place of Afrikaner nationalism in the development of South African capitalism. This question is of much more than historical interest. Its answer provides the basis for an explanation of the current crisis of the capitalist state in South Africa, and as such is of great contemporary political significance.

This study then seeks to explore the material conditions, contradictions and struggles in the development of capitalism in South Africa which gave rise to 'Afrikaner nationalism' as the (differentiated) form in which specific class forces came to be organised in the crucial formative period, 1934 to 1948. In doing so it aims both to remedy a lack in the Marxist literature on South Africa, and to lay to rest the myriad myths in the conventional understanding of Afrikaner nationalism. Following Marx's critique of the German philosophers that 'not only in their answers but also in their questions was there a mystification' (1968c: 29), the analysis proceeds in terms very different from those of the existing literature of Afrikaner nationalism. However, before elaborating the assumptions underlying the approach adopted here, it is necessary briefly to review this literature.

Introduction

Any review of the large and uneven literature on Afrikaner nationalism must necessarily be schematic and gloss over important differences and nuances. Nevertheless, it is possible to identify specific common elements and trends in this literature and examine them critically.

The first point to note is the tendentiousness of the great bulk of this writing. Almost without exception the literature in Afrikaans is written from a nationalist perspective. Much of it self-consciously seeks to construct political/cultural mythology. One leading author has gone so far as to claim divine appointment to this task (Scholtz 1967). This literature views 'Afrikaners' as much more than aggregates of people sharing a common language. Rather, they are seen as the constituents of 'Afrikanerdom' – a discrete, embattled nation, determined through a long history of struggle against external enemies to assert its separate ethnic identity and the social values inherent in the organic unity of the Afrikaner volk.

According to this mythology, 'Afrikanerdom' was shaped by its 300-year struggle to implant itself in the hostile South African soil, its roots constantly under attack from both the primitive inhabitants of the region and the relentless enmity of British imperialism. It was the resolute resistance to all attacks on Afrikaner identity, the assertion of a compelling and exclusive sense of self-identity (*eie*), and the history of suffering occasioned by these struggles, which forged the Afrikaner volk. United by the sense of *eie*, exhibiting an innate 'race consciousness', inspired by a sombre Calvinism, and far removed from the eroding effects of industrialisation, this volk is presumed to have developed for itself an exclusive, but democratic and classless form of social organisation, again undermined by the encircling enemies of British greed and black competition. With the electoral victory of the NP in 1948, the volk emerged from the wilderness. This represented its triumph over these forces of division and a glorious reassertion of the *eie*. Further, the 'cleansing fire' of long struggle, suffering and sacrifice, first tested and then sanctioned the historical mission of Afrikanerdom as the bearer of Christianity and justice in Southern Africa. Behind these ceaseless struggles, the human suffering, the fierce determination of the volk to resist, lurks 'the Hand which guides the fate of nations and men'. Like the prophets of Israel, the ideologists have elevated Afrikanerdom to the special instrument in Africa of their Calvinist God. Divine Will explains Afrikaner history. Divine Will forged Afrikanerdom into a discrete organic unity and converted it into its special instrument.

This at least is the nationalist mythology.[4] As such, it has been extensively criticised. The leading contemporary liberal historian of South Africa has condemned the 'bitter and humourless' mythology of Afrikaner historiography for failing to 'present the facts fairly and draw valid conclusions from them'. The result is a 'diseased' national outlook in which 'the capacity for formulating and pursuing a rational goal becomes vitiated by illusion'

(Thompson 1962:138, 125). Such a critique presumes of course that the work of the critic is untainted by such illusions. Yet, in questioning these myths, many histories in English likewise take for granted the discrete identity and organic unity of 'Afrikanerdom', and simply revise the moral assessment of Afrikaner nationalism from positive to negative. The central assumption here holds that Afrikanerdom (or 'the Boer race') and its associated social attitudes evolved 'in the long quietude of the eighteenth century' (de Kiewiet 1972:17). Isolated on the eighteenth- and nineteenth-century 'frontiers', far removed from the centres of colonial authority and the civilising ideas and influences of the Enlightenment and Industrial Revolution, and trapped in the conservative Calvinist dogma of the Synod of Dort, the migrating pastoralists who fathered the Afrikaner volk are presumed to have developed a chauvinist, backward, individualist *Weltanschauung* (de Kiewiet 1972:17). Honed in long battles against various African societies and regular confrontation with the British, this *Weltanschauung* became rooted in an idea of compulsion, a continuing sense of strife, notions of *eie*, racial hierarchy and a 'paranoid' fear of threats to 'Afrikaner existence' (de Villiers 1971:365). This developed in contradistinction to the blossoming of rationality and individual liberty in the urban centres of exchange. Characterised by the domination of 'non-economic' cultural values over the laws of the market, and a corresponding abhorrence of racial equality, this 'frontier tradition' is seen as the defining characteristic of the Afrikaner nationalism it fostered. The NP victory in 1948 is then taken to represent the triumph of the frontier over the forces of economic rationality – of ideology over economics.[5]

Accounts of Afrikaner nationalism in English have generally been written by people opposed to the NP. Some are openly disparaging in their view of Afrikaners, treating 'the Boer' as a backward, 'paranoid' simpleton, 'out of touch with reality', suffering from 'an inferiority complex' and the gullible tool of manipulating leaders (de Villiers 1971:365–6). One recent study concludes that Afrikaners are 'immature psychopaths' in a sociopathic culture (Lambley 1980:6–32). In the inherited pro-British spirit which inspires much of this writing, a number of non-Afrikaner authors have failed to read, or at least take seriously, what Afrikaners write about themselves (Marquard 1960), giving nationalist historians legitimate cause for complaint.

Not all histories of Afrikaner nationalism suffer from such obvious ideological limitations. However, serious problems remain with those works which do try to explain, rather than simply condemn, Afrikaner nationalism. I would argue that despite many differences at the level of conclusions, both the Afrikaner nationalist and liberal literature share uncritically the same principles of investigation and explanation – they operate within a similar epistemological framework. As a result, the liberal analysis of Afrikaner nationalism remains at the level of counter-ideological history. It presents but a pale, negative mirror-image of the assumptions of Afrikaner nationalist analysis. As this point is fundamental to my critique of this literature, and forms the point of departure of my own analysis, it is necessary to develop it.

Firstly, and most centrally, both Afrikaner nationalist and liberal traditions begin with the same assumption. Without exception their starting point and principal concept is the *a priori*, self-generating category, 'Afrikanerdom' or 'the Afrikaner'. This is taken as given and is subject to no historical, let alone critical, examination. 'Afrikanerdom' defines itself – it is Afrikanerdom 'because this is how Afrikaners see it' (de Villiers 1971: 365) – thus neatly and unquestioningly reproducing the basic tenet of Afrikaner nationalist ideology. The historically always disparate, differentiated and highly fractious Dutch- and Afrikaans-speaking populations are unproblematically reduced to a static and monolithic ethnic group. Here it is necessary to spell out the implications of the almost universal use of the category 'Afrikanerdom', as these impose themselves without exception on the existing literature.

Embedded within the category 'Afrikanerdom' are the questionable premises that all (white) Afrikaans-speakers are automatically integrated into the cross-class organic unity of the volk, instinctively share the presumably innate 'Afrikaner' conservative traditional cultural values, and are always available for ethnic mobilisation in terms of their common 'Afrikaner' interests. Now clearly, at specific junctures of South African history – and particularly from 1948 to 1978 – large numbers of Afrikaans-speakers have been politically mobilised and organised in a unified party on the basis of ethnically exclusive and racist ideologies. This is not in dispute. However, it is equally clear that at other junctures, Afrikaans-speaking whites of various classes have differentially resisted such 'ethnic mobilisation' and have been organised on other (and varying) bases. Moreover, the various Afrikaner nationalist movements in South African history were always constituted by a differentiated and shifting ensemble of social forces – each clearly articulating widely different conceptions and expectations of the 'volk' and what 'its' interests were.

Thus, periods of successful 'ethnic mobilisation' do not simply explain themselves. Nor are they explained by a notion of Afrikanerdom realising 'itself' or its 'civil religion' (Moodie 1975) in the 1948 election. The very concept of 'Afrikanerdom' rests on an extreme form of historicism. Only occasionally is this made explicit. Welsh, for example, states that 'as nearly 80 per cent of Afrikaners support the National Party and its extreme right-wing offshoot, the Reconstituted (Herstigte) National Party, I have used the terms Afrikanerdom and Afrikaners coterminously with Afrikaner nationalism' (1974: 249). This quote is of interest for a number of reasons. Firstly, as Heard's detailed electoral study (1974) makes clear, the first clause of Welsh's statement is probably true only after 1960, and not before. But more significant is the inference drawn from this claim and the subsequent function this inference performs in Welsh's analysis. A perceived aspect of South African politics of the period after 1960 (i.e. support for a political party) is sundered from its historically specific conditions of existence and unproblematically transformed into something else – into a timeless ethnic concept, 'Afrikanerdom'. This is then imposed backwards in linear historical time as a core concept to organise aspects of South African history as far back as the Great Trek of 1836–8. In these terms, the past becomes the inevitable movement to the present. The present explains the past. The development of Afrikaner nationalism becomes one all-embracing, teleological process in which an undifferentiated historical subject, 'nascent Afrikanerdom' (Welsh 1974: 250), realises its self-positing end. The history of the development of Afrikaner nationalism is the simple unfolding of 'what was there in embryo' (de Villiers 1971: 368). It matters little whether the historian invokes Divine Will (Scholtz 1967) or 'ethnicity' (Adam & Giliomee 1979) to explain this process of the self-realisation of 'Afrikanerdom'. In either case, the uncritical use of this historicist ethnic concept necessarily inscribes the result on the process from the very outset. Analysis then becomes the simple description of a predetermined unfolding.

This collapsing of the shifting, contradictory and historically specific bases of support for a political party (the NP, 1948–70) into the timeless ethnic categories of Afrikanerdom and 'the Afrikaner' is not the peculiar failing of Welsh's analysis, but is common to almost everything written on Afrikaner nationalism. Given that the NP has been in power since 1948, this conflation of party and ethnic group has led to the argument that 'Afrikaners' monopolise political power in South Africa, and so constitute a 'ruling ethnic group' or 'political class' (Adam & Giliomee 1979: ix, 36). The very different social categories of common language, ethnic group, political party, government and state are thus commonly used interchangeably, thereby simply obliterating the vastly different areas, levels and types of social action and organisation to which these categories refer.[6] This conflation closes a logical circle in which the South African state is reduced to an Afrikaner entity and seen as a simple instrument in the hands of this 'ruling ethnic group'. The logical confusion apart, what gets concealed in this view is precisely the character of the South African state as a capitalist state. Thus, the current crisis of the capitalist state in South Africa is reduced to a problem of 'the Afrikaner'. In asking 'can South Africa change without destroying itself?', a recent, influential treatise has answered its own question through an exclusive focus on 'the ruling Afrikaner ethnic group' (Adam & Giliomee 1979: ix).

The generalised historicism and logical circularity of liberal historiography likewise reflects the idealism characteristic of such analysis. By this I mean the tendency to treat ideas, ideologies, cultural values, belief systems – in short, all ideational phenomena – not only as 'independent... instances of social action' (Moodie 1975: 295), but also as sufficient explanation of social action. In these terms, historical processes, conjunctures and epochs are explained largely in terms of the expressed ideas, ideologies and values of social actors. In the literature on Afrikaner nationalism, such idealism is occasionally crudely ahistorical, in taking cultural values and ideologies as the unproblematic explanation not only of social processes, but also of themselves. 'Afrikaner traditions' are reified into an unchanging, timeless ethnicity possessed of the same essential 'pre-industrial' meaning and content in, say,

1875, 1915 and 1960. There is no need to explore the material conditions and struggles which produced these values: '*It came about* that the numerically small and widely dispersed Afrikaner people. . . gradually developed a group consciousness which, by the end of the 19th century, had grown into a national cohesion with its own distinct philosophy and way of life' (de Villiers 1971 : 366).

There do exist a few attempts to explore the historical generation, development, transmission and acquisition of the cultural values of Afrikaner nationalism (de Klerk 1975, Giliomee 1975, Hexham 1974, and Moodie 1975). Moodie's book in particular is an extremely well-researched and valuable analysis, the first serious study in English to explore systematically how Afrikaner nationalist ideologists interpreted the world for themselves and the volk. Yet, in common with the other studies cited, Moodie's analysis rests finally on the nationalist conception of Afrikaner culture and an undifferentiated Afrikanerdom. It fails to pose the questions, who were the differential constituents of Afrikanerdom, and what were the conditions and struggles which led to 'the rise of Afrikanerdom'? At best he distinguishes between the ideological 'elite' of the Bond, and the 'ordinary Afrikaners' who came to be mobilised by the visions of the former. The ideological redefinition of Afrikaner nationalism after 1934, the intense divisions of the 1940s and the victory of the NP in 1948 are all explained in terms of the internal political developments of Afrikaner nationalism. Yet, as Moodie now concedes (1980:xiv–xv), social reality cannot really be explained 'purely in terms of the conscious meanings of social actors'. To do so must finally reproduce Afrikaner nationalism's explanation of itself – an explanation which produces its own static and idealist conception of Afrikaner culture as the determining factor of social action. Ideology then becomes a simple elaboration of what is already present in fixed form.

The work of Adam and Giliomee (1979) recognises the need for structural explanations of the emergence of 'ethnic Identities'. However, they rely finally on an extreme form of idealism, arguing that 'psychological security rather than the material benefits attached to it must be seen as the secret appeal of nationalism everywhere' (p. 52). If Afrikaners huddle together because nobody likes them, exactly the same could be said of, say, communists in South Africa. All ideologies provide some form of 'psychological security' and emotional anchorage to those who believe in them. This tells us nothing and begs precisely the most important question – why, and under what conditions do differentiated collectivities of people come to be organised in terms of one ideology rather than another? This Adam and Giliomee are unable to explain, except through the highly circular concept of 'ethnic mobilisation' in which *a priori* 'ethnically organised groups' compete with each other for 'scarce resources' (1979:39).

The liberal critics of Afrikaner nationalism do not generally spell out the theoretical positions underlying their work.[7] None the less they clearly rely on an empiricist theory of knowledge and its assertion of a fundamental

8

theory/facts dichotomy in which the latter are innocent and neutral in a pre-existing givenness. Explanation is derived from the observation, ordering and cataloguing of facts, apparently without the intervention of a theoretical apparatus. In these terms, inadequate and incorrect explanation is attributed either to insufficient research and a failure to gather all the relevant facts (Thompson 1969: 3–6), or to the intervention of a theory (such as Marxism) which does not fit, and therefore distorts, the facts (Moodie 1977; Kuper 1974: 285; Kantor & Kenny 1976). In either case the primacy of facts is asserted outside of, and prior to, theory.

The idealism which permeates this work is but one form of such an empiricist theory of knowledge. As van der Berghe has argued, the primacy of ideology in South Africa is self-evident (1967: 267). Thus the primary terrain on which facts are collected is that of ideas. Social processes are then analysed predominantly in terms of the ideas held by different historical subjects – in this case, the unproblematic 'Afrikanerdom'.

Clearly, as social actors, both individually and collectively, people constitute (or if you like, define, interpret) reality for themselves through ideas, ideologies, values, belief systems, etc. Their actions in reality occur through such ideas. This is not in dispute. However, idealism rests on an unacceptable inference from this proposition to a completely different one which is in no sense axiomatic. Because objective social reality is constituted for people through ideas, idealism draws the conclusion that ideas (or ideologies, cultural values, etc.) explain the processes of social reality. In its most crudely Hegelian form, history is reduced to the movement of ideas (de Klerk 1975).

Whilst cultural values, belief systems, ideologies, etc. are crucial aspects of social reality, in no sense do such ideational phenomena constitute sufficient explanation either of reality or of themselves. For, as Wolpe has cogently put it:

> The failure to examine the changing, non-ideological conditions in which specific groups apply and therefore interpret and therefore modify their ideologies, results in treating the latter as unchanging [and undifferentiated – D.O.'M.] entities. By simply ascribing all action to generalised racial beliefs, prejudices or ideologies, the specific content of changing social relations and the conditions of change become excluded from analysis (1971: 101).

There does exist a body of literature on Afrikaner nationalism which seeks to go beyond such teleological and idealist circularity, namely, that operating within one or other model of fascism. There are generally two streams of such explanation. The first is broadly derived from the analysis produced by the Third International, and concentrates particularly on the racial themes in the perceived South African variant of fascism (Bunting 1969; South African Communist Party n.d.; Simons & Simons 1969; Slovo 1976). The second employs later Marxist theories of fascism, particularly influenced by the work of Poulantzas (1974) and Simson (1980). Both streams operate within the conceptual framework of class and class struggle, generally explaining

Afrikaner nationalism and its racial policy as the survival of pre-industrial relations under capitalism (Simons & Simons 1969) and/or as an alliance between the petty bourgeoisie and a fraction of 'big capital' leading to the hegemony of monopoly capital (Simson 1980). Yet there remain problems with both streams of explanation.

The first variant generally employs the term 'fascism' as a descriptive device rather than an analytical concept. Bunting, for example, offers no explicit definition of fascism and seems to regard the South African variant as an unproblematic combination of extreme racism and brutal repression. Here the concept of fascism operates by analogy to refer to the racist policies of the Afrikaner nationalist government. Great stress is placed on the similarity between statements made by the leaders of German and Italian fascism, and the pronouncements of the various spokesmen of Afrikaner nationalism. Explanation proceeds by elision rather than an analysis of the material conditions and struggles which produced such pronouncements. This leads Bunting in particular into idealist explanations.

The 1962 Programme of the South African Communist Party followed the Comintern in defining (South African) fascism as 'an open and terrorist dictatorship of the most reactionary and racialist section of the ruling class' (n.d.: 3) Although the relationship is not clearly explicated, this dictatorship is complemented by monopoly, as 'real power is in the hands of the monopolists who own and control the mines, the banks, the finance houses, most of the farms and major industries'. Their rule is maintained in a system of 'internal colonialism' which combines the 'worst features both of imperialism and of colonialism within a single national frontier [and] which determines the special nature of the South African system' (n.d.: 3 & 28).

The theory of internal colonialism in which white colonisers dominate and exploit the black colonised under a fascist dictatorship clearly situates the exploitation and oppression of black people in South Africa within a matrix of monopoly capitalist interests. Yet, I would argue, it rests finally on a racial polarity, and as such is a descriptive device rather than a theoretical concept. The analysis treats class on the one hand and race on the other as independent factors in South African history. The task is then to assign relative weight to each. The most recent elaboration of the theory acknowledges that as a 'useful shorthand' it is 'based on analogy' to deal with the obviousness of 'immediately perceived reality'. Here again, the primacy of race is taken as 'obvious' – that is, given by the empirical world (Slovo 1976: 118, 132). This begins at the wrong level and again begs the most important question. For Marxist analysis, the starting point is not the independence of 'racial factors', but the relations of production:

> It is always the direct relationship of the owners of the conditions of production to the producers . . . which reveals the innermost secret, the hidden basis of the entire social structure, and with it the political form of the relationship of sovereignty and dependence, in short, the corresponding specific form of the state. This does not prevent the same economic basis – the same from the

standpoint of its main conditions – due to innumerable empirical circumstances, natural environment, racial relations, external historical influences etc, from showing infinite gradations in appearance, which can be ascertained only by analysis of the empirically given circumstances (Marx 1971: 791–2).

The task is, then, to analyse the historical contradictions and processes of struggle around the development of capitalism through which these relations of production came to take the form primarily (though not exclusively) of racial categories.

More recent theories of fascism in South Africa draw heavily on the work of Poulantzas. This theorisation of fascism as 'an exceptional capitalist state form' is presented as a series of watertight social laws about the character of class struggle, the crisis confronting monopoly capital, and the alliances formed by the petty bourgeoisie (Simson 1980: 14–15). Apart from the damage this does to the historical variants of fascism,[8] these rigid formulations tend to produce what may be termed verificationist analysis. The first analytical step erects a model of fascism. Subsequent enquiry is directed towards gathering empirical proof of South Africa's fit into the model, rather than an investigation of the historical specificity of the South African social formation. The real comparative insights gained through the use of the concept of fascism do not compensate for the lack of historical specificity, nor, in my view, really extend the theoretical understanding of the South African social formation in general, and Afrikaner nationalism in particular. For these reasons it is not used in this study.

SOME BASIC ASSUMPTIONS

How then does the approach of this study differ from those outlined above? Firstly, it is assumed at the most basic level that 'we cannot judge such a period of transformation by its own consciousness: on the contrary, this consciousness must be explained from the contradictions of material life' (Marx 1968b: 182). The analysis presented here begins with broad, and changing, sets of social relations, contradictions and struggles at given historical conjunctures. It does so in order to answer the question why specific but differentiated collectivities of social agents, incorporated in specific but differing social conditions, came to be collectively mobilised in a particular historical conjuncture in terms of an ethnic ideology of Afrikaner nationalism rather than one or other of the competing ideologies of the period ('South Africanism', socialism, etc.). In doing so, particular emphasis is placed on the changing forms of differentiation of such social forces and the differences and conflicts between them. A constant theme is how the shifting constituent forces in the Afrikaner nationalist alliance were differentially affected by changing social conditions, and the implications of such changes for the nationalist alliance.

Thus the approach adopted here seeks to explain the development of Afrikaner nationalism from 1934 to 1948 through locating Afrikaans-speakers in the context of the social relations, conditions, contradictions and struggles consequent upon capitalist accumulation in South Africa. It is particularly concerned with what are seen as the (differing) real conditions of existence of Afrikaans-speakers of differing social classes – that is, with the ensemble of varying and changing economic, social, political and ideological relations in which they are differentially incorporated. The study seeks then to explore the changing ideological matrices which arose out of such conditions to constitute social reality for these differentiated collectivities – ideological matrices which form the lived and imaginary relation with such real conditions of existence.

It is perhaps necessary to spell this out a little more to meet the possible query of how an apparently 'ethnic' phenomenon such as Afrikaner nationalism can be explained through historical materialism with its emphasis on class. Does not such a Marxist approach either distort the facts or fail to take account of certain key facts, as various authors argue (Kuper 1974; Moodie 1977; Adam & Giliomee 1979)?

The problem of ideology is far from settled in Marxist theory. Indeed it remains the terrain of intense debate (Laclau 1977). Marx's celebrated claim that 'it is not the consciousness of men which determines their being, but, on the contrary, their social being which determines their consciousness' (1968b: 181) has often prompted a crude economic reductionism. More pertinently, however, it embodies the assumption that the ideas people hold about their world are not mere abstract formulations plucked from the air. Rather, for Marx, both the way in which people experience the world, and the ideas they derive from experience, are a function of the way the world actually is.[9] There is thus an (objective) experiential basis for all (subjective) cognitive categories, such as those of ideology. This implies firstly that if (as Marx argued) ideologies are in some way deceptive, and ideological categories are inadequate representations of reality, such mystification and fetishisation are not simply a question of faulty perception on the part of those who hold to such an ideology. On the contrary, given that such perception is based on experience of the objective nature of the way the world is, the inadequacies of ideology lie in the character of experience itself, as it is shaped by objective 'real underlying relations'. Thus the illusory or 'misrepresented' nature of ideology as a form of cognition must derive from the way in which the world, or reality, presents itself to experience, and not simply from inadequate experience of these forms. All this presumes, secondly, that the categories of ideology, though in some ways partial and misrepresentative forms of cognition, are not entirely inadequate. They must allow people to make sense of their experiences of reality and provide the framework for them to formulate courses of action in a way which enables them to survive and function as social beings. If they did not, such ideological categories would rapidly be vitiated by experience.[10]

Thus, if ideologies are partially adequate but misrepresented forms of cognition of the real world, the source of such misrepresentation remains to be established. As representations of direct experience which enable people to constitute reality for themselves, the categories of ideology are essentially practical, and arise out of the experience of everyday life. They begin with 'what is given'. However, the everyday experience of 'what is given' remains partial. Such everyday experience is neither the same as, nor necessarily simultaneously evokes, the conditions of existence of what is given – that is, the ensemble of material conditions, social relations and contradictions which make that kind of everyday experience possible.

To illustrate with a simple example drawn from everyday experience in South Africa. A black man wanting to travel from the outskirts of any city to its centre would have to wait for the arrival of a bus reserved for blacks. Even if five empty buses for whites passed him by, he would not be allowed to board them. At the everyday level he would experience this as yet another instance of white racism. It would confirm his probable interpretation of South Africa as a pervasively racist society, structured by white power and privilege. Now at the level of direct everyday experience, such racial categories of explanation adequately correspond to every black person's daily experience and provide a framework within which they can formulate courses of action to survive. However, such a common daily experience of intense racial discrimination is not the same as, and does not necessarily simultaneously evoke, an experience of the full ensemble of conditions which make such an experience both possible and common – that is, *inter alia*, the consolidation of capitalist production in a period of monopoly, the monopolisation of the means of production in the hands of white capitalists, the dispossession of African producers, etc.

Thus, if ideologies arise out of everyday experience and mirror and guide such experience in both a partially adequate yet misrepresented way, they do not adequately represent the conditions of existence of such everyday experience. Here is the source of the illusory character of ideology. The analysis of ideology then should not fall into the same trap by remaining at the level of the 'what is given' of everyday experience. Rather, it should seek to penetrate beyond the given to establish, firstly, the ensemble of prevailing underlying conditions which make the 'what is given' of everyday experience possible, and secondly, the forms and trajectory of social struggles which lead such conditions of existence to assume one ideological form rather than another.

Marxist theory identifies the relations of production as the primary (but not sole) condition of existence of ideology. As Marx argued: 'It is, in reality, much easier to discover by analysis the earthly kernel of the misty creations of religion than to do the opposite, i.e. to develop from the actual given relations of life the forms in which these have been apotheosised. The latter method is the only materialist, and therefore the only scientific one' (1976: 494). In these terms, an analysis of ideology must begin with the historical development of capitalist production relations – the concrete processes of class formation and class struggle, and the political and ideological forms these took.

To begin at this level is to insist that classes are neither serried ranks of homogenous individuals, nor are they immaculately conceived. Rather, as heterogeneous collectivities, classes are fathered in struggle. Born under specific historical conditions, and into and as a result of particular struggles in concrete social formations, classes carry their birthmarks with them as defining characteristics. In the historical processes of class formation, the various agents of the same class are incorporated in varying sets of social relations and are subject to differing conditions and pressures. They undergo differential experiences, engage in differing struggles and form widely differing mental conceptions of these experiences. Thus, for example, the process of proletarianisation 'frees' producers from their means of production and means of labour, transforming them into wage labourers. But it does so unevenly. Peasants on the one hand and urban petty commodity producers on the other may well finally end up as members of the same (working) class. Yet they travel there by very different economic, political and ideological routes. In the process they are subject to very different economic pressures, are engaged in widely divergent struggles and forms of political organisation, and form varying cultural and ideological conceptions of the processes involved. They carry with them, as an integral part of their (now proletarian) existence, these different (and often contradictory) conceptions and representations of their different experiences. Such conceptions and representations provide the cultural and ideological framework within which the new position is experienced, interpreted and mediated.

Thus the very process of class formation itself – the particular ways in which capitalist relations of production are established in class struggle – gives rise to divergent ideological and organisational forms through which the class struggle is fought out. This is surely the import of Marx's famous declaration: 'Men make their own History, but they do not make it just as they please; they do not make it under circumstances chosen by themselves, but under circumstances directly encountered, given and transmitted from the past. The tradition of all the dead generations weighs like a nightmare on the brain of the living' (1968a : 95). If analysis begins at this level, then, ideology is neither reduced to a simple 'superstructural' reflex directly readable from 'the economy', nor to a deliberate mystification of real relations manufactured with manipulative intent in the minds of capitalists or bourgeois politicians (e.g. Rich 1977). Rather, ideology is seen as an objective systematised representation of social relations embodied in real material institutions. As such it has a real determinate presence.

In this conception then, the ideas, the mental images, the systems of representation which social agents hold of the material world form a vital part of the processes of social reality. As both products and representations of material reality and struggle, ideologies constitute the system of representation through which various collectivities of social agents define for themselves the parameters and limits of social interaction (class struggle) and so mediate their positions within that process of class struggle. As such, ideologies form the lived and imaginary (i.e. ideational) relation with their real conditions of existence – the ideational forms of representation through which the economic, social and political relations and contradictions are lived and fought out by men and women. As ensembles of past and present practices, and comprised of contradictory and differentiated elements, ideologies ideationally embody their conditions of existence in a partial but misrepresented way. The particular and varying forms of such embodiment can only be shown through concrete analysis.

However, before undertaking such concrete analysis two further aspects should be stressed. Firstly, as Gramsci pointed out in a slightly different context (1971:197), the general term 'ideology' encompasses at least two levels: the 'scholarly' or 'literary' on the one hand, and the 'practical' or 'popular' on the other. At the 'literary' level, ideology appears as the product of intellectuals – as a systematised and apparently non-contradictory set of ideas making up a coherent world-view. The 'popular' level of ideology refers to the often contradictory forms of popular consciousness in and through which bodies of people act socially.

This distinction between the literary and popular levels of ideology poses the question of the relationship between the two levels. What unites, say, the social theory of Parsons (literary level) with pop music, as elements of an ideological discourse with the same class connotation? To answer this question it is necessary to point to a second aspect of ideology – that which Althusser has termed the 'interpellation' or constitution of subjects. By this is meant the way in which ideologies transform individuals as the bearers of objective structures into subjects – into social agents with a defined social role:

> Ideology 'acts' or 'functions' in such a way that it 'recruits' subjects among the individuals (it recruits them all) or 'transforms' the individuals into subjects (it transforms them all) by the precise operation of interpellation or hailing, and which can be imagined along the lines of the most common everyday police (or other) hailing: 'Hey you there . . .' (Althusser 1971:162)

Different ideologies interpellate different subjects. Thus, for example, both the literary and popular forms of one ideology may hail individuals as 'Hey there, you Afrikaner', whilst in a different ideology the same individual may be hailed (or constituted) as a different subject: 'Hey you there, fellow worker'. In this conception, ideology is the means through which individuals live out their relation with their real conditions of existence 'as if they themselves were the autonomous principle of determination of that relation'. The mechanism of this 'characteristic inversion' (Laclau 1977:100) is interpellation. Thus, that which constitutes the unifying principle of an ideological discourse – that which unites the social theory of Talcott Parsons and the pop music of the Abba group as part of a common ideological discourse with the same class connotation – is the subject interpellated and thus constituted through this discourse. The significance of this stress, firstly on the distinction between the

15

literary and popular forms of ideology and secondly on the interpellation of subjects, will become clear in chapter 5.

This study then operates at two levels of analysis. Firstly, it seeks to analyse the specific contradictions of and struggles around the development of capitalism in South Africa which gave rise to the highly differentiated phenomenon 'Afrikaner nationalism' as one of the ideological and political forms of struggle. It concentrates on the crucial formative period from 1934–1948. As here conceived, 'Afrikaner nationalism' is an historically specific, often surprisingly flexible, always highly fracturated and differentiated response of various identifiable and changing class forces – in alliance – to the contradictions and struggles generated by the development of capitalism in South Africa. Yet this characterisation is still inadequate. Afrikaner nationalism was more than a passive response to class struggles. It developed as one of the organisational and ideological forms through which these struggles were fought out.

Existing accounts have so posed their questions that the focus has been placed almost exclusively on the party political and ideological dimensions of Afrikaner nationalism. In doing so, they have defined out of consideration, or relegated to a peripheral position, perhaps the most important aspect of the development of Afrikaner nationalism between 1934 and 1948 – the so-called 'economic movement'.[11] The second level of analysis of this study, then, involves a detailed examination of this neglected aspect of Afrikaner nationalism. The 'economic movement' refers to an organised attempt by specific class forces after 1934 to secure a base for capital accumulation in the industrial and commercial sectors of the economy. Put another way, specific petty-bourgeois groups sought to transform themselves into an industrial and commercial bourgeoisie utilising a broad set of organisational, ideological and political means to mobilise mass support from Afrikaans-speakers of other classes for this attempt. As here conceived, the economic movement provided the core around which the Afrikaner nationalist class alliance developed in the years 1934 to 1948 (and indeed after 1948). In effect, it is argued, it was within and through the economic movement that this alliance was first forged, thereby making possible its elaboration at a political level by the NP. Thus, an investigation of this economic movement lays bare the character and structure of Afrikaner nationalism as a shifting class alliance; it makes comprehensible the complex ideological struggles and the development and transformation of nationalist ideology during these years; and it provides the basis for an understanding of the development of the various forms of political organisation of these class forces.

Taking these two levels of analysis together, this study seeks to answer the question, how various class forces came to organise themselves to pursue particular interests vis-à-vis other class forces under the banner of a differentiated nationalist ideology. It is divided into five parts. Part I examines how the particular place South Africa occupied in the capitalist world system gave rise to specific but differing barriers to the accumulation of capital during the Great Depression. This led to the political and ideological reorganisation of the capitalist class and the emergence of the 'purified' NP as an alliance between specific agricultural capitals and the Afrikaans-speaking petty bourgeoisie. Part II explores the reorganisation of this petty bourgeoisie in the Afrikaner Broederbond, together with its ideological development and areas of struggle, leading to cooperation with specific capitals to organise the Afrikaner economic movement. In Part III are analysed the politics, organisation and ideology of the economic movement in the 1940s, to assess its particular place within the development of Afrikaner nationalism. Part IV traces the accumulation of Afrikaner capital in the 1940s, while Part V analyses the class struggles which led to the election of the NP government in 1948 and concludes with a brief assessment of the development of the Afrikaner nationalist class alliance after 1948.

Part I

The Great Depression and the collapse of Hertzog Afrikaner nationalism

1

The Depression and the class basis of the Nationalist Party

During the years 1933 to 1934, the differential impact of the Great Depression on various branches of capitalist production precipitated significant party political realignments in South Africa. Commonly referred to as 'fusion', this local political and ideological reorganisation of various class forces reflected the economic, political and ideological restructuring of capitalism internationally. The early 1930s marked the climax to an extended period of deep crisis for imperialism.[1] Notwithstanding a temporary economic upswing from 1924 to 1929, the long stagnation in the accumulation of capital since 1913 culminated in the Great Depression of 1929 to 1932. These were years of deep social ferment. Capitalist rule was shaken by the 1917 Russian revolution and the revolutionary situation throughout Europe between 1918 and 1923. Even following the reconsolidation of bourgeois rule, in many leading capitalist countries combative and well-organised working-class parties were transforming the character of traditional politics. This widespread combination of protracted economic difficulties and intensified class struggles weakened the hold of traditional bourgeois ideology over all classes. The drawn-out ideological crisis of the 1920s – most obvious in the German Weimar Republic, but present to varying degrees in all the major capitalist states – was particularly significant in undermining traditional class alliances, giving rise to new political alignments and intense ideological conflict.

Economically, the resolution of this crisis occurred on the basis of a significant restructuring of capital both nationally and internationally. Particularly important here was the general trend towards the reorganisation of all sectors of capitalist production on a more capital-intensive basis under increasing monopoly and cartelised control. This permitted both the introduction of new technologies and an effective reduction of labour costs. Large-scale rearmament programmes undertaken by the leading imperialist powers provided the crucial *via media* out of the economic crisis. This national and international restructuring of capital ushered in a period of heightened competition and conflict between the major imperialist countries which led ultimately to the Second World War.

Such economic reorganisation was made possible by important shifts in bourgeois politics and ideology and and significant changes in the form of the capitalist state. Most notably this period saw the full development of the interventionist state to secure the necessary economic, political and ideological conditions for the dominance of monopoly capital and to ensure its profitable operation. The specific forms of these interventionist states, their ideological character, the class alliances on which they rested and the nature of political organisation within them ranged from fascism in Italy, Germany and Japan, through the 'National Government' in Britain to the New Deal in the USA. Yet despite this variety of state forms, most reflected sharp break with the traditional alignments and forms of organisation of bourgeois politics.

This generalised crisis of imperialism had its echo in South Africa. In the 1929 elections the NP under General J.B.M. Hertzog secured an absolute parliamentary majority. The Nationalists had previously governed from 1924 in a coalition – known as 'the Pact' – with the Labour Party. This 1929 triumph was the last ever independent victory for the NP. At the height of the Depression, in February 1933, Prime Minister Hertzog overrode vociferous objections from a powerful minority in his party and formed a new coalition government with the South African Party (SAP), led by his political arch-rival, General Jan Christian Smuts. In June 1934, the majority of each of the two coalition parties 'fused' to form the United Party (UP). Opposition elements in each of the coalition parties drew back from 'fusion' to organise themselves in the pro-imperialist Dominion Party and the Gesuiwerde (purified) Nationalist Party (hereafter G/NP).

Fusion transformed the party political and ideological organisation of specific class forces in South Africa. It temporarily resolved the political crisis of the Depression, and led to state intervention to effect crucial economic reorganisation. From the viewpoint of this study, fusion marks a fundamental break and turning point in the development of Afrikaner nationalism. The 'Afrikaner nationalism' which developed after 1934 differed markedly in its class basis, ideological orientation and organisational structures from the pre-1934 varieties. The prevailing view which presents *gesuiwerde* Afrikaner nationalism as the continuation of a 'pure' nationalist tradition fundamentally obscures its development at each of these three levels. In order to grasp the pattern of development of Afrikaner nationalism over the following four decades, it is essential that this break-up of the old NP and the general political realignment of class forces in South Africa be correctly interpreted. Given the crucial position of agricultural capital in Afrikaner nationalism and its central role in the fusion crisis, such an explanation should be situated in an examination of aspects of the development of capitalist agriculture in South Africa, the political struggles around it, and the character of the NP.

CAPITALIST AGRICULTURE AND THE STATE

The years 1870 to 1920 saw the transition to capitalist production in South African agriculture. Its particular path was one of transformation 'from above'. Through a process of protracted rural class struggle, both the large and small estates of white *rentier* landlords were largely transformed into capitalist farms, whilst the rent-paying, but economically relatively independent, African peasants were almost universally reduced to wage labourers and/or labour-tenants. The state played a decisive role in the process.

This broad characterisation should not hide the fact that this process of rural transformation was marked above all by its extreme unevenness. In the period under review there were wide regional and sectoral variations in the character of farming, the production relations and labour processes involved, the technical and organic compositions of capital, the market conditions – in short, extremely wide disparities in the levels of development of capitalist agriculture. These differences had important effects on the forms of political and ideological organisation of white farmers.

By the end of the nineteenth century, capitalist production was firmly taking hold of agriculture in the self-governing British colonies of the Cape and Natal. Here agricultural commodities were produced primarily for export – wool, wine and deciduous fruits in the Cape, sugar in Natal. The economic interests of Cape and Natal farmers were thus firmly meshed in the nexus of imperialist trade. In other ways too they were dependent on British imperialism. Firstly, through the colonial conquest of African pre-capitalist societies and then through a gathering legislative assault on the economic independence of the African peasantry, coupled with a great many labour measures, the colonial state played the crucial role in securing from above the conditions of accumulation for such agriculture (Murray 1979: 12–46). British imperialism was thus viewed by most agricultural capitalists of the Cape and Natal as a pre-condition of their existence. However, significant differences developed in the political and ideological orientation of farming interests between the two colonies.

After 1880, the predominantly Afrikaans-speaking farmers of the Cape were organised through the Afrikaner Bond (Afrikaner League) in a cautious contradictory alliance with merchant and mining capital. This fell apart between 1895 and 1902 and, largely as a result of the Anglo-Boer War, a mild form of cultural nationalism emerged at the Cape, dominated by the Bond and the various language movements (Davenport 1966). When the Cape section of the NP was formed in 1915, it quickly won support from most branches of Cape agriculture – though in some of the wheat-farming areas there was strong support for the SAP.[2]

The British settlers who farmed the sugar plantations of Natal, on the other hand, developed a colonial jingoism worthy of Rudyard Kipling. Following the union of the four colonies in 1910, they supported the ultra-imperialist Unionist Party. When the Unionists merged with Smuts' SAP in 1921, they gave the SAP their grudging backing. Yet a strong Natal separatist movement mushroomed during the 1920s. It was based on powerful sugar interests, determined to maintain the cosy relationship with Britain (and the high preferential rates Natal sugar enjoyed on the British market) (Nicholls 1961: Part 2).

The situation in the former Boer republics of the Orange Free State (OFS) and the Transvaal was more complex. Prior to 1870, 'traditional' Boer pastoralism in these regions was based mainly on the extraction of surplus in the form of rent (in kind and labour) from African tenants on the large farms of Boer landlords. The opening up of the diamond fields in 1870, and the Transvaal goldfields in 1886, stimulated a change in Boer farming, leading to new struggles between Boer landlords and African peasants.

In the OFS, Boer landlords slowly began to produce agricultural commodities, particularly maize, for the huge market provided by the diamond fields. Simultaneously, a relatively prosperous African peasantry developed in the OFS, also marketing its surplus product. Much of this peasant production rested on a form of share-cropping on white farms, known as 'farming on the half'. In the last decades of the nineteenth century a major rural class struggle developed in the OFS between this African peasantry and the Boer landlords, who were turning to commodity production (Bundy 1972).

In the Transvaal, the growing differentiation of the Boer community was exacerbated by the impact of goldmining after 1886. By the mid-1890s the Boer population was divided into three distinct socio-economic groups. Large, *rentier* landlords or 'notables' (Trapido 1978) dominated the Boer state. In the absence of well-defined markets in land, labour and capital most notables shunned commodity production, finding it more remunerative to have rent-paying African squatters on their large landholdings. Within this group a weak impulse towards the development of commodity production did spring up around such 'progressive' figures as Louis Botha and Piet Joubert – who provided the focus of Boer opposition to Kruger's government. However, before the outbreak of the Anglo-Boer War in 1899, commodity production in Transvaal agriculture remained extremely underdeveloped, and most foodstuffs for the mining market were imported.

The largest number of Boers fell into the second group of smaller landowners, also living off the rents of (far fewer) African tenants. Boer politics were marked by sharp struggles between the notables and smaller landlords. The latter succeeded in enacting the Plakkers Wet (squatting law) of 1887, amended in 1895. This sought to secure a stable source of rent for smaller landowners by limiting the number of African tenant families on any farm to five – thereby depriving the notables of much of their source of income. Such was the notables' domination of the Boer state, however, that the Wet was never effectively implemented. With the consolidation of goldmining, thousands of Boers either sold their farms or themselves went prospecting. By the mid-1890s, almost half the surveyed farms in the Transvaal were owned by absentee landlords, either notables or, increasingly, mining companies (Bleloch 1901:395). This intensified the pressure on land and the shortage of African labour. A relatively large and growing group of landless Boers developed after 1886. These either squatted as tenants (the so-called *bywoners*) of Boer landlords, or drifted to the mining centres to swell the army of unemployed whites.

Thus, although commodity production was developing, in both the former Boer republics the prevailing agrarian property relations acted as barriers to the development of fully capitalist production in agriculture. On the one hand, Boer landlordism was based on the extraction of rent from an African peasantry, rather than on the production of commodities. The African peasantry, on the other hand, though now subject to increasing economic pressures, still largely retained their means of production and hence a relative economic independence. The Boer landlord class lacked the strength to effect the transformation in property relations necessary to establish capitalist production. The impetus to such transformation came from outside Boer agriculture, through the profound effects of the Anglo-Boer War of 1899 to 1902. Yet the trajectory in the two republics was uneven and had differential political effects.

During the Anglo-Boer war there were widespread seizures of Boer land by African peasants. These were rapidly overturned, after the Peace Treaty of Vereniging, by special Boer commandos, armed for the purposes by their erstwhile British enemies (Trapido 1975). The colonial state thus intervened decisively to enforce the property rights of Boer landlords over African peasants. Hereafter the transformation of agriculture in the former Boer republics was a clear priority of colonial administrative policy. Numerous measures were introduced to facilitate the development of commercial agriculture (Marks & Trapido 1979). Their combined effect was to consolidate the dominance of larger landowners, now emerging as capitalist farmers. A number of aspects of this process are noteworthy.

British scorched earth policy during the war had devastated Boer agriculture. Approximately 30,000 homesteads were burned down, and livestock and crops destroyed. The herds of OFS Boers were reduced by over 50 per cent, involving the loss of more than half a million cattle and some three and a half million sheep. In the Transvaal, some 75 per cent of Boer livestock was lost (Breytenbach 1949:46). Thousands of *bywoners* and small landlords could no longer survive and were driven off their land. In the immediate post-war years most Boer landlords were able to survive only by populating their farms with ever larger numbers of cultivating African tenants – in many cases driving off Boer *bywoners* to accommodate them (Trapido 1978:50–2). In many areas this led to a significant shift from the pastoralism traditional in Boer farming to arable production, primarily of maize. Moreover, after the immediate post-war crisis had been weathered, many larger landlords now began to shift from *rentier* to commercial production. The long-delayed payments of war reparations to the Boers were secured only by those who had managed to cling to their land. The introduction of landbanks in the Transvaal in 1907 and in the OFS in 1908 made capital available to those with security in land. By 1908, in both former Boer republics the larger landowners, who had long blocked anti-squatting legislation as a threat to their rent, were now in the forefront of those demanding measures to remove African tenants from their land (Keegan 1978; Moodie 1980), thus freeing it for commercial production. This had the active support of the British colonial administration, which viewed all tenancy arrangements as an obstacle to the development of commercial agriculture and sought to replace them with wage labour (Marks & Trapido 1979). In practice, in line with the recommendations of the 1905 Native Affairs Commission, a widespread system of labour tenancy evolved as a transitional form of wage labour. This attempt of landlord and state to transform African peasants into wage labourers led to a gathering assault on all forms of African access to land in the northern provinces. It culminated in the 1913 Land Act, forbidding African land ownership outside delimited 'native reserves' covering but 8 per cent of the total area. The Land Act finally undermined large-scale access to the means of production and began a process of rapid proletarianisation of African producers.

The development of capitalist production in agriculture also accelerated the proletarianisation of white petty-commodity producers.[3] This rural impoverishment of large numbers of white farmers produced large-scale migration to the cities. By the 1920s an annual average of 12,000 whites was leaving the rural areas, creating a vast army of white urban unemployed, known as 'poor whites'. The 1932 Carnegie Corporation Commission blamed this 'poor white problem' directly on the development of capitalist agriculture. It 'conservatively' estimated the number of these unfortunates at 300,000, out of a white population of just over one and a half million (Part III, 217–22). Though the largest absolute number of 'poor whites' was found in the Cape Province, by 1932 the rate of such rural impoverishment and proletarianisation was most rapid in the swiftly changing rural areas of the Transvaal. The uneven development of capitalist agriculture in the north thus produced a rapid differentiation of the Afrikaans-speaking rural communities, as some were driven into penury and others began successfully to emerge as capitalists. Once again, this had differential political and ideological effects in the northern provinces.

In the Transvaal, following the Anglo-Boer war, emerging capitalist farmers led by the Boer generals Louis Botha and Jan Smuts, dominated the newly established Het Volk (The People) party (Garson 1966). They were the real beneficiaries of the responsible government granted by the Liberal Party administration in 1906. As capitalist production took hold of Transvaal agriculture, its major market was provided by the mines. Political co-operation soon developed between the wealthier farmers who dominated Het Volk and the mineowners – a cooperation carried over into the SAP formed by Botha and Smuts after Union in 1910.[4] When the SAP split in 1913/1914 on the issue of the relationship with imperialism, the wealthier farmers of the Transvaal supported the 'conciliationist' pro-British policies of Botha and Smuts. These maize-producing capitalists were the real rural anchor of the SAP. On the other hand, the formation of the NP in the Transvaal in 1915 was based on the strong republicanism of the stock farmers of the Northern Transvaal and of the smaller farmers, who were most subject to pressures of proletarianisation.

26

In the OFS the situation was somewhat different. At the Vereniging Peace Conference, the OFS delegation had strongly opposed surrender to the British. The wartime devastation of agriculture was much more severe in the OFS and the development of capitalist production in agriculture was now even slower than in the Transvaal. The major barriers were a strong and productive African peasantry on the white farms and a shortage of credit. It was the OFS leader, General Hertzog, who framed the legislation to drive Africans off white farms in what became the 1913 Land Act. But the emerging political cooperation between wealthier Afrikaner farmers and mineowners in the Transvaal did not develop in the OFS. The Oranje Unie party of Abraham Fischer and General Hertzog was much more anti-'imperialist' than its Het Volk counterpart in the Transvaal. With the unification of the four colonies in 1910, these two Afrikaner parties merged with the Afrikaner Bond in the Cape to form the SAP led by Louis Botha. Yet relations within this new party were uneasy. Prime Minister Botha sought to keep Hertzog out of his Cabinet because of the latter's opposition to Botha's strongly pro-British policies. When the issue of the relationship between the South African state and British imperialism precipitated a split between Botha and Hertzog in 1913, most Afrikaner farmers of the OFS followed the latter out of the SAP. In the 1915 general elections the OFS was solidly behind Hertzog's newly formed NP.

With Union in 1910, the SAP government continued the policy of state action to secure the development of capitalist agriculture. This involved on the one hand the attempt to transform relations of production through the Land Act, and, on the other, the provision of credit and other facilities. The establishment of the state-run land bank in 1912 made short- and long-term credit available to farmers and was a vital step in the slow transformation of agriculture.

In 1924 the Nationalist/Labour Party 'Pact' government was voted into office on a platform pledged, *inter alia*, to stronger state action to transform agriculture. The agricultural policies of the Pact contained an inherent contradiction. On the one hand, through special credit facilities, land settlement schemes, etc., the Pact sought to arrest the proletarianising effect of the development of capitalist agriculture and to keep smaller (white) farmers on the land. On the other hand, however, its policies were primarily designed to facilitate the rapid transition to capitalist agriculture through, *inter alia*, the extensive supply of large-scale credit, various marketing measures, state provision of seeds, stock registration, fencing and drought-relief measures. Yet the most important of these policies, the attempt to speed up the dispossession of rural Africans through legislation to transform African labour-tenants on white farms into wage labourers, was consistently frustrated (see p. 30 below). These were years of swift change at all levels. The concentration of capital fostered by the Pact's industrial and agricultural policies heightened the contradictions and struggles within the social formation, both between the exploited and exploiting classes, and within the capitalist class itself. The African peasantry were steadily impoverished during this period, leading to the rapid emergence of a growing urban African proletariat. The Industrial and Commercial Workers' Union (ICU) 'spread like wildfire' through urban and rural areas. It sought to organise both African workers and peasants around a contradictory, though 'radical' and rhetorically militant platform. Moreover, the Pact's policies further reflected the divisions within the capitalist class. The myriad forms of state assistance to agriculture (and industry) were possible only through various direct and indirect taxes, levies, etc. on the goldmining industry. In effect, this involved the state transferring the surplus value generated in the mining industry to agricultural (and industrial) capital. The result was a bitter political and ideological struggle at all levels between these capitals, together with their political and ideological representatives.[5]

This transfer of surplus value by the state was possible not, as conventional wisdom (and mining-house ideology) would have it, because the state was an instrument of backward, self-interested 'Boers', but because the Pact represented an unstable class alliance between sections of agricultural and industrial capital, together with important strata of organised white labour. This point is of fundamental importance in the analysis of the politics of the period. Such was the balance of class power in the social formation that, on its own, agricultural capital lacked the political and ideological weight effectively to implement such policies. It was forced to sustain political alliance with other class forces in order to do so. It was precisely these alliances which first began to crumble during the Depression, threatening the isolation of agriculture and so a collapse of state support for its interests. For all the Pact's attempts to foster the interests of farmers, such was the balance of class forces that its agricultural policies were only partially successful. Two barriers to the accumulation and concentration of capital in agriculture existed, which the class alliance of the Pact was too weak to shift. Both had uneven effects within agriculture.

In the two former Boer republics in the north during this period the rural relations of production were themselves in transition. As the impact of the Land Act drove African peasants into wage labour, the size of the African agricultural labour force in the Transvaal grew by 75 per cent between 1918 and 1930 (from 69,968 to 122,426). In the OFS, where the changes were not as rapid, the corresponding figures were 59,638 and 81,046 (Department of Agriculture 1961: 11). Morris (1976) has shown that this involved the transformation and disintegration of the predominant system of labour-tenancy. The survival/disintegration of the labour-tenancy system was a site of intense rural class struggle as farmers strove to limit their workers' access to land and to make them solely dependent on wage labour. Above all, this required further legislation both to restrict such access to land and to tighten the largely ineffective measures which were designed to limit the influx of African workers to the cities. Yet this was now primarily a concern of northern agriculture, particularly the Transvaal, where the labour-tenant system was most firmly established. In the Cape, on the other hand, labour-tenancy had almost entirely been superseded by wage labour by the 1930s.

Secondly, the Pact's policies were unable to resolve the fundamental structural contradiction into which agriculture was locked as a result of South Africa's place in the imperialist chain. South African agriculture was not competitive on world markets – as early as 1883 the government of the Cape colony had to erect protective tariffs around its wheat farmers. However, whilst the state could and did take various measures to stabilise the prices and protect the internal market for agricultural commodities, it could do very little about conditions on the export markets. Again, an uneven pattern is evident. While the various internal price stabilisation measures undertaken by the Pact were reasonably successful in sustaining price levels between 1926 and 1930, during the Depression and the subsequent drought of 1933 they proved virtually ineffective. The price of the principal agricultural commodity on the internal market, maize, tumbled from an average of 11/5d per 200 lb bag between 1926 and 1930, to 4/11d for the best grades by 1933 (Department of Agriculture 1961:183).

Thus, led by the maize producers (who comprised the largest single group of white farmers), organised agriculture began to agitate for higher subsidies and producer controls of the market through a single-channel marketing scheme (Finlay 1976). Yet such reforms implied a further attack on mining profits through higher food prices for its 300,000-strong work force. As furor over the Excess Profits Tax (below, p. 46) was to show, the class basis of the Pact was too narrow to allow assistance to agriculture to be intensified. To do so finally required some form of collaboration with mining capital, and hence a quid pro quo. Again, this became very clear as support for the established parties began to wither away during the Gold Standard crisis.

On the other hand, many of South Africa's agricultural commodities, such as wine, wool, deciduous fruits and sugar, were primarily produced for export. As analysed below (p. 36), export producers were generally more severely affected by the Depression than farmers whose commodities were sold on the internal market. In October 1931, the government introduced export subsidies, which were doubled barely three months later. By 1933/4 these subsidies comprised one third of the total state support for agriculture, yet had little effect. Export producers were subject to the dual liabilities of the international commodity market and the Imperial Preference System.

Britain was the vital market for most of South Africa's export produce. In the classic understatement of an economic historian of the British Empire, the South African state was 'lacking in any real power over prices in the British market' (Drummond 1972:24). However, even in this area it is crucial to recognise the uneven character of this relationship. Some of South Africa's agricultural export commodities enjoyed favourable preferences under the scheme, for example, sugar, some fruits, and wine. Others, most notably wool, did not (Marais 1958:154) The full significance of the question of Imperial

Preferences is dealt with in the following chapter. The point to note here is that, on the one hand, the capacity of the capitalist state adequately to secure and stabilise the internal market for agricultural commodities posed the question of the political relationship between specific agricultural capitals and mining capital. On the other hand, and over and above this question, the very incapacity of the South African state to do much about the prices of export commodities raised the very relationship between the South African state and imperialism itself as a central political question for certain agricultural capitals.

Here again, the regional differences in agricultural production are significant. Transvaal and OFS farmers produced primarily for the internal market, and were increasingly concerned with the first of these questions. Cape agriculture (with the exception of wheat) was mainly geared around the export market, and was vitally interested in the second of these questions. Thus, the development of agriculture under the Pact government increasingly posed different political and ideological questions for the Afrikaans-speaking farmers of various provinces.

By the 1930s, both the prevailing property relations and the conditions of the market operated as barriers to accumulation for specific agricultural capitals. The uneven development of capitalist agriculture brought both these questions to the forefront of political struggle. Yet it did so in a manner which expressed deep regional disparities. Moreover, the Pact government had gone as far as it was politically able. Firstly, its attempts to transform the system of land tenure had, since 1926, been thwarted by the political strength of the SAP. Since the so-called 'Hertzog Bills' proposed to alter both the franchise provisions and the land tenure system in the Cape Province, they required a constitutional amendment by a two-thirds majority of a joint sitting of both Houses. With some of its MPs dependent on the African vote in the Cape, the SAP opposed the bills and forestalled this majority. However, Smuts was under strong pressure from his Transvaal supporters to back the Land Bill which would empower farmers to expel African squatters from the farms and lengthen the period of obligatory service for labour-tenants, while limiting the size of their plots. Secondly, the Hertzog government was unable to introduce the central maketing system favoured by northern agriculture, as it faced too powerful an alliance against the rising food costs this would entail (mining and industrial capital, together with organised white labour). Thirdly, its attempts to redefine the economic relationship between South Africa and Britain met with total intransigence from both Conservative and Labour Party governments at the 1926 and 1930 Imperial Conferences. The few concessions wrung from the Ottawa Conference altered nothing.

The growing paralysis of the Pact regime on these central issues began to pose anew the question of political alliances. Moreover, accentuating regional differences in the interests of agriculture were loosening the ideological cohesion of the NP itself. The contradictions between the forces represented in firstly the NP and secondly the Pact were exacerbated by the Depression, steadily undermining both groupings.

THE HERTZOG NATIONALIST PARTY

The label 'Nationalist Party' is, in a sense, a misnomer.[6] This was no single 'national' party, but a loose federation of four autonomous provincial NPs, each with its own distinct social base, party organisation, membership, press, interests and ideological style. The NP as a party had a 'national' existence only through four institutions: a Federal Council which met but rarely; the parliamentary caucus; the national leader (Hertzog); and, when in office, the Cabinet (though this always contained Labour ministers).

Each of the national institutions of the party was a site of differing kinds of political struggles and represented varying sets of interests. This much-neglected structure of the NP is central to an understanding of its history, as the real locus of power in the party itself lay in the provincial party organisation rather than the national institutions. The provincial leaders often had greater influence within their provincial parties than the national leader. Within the party (as distinct from the Cabinet) they wielded almost as much influence as the nationalist leader himself.[7] These provincial parties jealously guarded their interests, prerogatives and identities both from each other and from the national institutions of the party. The composition of a NP Cabinet had always to pay due regard to the relative weight of the provincial parties.

The 'regionalist' or 'provincialist' struggles which always plagued Afrikaner nationalist politics thus rested at one level on these four distinct party political and ideological structures. More fundamentally, however, such regionalism and often wide policy and ideological differences between the provincial parties are explained by the fact that each party had distinct class basis – each was the institutionalisation of a distinct form of class alliance which differed in important respects from those of its federal partners. Thus, as separately-organised, separately-financed and separately-led political institutions with different social bases, the four provincial NPs acquired distinct institutional practices, ideological styles and interests. Far from being monolithic organisations, they changed significantly over time.

The Cape NP was led by Dr D.F. Malan. It organised a political alliance between the capitalist wine and fruit farmers of the Western Cape and Boland; the wool and ostrich farmers of the Karoo; the Afrikaans-speaking petty bourgeoisie; and a very small, but extremely powerful, financial capital in the Sanlam companies led by W.A. Hofmeyr. This latter group controlled the Party's press and critical sections of its organisation.[8] The Cape Party also drew support from the 'poor white' areas around Knysna and George.

In the OFS, the NP was based overwhelmingly on the maize farmers, who accounted for most of the province's white agriculturalists. A growing petty bourgeoisie in the small towns of the OFS was also a significant base for the party, which was led by Hertzog himself.

The class basis of both the NP and the SAP was at its most fluid in the Transvaal, reflecting the rapid and fundamental changes in both town and countryside wrought first by goldmining, and then by the development of capitalist agriculture and industry. Whoever captured the shifting rural support in the Transvaal was the master of Parliament. As a generalisation, however, the stock farmers of the north and the middle and small agriculturalists were the real base for the Transvaal NP. The wealthier capitalist farmers in the maize areas of the west and south-east, on the other hand, were generally Sappe (SAP supporters). The Afrikaans-speaking petty bourgeoisie in the Transvaal were solid in their support for the NP. This was the province in which the rate of proletarianisation of white farmers was the most rapid. Under the leadership of its mercurial founder, Tielman Roos, the Transvaal NP competed with the Labour Party for the support of the growing number of urban 'poor whites'. Paradoxically it did so through a formal alliance with the Labour Party (the real heart of the Pact was in the Transvaal) through which it stole much of the political thunder of the deeply-divided Labourites.

These diverse bases of support for the NP were expressed through differing ideological emphases, political styles and priorities. One example will suffice. In their early years, the NPs of the former Transvaal and OFS republics were solidly republican. As late as 1919, Hertzog led a delegation from the Transvaal and OFS to the Versailles Peace Conference to demand, in accordance with the Fourteen Points, the restoration of the independence of the old republics. The Cape Party, on the other hand, reflecting its 'colonial heritage' view of itself as the old Afrikaner Bond resurrected, and the dependence of Cape farmers on the British market, was at best lukewarm over this issue.

Thus, as it slowly developed after the founding of the OFS NP in 1914, the 'Nationalist Party' represented widely differing social forces, subject to very different socio-economic pressures. It was rent with internal contradictions, ideological disputes and strong personal antipathies among its leadership.[9] Even to bring about the Pact with the Labour Party in 1923, the constituent parties had been forced to water down key parts of their programmes. The Nationalists agreed to freeze any moves for a republic, while the Labour Party abandoned the socialisation of the means of production. These compromises alienated important minorities in both parties – the very minorities which continued to stress the contradictions between the partners to the Pact, and were the first to move towards an open splitting of their own parties.

Coalition regimes generally represent an unstable balance between contending class forces, in which neither are independently able to assert the upper hand. Following the assumption of office by the Pact in 1924, the contradictions within the regime were given full play and began to undermine the unity of both parties. This was immediately obvious in the deep divisions within the Labour Party, leading to an open split between the so-called

Councellite and Cresswellite factions in 1928. The slow disintegration of the NP was less obvious, only becoming clear in the coalition crisis itself. However, like all political crises and splits, the rapid disintegration of the NP into coalition and then fusion merely expresses, in more or less dramatic form, the concentration to a point of open rupture of underlying contradictions.

This stress on underlying contradictions, however, should not obscure the highly visible side of the coin. In the years from 1924 to 1929, the Pact government pursued a bold and vigorous programme of industrial protection and infrastructural development, agricultural subsidisation and the protection of employment for white workers. Over and above these numerous concrete measures, the first Hertzog government identified 'three great issues' as a concentrated expression of the interests of its heterogeneous social base. These were: the pursuit of 'sovereign independence' from the imperial power; the achievement of complete equality in the state between the English and Afrikaans languages; and the economic nationalism of 'South Africa first'.[10]

Despite the contradiction between the class forces represented in the Pact, their alliance sprang from a common, violent clash of interests with monopoly capital as it was represented primarily in the mining industry, but also in the great import houses and the banks. Ideologically, however, this common enemy represented different things and expressed a different set of social relations to the supporters of the Pact parties. To the skilled, largely English-speaking workers of the Labour Party, monopoly capital represented the bosses and the domination of capital, against which they had been involved in a bitter and often bloody struggle since the 1890s. To the Afrikaans-speaking farmers in all areas, the petty bourgeoisie and 'poor whites', monopoly capital meant above all the British and the political domination of British 'imperialism'. To those class forces which comprised the base of the NP, and to the Anglo-Boer War veterans who dominated its leadership, the mining houses, the banks, the great import houses, the 'English' press and the senior state officials were all synonomous with 'imperialism'. In a notorious 'Century of Wrong' (Smuts 1900), these partners, marching together under the hated Union Jack, had murdered the martyrs of Slagtersnek, driven the Boers into the Great Trek and then annexed their Republic of Natalia after but three years. With a cheap legal trick they stole the diamond fields of the OFS and violated the Sand River Convention to annex the Transvaal in 1877. Defeated by the Boers at the Battle of Majuba and forced to recognise Boer independence, these fortune hunters bled the Transvaal white and then trampled into dust the independence of the Boer republics, killing 25,000 women and children in their concentration camps in the process. Under Milner they even tried to destroy the Afrikaans language whilst driving poor Afrikaner farmers off their land into the Sodom and Gomorrah of the cities and (most heinous of all) into economic competition with the black man. These foreign devils had corrupted once-heroic Boer generals like Botha and Smuts, turning them into tools of the mineowners and 'handymen of the Empire' so that, but four years after Union in 1910, South Africa had been dragged into Britain's war with Germany and Afrikaner had fought Afrikaner in the ensuing *Rebellie*. Their 'imperialist' policies were destroying the rural communities, transforming proud rural patriarchs into pitied and despised 'poor whites' and dividing the volk in the full bitterness of class warfare. Finally, their relentless pursuit of profit and domination led them to substitute cheap black labour for white miners in 1922, and, when a great mine strike ensued, butchered nearly 300 people whilst they bombed and shelled the miners into submission.

The varying and often contradictory interests of all the forces represented in the NP were ideologically condensed and found expression in a broad 'anti-imperialism', cast in an anti-capitalist rhetoric. In its widest sense, this general ideological conception of 'imperialism' and 'imperialist domination' referred to the ways in which both South Africa's constitutional position in the British Empire and the economic domination of (largely British) monopoly capital within the economy, inhibited the capacity of the South African state to foster the interests of the class forces represented in the NP, and led to a general discrimination in state and market against the Afrikaans language. These complex associations compressed many levels of meaning and symbols of 'imperialism' – from the British state itself, through its representative in South Africa, monopoly capital, to the SAP. The use of the term 'imperialism' in Afrikaner nationalist ideology implied all these senses, and all were concentrated in its mythical ideological personification, 'Hoggenheimer'.[11] The 'three great issues' of sovereign independence, language equality and 'South Africa first' crystallised the opposition to these forms of 'imperialist' domination. But, to many Afrikaner nationalists, they did not go nearly far enough.

In histories of Afrikaner nationalism written in English, this form of anti-imperialism is often dismissed as backward Afrikaner chauvinism – perhaps understandable immediately after the British atrocities of the Anglo-Boer war, but distinctly outmoded by the 1920s. Yet a proper understanding of its meaning and persistence must locate it in the development of British imperialism of the period. The First World War had transformed Britain from the world's financier into a debtor of the USA. In the following years British imperialism was under intense competition (particularly in Latin America and China) from an aggressive US imperialism and its 'equal weight' and 'open door' policies. By the late 1920s competition from Germany again loomed large. All this occasioned intense economic and ideological debate within Britain over the economic policies to be pursued in the Empire. In Drummond's words the 'Imperial Visionaries' did battle with *'laissez faire* free traders' (1972:36). Neither offered much solace to the NP. This imperialist bickering revolved around questions of the implications for Britain of the industrial development of the Dominion through import substitution, protection of the access of British industrial commodities to the markets of the Empire, and the development of preferential tariffs for the raw materials and foodstuffs produced in the Empire. This was a period of continuing massive unemployment in Britain which the 'imperial visionaries' sought to resolve by exporting the surplus population to the rural areas of the Dominions. Lord Beaverbrook waged an energetic campaign for 'Empire Free Trade', and in 1931 the British National Government abandoned nearly a century of dogmatic free trade ideology to impose protectionist tariffs. Further, during the 1920s the erection of 'machinery for economic cooperation' and the creation of various imperial economic boards to regulate imperial tariffs frightened both the South African and Canadian governments into expecting an attack on their trappings of national sovereignty and a re-centralisation of the Empire (Drummond 1972: chapters 2–3).

In this context then, the 'anti-imperialist' stance of the NP and its particular constitutionalist stress on sovereignty was much more than a simple ideological straw man, and reflected the real economic interests of NP supporters. The concessions on national status and Dominion sovereignty won by Hertzog at the 1926 and 1930 Imperial Conferences were significantly accompanied by a blank refusal to expand concessions on preferential tariffs for South African agricultural exports. The question of the relationship between South Africa and the Empire – in Dr Malan's phrase, 'nationalism or imperialism' – went to the heart of the economic interests of all classes in South Africa. Whenever it was raised, it would provoke fierce political struggle. As the Depression deepened in South Africa, it was this issue which was posed ever more sharply, in a form which was to dissolve existing political alliances.

THE DEPRESSION AND THE ACCUMULATION OF CAPITAL IN SOUTH AFRICA

From the comfortable vantage point of the middle-class academics writing on South Africa's economic history, the country's experience of the Depression appears as 'relatively mild' (De Kiewiet 1972:156; Houghton 1971). This echoes the pigs' interpretation of the Animals' Charter of *Animal Farm* – for some, the mildness was more relative than for others. Reliable statistics on the Depression are 'relatively' scarce. The Industrial Census returns for 1931 and 1932 have never been published. Measured in terms of millions of pounds and percentages of available economic indicators, the Depression may, in retrospect, indeed appear to have been relatively mild. Yet this misconceives the nature of the economic crisis for capital and hides its dramatic and harsh, though uneven, effects on the producing classes.

As a crisis of capitalism on a world scale, the Great Depression led to stagnation in activities promoting the valorisation and accumulation of capital. The particular form and effects of this crisis in South Africa were determined above all by South Africa's position in the world economy as an exporter of minerals and agricultural commodities. By 1932, the value of national output was £26.5 million lower than that of 1920 (US 1960: S-3). Yet this crisis took the form of uneven and differing barriers to accumulation for different capitals.

The monopoly goldmining industry was the least affected. The mining of gold was the direct production of the money form of value – the industry had no worries about realising surplus value. Unemployment in other sectors freed labour for the mines. The prices of much of the industry's technical and other requirements fell. Throughout the Depression the money value of goldmining production actually increased (Houghton 1976:283). However, the British abandonment of the Gold Standard in September 1931 devalued the British pound. The South African government declined to follow suit. Initial mining industry support for this policy soon gave way to strong opposition as the expected cheaper imports and lower internal price structure was offset by heavy state subsidies to agriculture – subsidies effectively financed by the mining industry. This 'Gold Standard crisis' was to be the issue which sparked off political realignment.

The barriers to capital accumulation for local industry were more severe, as the collapse of credit and the shrinking market meant that the value of its products could not be realised. The years 1930 to 1933 saw a big cutback in industrial production. Total income from private manufacturing declined by almost 20 per cent, bankruptcies were frequent and the fall in employment matched that in income. Similarly, the general cutback in production and investment, massive unemployment, and the resultant shrinking market, all had their effects in the sphere of circulation. The commercial sector generally was severely hit by the Depression. In the three years from 1930 to 1932, its contribution to national income fell from £36.7 m to £25.8 m (US 1960: S-3, L-3).

Of all the sectors of capitalist production, agriculture was the worst hit by the Depression.[12] As Marx pointed out (1971:117), the 'interruptions, great collisions, even catastrophes, in the process of reproduction' of capital induced by violent price fluctuations have an effect on agriculture far worse than that of other spheres of capitalist production. During the Depression, tumbling export prices, a shrinking internal market and the worst drought of the century produced a fall in the total value of all agricultural crops of 42 per cent. Yet the impact of the Depression on agriculture was extremely uneven. Farmers producing for export were generally worse off than those producing for the internal market. In 1932, the value of South Africa's agricultural commodities sold on the external market was barely 36 per cent of their 1928 value, whereas the corresponding average value of internal prices was 60 to 70 per cent of the 1928 figure. On the other hand, the total value of the annual crop of the major internal agricultural commodity – maize – halved between 1928/9 and 1932/3, whilst in other sectors such as viticulture, sugar (both primarily export commodities) and wheat, the corresponding declines were 'relatively mild'. Livestock farmers too were badly hit by the Depression – the total value of all livestock products

36

was halved. Sheep farmers, for example, sought in vain to counter the dramatic fall in wool prices through a massive increase in production. Though the total wool clip doubled between 1928/9 and 1932/3, its value fell by over 70 per cent. Furthermore, the huge increase in flocks in so short a period produced an ecological crisis in the sheep farming areas which wiped out 30 per cent of the total sheep population (or 13 million sheep) in 1933/4 (Department of Agriculture 1961:51, 25). Thus, though highly irregular in its effects, the Depression produced severe hardship for white farmers. The Secretary of Agriculture described the period as 'the darkest and most difficult experienced for the last 30 years' (Finlay 1976:10). For most, these were years of desperate struggle for economic survival against the seemingly merciless attempts of both the market and nature to drive farmers off their land.

This uneven crisis in the reproduction and accumulation of capital produced massive unemployment amongst workers of all races. By September 1933, approximately 22 per cent of all white and coloured males (188,000 men) were officially registered as unemployed (Department of Labour 1933:11). The ranks of the unemployed were swollen by the thousands of white farmers driven off the land and into acute poverty by the Depression. In December 1932 it was conservatively estimated that one-sixth of the white population was 'very poor'. A further 30 per cent of all white families was classified as 'poor' – as 'so poor they cannot adequately feed or house their children' (Carnegie Corporation Commission 1932: vi–vii, Part III, 217–22).

There exist no statistics whatsoever to measure African unemployment and poverty. Yet in reality both were acute. During this period, the 'civilised labour policy' of the state sought to remedy white unemployment by replacing black workers with white labour. In all sectors of the economy, except mining, the ratio of black to white workers fell dramatically. Unemployed Africans were forced back into the overcrowded, impoverished 'native reserves'. With almost monotonous regularity, government reports and commissions of this period warn of 'appalling poverty' in these reserves and raise the spectre of 'mass starvation' (NEC 1932: para. 69).

This was a period of intensified class struggle. The 1920s had seen gathering rural struggles against the proletarianising effects of the 1913 Land Act. African workers too were increasingly organised as the ICU rapidly established itself throughout the rural and urban areas. Though seriously weakened by internal contradictions and splits, by 1928 the ICU claimed 100,000 members. The onset of the Depression saw increased ICU agitation and struggles in the cities. A frightened Hertzog government introduced a battery of repressive legislation in 1929 and 1930, specifically to deal with the ICU and a growing Communist Party (CP). Led by the Minister of Justice himself, machinegun-toting police squads raided the townships, tear-gassed crowds, smashed up meetings and terrorised workers. This extreme repression culminated in the murder of Communist militant Johannes Nkosi. Moreover, the vast numbers of black and white unemployed were increasingly restive. The efforts of the CP to build a multi-racial movement of the unemployed began to meet some success – despite a bitter factional struggle raging within the CP.

In this conjuncture of an uneven accumulation crisis and heightened class struggle, the specific interests of certain identifiable capitals were increasingly unable to be contained within the party political structure. Similarly, existing political alignments were further undermined by a general weakening of the prevailing ideologies. The result was an extended political and ideological crisis which culminated in fusion.

2

The disintegration of the Nationalist Party, 1927 to 1934

It was argued in the previous chapter that the varying and contradictory interests of the forces organised in alliance by the NP were ideologically condensed and found expression in a broad anti-imperialism. However, precisely the visible success of the Pact regime on the 'three great issues' of 1924 to 1929 began to weaken this anti-imperialism amongst certain elements – most notably in the government and NP bureaucracy. The fruitful coalition with the 'English' Labour Party, the rapid growth of industrial production, the de-escalation of industrial conflict, and the period of agricultural prosperity in the mid to late 1920s – all began to blur the lines of conflict and dampen ideological fervour. The Language Act of 1925 and the rapid promotion of Afrikaans-speakers in the state bureaucracy did much to take the steam out of the language issue. Paradoxically, the unsuccessful attempts to enact the 'Hertzog Bills' (p. 30 above) brought close the rural interests of both the NP and SAP. But above all, the developments on the constitutional front both muted the anti-imperialist ardour of important sections of the NP and opened wide divisions within it.

The growing contradictions within the NP and the extended ideological crisis leading to its disintegration in August 1934 can be traced in four stages: 1927 to September 1931, which marked a growing ideological accommodation with 'imperialism'; September 1931 to December 1932, the Gold Standard crisis; January to February 1933, the collapse into coalition; and March 1933 to August 1934, coalition leading to fusion and rupture. It is necessary to examine these in some detail, as each marks a distinct shift in the balance of political forces in the state.

1927 TO DECEMBER 1931

At the 1926 Imperial Conference, Hertzog wrung the Balfour Declaration from a reluctant Conservative British government. This declared all the Dominions 'autonomous communities', enjoying complete equality of status with Britain herself. On his return to South Africa, without consulting his colleagues, Prime Minister Hertzog proclaimed the constitutional aims of his party satisfied. It would now abandon republicanism. Against strong opposition, Clause 4 of the OFS Party's constitution was amended to remove reference to a republic. These actions outraged many sections of the nationalist opinion, sharpening the polarisation within the NP. Though least apparent at the time, by far the most significant of its long-term effects was the decision of the small, secret Afrikaner Broederbond to 'take an active life in the community, leaving no avenue neglected'. Henceforth, the Bond sought to redefine Afrikaner nationalism and to assume the role of its watchdog and vanguard (see chapter 4 below).

This ideological polarisation deepened following the 1930 Imperial Conference and the resultant Statute of Westminster conferring Dominion status on South Africa. For Hertzog, this finally closed the constitutional issue. Alarmed republicans cried that the general 'predicts peace between imperialism and nationalism. Let us say at once this is a false peace' (*Die Volkstem* 6/12/30). After consultations within the Broederbond, Dr N.J. van der Merwe formed a formal republican ginger group (Die Republikeinsebond) within the NP, and intrigued with extra-party forces to get rid of Hertzog (van den Heever 1946:232–3).

These widening ideological divisions within the NP were accompanied by other significant developments. Since 1928 there had been persistent rumours of attempts, particularly in the rural areas of the northern provinces, to bring the two major parties together (Moodie 1975:120). Hertzog himself expressed this undercurrent in a provocative speech to the 1930 congress of his party.

> What I have felt for a long time now, and have also long been working for, is that the time has come for us South Africans, Dutch- or English-speaking, to recognise and acknowledge the fact that so long as we stand apart and try to reach our goal along different paths we must expect that a great deal of what we wish to achieve as a nation will not be attained. . . . After what has been achieved at the Imperial Conferences in 1926 and 1930, there no longer exists today a single reason why, in the constitutional and political fields, Dutch- and English-speaking South Africans cannot feel and act in the spirit of a consolidated South African nation. . . . This will come to pass. That it should, is the task to which the Nationalist Party is now called. Is the Nationalist Party equal to this task? *If not, it has served its time*! Nationalists! Let us accept this task. Today as never before, English- and Dutch-speaking South Africans stand ready to extend a hand to each other in a spirit of reciprocal sincerity, as equal and equally-righted Afrikaners (van den Heever 1946 :600).[1]

By 1931, the Depression was biting deeply. At the precise juncture when the distress of capitalist agriculture called for new state policies, contradictions within the NP's class base were weakening its ideological cement and political cohesion. The Gold Standard crisis finally intensified these contradictions to the point of rupture.

SEPTEMBER 1931 TO DECEMBER 1932

In September 1931, the British National government went off the Gold Standard. The Hertzog government was subjected to growing pressure to follow suit. Yet for fifteen months of rapidly deepening economic crisis, particularly for farmers, the government stressed its resolve to fall rather than leave gold. Above all, the NP represented agricultural interests. Why did it cling so determinedly to a policy which, through tumbling export returns and rocketing import bills, hit agriculture far harder than any other branch of capitalist production?

Hertzog, Finance Minister Claas Havenga, and most Cabinet members were themselves large-scale farmers. Acutely aware of the disastrous condition of agriculture, they were convinced that only by remaining on the Gold standard could the state foster its interests. The NP concentrated its representation of agricultural interests in a particular form of anti-imperialism. The NP government interpreted the wider interests of its supporters in terms of the ability of the South African state to act independently of Britain. Enshrined in the Statute of Westminster, this hard-won constitutional independence was put to the acid test with the Gold Standard crisis. As it confronted the NP government, the issue was absurdly simple. Was the South African state, like Mary's little lamb, meekly and dutifully to tag behind every unilateral twist of imperialist policy – as Smuts and the SAP urged? Or were the interests of those it represented best served through a steadfast assertion of independence and a refusal to go off gold? To the government these were rhetorical questions.

The decision to remain on gold was initially supported by the mining industry and the SAP. Yet this soon gave way to vigorous opposition as heavy state subsidies to agriculture offset the expected cheaper imports and lower internal price structure induced by remaining on gold. As the SAP, the Chamber of Mines, and the English language press mounted a determined campaign against the Gold Standard, Hertzog's pleas for cooperation were again moderated by frequent warnings of the imperialist threat. He argued that by opposing agricultural subsidies and the Gold Standard the SAP was selling out both the farmers and the national interest in a stable currency to the demands of 'Hoggenheimer'. NP dissidents like Dr van der Merwe rallied around the government's firm and aggressively nationalist position. Moreover, despite its increasingly desperate position, organised agriculture refused publicly to associate itself with Smuts' and Hoggenheimer's demand to link up with sterling. While the logic of its evidence to the Gold Standard Commission implied abandonment, this the South African Agricultural Union (SAAU) would not recommend. It did not want to get 'mixed up' in party politics, claiming this was 'purely a matter for the state' (Kaplan 1976: 152).

Throughout this crisis, the regime sought to shore up the perilous position of agriculture through various forms of subsidies. Yet nothing seemed to stem the tide of falling prices. It was precisely this apparent ineffectiveness of government policy, coupled with the already weakened ideological cement of the NP, which now began slowly to dislodge agriculture's support for both the traditional parties. During this period the demand from the rural areas, particularly the Transvaal, for a *rapprochement* between the Nationalists and

Sappe increased considerably. Here it is crucial to note that these demands were for *hereniging* (re-union) of the rural interests rather than for *samesmelting* (fusion) of all the class forces represented in both parties. It was expected that the Unionist element of the SAP (seen as the representatives of 'Hoggenheimer') would be excluded. Two by-elections showed the extent of this erosion of support. At Colesberg the NP came within a hair's breadth of losing one of its safest seats. Early in December 1932, the SAP captured the 'safe' Germiston constituency from the Creswell wing of the Labour Party, still in the government. Germiston particularly was widely interpreted as a major defeat for the government.

The jubilant SAP leadership began to anticipate a sweeping victory in the elections which NP policy must surely precipitate. However, the SAP was itself in serious political trouble with a powerful devolution movement undermining its support in Natal. It soon became clear that these by-election results signified a more profound shake up of party political representation than a swing towards the SAP. A catalyst was needed to break what local commentators delighted in labelling 'the party political log-jam'. This soon appeared in the portly shape of Tielman Roos.

Following the 1929 elections, Roos had resigned from the Cabinet and from leadership of the Transvaal NP on grounds of ill-health. Appointed to the Appeal Court, he spent three years intriguing against Hertzog and seeking ways of returning to the Cabinet. This Hertzog flatly refused to countenance (van den Heever 1946:234–40). Finally, in a major speech delivered on 16 December 1932, the Afrikaner nationalist holy day, Roos urged the abandonment of the Gold Standard. Six days later he resigned from the Bench and dramatically re-entered politics.

Roos' lightning campaign against the Gold Standard had two effects. Firstly, it precipitated massive speculation and a rush to convert banknotes to gold. In three days £3m flowed out of South Africa. On Boxing Day the Minister of Finance was informed that unless the convertability of the South African pound was terminated the commercial banks would be forced to close. A mere six days after Roos re-entered politics, South Africa left the Gold Standard.

Hertzog's bitter attack on 'organised finance power', but more particularly 'Afrikaner treachery' in the guise of Roos (*Die Burger* 31/12/32), points to the second of these effects. Roos' actions finally eroded the political support for the government's position amongst Transvaal farmers, hardest hit by plummeting agricultural prices. The flood of ink spilled on this affair has blotted out one crucial fact. In the six days between his political resurrection and the abandonment of the Gold Standard, Roos campaigned as an NP politician. His programme won wide support within the Transvaal NP. Fifteen of its MPs and one senator rallied to their former leader. Piet Grobler, Roos' dour successor as Transvaal leader, had long promised to stand down in his favour. Roos' nationalist credentials were impeccable. His return to politics and the programme he put forward appeared to offer a way out to those whose daily deteriorating economic position seemed to necessitate the abandonment of the Gold Standard, but who could not support this demand coming from the SAP, as they dreaded its probable return to power, dominated by its Unionist element.[2]

JANUARY TO FEBRUARY 1933

The year 1932 ended with the NP in disarray. Its ideological cohesion had long since collapsed. Now its rural base in the Transvaal was wasting rapidly away. In a House with a nominal NP majority of fourteen, Roos and his fifteen MPs held the balance of parliamentary power. The 'Lion of the North' now changed his roar, demanding the formation of a National Government headed by himself. Hertzog refused to deal with him. The Cabinet was divided. Malan called for immediate elections. Hertzog's man in the Transvaal, Oswald Pirow, taking measure of the demands of Transvaal farmers, favoured an approach to Smuts (Crafford 1943:236). During this period, while the party leaders and other powerful interests courted and were courted by Roos, Parliament was in recess.

The most significant immediate result of leaving gold was an increase in the price of gold from 85/- to 120/- per fine ounce – a 'premium' 35/- per fine ounce. A struggle over this premium instantly erupted. Three days after leaving gold, the official organ of the Cape NP declared that the 'greatest part' of the premium 'belonged to the people of South Africa' and not to the gold shareholders (*Die Burger* 31/12/32). Smuts retorted that 'following the abandonment of the Gold Standard, extra-ordinary assistance to the farming population must cease' (*Die Burger* 3/1/33). Early in 1933, the government announced proposals to tax most of the gold premium. From this moment, the Chamber of Mines began to prod the SAP towards coalition with either Roos or the Nationalists.[3]

As the last week of January and the re-opening of Parliament drew near, the SAP was, if anything, in deeper disarray than the Nationalists. Its rural base in the Transvaal, without which it stood no chance of ever returning to office, was white-hot with agitation for *hereniging*. Its sixteen Natal MPs were increasingly restive over the devolution issue, as the sugar interests feared that any collaboration with the Nationalists would sacrifice their special preferential tariffs (Nicholls 1961). And finally the proposed gold premium tax, coupled with the rural demands for *hereniging*, awoke the mineowners and their press to the real possibility of a new, united, rural party, committed to even higher protective tariffs. As Sir Abe Bailey warned, such a party would have an automatic parliamentary majority (*Die Burger* 13/1/33).

Smuts had rejected Roos' approaches early in January, declaring the proposed Cabinet unacceptable.[4] Yet the rapid withering away of support both for the SAP, and for Smuts within it, compelled a resumption of negotiations just before Parliament re-opened. Roos made concessions, and the issue was referred to the SAP caucus. It was widely reported that thirty of its sixty-one MPs, including the mining representatives, Sir Ernest

43

Oppenheimer, Sir Abe Bailey and Sir Harry Graumann, favoured accepting Roos' offer even though it meant dumping Smuts.[5]

Thus, by the re-opening of Parliament on 24 January, the party representation of classes was in a state of extreme flux. Extra-parliamentary pressure had forced the government to abandon its strong attachment to the Gold Standard. With its support dwindling, the governing party was dazed and disorganised by the rapidity of events, and deeply divided over what course to follow. Yet the opposition was in no position to seize the initiative as it too was in disarray. The erosion of crucial bases of support for the two major parties was everywhere evident. The two party leaders had suffered an enormous loss of prestige in the process. But neither had Roos been able to gather to himself sufficient support for a decisive break. At precisely the stage when the country was deep in economic crisis and a state of high political ferment, a profound stalemate between the political parties had been reached.[6]

At this stage, no doubt acutely aware of his own precarious political position, Smuts made what developed into the decisive initiative. On 24 January, during the no-confidence debate, and a full week before his caucus was to vote on Roos' proposals, he called for a coalition of the Nationalist and South African Parties. The immediate response from the government benches was unanimously reluctant and derisory. Justice Minister Pirow (later to follow Hertzog into fusion) chided the opposition that 'it is since the time when it became known that . . . the state was going to take a reasonable share of the profits on the mines that their demands became so urgent' (*Die Burger* 26/1/33).

However, the ritual rejection of Smuts notwithstanding, the NP had no real alternative. The ability of the NP to present itself as the personification of national will and interest, and to unite both class power and state power in itself, had been mortally undermined. The Depression unevenly and differentially intensified the barriers to accumulation for different capitals. As discussed in chapter 1, these uneven effects thus required different state policies to restructure some of the conditions of accumulation for various capitals, particularly branches of agriculture. Given the existing balance of forces in the state, on their own these agricultural capitals were too weak to implement such policies through the NP. The resulting political crisis thus led to a rapid realignment of class forces outside the existing parties. Both the NP and SAP were increasingly by-passed and seriously weakened. Increasingly abandoned by part of its rural base, with its ideological cohesion shattered, the NP lacked the political support to continue to rule on its own. Some form of party political realignment was essential.

The very day the SAP caucus vetoed cooperation with Roos in favour of continuing initiative to the NP, Hertzog proposed such negotiations to his own caucus. This proposal had earlier been communicated to Smuts. It is difficult to escape the conclusion that this finally enabled Smuts to sway a three-day debate in the SAP caucus (Pirow 1957:148, 243). Hertzog told his caucus that the NP had no choice. Four factors compelled his personal volte-face. Firstly, in reply to Malan's insistence on an appeal to the country, the NP would lose any elections. Secondly, failure to achieve coalition would drive Smuts back into the 'imperialist' wing of the SAP, undoing all the NP's achievements since 1924. Thirdly, the economic situation, particularly the agricultural position, demanded a national government. Finally, calls for unity from the volk could not be ignored.[7]

The caucus was deeeply divided. Most Cape representatives and many Free State MPs strongly opposed any dealings with the party of Hoggenheimer. Hertzog was requested to spell out his terms for coalition before negotiating with Smuts. He would not be bound by the caucus, however, and negotiated with Smuts, independent of caucus or Cabinet (Krüger 1960:81). On 15 February, in his personal capacity, Hertzog issued a statement of agreement with Smuts on seven principles: the maintenance of sovereign independence; the maintenance of the Union and the Flag (there were demands for secession in Natal); protection of agriculture; 'civilised labour' policy; the solution of the 'native question' (legislation had been stalled since 1926); equal language rights (also under attack in Natal); and the protection of South Africa's monetary system and position (*Die Burger* 15/2/33). Nine days later, coalition was announced on the basis of these proposals.

This finally doused the flickering political hopes of Tielman Roos. The 'Lion of the North' had seen himself as South Africa's political messiah, but his Centre Party won only two seats in the 1933 general elections. Politically broken, Roos retired to his large debts and an early death two years later. Other splinter groups aside from the Centre Party were thrown out by coalition. The Natal Federal Group within the SAP was later to form the nucleus of the Dominion Party. Hertzog's autocratic leadership provoked the formation of a Republican Party and a Farmers' and Workers' Party by dissident Nationalists. But, above all, coalition widened the divisions within the NP, particularly between the provincial parties, almost to the point of formal breach.

With individual exceptions, the Transvaal NP welcomed coalition as it arrested the withering away of its rural support. The OFS party referred to the 'economic pressure' experienced by farmers and, despite strong objections from some MPs, supported its leader in the hope that coalition 'would lead to a relief of this situation' (*Die Burger* 25/3/33). But reaction from the Cape was very different. Malan declared coalition a question of the relationship between nationalism and imperialism. It would 'throw together in the same camp, people whose inner convictions differ' (*Die Burger* 16/3/33). The Cape party 'laid itself down under protest' before the '*fait accompli*' of coalition as 'a purely temporary measure'. It would support the new government only in so far as its policies did not conflict with the principles of the NP (*Die Burger* 25/2/33).

For Transvaal and OFS farmers, the Depression compounded the con-straints on the accumulation of capital presented by the persistence of labour-tenancy and the state of the internal market. The further concentration of agricultural capital required state action to restructure both. An NP government had proved unable to effect this. If the price was cooperation with Smuts, so be it. Cape farmers on the other hand were not short of African labour. Export prices were their major concern. At the 1926 and 1930 Imperial Conferences, and again at the 1932 Ottawa Conference, successive British governments showed marked opposition to any improvement in these terms of trade. Furthermore, South Africa's trade with Germany – a major and growing market for Cape wool farmers – had come under powerful attack at Ottawa (Nicholls 1961: chapter XVI). Cooperation with 'Hoggenheimer' seemed to promise only an intensification of 'imperialist' domination and worsening terms of trade for Cape farmers.

Despite Cape opposition to fusion, Malan was in no position to break with Hertzog. The coalition agreement called for early elections and guaranteed sitting MPs their seats. This provided the Cape Party with a powerful base from which to oppose cooperation. Malan refused a portfolio in the coalition Cabinet, and the Cape NP machinery began an intensive anti-coalition campaign. In the general elections of May 1933, the coalition swept 136 of the 150 seats. The 74 seats won by the NP included those of Malan and his supporters. Yet Malan himself came uncomfortably close to losing his Calvinia seat to the Farmers' and Workers' Party formed by a former fellow Nationalist NP disillusioned by Malan's failure to break with Hertzog. The uncharitable have suggested that it was only Smuts' intervention on his behalf which kept *Die Doktor* in parliament (J.C. Smuts Jnr 1952:327; Pirow 1957:154–5).

MARCH 1933 TO AUGUST 1934.

The coalition government continued to give assistance to agriculture. Hertzog further managed to enshrine the constitutional position of South Africa *vis-à-vis* Britain in the 1934 Status Act. This, he considered, finally secured South Africa's full sovereign independence – a view which drew him even further away from the NP republicans (Scholtz 1975:110). Equally significant were concessions on taxation of the gold premium made in the 1933 Budget. The initial aim was to take most of the extra profits accruing to the mines. Under the compromise '50/50 arrangement', however, whilst the scale of taxation soared the post-tax profits of the gold mines increased from £10.7m in 1933 to £16.6m in 1934.[8] These concessions aroused further fury within the NP (*Die Burger* 23/5/34). A sympathetic biographer of Smuts argues that on this issue 'Hertzog guarded the interests of the capitalistic mining industry' (Crafford 1943:248).

Coalition did not resolve the party political organisation of class forces. Throughout 1933 and 1934 pressure mounted both to end the arrangement, and for a more permanent merger. The impulse for some form of union came from two sources. The Unionist element of the SAP was eager to wean

Hertzog away from the 'extreme' nationalists – that is, those who wanted to take the whole of the gold premium.[9] Secondly, demands for closer union came from the rural branches of both parties in the northern provinces, especially the Transvaal. A grass-roots movement swept the province and soon after coalition party branches began to amalgamate at the local level. The August 1933 Congress of the Transvaal NP authorised Hertzog to take steps to seek closer Union with the Sappe. The OFS Party Congress followed suit in October. Again, it must be stressed that these moves from the rural party branches were for *hereniging* rather than fusion (see above, p. 42). They were premised on the understanding that the Unionists would be excluded. So strong was this movement that Smuts was obliged to issue a statement that he would only contemplate fusion if the Unionists were included (*Die Burger* 15/9/33).

All this left the Cape Party in a difficult position. The argument that Hertzog had compromised with 'Hoggenheimer' received solid support in the Cape. Yet, the strength of the northern rural demand for *hereniging* isolated the Cape Party. Malan thus emphasised the need for the *hereniging* of all Afrikaans-speaking rural interests, and total opposition to *samesmelting* (fusion) with 'Hoggenheimer'. Unlike the NP, which was a farmers' party, the SAP was no 'inner unity', he argued, but represented antagonistic interests. The NP should deal only with its 'national' element. *Samesmelting* with the financial interests of the Rand would realign the parties along class lines and toll the death of Afrikaner nationalism (*Die Burger* 2/12/33 and 17/12/33). The Cape NP Congress made it clear to Hertzog that it was only prepared to consider *hereniging*, but never *samesmelting* (*Die Volksblad* 5/10/33).

Throughout early 1934 the Cape Party negotiated with Hertzog, who adopted the compromise slogan of *vereniging* (union). In the wake of the Status Act, Malan dropped his opposition to negotiations with Smuts, and Hertzog's speeches took on a decidedly more anti-imperialist tinge. For a while it appeared as if the Act had restored some unity to the NP. However, as Smuts' private letters make clear, powerful forces were working to detach Hertzog from Malan (Hancock 1968:253–4). In an (in)famous speech to the Rotary Club, Smuts declared that the Status Act had tightened South Africa's ties with the Empire. 'We see the birth of a new system which is designed to continue for centuries to come. . . . In the Empire the Freedom of the parts is making for the salvation of the whole' (*Cape Times* 25/5/34). Malan regarded the Status Act as a victory for nationalism. To Smuts it conferred 'full sovereign status, freedom to the utmost without limit, but always in the group of *comrades and friends* with which *we* have marched hitherto in *our* history' (HAD 11/4/34; my italics). Clearly, the definition of 'us' differed widely. Many nationalists viewed Smuts' 'comrades and friends' in a distinctly more jaundiced light. Malan was quite correct. There was no room for his type of nationalism and Smuts' imperialist vision in the same party.

The 'Rotary Club speech' terminated Malan's willingness to treat with Smuts. At the meeting of the NP's Federal Council, called to approve fusion,

Malan again cried *fait accompli*. With six other members he voted against the thirteen in favour of fusion. A statement by the seven dissidents declared that the existing fusion proposals would make the new United South African National Party (UP) 'a bulwark of imperialism and capitalism, and that, in the long run the farmer, the worker, and the poor man would be unable to feel themselves safe in it'. They demanded an immediate programme of action from the new party to deal with agricultural credit and mortgage debts, the 'poor white' problem, immigration controls, the 'Indian question', conditions of labour, and 'the native question'. Since these issues were not included in the fusion principles, they declared their resolve to maintain a 'virile' NP to attack 'the economic problems of our people and ensure full sovereign independence' (*Die Burger* 22/6/39).

And that was the end of the old NP. It split into *smelters* (fusionists) who followed Hertzog into the UP and *gesuiwerdes* (purifieds) who stayed with Malan as the leader of the now '*gesuiwerde*' NP. The major strength of the *gesuiwerdes* lay in the Cape. The Cape NP congress rejected fusion by 164 votes to 18 (*Die Burger* 27/7/34). In the north, the *gesuiwerdes* were very much weaker. The OFS Party Congress had voted to dissolve itself into the UP by 107 votes to 27 (*Die Burger* 1/8/34) and the Transvalers followed suit by 281 to 38 votes.[10]

3

The Gesuiwerde Nationalist Party and the class basis of Afrikaner nationalism

Afrikaner nationalism was transformed in the decade following fusion. The key to understanding this transformation lies in an explanation of the class basis of the Gesuiwerde party. Like its Hertzogite predecessor, the G/NP was no single, 'national' party, but a federation of four separate provincial parties. Its only real 'national' structures were the *hoofleier* (chief – or national – leader, Dr Malan), the Federal Council, and the parliamentary caucus. The significance of this fact has been emphasised (above, p. 31). Here it should be noted that, following fusion, this distinction between the provincial parties was even more sharp. They were highly disparate bodies, representing widely varying interests. Each was the institutionalisation of a distinct form of class alliance, differing significantly from its federal partners. This point is of paramount importance in the explanation of the development of Afrikaner nationalism and the emergence of deep north/south antipathies in the following decades.

The Cape NP required very little *suiwering*. In terms of organisation, personnel, its class basis and ideological expression, the G/NP was the old NP in the Cape. Though twelve of its twenty-six MPs went over to the UP, the branches and membership remained solidly behind Malan. Returns from local branches showed that less than three per cent of the membership joined the UP (*Die Burger* 1/12/34). The Cape party retained the support both of most of the province's agricultural interests, and the Afrikaner petty bourgeoisie.

For most Cape farmers, the crucial political question centred around the capacity of the South African state to influence the prices paid for their exports. This question, however, was inextricably linked with the wider constitutional question of sovereign independence. Prior to the 1926 Balfour Declaration, the constitutional position of South Africa did not include the right to establish independent trade agreements with states other than Britain. After 1926 the Hertzog government began to send trade missions to Europe and America, seeking trade agreements outside the Empire. On the conclusion of such an agreement with Germany, Smuts, the 'Handyman of the Empire', complained that this showed 'there is not that *friendship* and *cooperation* which I think should exist in a partnership [Britain being the "senior partner" in "our great firm"], in a comradeship such as we have in the Commonwealth' (*The Star* 10/11/28). Given the effect of this 'comradeship' on export prices, the arrogant refusal of the comrade senior partner to renegotiate preferential tariffs and its attack on South Africa's German trade, the constitutional relationship between the South African state and British imperialism was of crucial significance to Cape farmers. The very congress of the Cape party which decisively rejected fusion, attacked 'the threat to our wool and other markets posed by the one-sided trade with Britain and the British connection'. It further demanded that the government restore trade with Germany and end the import restrictions which posed 'a huge threat' to wool farmers (*Die Burger* 27/7/34).

Thus despite the historic association between the Cape and Britain, the issue of sovereign independence encapsulated the direct economic interests of Cape farmers. They generally favoured any extension of South Africa's constitutional independence which did not threaten to close the British market to them. Malan's claim that Hertzog had compromised with Hoggenheimer won much support. The first G/NP programme was in effect the programme of Cape agricultural capital. It demanded strong state measures to establish new export markets, especially the German, the abolition of Imperial Preferences hindering the development of such markets, and a continued struggle for 'independence' from 'imperialism' (*Die Volksblad* 24/11/34).

In the OFS, the situation was very different. Despite intense loyalty to Hertzog, the campaign against *samesmelting* won wide support. Hertzog made fusion a question of personal confidence. The Nationale Pers newspapers, *Die Burger* and *Die Volksblad*, hinted darkly at 'manipulation' of the fractious fusion Congress. But as the resolution approving coalition had shown, it was above all the appalling condition of agriculture, and farmers' needs for state action on the labour and marketing questions, which ultimately won the support of most OFS farmers for fusion. When the Congress approved the fusion proposal by 107 votes to 27 the dissidents withdrew, proclaiming themselves the 'legitimate' OFS NP (*Die Burger* 2/8/34).

While some farming support for the anti-fusion position remained, the real base of the OFS G/NP was the petty bourgeoisie – the rural traders, lawyers, teachers, civil servants, etc. (see below, pp. 52–8). Much organisational rebuilding was required. At the first congress of the OFS *gesuiwerdes*, their leader, Dr N.J. van der Merwe, indicated the ideological direction to be taken when he condemned fusion as a 'fatal collusion with the forces of capitalism and imperialism'. The G/NP, he declared, was the only reliable opponent of 'autocratic government and domination by large capital'. Echoing an earlier characterisation of the G/NP as the 'champion of the worker and the farmer' (*Die Volksblad* 24/11/34), van der Merwe stressed its strong republicanism. The party would 'break all foreign ties, whether constitutional, economic, or any sort, to develop a clear policy for the advancement of the white population' (*Die Burger* 7/12/34).

The impulse to *hereniging* had always been strongest in the Transvaal. Given the dire straits of the Transvaal farmers, such was the support for fusion that the NP was purified almost out of existence. The G/NP had to be built from scratch by its new leader, J.G. Strijdom – the only one of the Province's thirty-two Nationalist MPs who did not join the UP. The party, he declared, 'must go back to before 1926 [i.e. the Balfour Declaration] and combat capitalism. The strength of capitalism lies in the mines, and the means by which to oppose it lie in the gradual, but inexorable nationalisation of the mines. The power of the great banks must be curtailed, and at the same time, capitalism in agriculture must be fought' (*Die Burger* 7/12/34).[1] In an attempt to build up a rural base Strijdom articulated the most extreme agricultural demands over the next years, particularly on labour issues. The small rural support which did exist for the G/NP was confined to those more pressured by the development of capitalist agriculture, and to the tobacco and stock farmers in northern Transvaal whose discontent over the labour-tenancy system was most acute.

But even more than in the OFS the core of the Transvaal G/NP was the petty bourgeoisie – the academics of Pretoria and Potchefstroom Universities, the clergy of the Dutch Reformed Church, civil servants, teachers and lawyers, etc. Until the outbreak of the Second World War, the petty bourgeoisie were virtually the sole source of support for the G/NP in the north, and dominated the development of Afrikaner nationalism in these provinces.

This petty-bourgeois dominance in the north is central to an understanding of the development of Afrikaner nationalism after 1934. Given the extremely weak parliamentary representation of the northern G/NP (but five of a total of seventy-three MPs), Afrikaner nationalism in the north began to be dominated by extra-parliamentary and extra-party activities and organisations. The Broederbond emerged as the key policy co-ordinating body of northern Afrikaner nationalism after 1934 (chapter 4 below). Throughout the remainder of the 1930s, the Bond was far more powerful and important than the party itself in the Transvaal and, to a slightly lesser extent, in the OFS. Both this petty-bourgeois dominance and extra-parliamentary focus of northern Afrikaner nationalism brought it into conflict with the Cape. The prestige of Dr Malan, and the numerical preponderance of the Cape party and the interests it represented, gave it a national predominance which, coupled with a strong holier-than-thou attitude towards the erring volk of the north, was much resented. Further, unlike the petty-bourgeois-dominated northern parties, the Cape G/NP remained a party of (agricultural and financial) capital. It did not thus undergo the same ideological transformation as the northern parties. The republicanism of the Cape was decidedly weaker than that of the north. Malan was an extremely belated convert to the republican cause, reflecting the reluctance of Cape farmers to isolate themselves completely from the British market. Finally, given the ideological and organisational continuity in the Cape, and the relative strength of the Cape party, the Broederbond had no vacuum into which to rush. Thus, the redefinitions it wrought in the north were never as far-reaching in the Cape, and the Bond never achieved the position of controlling influence in the Mother Province. Rather, this role of the mafia of Cape Afrikaner nationalism developed upon Keeromstraat and Belville – the Nasionale Pers and Sanlam groups both dominated by the ubiquitous W.A. Hofmeyr (chapter 7 below). Thus the 'regionalism' long characteristic of Afrikaner nationalism became even more acute.

SOUTH AFRICAN CAPITALISM AND THE AFRIKAANS-SPEAKING PETTY BOURGEOISIE

The ideological transformation of Afrikaner nationalism into 'Christian-nationalism' in the north after 1934 was essentially the work of the petty bourgeois intellectuals organised in the Broederbond. It is thus necessary to analyse the specific social position of the Afrikaans-speaking section of the South African petty bourgeoisie to explain their support for the *gesuiwerdes* and their central role in developing Christian nationalism. There were two elements in this petty bourgeoisie: those actually engaged in petty commodity production on the one hand, and various types of intellectuals on the other – clergy, teachers, academics, lawyers, journalists, etc.

The historical trajectory of capitalist development in South Africa placed the Afrikaans-speaking petty bourgeoisie in a structurally different set of roles, alliances, pressures and struggles, from those of the English-speaking members of this class. These structural differences expressed the widely divergent historical processes which formed the English- and Afrikaans-speaking sections of the petty bourgeoisie, and the differing class forces with which each was identified and allied.

This is seen firstly in the ownership structure of the economy. As Table 1 makes clear, as late as 1938/9 Afrikaans-speakers controlled an insignificant proportion of the total production in all spheres of the economy except agriculture (where Afrikaner farmers produced 87 per cent of all marketed agricultural and livestock produce). The overwhelming majority of Afrikaner business undertakings were small one-man or family operations, with cooperatives comprising the bulk of the remainder. With few exceptions (e.g. Die Nasionale Pers, and the insurance companies Santam and Sanlam, see chapter 7) these establishments were either directly involved in petty commodity production or provided petty commercial and financial services to such producers. Thus, within 'manufacturing', blacksmiths and cheese and butter makers comprised the largest groups. Within 'finance', with the exception of Sanlam and Santam, these institutions were all small cooperative credit institutions. In no sense can they be considered finance capital. The

Table 1. *Afrikaner business undertakings in 1938/9*

Sector	Number of undertakings	Turnover (£m.)	Percentage of Union total
Commerce	2,428	28	8
Manufacturing	1,293	6	3
Mining	3	1	1
Financial	40	27	5
TOTAL	3,764	62	5

Note: The £27m. under 'financial' refers to funds under administration. There are discrepancies between the figures cited in this table and those of the census, as the table includes undertakings with less than three employees, normally excluded in the census.
Source: *Volkshandel* September 1950.

commercial undertakings were almost exclusively concentrated in the small towns of the rural areas. Even the three 'mining' establishments were involved in sifting the left-overs of worked-out gold mines bought for next to nothing. The overwhelming majority of these operations provided no real basis for the accumulation of capital. Their owners and operators were in no sense part of the capitalist class, but rather comprised a petty bourgeoisie pure and simple. Most struggled desperately for economic survival as capitalist production increasingly took hold in all spheres, driving out independent producers.

There is a further aspect to this. Again, virtually without exception, these undertakings were directly or indirectly linked to agriculture – through the provision of services and credits or the circulation and processing of part of the product. The fortunes of this petty bourgeoisie thus rose and fell with those of Afrikaner farmers. If it had no basis for the accumulation of capital, without agriculture it had no economic existence whatsoever. The interests of this petty bourgeoisie, economic and political, were thus inextricably tied up with those of agriculture. This too was changed by fusion.

For these commodity producers, the extreme economic and social pressures to which they were subjected stemmed from one source – the monopoly interests which dominated the economy – in a word, 'Hoggenheimer'. With fusion, most northern agricultural interests were now organised in an alliance in the UP with the arch-enemy, an alliance which most petty commodity producers could not support, as it offered them nothing but threatened much. Thus, despite their total economic dependence on agriculture, the northern petty bourgeoisie overwhelmingly supported the *gesuiwerdes*, providing the G/NP with its only real base in the north. But, more than any other group, it was they who felt most keenly the barbs of division (summed up in the dreaded word *broedertwis* – division between brothers), and who stood behind the appeals for unity of the volk against 'imperialism'. This is seen even more clearly in an examination of the social position of Afrikaner intellectuals.

The Afrikaans-speaking intelligentsia developed historically in the north in the interstices of the small, scattered *platteland* (rural) communities. They were truly 'organic intellectuals' in the Gramscian sense. Their economic and social activities as intellectuals were inextricably linked with the activities and interests of agriculture. They gave northern agriculture an 'homogeneity and an awareness of its own function not only in the economic, but also in the social and political fields' (Gramsci 1971:5). Before the Anglo-Boer war of 1899–1902, a high degree of economic differentiation had developed within the 'Boer' population. Yet a strong sense of community survived, built around a solidly Calvinist, petty-commodity-producer *Weltanschauung*. Following the defeat of the Boer republics in 1902, northern agriculture underwent a process of transition to capitalist agriculture. This proletarianised many white farmers on the one hand, and saw the gradual emergence of a class of capitalist farmers on the other.

This slow, but inexorable disruption of the old, 'traditional', *platteland* communities had contradictory ideological results. At one level, it saw the apparent persistence of the ideological structures of the swiftly changing *platteland* communities. Capitalist farmer, 'poor white' and intellectual all came from the same *platteland*. Their values, beliefs, ideas and expectations were formed in the old world view. In the early years of transition, they all mediated these changes through its spectacles. Thus, as the 1919 to 1920 *hereniging* attempts showed, much ideological common ground existed between the NP and the rural wing of the SAP (D.J.J. Coetzee 1975).

At other levels, however, the profound changes wrought by the uneven development of capitalist agriculture slowly undermined the basis of these ideological structures, transforming the 'organic' character of Afrikaans-speaking intellectuals. The rapid differentiation of northern agriculture, and its political and ideological polarisation between the Nationalist and South African parties, sharply divided the intellectuals. Some supported Botha and Smuts, still more followed Hertzog and Roos. Yet the predominant intellectual response by both groups was precisely a nostalgic affirmation of the disappearing organic character. Most Afrikaner intellectuals sought to paper over this social differentiation and political polarisation by appealing to a mythical and mystified unity of the Boer rural republican past – and validating these appeals in terms of the symbols, myths and ideologies of that mystified past.

Finally, the demography of the Afrikaner petty bourgeoisie was itself changing. By the late 1920s the intelligentsia had been increasingly driven into the urban areas by the disintegration of the *platteland* communities. The majority of the 'Afrikaners' they confronted here belonged to the dispirited army of proletarianised – the 'poor whites', who comprised over 25 per cent of the white, Afrikaans-speaking population (Sadie 1975:88).

The intellectuals' response to the 'poor white' problem was one of acute horror at the poverty and degradation, coupled with a recognition that it was caused by the effects of capitalist development on agriculture, and a desperate search for measures which would arrest both the process of proletarianisation and the threat it posed to the position of both the intellectuals and petty commodity producers.

Thus by 1930 the process of agricultural differentiation was increasingly detaching all elements of the Afrikaans-speaking petty bourgeoisie from its traditional alliances, leaving it disorganised, confused and isolated. The process of capitalist development had subjected this class to direct economic pressure. The rural exodus drove much of the clientele of lawyers and traders from the rural towns. Shrinking rural congregations, coupled with the rise of the apostolic churches in the urban areas and the attraction of the proletarianised to the godless labour movement, effected both the purses and the faith of the rural clergy of the three Dutch Reformed Churches. Furthermore, the structure of South African capitalism offered few opportunities to those whose home language was Afrikaans. The economy was dominated by 'imperialist' interests. Its language was English, and Afrikaans-speakers were powerfully discriminated against. Promotion and advancement required both proficiency in a foreign language – that of a conqueror – and virtual total acceptance of the structure of values dominant in the economy. Many Afrikaners around Smuts did make these leaps – most notably J.H. Hofmeyr. But for those Afrikaners who owned no land, yet who possessed a modicum of training or education rendering them unsuited to manual labour, or who were unable or unwilling to make these leaps, the only avenues of employment open were as teachers, clerics, academics, lawyers, journalists and clerks. And these professions limited their daily professional activities to areas which involved only other Afrikaans-speakers. All the obstacles to economic advance and the severe pressures induced by the structure of South African capitalism were experienced as discrimination against Afrikaners on behalf of the monopolies and 'imperialism'. In the Afrikaans language and culture itself seemed to be concentrated the experience of political oppression from Slagtersnek to the *Rebellie* and the continuing economic woes of most Afrikaans-speakers. Thus, for the petty bourgeoisie, the affirmation and assertion of both language and culture came to symbolise the struggle against all the discriminatory 'imperialist' structures.

There is another aspect to this. Precisely in the daily productive lives of Afrikaner intellectuals, as the thinking and organising element of an increasingly polarised class, were synthesised and concentrated the manifold and contradictory effects of capitalist development on capitalist farmer, small trader and 'poor white' alike – that is, on *all* Afrikaners. The Afrikaner intellectual taught the curriculum of 'imperialism' to the children of the rural bourgeoisie and the dispossessed. He administered its policies and interpreted its laws for farmers and workers. As an academic he was particularly concerned with the causes of these transformations and as a cleric he had to explain them to a confused flock in cosmic, symbolic and purposeful terms. Like the 'educated elite' of colonial Africa, the Afrikaner petty bourgeoisie identified 'imperialism' as the source of all its ills. They too saw themselves as 'the interpreters' of its effects on all the social classes of the 'Afrikaner nation', asserted the glory of 'their' culture, and generally organised themselves into a myriad cultural associations, self-help groups, agitational unions and open and secret societies.

The Pact government had introduced numerous measures to foster the particular economic interests of the Afrikaans-speaking petty bourgeoisie – equal language rights, compulsory bilingualism in the civil service, the appointment of Afrikaner intellectuals to senior civil service positions, their large-scale employment in senior and middle-management positions in the expanding infrastructure of state-run industries, etc. Equally significant, at just the time when Afrikaner intellectuals were being detached from their traditional alliances by the effects of capitalist development, NP rule offered them an ideological role within the state which went far beyond this old rural constituency. All these measures thus secured for the Afrikaner petty bourgeoisie a sheltered niche against 'imperialism'. Yet this protection rested on NP control of the machinery of government. In ending this, fusion threatened the complete isolation of the petty bourgeoisie.

Fusion was a response to the changing structure of South African capitalism. It represented, *inter alia*, a recognition by particular agricultural capitals that their interests were no longer irreconcilable with those of the 'imperialist' mining industry. This was reflected in General Hertzog's regular claim after 1934 that 'South Africa's' interests were best secured in the 'cooperative structure' of the Commonwealth.[2] But the ideological and political crisis of fusion profoundly disorganised and confused the petty bourgeoisie. It threatened both their economic and ideological interests, eroding their particular ideological function as they were displaced by the monopoly mining industry as agriculture's primary class ally.

If fusion divided and disorganised the Afrikaner petty bourgeoisie, once again the uneven effects of these processes must be emphasised. The Afrikaans-speaking petty bourgeoisie in the north and south were in different positions, and their political and ideological response varied. Given agriculture's continued support for a vigorous G/NP in the Cape, the political alliance with the petty bourgeoisie was maintained. In the Transvaal and the Free State on the other hand, confused, disorganised and despondent, some petty-bourgeois Afrikaners tagged reluctantly behind the UP. Others, but particularly the younger intellectuals who would have to wait long for any hope of advancement through the state, began for the first time to assert a petty-bourgeois position independent of other classes. It was academics at Pretoria, Potchefstroom and Bloemfontein Universities, teachers in the Transvaal and the OFS, organised through the Broederbond, who began the first tentative ideological redefinitions of Afrikaner nationalism following fusion. This is explored in following chapters.

Part II

The Afrikaner Broederbond and the beginnings of the economic movement

4

The Afrikaner Broederbond

The Afrikaner Broederbond grew out of a grouping calling itself Jong Suid-Afrika (Young South Africa), formed in May 1918. In July of that year it changed its name to the Afrikaner Broederbond. It was a time of political crisis and depression when, according to the Bond's later secretary, 'The Afrikaner soul was sounding the depths of the abyss of despair' (quoted in Serfontein 1979:31). The 1913 split in the SAP produced confusion and bitterness amongst Afrikaners, particularly in the northern provinces. This was compounded by the violent suppression of the *Rebellie*, the execution of Jopie Fourie and the imprisonment of its leaders by Botha's government. Agriculture was depressed and the influenza epidemic raged. The squeeze on land and the effects of the *Rebellie* drove increasing numbers of rural whites into the cities, accelerating the problem of 'poor whiteism'. All writings on the Bond stress the significance of this period when 'politically and economically the Afrikaner had been reduced to a slave in the land of his birth' (Oelofse 1964:7–8).

These conditions generated many organised responses. In the OFS General Hertzog formed the NP in 1914. Similar parties were formed in the Transvaal and the Cape the following year. The Helpmekaar (Mutual Aid) organisation was conceived to pay the fines of the imprisoned leaders of the *Rebellie*, and its mobilisation of the savings of Afrikaans-speakers was partly to inspire the formation of the two future insurance giants, Sanlam and Santam (chapter 7 below). The growth of the cooperative movement dates from this period. In the Cape the cultural nationalism of the Afrikaans language movement was given political and economic muscle. In three full years a handful of Cape Town and Stellenbosch professional men formed Die Nasionale Pers (National Press), the Cape NP, and Sanlam and Santam. But the Western Cape was little affected by the economic and political crises which wracked the northern provinces. The well-off, educated Afrikaners who formed these groupings were in a very different position from those in the north. The bitter words of a later anti-Cape survey of the formation of the Bond echo the recurring conflict between north and south in nationalist politics: 'compared with the acute stress raging in the northern provinces, there was little need south of the Hex River' (*Veg* November 1968).

This important point highlights what were in effect the different class bases of the nationalist movement in the Cape and the Transvaal. While this was analysed at length above, here it is vital to note that, from the outset, as a predominantly Transvaal organisation, the Broederbond differed from the mainstream of that province's nationalist movements. Whereas Transvaal Afrikaner nationalism was then overwhelmingly rural in its social basis and concerns, the Bond was a determinedly urban grouping of the petty bourgeoisie. It was founded by fourteen railway clerks, policemen and clergymen (CESO 1965: para. 32). While its membership always reflected the domination of petty bourgeois elements (see below, p. 63), two groups in particular played a central role in its early years. The Bond involvement with the question of Afrikaans schools after 1921 attracted a large number of teachers into its ranks (Louis J. du Plessis 1951). They soon infused life into the Bond, and through men such as L.J. Erasmus and, particularly, I.M. Lombard and J.H. Greijbe, dominated its leadership.[1] By the later half of the 1920s, however, large numbers of academics from the Calvinist University of Potchefstroom had joined the Bond and were displacing the teachers from the leadership. Men such as Professor L.J. du Plessis, J.C. van Rooy and H.G. Stoker brought to the Bond a developed and rigorously conservative Calvinist *Weltanschauung*. They infused new vigour into the organisation and self-consciously operated as its ideologues. By the late 1920s they were without doubt its guiding force. L.J. du Plessis became deputy chairman in 1928, and chairman in 1930, to be succeeded by J.C. van Rooy in 1932. In the confused days of coalition and fusion the influence of the Potchefstroom academics kept much of the Afrikaner intelligentsia out of the UP and provided some ideological credibility for the very weak G/NP in the north.

However, in its very early years, according to the then secretary, the Bond was 'little more than a semi-religious organisation'.[2] The official Bond history makes clear that prior to 1927 the organisation had no real conception of its function or role. Wracked by dissension and disagreement, it struggled to clarify its purpose and establish itself as a disciplined body. In 1919 the first purge occurred when only nineteen of the over a hundred members undertook to make a 'declaration' of loyalty. A second purge followed an acrimonious split from 1923 to 1925, mainly over the Nationalist/Labour Party Pact. Late in 1921, in an attempt to enforce discipline, the Bond decided to transform itself into a secret organisation. Again, its official history details the strong internal opposition to this policy, leading to a number of expulsions and even the dissolution of the West Rand Division in 1926. The struggle over the secrecy ruling seems only to have been resolved in 1932 (Pelzer 1979: 14–16, 55).

For much of the 1920s the Bond functioned in semi-Masonic fashion (and for a while seems to have modelled itself on the Freemasons), operating almost exclusively in the cultural field. Within the bounds of its limited resources it sought both to foster its members' direct interests by finding them employment and to debate the economic, social and political issues confronting them—issues such as 'the native question, immigration, profiteering, home language education and library affairs' (Military Intelligence 1944: section V, para. 8). Its 'cultural action' sought to promote Afrikaans in schools and commerce, encourage mother-tongue education and develop Afrikaans literature (Pelzer 1979:90). Although it began slowly to move out of its Transvaal base, establishing the first division in the OFS in 1926 and in the Cape in 1931, it remained overwhelmingly a Transvaal organisation with but 212 members in nine divisions by 1927. During these first ten years of its existence it cannot be said to have been a significant force in either Afrikaner cultural life or nationalist politics.

Two traumatic events in the 1920s and 1930s decisively altered the Bond's role and led to its relatively rapid development into the highly disciplined vanguard organisation of northern Afrikaner nationalism. The first occurred in 1927 when General Hertzog abandoned republicanism following the 1926 Balfour Declaration granting South African Dominion status. This 'betrayal' prompted a Bond decision to 'expand activities and take an active part in the life of the [Afrikaner] community leaving no avenue neglected' (Military Intelligence 1944: section V, para. 8). The divisions were instructed to increase their influence in local affairs, so that in every district Afrikaners would be aware of a 'moving force, even if its source could not be precisely located'. This marked the end of the 'youthful phase' of the Bond and the start of its attempt 'systematically to infiltrate every arena of importance to the continued existence of the Afrikaner and to make the AB's influence felt' (Pelzer 1979: 95–6).

The effect of the Balfour Declaration on nationalist politics likewise brought home the Bond's need for a 'public front' (Pelzer 1979:119). This led to its establishment in December 1929 of the Federasie van Afrikaanse Kultuurverenigings (Federation of Afrikaans Cultural Association, hereafter FAK). Under the chairmanship of the OFS Nationalist Party MP, Dr N.G. van der Merwe, the FAK was an umbrella body designed to provide 'central organisation' and 'clear direction' to the myriad Afrikaner cultural groupings. The Bond's paternity of the FAK is undisputed. Its official history acknowledges that as 'a creation of the AB, the FAK is regarded by the mother-organisation as its public arm' (Pelzer 1979:120). The FAK was to be the most important and influential of the Bond's numerous public fronts. With token exceptions the two bodies shared the same executives and officials who publicly implemented the FAK policies secretly decided upon in the Bond. By 1937 almost 300 cultural bodies were affiliated to the FAK. Now, in effect, the Bond's early concern with routine cultural work was openly undertaken by the FAK, freeing the Bond to concentrate on other issues. In the words of its chairman in 1932:

> We find the AB is slowly handing over the cultural work to its much bigger son, the FAK ... [But] national culture and the welfare of the volk will only flourish if the South African people break all foreign bonds. After the cultural and economic needs, the AB will have to devote its attention to the political needs of our people (*Rand Daily Mail* 8/11/35).[3]

In the period between the formation of the FAK in 1929 and coalition in 1933, under the leadership of the Potchefstroom academics the Bond strove to strengthen its organisation, tighten discipline and extend its membership 'to the Afrikaner elite throughout the country' (Moodie 1975:146–7). Membership rose from 212 in nine divisions in 1927, to 362 in 17 divisions in 1929, reaching 1,023 in 55 divisions by 1933 (Pelzer 1979:32). Internal opposition to the Potchefstroom academics and their reorganisation of the Bond during this period led to the formation in 1930 of a breakaway Handhawersbond by one-time Bond secretary L.J. Erasmus and other members of the Transvaalse Onderwysersvereniging (Transvaal Teachers' Association, hereafter TO).[4]

In these years the Bond also began for the first time to intervene in the growing conflict within the NP. In 1930, following discussions in the Bond, FAK chairman and Nationalist MP Dr N.J. van der Merwe formed the Republikeinsebond (Republic League) as a ginger group within the NP, agitating against Hertzog's leadership. Yet whatever the dissatisfaction with Hertzog, given both the class alliances underlying the NP and the general's enormous political stature, the Broederbond was in no position to mount an open challenge until he himself precipitated a break. The long coalition/fusion crisis of 1933/4 was the second catalyst which finally transformed the Bond. As analysed above, fusion disorganised the Afrikaner petty bourgeoisie and detached it from its traditional political alliances. In the political vacuum following the collapse of the NP in the north, the Bond progressively assumed for itself the role of the directing body – or in its own words 'war council' (Pelzer 1979: 12) – of Afrikaner nationalism.

As the fusion crisis ripened in 1933/4, the leadership again tightened discipline and 'purified' the Bond. Its 1934 annual congress decided to infiltrate members into 'key positions' in all leading institutions. New regional councils were introduced to strengthen local and national coordination (Pelzer 1979: 55, 109, 36). And according to a later Bond chairman, in 1934 a campaign was begun to recruit 'Afrikaans national political leaders'. Dr D.F. Malan, the Transvaal G/NP leader J.G. Strijdom, and leading OFS *gesuiwerde* C.R. Swart, now joined (Serfontein 1979: 40), to be organised into a Bond parliamentary group. At the end of 1934 a Bond 'Political Commission' was appointed with L.J. du Plessis as 'Political Commissar' – though this title was later dropped and the Commission was renamed the Parliamentary Commission (Pelzer 1979: 148, 174). Professor du Plessis soon also became the chairman of the Transvaal G/NP.

Who did this reorganised Bond represent, and how did it function? It must be stressed that it remained based predominantly in the urban areas of the northern provinces, especially the Transvaal. The Bond's influence and membership in the Cape was always slight compared with the north. In the 1930s the Afrikaans-speaking urban white population was overwhelmingly working-class. Membership of the Bond was constitutionally required to reflect the occupational structure of the local Afrikaans communities, giving the Bond the 'right' to speak in their name. In practice, membership was confined largely to the professions. A stiff annual membership fee (£12.10.0), a system of regular financial levies and a strict requirement that members be 'financially sound', ruled out anything but token working-class membership. One long-time member and former divisional chairman told me that workers as such were never involved, as it was felt 'there was no specific need for workers in the Broederbond'. Bond membership remained almost exclusively petty bourgeois. In 1944, the first year for which a reasonably reliable breakdown of members' occupations exists, teachers, academics, clergymen and civil servants accounted for over fifty per cent of members, with lawyers, journalists, politicians, farmers and assorted businessmen as other large occupational groupings (Military Intelligence 1944: section V; *Die Transvaler* 14, 20 December 1944 and 3 January 1945). This heavily petty-bourgeois membership comprised in effect the cream of the northern Afrikaner intelligentsia, and came to be regarded – and so regarded itself – as the self-chosen elite of 'Afrikanerdom'.

This elitism was a crucial aspect to the functioning of the Bond. Membership was constitutionally restricted to financially sound, white, Afrikaans-speaking, Protestant males over twenty-five years old. These had to be of 'unimpeachable character' and actively accept South Africa as their sole homeland, containing 'a separate Afrikaner nation with its own language and culture' (Oelofse 1964: chapter 3, para. 11–56). Nobody could apply to join. The extremely stiff, complex selection procedure was designed to ensure secrecy and to control and maintain ideological purity and rigid discipline. Candidates could only be proposed from within the local divisions. Every single Bond member and the Executive Council vetted each candidate, who could be rejected by a simple blackballing procedure. In effect, then, most members were known to each other, and in this sense the Bond clearly was a self-chosen, self-reproducing elite.

The Bond was a policy-making, coordinating body. It determined fields of action and their parameters without itself directly implementing policy. This was left to the front organisations and individual members. It was organised into local divisions of between five and fifty members. A twelve-member Executive Council presided over daily affairs and administration. The divisions were required to meet monthly to 'discuss everything to do with Afrikaners in its particular area, especially economic life'. Issues and proposals were thoroughly discussed and criticised and then referred to other divisions. If necessary the Executive Council appointed 'a committee of experts' to consider particular issues. According to a former member, the complex policy-making process generated 'a feeling of intense comradeship'.

As the old boy network *par excellence*, the Bond set up 'ongoing machinery to handle everything'. Once 'fully worked out policy' had emerged from the consultation process it was either implemented by mandated individual members working through front organisations, or 'laid before the volk' in a volkskongres (congress of the volk) – themselves organised by a Bond front organisation (CESO 1965: para. 39).

A picture emerges of an immense informal network of influence in all regions and all sections of the Afrikaner community, together with a powerful organisational bond forging very strong group loyalties. The vital significance of the Bond as it developed after fusion lay in the fact that through it the intellectual cream of the Afrikaner petty bourgeoisie was independently organised into a militant, highly disciplined body. Through the coordination and direction of the disparate individual talents of this class, and their 'systematic infiltration' into all 'key bodies in national life' where they could exercise 'quiet influence', the Bond provided a superb vehicle for the discussion, elaboration, adoption and eventual execution of what, after fusion, amounted to the independent programme of the Afrikaner petty bourgeoisie.

Given the extreme weakness of the northern G/NP, especially in the Transvaal, the extra-parliamentary Bond became clearly the most significant and influential northern Afrikaner nationalist organisation. In contrast to the Cape, where the party remained the dominating force, in the Transvaal and the OFS the Bond acted to a large extent independently of the party and, at least in the 1930s, effectively controlled the northern G/NP. Whilst in the Cape the old generation of political leadership formed in the early twentieth century retained firm control, in the northern provinces a new generation of intellectuals assumed the leadership of Afrikaner nationalism through the Bond. These younger men had not fought in the Anglo-Boer War and had lived most of their lives in a unified South Africa. Given a chance of leadership and an influence they would otherwise have had to wait long for, they brought to Afrikaner nationalism new vigour, ideas and perspectives. To the influence of the young Potchefstroom academics was soon added that of four celebrated doctors, N. Diedrichs, P.J. Meyer, H.F. Verwoerd and A. Hertzog (the general's son). All were newly returned from overseas study in the early 1930s, and, Diedrichs and Meyer in particular, strongly influenced by European fascism.[5] With the Potchefstroom academics, they led the post-fusion ideological redefinition of Afrikaner nationalism.

Soon after coalition, a new Journal, *Koers* (Directions), appeared from Potchefstroom. Its first editorial expounds its self-conscious ideological role: 'Indeed, in our country and throughout the entire world, there prevails the greatest confusion on religious, moral, educational, social, political and economic issues. However weak and impotent it may be in many respects, with the mercy and help of God *Koers* will try to give direction in all these areas' (August 1933).

During the 1930s *Koers* was effectively the theoretical journal of a major faction of the Bond. It raised all the contemporary issues, answering them in policy terms. Through his regular column *Die Loop van Dinge* (the passage of things), 'Political Commissar' L.J. du Plessis kept up a running commentary on political affairs. His analysis of coalition in the first issue clearly illustrates the economic basis of Bond nationalism and well sums up the fears of the Afrikaner petty bourgeoisie generally:

> General Hertzog has achieved what neither General Botha nor General Smuts could accomplish. He has reconciled the great majority of Afrikaners with the idea of the British Empire.... When, with Sovereignty [i.e. in the 1926 Balfour Declaration and the 1931 Statute of Westminster] General Hertzog also accepted cooperative Imperialism, in practice the differences between the two large parties on this issue fell away.... It is therefore certain that under the new regime less emphasis will be placed on sovereignty than on mutual cooperation within the Empire. Once again Imperialism will stride triumphant throughout the land. Under present international conditions, cooperative Imperialism will mainly, though not exclusively, take the form of economic collaboration. Our monetary system, our commercial and banking policy, our industrial sector will remain Imperialist oriented and grow increasingly so. In place of the old political subjugation we now enter a period of economic dependence. And the golden chains so forged are much stronger and more dangerous than the old [political] chains because they are more difficult to recognise, and once forged, are not easily discarded. The apparatus of this collaboration is already largely extant, particularly in the banking and commercial sectors. Only a government fully committed to South Africa's economic independence could escape this octopus grip. What will happen under a government sympathetic to [Imperialism] is impossible to predict (*Koers*, August 1933).

In this environment of perceived 'imperialist' domination, the Bond strove to interpret the world and formulate counter-policy for its petty-bourgeois membership. Political power was seen as one of the keys to the ending of this domination. Recognising its isolation and weakness the Bond sought allies by again appealing to agricultural interests and to Afrikaner workers, and fighting for what it termed 'the small man' in all sectors against the threat of 'imperialism'.

Yet such allies could not simply be appropriated by mystic appeals to the unity of the Afrikaner volk. As the enthusiastic rural support for fusion in the north indicated, poorer farmers tended to follow the lead of larger landowners and Afrikaner workers displayed an unhealthy attraction for class organisations. Given the existence of a very large group of 'poor whites', a real danger existed that they could be mobilised by working-class organisations, thereby undermining any potential mass base for Afrikaner nationalism. An obsession with the dangers of class division and class mobilisation and the pressing need for the unity of Afrikaners of all classes is thus a major theme of the Bond ideologies during this period. These groups had to be saved for the volk and mobilised as Afrikaners.

Yet underlying all these problems was the almost total exclusion of Afrikaners from control in any sector of the economy except agriculture (see above, pp. 52–4). If, as *Koers* argued, the basis of imperialist domination was economic, the mere capture of government would not end it. That was the discredited Hertzog panacea. The collapse of the Hertzog NP, reinforced by the urban experience of capitalism, had taught one profound lesson: it was economic strength which counted above all. From now on, the overriding aim of the Bond intellectuals would be the transformation of the economic position of the Afrikaner petty bourgeoisie – to transform this petty bourgeoisie into a bourgeoisie on the savings of Afrikaner workers and farmers. This was the now proven Cape formula. Thus the Bond strove to break the economic dependence of the petty bourgeoisie on other classes and burst open the doors of economic advance now barred to them by the use of their mother-tongue. Together with the Afrikaner finance capital in the Cape, the Bond began the task of generating explicitly Afrikaner capital, to enable the Afrikaner petty bourgeoisie to participate in the industrial capitalist economy through the medium of their own language. This was seen as a direct assault on 'imperialism' and its *alter ego*, 'capitalism'. The Afrikaans language and culture provided the primary focus for the ideological redefinition of Afrikanerdom and its nationalism in the 1930s and 1940s, as the petty bourgeois militants of the Bond in a wary alliance with the Sanlam mafia, sought to mobilise Afrikaans-speakers of other classes in support of their vision. Thus, throughout the thirties, as the Bond concentrated its attention on these problems it operated in three broad areas: the ideological redefinition of Afrikanerdom and Afrikaner nationalism; the organisation of Afrikaner workers into ethnic trade unions; and the establishment and promotion of Afrikaner business interests. These are explored in turn in the following chapters.

5

The Afrikaner Broederbond and the development of Christian-nationalist ideology

The ideological debates which redefined Afrikaner nationalism into 'Christian-nationalism' during the 1930s took place within a general framework of Calvinist ideas. A brief outline of developments within South African Calvinism is thus necessary.

The years after 1870 witnessed profound and violent transformations in South Africa. Old patterns of life were shattered, and men and women were hurled into new, foreign, and threatening economic, social and political environments. The rapid development of industry and the large-scale proletarianisation of both black and white rural producers intensified these social disruptions in the 1920s and 1930s. Old certainties were destroyed, old world views and moralities undermined; men and women were forced to adapt their values and ideas to totally new social relationships, new patterns of life.

Reflecting these processes, there developed a growing conflict within the various streams of South African Calvinism. The steady erosion of the rural communities and the exodus to the cities, the rise of working-class politics and the growth of apostolic churches amongst 'poor whites', all led to a gathering theological crisis. The churches, too, had to adapt their theology and sermons to the new conditions and values of industrial society. These conflicts are well-documented elsewhere.[1] Of concern here are not the theological niceties and minutiae of interpretation, but the generally-ignored fact that these theological struggles posed in highly abstract and abstruse form the economic, social and political questions of the day. In this context of rapid social change and intensified class struggle were raised issues affecting all Afrikaans-speakers.

Briefly, however, the conflict boiled down to a struggle between an evangelical tendency in the tradition of Andrew Murray, and a more narrowly 'reformed' theology drawing heavily on the Dutch theologian/politician, Abraham Kuypers. Of the three existing Dutch Reformed churches, the small, theologically liberal Nederduitsch Hervormde Kerk (NHK) remained largely outside these struggles. The rigidly conservative and equally small Gereformeerde Kerk (GK) was the very site of developing Kuyperian theology. Within the largest of these churches, the Nederduits Gereformeerde

67

Kerk (NGK), this conflict was at its most acute throughout the 1920s, leading to the heresy trial and dismissal from the Stellenbosch Seminary of Professor J. du Plessis in 1928. By 1935 a prominent evangelical publication mourned the 'two directions in our [NGK] church' (Bekommerd 1935), whilst the Kuyperian tendency published a series of books aimed at giving 'direction in the crisis' (*Koers in Die Krisis* 1935, 1940, 1941).

Rooted in an individualistic liberalism, the evangelical tradition emphasised the redemption of all, and the task of all Christians to bring in all who could be saved. To the Kuyperians this was unreconstructed methodism. They counterposed the doctrine of elective grace as distinct from common grace. At the heart of the Kuyperian schema lay the doctrine of *sowereiniteit in eie kring* – the principle of the absolute sovereignty of God in every sphere (*kring*) of life, each independent of the others. Many NGK theologians supported neither the evangelical nor the Kuyperian extremes, but emphasised the organic relationship between volk and *kerk* (church).

Prevailing idealist analyses of Afrikaner nationalism take these theological debates as the source and explanation of Afrikaner nationalism. At best, there is dispute over which Calvinism was the most influential.[2] My stress on the theological struggles of the period begins from a very different premise. As responses to a rapidly changing world, these Calvinist reinterpretations provided the ideational and symbolic framework within and through which the redefinition of Afrikaner nationalism into Christian-nationalism began. The ideologues who sought to redefine Afrikaner nationalist ideology in the 1930s and 1940s did not pluck timeless conceptions either from the air, or (as occasionally claimed) from the hand of providence. The moral principles, symbolic structures, concepts, terms of reference, and system of validations through which Christian-nationalism was elaborated, were neither dreamed up nor invoked through mysticism. As men concerned to explain a changing world, these ideologists drew on and further elaborated their existing structure of ideas – a broadly Calvinist *Weltanschauung*. Whatever the contorted discussions of *sowereiniteit in eie kring, kultuur*, volk, nation, etc., these were the concepts through which the ideology posed such problems as, *inter alia*, the developing crisis in agriculture, the proletarianisation of small farmers, the acute poverty of 'poor whites', the continuing imperialist domination of the economy and economic discrimination against Afrikaans-speakers. A reading of the key journals, books, pamphlets and newspapers of the time reveals a desperate concern with the real issues of material life, not mere spiritual delvings. It reveals both an attempt to understand the issues and bewildering changes of the time, and a determination to translate understanding into concrete action, concrete policies.

The pre- and post-fusion ideological definitions differed firstly in their delimitations of 'Afrikanerdom' and secondly in the character of 'its' nationalism. The 'Hertzogist' conception of 'Afrikanerdom', which thoroughly dominated the old NP, was subjective. An individual's personal attitude decided whether or not she/he was an 'Afrikaner'. All white South Africans,

Afrikaans- and English-speaking, who viewed South Africa as their sole homeland, who accepted absolute language equality and the principle 'South Africa first', were regarded as Afrikaners. Hence Hertzog's regular reference to Afrikaans- (or sometimes Dutch-speaking) and English-speaking 'Afrikaners' (Note 1, p. 258). The 'Afrikanerdom' the Hertzog NP sought to mobilise was never seen in terms of a rigid ethnic and culturally defined volk. So far as the NP concentrated on cultural issues, this was in the context of consolidating equal language rights. Even in the early days of the 'two stream policy' Hertzogism emphasised above all else a South Africanist ideology as a counterpart to British 'imperialism'. This broad South Africanism remained the dominant ideology of the UP under Hertzog's leadership. The ideological basis of fusion lay in Hertzog's argument that most elements in the SAP were now South Africanist. Moreover the Hertzog NP further implicitly accepted the class divisions within the white population as the natural basis of political organisation. It was generally content to leave the organisation of white workers to the Labour Party (Nasionale Party 1931:101–16).

To the Broederbond it was Hertzogism's subjectivism and consequent ideological looseness, lack of ethnic consciousness and acceptance of 'foreign' notions of class division which explained the general's 'sell out' to 'imperialism'. If not to be repeated, such subjective criteria had to be replaced by 'objective' ones. The concepts and constituents of Afrikanerdom, together with the significance of class divisions in social and political life, required extensive redefinition. At the outset, English-speakers could be excluded as 'foreign elements'. Not meshed in the cultural unity and loyalties of the volk, they were always susceptible to 'imperialist' blandishments. The Bond's new, ethnically exclusive delimitation of 'Afrikanerdom' then involved the definition of what was peculiarly 'Afrikaans' about 'Afrikaners' – an intensive analysis of the inter-relationships between the individual, volk, culture and the state.

Thus the 1930s saw intense and wide-ranging debate amongst Bond intellectuals seeking to reinterpret the experience of capitalist development into new ideological forms. Within this debate a number of intersecting yet subtly different streams of influence, each with many permutations, can be identified. Through *Koers* and the individual writings of men like L.J. du Plessis, J.C. van Rooy, H.G. Stoker, J.D. du Toit (the poet Totius) and C. Coetzee, the Potchefstroom academics who dominated the Bond in the early 1930s elaborated an explicitly Calvinist *Weltanschauung* rooted in the Kuyperian doctrine of *sowereiniteit in eie kring*.

For these Kuyperians, culture was a divine product, which, together with race, history, fatherland and politics, distinguished the various nations from each other. As a divinely created entity, each volk was a separate social sphere (*kring*), each with a God-willed structure, purpose, calling and destiny:

> God willed the diversity of Peoples. Thus far He has preserved the identity of our Volk. Such preservation was not for naught, for God allows nothing to happen for naught . . . He maintained the identity of our Volk. He has a future task for us, a calling laid away. On this I base my fullest conviction that our Volk will

69

again win back its freedom as a Volk. This lesson of our history must always be kept before our eyes. . . . If He wishes to make us one Volk again and to give us our freedom, He will create the necessary circumstances. If we get our free republic it will not be from the hand of man, but will be gift of God . . . [b]ecause God, the Disposer of the lot of nations, has a future task laid away for our Volk. Let us thus become conscious of our calling (Stoker 1941:250-1).

This Kuyperian 'Christian-nationalism' was soon refined in extensive debate with a more secular nationalism developed by other academics and intellectuals outside Potchefstroom. Labelled 'neo-Fichtean' by Moodie (1975:154), this was elaborated amongst others by men such as Drs N. Diedrichs, P.J. Meyer, H.F. Verwoerd, A. Hertzog, G. Cronje, T.J. Hugo, and J. de W. Keyter. It received its most explicit statement in Diedrichs' *Nasionalisme as Lewensbeskouing* (Nationalism as *Weltanschauung*), published in 1936. For Diedrichs, too, God ordained the division of nations, each with its own specific calling. Service to the nation is thus service to God. The nation is the only true reality. Any attempt to obliterate national differences abrogates God's natural law. Hence the implacable rejection of notions of human equality (Diedrichs 1936: *passim*).

This 'neo-Fichtean' group soon emerged as the ideological leader of the Afrikaans-Nasionaal Studentebond (Afrikaans National Students' Union, hereafter ANS). The ANS newspaper, *Wapenskou* (Review of Arms), became their regular organ. A modified 'neo-Fichteanism' was propagated by Verwoerd as editor of *Die Transvaler* after 1937. Their move into the Bond leadership was rapid. P.J. Meyer became Bond deputy secretary in 1937. By 1938 Diedrichs' ideological prominence enabled him to displace Kuyperian J.C. van Rooy as Bond chairman. Verwoerd was elected on to its Executive Council in 1940, at about the same time as Albert Hertzog.

The third important stream of ideological influence stemmed from NGK theologians who supported neither Evangelists nor Kuyperians in the theological controversies of the period. Emphasising rather an organic relationship between volk and church, they urged the church to play a more active role in the life of the volk – now defined in ethnically exclusive terms.[3] Increasingly concerned with the pragmatic problems of poverty and anglicisation of their congregations, they placed great stress on education as the panacea for both. This grew into an emphasis on Afrikaans education and the need to preserve the national character and culture of Afrikaners. NGK theologians such as Dr D.F. Malan had been the moving spirits behind the language movement. As early as 1911 he wrote: 'God wills the difference between nation and nation. And he Wills these because he has placed before each People a unique destiny, a unique calling . . . He has a unique calling for our People with its own Ethnic nature' (Moodie 1975:71).

The Depression transformed this concern with poverty and Afrikaner education into burning issues around which the NGK increasingly began to organise. In the bitter schism over fusion, the NGK redoubled its emphasis on unity. Through men like W. Nicol (Bond Chairman 1924–25), P.K. Albertyn, and Malan himself, the pragmatic *volkskerk* NGK tendency found much common ground with the strongly Kuyperian *kultuurpolitiek* of the period, leading to increasing cooperation.

Despite the many differences within and between these groups, sufficient common ground existed to enable ideological debate to take place within agreed parameters. Four broad areas of agreement emerged: the relationship between culture and nationalism; the dangers of class divisions; the need for the economic mobilisation of Afrikaners; and republicanism. (Significantly, during the thirties this ideological elaboration of Christian-nationalism did not involve detailed debate or discussion of policy on the 'native question'. White supremacy was taken for granted. The detailed development of the concept of apartheid only began in the 1940s – see chapter 12 below.)

All groups agreed that the nation is the primary social unit from which all individuals draw their identity. As products of Divine Will, each with an allotted task and calling, nations are distinguished from each other by 'culture'. The development of culture and the protection and promotion of its unique, exclusive values is thus a divinely-ordained duty. Hence the Bond's assertion: 'The Afrikaner Broederbond is born out of the deep conviction that the Afrikaner nation has been planted in this country by the Hand of God, destined to survive as a separate nation with its own calling.'[4]

During the 1930s, this divinely-created Afrikaner nation was politically divided, culturally disunited and wracked by severe class divisions. Afrikaner workers displayed scant interest in the culture and the politics of the volk, and behaved economically and politically in class terms. The huge 'poor white problem' was the most glaring manifestation of this division. Rapid 'de-nationalisation' of urban Afrikaners, particularly 'poor whites', disturbed all ideologues. They agreed on the major theme of the period, the overriding need for unity between Afrikaners of all classes (*volkseenheid*), and more particularly, the need to win workers to Afrikaner nationalism. In the words of Diedrichs: 'If the worker is drawn away from our nation, we may as well write Ichabod on the door of our temple.... He must be drawn into his nation in order to be a genuine man. There must be no division or schism between class and class' (Moodie 1975: 168).

Hankering after the idealised 'unity' of the Great Trek and the republics, in terms of whose mythology all were farmers united against external enemies, class divisions were seen as the product of 'imperialism', and its *alter ego*, 'foreign' capitalism. While Afrikaners had suffered under capitalism, the solution lay in improving their position in the industrial economy, to take control of South African capitalism itself and develop a *volkskapitalisme*. This economic movement aimed 'to prevent the further destruction of the Afrikaner volk in the attempt to adjust to a foreign capitalist system; but to mobilise the volk to capture this foreign system and transform and adapt it to our national character' (L.J. du Plessis, quoted by E.P. du Plessis 1964:104).

This transformation of *kultuur*, classes and the economy was to be

71

encapsulated in a republic, freed from British political domination, 'independent' of the golden chains *Koers* so regularly warned of. This republic would be based not on the 'mechanical' liberal parliamentary system, but rather on 'organic' *volksregering* (people's government) (Meyer 1941:116). In this organic volk's republic, the state would become a positive moral instrument for the creation of a truly Christian-national society. On this, too, there was unanimity – though Malan's conversion was belated and, some would argue, hesitant. The Bond's vision of Republican nirvana received its apotheosis in the controversial Draft Republican Constitution published 'for discussion' in 1942.[5]

The common ground between these different ideological streams was summed up as 'Afrikanerism' by L.J. du Plessis as early as 1935. It aimed at the 'Afrikanerisation' of South Africa so that:

> there should be Afrikaners; that they should be ineradicably strong through unity; that they should outwardly establish and maintain their own nature (that is culture); that they should live out this nature (that is independence); that they should be unimpeded without (that is freedom); that in view of this they should have control over the soil and riches of South Africa (that is solvency and domination); and that finally, in unity, with their own culture independently realised, freely and as owners they should bring forth by their own power their own Afrikaans constitutional organisation as armour and shield for their Afrikanerisation of South Africa' (L.J. du Plessis, Hugo, T.J. & F.J. Labuschagne, n.d.: 3).

As shown in Part I, the uneven effects of rapid capitalist development eroded the material base of the 'Hertzogite' NP. These swiftly-changing material conditions themselves gave rise to the ideological debates within the Bond as an attempt to comprehend and respond to such changes. A new 'Christian-nationalist' ideology emerged in the very process of the intellectual mediation of this new urban experience of rapid capitalist development. Here lies the core of the break with the ideology of the old NP, which was primarily concerned with the rural impact of capitalism.[6] Thus, despite Hertzog's attacks and powerful counter-claim to be the true representative of 'Afrikanerdom', the ideological debates in the Bond did succeed precisely in redefining 'Afrikaner' culture in the very process of conceptualising rapidly changing economic, social and political conditions.

But the ideological debates within the Bond during the 1930s were essentially elitist. In obscure journals and pamphlets, small groups of intellectuals argued amongst themselves in complex, abstruse language. The volk as such displayed scant interest, let alone understanding. The vast majority of Afrikaans-speakers clearly still clung to Hertzogism. Yet the dauntingly intellectual debates in the Bond during the 1930s clearly con-stituted the 'literary' aspect of a new ideology (see p. 15 above). Although it drew on the symbolic structures, moral principles, concepts and system of validations present in both the literary and popular aspects of existing nationalist ideology, these were elaborated in such a way that, at the literary level at least, a clear break was made with this Hertzogist ideology.

It is important to be clear on this. I argued in the Introduction (p. 15) that the axis and organising principle of any ideology, and that which distinguishes ideologies from each other, is the specific interpellation – the subject interpellated – of each ideological system. In effect, then, the intellectual ideological debates in the Bond succeeded in the elaboration and development of the concept of a new historical subject – an organically united Afrikaner volk. Though the term Afrikaner volk was widely used in Hertzogism, the Bond ideologues effected a complete transformation of its content and conceptions of its historical development. It was now defined in culturally exclusive terms, an exclusivity fired in past struggles and destined to be realised in a republican nirvana. This organic volk was now declared a divine product and assigned a divinely allotted calling. Yet the ideologues' concept of an organically-united Afrikaner volk was confronted with the reality of intense cultural, class and political divisions amongst Afrikaans-speakers. In the abstract schemas of the intellectuals these real divisions were overcome at the literary level through the ideological neutralisation of existing antagonisms, and their replacement, in thought, by other antagonisms. The real class, political, religious and cultural antagonisms within the volk were conceptually neutralised by reducing them to simple differences. To take the most important of these. While the existence of class divisions was recognised and regretted, within the intellectual schemes these were treated as mere differences – as the various components of an organic whole. Each constituent part of the whole was accorded equal weight, the antagonism between them denied, and thus the meaning of these class differences at the political level neutralised through the denial of the class struggle. Yet if antagonisms within the historical subject – the volk – were ideologically neutralised, those between the organically-united volk and other groups were developed. Hence, the ideologues argued, the existence of intense and irreconcilable antagonisms between the volk on the one hand and various and numerous external forces on the other: 'The Afrikaner Calvinist can only seek and find power in cooperation with other Christian members of the volk because our existence as a volk was threatened in various ways by imperialists, Jews, coloureds, natives, Indians, Afrikaner renegades and so on.' (H.G. Stoker, *Koers* December 1942)[7]

Thus, during the 1930s, the ideologues were successful in redefining ideology only at a literary level, in the forms of thought of groups of intellectuals. The vast majority of Afrikaans-speakers clung to Hertzogism. In other words, it was Hertzogism which interpellated individual Afrikaans-speakers as subjects. Hertzogism 'hailed' them not as Christian-national Afrikaners, but as 'Hey, you Afrikaans-speaking South Africans!' Thus the success of the Bond intellectuals was partial. While they had arrived at the concept, or idea, of a new subject, individual Afrikaners were not interpellated as this subject. Christian-nationalism had not yet entered popular consciousness, it did not yet in practice combine the literary and popular levels of ideology, it had not succeeded in interpellating – as distinct from defining – this new Christian-national Afrikaner subject.

This is a crucial point. 'Christian-nationalism' or 'Afrikaner-nationalism' was much more than a complex intellectual–ideological framework representing certain views of the world. The terms also encompassed the mass social and political movement which emerged, comprised of widely disparate groups, mobilised through this ideology. It is not enough simply to trace the literary forms of development of the ideational structure and simply assume its inherent appeal to all Afrikaans-speakers. The actual translation of such literary forms of ideology from intellectual journals and the debates of elite groups into a form of mass consciousness – the process by which the new subject was successfully interpellated – has to be investigated. This was achieved only through various protracted struggles, and the development of new forms of organisation. In this process, the Bond's control of organised Afrikaner culture was a powerful weapon.

The Bond began life as a cultural organisation. During the 1920s it devoted the bulk of its energies to cultural issues. Its control of the Afrikaner Teachers' Association (TO) in the Transvaal in the 1920s, and then later in the OFS, together with its growing influence in the GK and NGK, provided a vitally important base from which to influence the cultural lives of many Afrikaans-speakers. General Hertzog's 1935 attack on the Bond made much of the 'improper influence' Bond-inspired teachers exercised on children. However, the greatest success of the Bond lay in establishing control over the vast majority of Afrikaner cultural associations. The vital steps had been taken even before fusion, with the formation of the FAK as the bond's public front (pp. 61–2 above).

One of the first and most important tasks undertaken by the FAK was its language project. Its conscious goal was to modernise Afrikaans, adapting it to industrial society, transforming it from the language of the veld and farm to the language of city, factory and commerce. In doing so it drew together, coordinated, directed, and planned the full resources of Afrikaner intellectuals. FAK committees drew up and issued authoritative booklets of new words, new terms and new concepts on everything from the component parts of the internal combustion engine to the laws of cricket. Because it came to dominate the development of the language itself, to guide the terms in which Afrikaans-speakers of all classes conceptualised the profound social transformations of the early 1930s, the Bond's public front exercised enormous influence over all aspects of daily life.

The language issue affected Afrikaans-speakers of all classes, in all walks of life. The Hertzog NP had fought for language equality within the state, an equality enshrined in the 1925 Language Act. But with the rapid break-up of the *platteland* communities and the increasing urbanisation of Afrikaners, by the 1930s the language struggle had shifted to the centres of industrial production, the cities. The cities of South Africa were overwhelmingly English. English was the language of the urban economy and culture. On the factory floor, in shops and banks, Afrikaans was hardly ever used but was derided as a 'kitchen language'. This was experienced by all Afrikaans-speakers as intense discrimination against both their language and themselves. Whatever their class position, simply to conduct their daily lives they were forced to use a foreign language, that of a conqueror. Thus, while the FAK was adapting the Afrikaans language to industrial society, the Bond sought to organise all Afrikaans-speakers to struggle for the right to use their own language, to fight the discrimination against Afrikaans. Under Bond direction many local organisations were formed, many campaigns waged. Typical of these was the call by the ANS: 'Never shop where you are not served in Afrikaans, and where Afrikaans is not accorded its rightful place on notices and signboards – and tell the trader why. Pay no accounts which have not been issued in Afrikaans, and patronise no firm which does not advertise in Afrikaans newspapers and magazines' (*Wapenskou* February 1936). The language struggle was given a firmly nationalist direction by the Bond. It was seen as part of the assertion of a separate Afrikaner identity (*eie*). The Bond's leading role in the language struggle gave it great influence over all Afrikaans-speakers.

Nowhere was this more evident than in the field of culture itself. The FAK rapidly established the desired 'central control' over cultural matters to emerge as the supreme cultural arbiter of things 'Afrikaans'. By 1937, almost 300 cultural bodies, church councils, youth and students' associations, and charitable, scientific and educational groups were affiliated to it. This domination of Afrikaner cultural life through the FAK was the Bond's major political weapon. Following fusion, the Bond itself was unable to espouse support for the G/NP. Clause 6 of its constitution banned party politics. The open introduction of party politics into Bond deliberations and those of its front organisations would have alienated the mass of Afrikaners in the north who supported Hertzog. In any case, the Bond was better organised and more powerful than the pathetically weak northern *gesuiwerde* parties. In the midst of the fusion crisis, the Bond chairman and secretary wrote to all members:

> Brothers, your executive council cannot say to you: 'further party-political fusion or Union or Re-union or fight against it'. . . . But we can make a call on every *Broer* [Brother] to choose in the sphere of party politics what, according to his fixed conviction, is most profitable for the object of the Bond and the Bond's ideal, as recorded above and as known to all of us [the Afrikanerisation of South Africa in all spheres of life – DO'M]. Let us keep the eye fixed on this – that the main object is that Afrikanerdom shall reach its ultimate destiny of domination in South Africa. . . Brothers, our solution for South Africa's troubles is not that this or that party shall gain the upper hand, but that the Afrikaner Broederbond shall rule South Africa (*Rand Daily Mail* 8/11/35).[8]

Throughout the 1930s, the Bond publicly eschewed party politics. Instead, through the FAK, it placed great emphasis on cultural organisation. It fostered the formation of separate, parallel, Afrikaans cultural organisations in all possible spheres – from the Voortrekkers, who replaced the Boy Scouts, to the Noodhulpliga, which substituted for the St John's Ambulance Brigade. These aimed to subvert the ideological hegemony of Hertzogism by physically removing Afrikaans-speakers from cultural contexts where Hertzogism prevailed. Through the separate, aggressively Christian-nationalist cultural organisation of Afrikaans-speakers, a new consciousness would be formed – a new subject would be interpellated. Through this strong emphasis on *kultuurpolitiek* (cultural politics) rather than *partypolitiek*, the Bond was increasingly able to delimit the legitimate parameters of Afrikaner culture, and to develop and direct mass campaigns on cultural issues. This culminated in the Bond-organised celebration of the centenary of the Great Trek.

The *Eeufees* (centenary), or *Tweede Trek* (Second Trek), was the Bond's largest attempt at mass mobilisation along a cultural issues. After the proposals had been approved in Bond discussions, the *Eeufees* was organised by the Bond founder and first chairman, Henning Klopper, working through the Afrikaanse Taal en Kultuurvereniging (Language and Cultural Union) of the South African Railways and Harbours. By any standards the four-month event was great political and cultural theatre. Though initially there was little popular enthusiasm, by the time the *Tweede Trek* began, the Bond had prepared the ground for a massive cultural orgy.

Nine replicas of the oxwagons of the Voortrekkers, each named after a Voortrekker hero, travelled slowly from Cape Town to Pretoria, visiting as many towns as possible. All along the route ever larger crowds met the wagons with passionate enthusiasm. Moodie's description (1975:180) conveys this:

> Men grew beards and women donned Voortrekker dress; street after street in hamlet after hamlet was renamed after one or other Trek hero; babies were baptised in the shade of the wagons – one was christened '*Eeufeesia*' (best translated 'Centennalia') – and young couples were married in full trekker regalia on the village green before the wagons. With tearful eyes old men and women climbed onto the wagons – 'Lord now lettest thy servant depart in peace', said one old man – and the young ones jostled with one another in their efforts to rub grease from the wagon axles onto their handkerchief. Monuments were raised up and the wagons were pulled through freshly laid concrete so that the imprint of their tracks could be preserved forever.

The *Eeufees* culminated in the anniversary of the Battle of Blood River on 16 December. *Die Burger* calculated that over 100,000 Afrikaners gathered on Monument Koppie (hill) in Pretoria for the festivities around the laying of the foundation stone of the Voortrekker monument by three women descendants of the Trekker leaders Retief, Potgieter and Pretorius. (General Hertzog had initially been asked to do it, but withdrew when the *gesuiwerdes* accused him of playing party politics.)

The overwhelming emotional message of the *Eeufees* was unity (*volkseenheid*) in the face of party political divisions. This meant different things to different people. Some republican firebrands dreamed of a *coup d'etat*.[9]

Professor A.C. Cilliers, the leading ideologist of Hertzogism, proposed the formation of a new, specifically 'Afrikaner' party on the basis of the 'ox-wagon sentiment' (p. 120 below). More significantly, the *Tweede Trek* gave rise to the Ossewa Brandwag (Oxwagon Sentinels, hereafter OB), formed in February 1939. The OB grew into a mass movement in the early 1940s and challenged the position of the NP itself (chapter 8 below).

But the *Eeufees* did largely succeed in mobilising Afrikaans-speakers in terms of a cultural and ethnically exclusive vision. It united Afrikaners as Afrikaners, transcending the bitter divisions between the UP and G/NP. This was the real attraction of the OB. By the beginning of 1939, the Bond's persistent emphasis on *kultuurpolitiek* was slowly beginning to politicise the issue of Afrikaner culture. Hertzog was deprived of his previously un-challenged title as the defender of Afrikaner culture. Through its dominance of the development of Afrikaner culture and the Afrikaans language, the Bond was able to exercise great influence over all aspects of the daily lives of Afrikaans-speakers. In many respects its influence over the terms of thought enabled it to direct the patterns of thought. In the absence of a powerful rival organisation which could lead the cultural struggle in other directions, the Bond-controlled cultural organisations were able to pose as the legitimate representatives of all Afrikaners, as the guarantors and defenders of its 'national' treasures. This had vitally important effects in the elaboration of Afrikaner nationalist ideology, as it was Bond intellectuals who appropriated the now legitimised 'Afrikaner' culture and transformed it into a radically revised ideology.

Yet, whilst *kultuurpolitiek* provided an ideological framework within which to forge *volkseenheid*, mass support for political groups does not finally grow out of 'pretty speeches and large cultural gatherings', as Albert Hertzog recognised (Naude 1969:13). During the 1930s the Bond initiated two movements which were to give *kultuurpolitiek* a specific class content, politicising class cleavages in cultural terms and finally succeeding in the interpellation of the new subject – the Afrikaner volk. These were the assault on the trade unions, and the economic movement. The first mobilised working class support, whilst the second made explicit the economic basis and petty-bourgeois character of Afrikaner nationalism. They are discussed in the following chapters.

6

The Afrikaner Broederbond and Christian-national trade unionism

The years 1933 to 1948 saw the development under Bond supervision of new forms of labour organisation in South Africa. Labelled 'Christian-national', they sought to organise Afrikaans-speaking workers so as to 'free our fellow members of the volk from the exclusively materialistic labour organisation under foreign control, and to bring our people into an economic – cultural organisation which makes provision for economic and spiritual needs' (Pelzer 1979: 151). This involved active combating of any notion of class struggle – replacing it with the principle of mutual cooperation and interest between workers and employers. The result was a protracted assault on the existing white labour movement.

Prior to 1948, the Christian-national assault on the white labour movement sought both to take over specific trade unions or industrial organisations, and, more broadly, to wean workers away from ideologies of class. The assaults on specific trade unions concentrated on the railways, and the mining, building, iron and steel, clothing and leather industries. An alternative organisation, Spoorbond, established itself as the largest of the railway unions. The struggle for power within the Mine Workers' Union finally resulted in success for a Christian-nationalist-inspired 'Reform Movement' in 1948. Achievements in the iron and steel industry were limited and the assaults on the Garment Workers' and Leather Workers' Unions were dismal failures till the NP government enacted the Suppression of Communism Act in 1950. In addition to the struggles within individual unions, broad mobilisational organisations such as the Nasionale Raad van Trustees (National Council of Trustees, hereafter NRT), Blankewerkers se Beskermingsbond (literally, White Workers Protection League), the Reddingsdaadbond (Rescue Action Society, hereafter RDB), and the Ossewa Brandwag Arbeidsfront (Labour Front of the Oxwagon Sentinels) arose. These were designed to break the ideological and organisational hold of class groupings such as the Labour Party and the South African Trades and Labour Council. Though they were not as successful as their ideologists claimed, by 1948 the unity of the white labour movement had been undermined.

The 1930s and 1940s were periods of profound change in the structure of

South African capitalism, witnessing a particularly rapid process of secondary industrialisation. The contribution of manufacturing to National Income first surpassed that of agriculture in 1930 and outstripped mining by 1943. Within manufacturing itself, a fundamental shift in the emphasis of production towards heavy industry occurred. Even before the war, the industrial group, consisting of metal products, machinery and transport equipment, emerged as the largest group within the manufacturing sector, its contribution to total manufacturing output rising from 17.6 per cent in 1930 to 26.6 per cent by 1940, and reaching 30.3 per cent by 1950. This industrial expansion brought with it far-reaching changes in the labour process. The total number of white production and related employees in private industry more than trebled between 1933 and 1950 (from 32,718 to 104,913). Yet despite this absolute increase, so rapid was the growth of the African industrial labour force that white industrial employees as a percentage of total production workers fell from 35.9 per cent in 1933 to 24.4 per cent in 1950 (US 1960: S-3, L-4, G-8). Moreover the nature of white industrial employment was changing. During the 1920s, industrial production was largely based on the artisan/unskilled division of labour. Under the Pact government, state intervention through a variety of measures – most notably the Wage Act – had promoted more mechanised forms of industrial production (Davies 1977: 195). The artisan/unskilled division of labour was increasingly replaced by that of semi-skilled operatives working machines (BTI 1945: 42–6).

The expansion of industrial activity during the 1930s, and particularly during the war, accelerated this process. As a crude index of mechanisation, the capital to labour ratio of private manufacturing rose from £794 per worker in 1932 to £981 in 1939 and £1,156 in 1946 (US 1960: G-8). In the face of full white employment during the war, 'large numbers' of Africans began to move into operative positions 'in a wide range of industries' (BTI 1945: 46). Yet this was no frontal attack on the racial division of labour. State policy during this period was ambivalent. On the one hand, through a series of incentive schemes, the extended use of female labour, and the orderly transfer over time of whites into supervisory positions, it sought to protect the existing racial division of labour (Department of Labour 1947 and 1948). On the other hand, the requirements of industrial production compelled the state to allow the employment of Africans in operative positions. Both the Board of Trade and Industry and the Van Eck Commission advocated further mechanisation and increased use of 'low-paid' African operatives for industry (BTI 1945: 46; AIRC 1941: para. 191).

The period under review thus witnessed two vital changes in the labour process which were to affect the organisation of white workers. Firstly, the emergence of operative labour during the 1930s tended to lead either to the displacement of artisans, or to a reduction in their status from 'craftsman' to supervisor. The craft unions bitterly resisted this undercutting. There were continual complaints and a number of strikes by craft unions against the employment of white operatives in positions previously occupied by

79

'craftsmen' – the anti-strike provisions of the Industrial Conciliation Act were much used during the 1930s (Simons & Simons 1969: 508). The large army of unemployed 'poor whites' exacerbated the fears of the craft unions. The Trades and Labour Council (TLC) delegates to the 1934 National Conference on the 'poor white' problem reported that attempts were being made to relax apprenticeship rules and other 'safeguards' against labour dilution. Skilled workers were in danger of being undercut by 'the less skilled, lower paid, rural migrant', that is, newly-proletarianised Afrikaans-speakers (*Forward* 2/11/34).

Following the defeat of the 1922 white miners' strike, trade union membership had fallen from over 113,000 in 1919 to 67,000 in 1926. During the 1920s, craft unions formed the backbone of the trade union movement and the Labour Party. The 1930s also saw a very rapid increase in industrial as opposed to craft unions – a result of 'the continuous changes which are taking place in industrial techniques' (ILC 1935). By 1934, registered trade union membership had climbed slowly to 89,000. In the wake of the expansion of industrial activity following the abandonment of the Gold Standard, membership of registered unions rocketed by 100,000 between 1933 and 1937, to exceed a quarter of a million in 1942. By 1948 the figure stood at 339,895, of whom 230,980 were white (US 1960: 6–11). This reflects the rise of industrial unions, engendering acute tension within the trade union movement itself. The craft unions persistently failed to organise new industrial recruits during the 1930s – a task increasingly undertaken by various 'left' groups ranging from individual communists to a newly emerging social democratic group within the Labour Party. The left generally offered militant struggle on wage issues while the craft unions continued their struggle to maintain craft privileges.

The tensions between the two groups within the TLC were acute throughout the 1930s and 1940s. This was reflected in the continuing crisis of the Labour Party. Davies (1977: 211–13) has traced the 1928 split between the 'Creswellites' and the 'Councillites' to divisions between the older craft unions and the less skilled. Though Creswell faded from the scene, the Party remained racked by these tensions throughout the 1930s. A further factor operated against the Labour Party during this period. The vast majority of new industrial white employees were recently-proletarianised Afrikans-speakers. Albert Hertzog claimed in 1939 that over 80 per cent of trade union members were Afrikaners, compared with only 10 per cent of the trade union secretaries (Naude 1969: 265–6). Though this was probably an overestimate, it highlights an important point. The leadership of the Labour Party was still largely English-speaking and drawn from the older craft unions – from those groups antagonistic towards newly employed white operatives and unsympathetic towards the problems of 'rural migrants'. Only in the late 1930s did important Afrikaans-speaking leaders begin to emerge within the Labour Party. By this stage Christian-national activists had been able to label the party 'anti-Afrikaans' (Naude 1969: 29).

The second change in the labour process which crucially affected the position of white workers and the trade union movement was the occupational mobility of Africans during the war. Their movement into operative positions further aggravated the tensions of the 1930s. Some of the new industrial unions had begun to organise Coloured and Indian workers who were eligible for membership of registered trade unions. More significantly, during the 1930s an independent African trade union movement emerged, to mushroom during the war. By 1945 nearly 40 per cent of the African industrial labour force was 'unionised' in one sense or another (O'Meara 1975b: 153). These unions received virtually no assistance from organised white labour, despite appeals from individuals within the TLC for assistance (MUJC 28/9/42). State proposals to expand the utilisation of African operatives explicitly recommended their 'cheapness' relative to white labour (BTI 1945: 42–6; AIRC 1941: 19). Both the expansion of African unemployment in operative positions and the emerging organisation of Africans in militant unions, presented the potential of undercutting white operatives. Indeed, during the war years, the earnings gap between white and African industrial employees actually closed slightly (Steenkamp 1962: Table 1). Particularly during the war, specific strata of white workers began to perceive themselves as threatened by the influx of African labour and by the continuing ambivalence of the UP government on issues such as migrant labour, pass laws and influx control. These fears too provided Christian-national organisers with powerful weapons.

These twin changes in the labour process, and the festering divisions they prompted within both the trade union movement and the already divided – though still powerful – Labour Party, were the sores exploited by the Christian-nationalists. However, the specific position of Afrikaans-speakers in the labour process and class relations were further factors rendering them susceptible to these assaults.

THE POSITION OF AFRIKANERS IN INDUSTRY

One of the shibboleths of South African history holds that the proletarianisation of 'rural' Afrikaners began with the Anglo-Boer War. While the process accelerated dramatically after 1902, the Dutch Reformed Church synod discussed 'the poor white problem' as early as 1886 and a church conference on the subject was held in 1893. Though evident in all the colonies and republics, the rate of proletarianisation of white Afrikaans-speakers was highest in the Transvaal prior to the Anglo-Boer War. Given the Chamber of Mines' policy to import the skilled labour needed for the mines, opportunities to acquire skills were virtually non-existent. Proletarianised Afrikaners were almost totally unskilled and lived in extreme poverty. A large part of the 1897 Volksraad session was devoted to the problem and the Republican government instituted special schemes, such as the Brickfields project, to provide employment for such Afrikaners. The years following the Anglo-Boer War saw a 'phenomenal rise' in the birth-rate of Afrikaans-speakers in the northern colonies. Coupled with the devastating effects of the British scorched earth policy during the war and three major agricultural depressions (1903–8, 1920–3, 1929–34), this population explosion created intense rural pressures, provoking rapid proletarianisation. In the period 1921 to 1936 an average of 12,000 whites left the rural areas for the cities each year; but such was the effect of the population increase, that only after 1936 did the absolute number of Afrikaans-speakers living in the rural areas begin to fall (Pauw 1946: 85–90, 135). In the wake of this rapid proletarianisation came acute poverty and unemployment. By 1931 most of the 300,000 whites (or one-sixth of the white population) classified as 'very poor' by the Carnegie Commission (p. 37 above) were Afrikaans-speakers. By September 1933 the number of registered unemployed adult males had reached 188,000 (Carnegie Corporation Commission 1932: para. 9; Department of Labour 1933:11).

This highlights an interesting discrepancy between the ideology of Christian-national trade unionism and its actual operation. The ideologists always claimed that they were in the business of 'rescuing' Afrikaner workers from 'poor whiteism'. In practice, few or no attempts were made to organise 'poor whites'. The majority of attacks on trade unions were directed at those whose members could in no way be considered 'poor whites', but were in fact chosen for their relative prosperity – the single exception being the Garment Workers' Union (hereafter GMU, see below). By 1940 the Department of Labour reported that the 'poor white' problem had largely been solved by the industrial expansion prompted by the war (1940: 8). Yet the existence of the large, predominantly Afrikaans-speaking 'poor white' population served a useful function for the Christian-national activists. They constantly exhorted Afrikaner workers that only through Christian-nationalist organisations could they avoid the yawning trap of 'poor whiteism'.

Given the trajectory of the pattern of proletarianisation in South Africa, skilled artisans in industry were overwhelmingly English-speaking. However, the vast majority of the influx of white labour into industry and operative positions during the 1930s was Afrikaans-speaking. Newly proletarianised Afrikaans-speaking workers tended to occupy positions at the lower levels of skill. In 1939, for example, almost 40 per cent of adult male white Afrikaans-speakers were clustered in the four occupational categories: unskilled labourer, mineworker, railway worker and bricklayer. This compares with just 10 per cent of 'other whites' (Pauw 1946:235). Thus, relative to English-speaking industrial workers, Afrikaners found themselves either in the large army of unemployed 'poor whites' and/or as operatives in the least skilled, lowest paid roles assigned to white labour. Occupational mobility was limited by the widely resented apprenticeship system, zealously guarded by the (English-speaking) craft unions. Indeed, the tension between English-speaking artisan labour and newly proletarianised Afrikaners had a long history. The first large-scale movement of Afrikaners into any industry occurred during the 1907 strike by white miners, when Afrikaners were employed as scab labour. Throughout the 1930s Afrikaners were feared by the craft unions as a real and potential source of undercutting.

This relatively disadvantaged position of Afrikaans-speakers in the white labour force, coupled with the antagonism of the craft unions, gave Christian-national ideologues two powerful weapons. They could claim deliberate discrimination against Afrikaner workers by an alliance of 'foreign capitalist bosses and foreign trade union leaders', designed to line the pockets of both (Naude 1969:267–8). Further, given changes in the labour process, particularly the movement of Africans into operative positions during the war, they could claim that the 'imperialist' state, aided and abetted by 'foreign/communist' trade union leaders, sought to replace Afrikaner workers with cheap African labour, forcing them back into the morass of 'poor whiteism' (*Inspan* April 1947:36–7). In the long struggle within and around the trade unions it is the particularly disadvantaged position of Afrikaans-speakers in the labour process, and the resulting class relations, coupled with the persistent refusal of the white labour movement to tackle these issues, rather than 'nationalism' or appeals to the mystic unity of the volk, which provides one of the keys to an understanding of the successes and failures of Christian-national trade unionism. The other key lies in an understanding of the character of the groups and organisations which sought to mobilise Afrikaner workers.

CLASS INTERESTS AND CHRISTIAN-NATIONALISTS

Two points must be made clear from the outset. First, neither the broad assault on the ideology and organisations of the registered trade union movement nor the attacks on specific trade unions were emanations of a self-consciously 'Afrikaner' faction of white workers. Both were initiated, inspired, led, financed and maintained by petty-bourgeois groups. Secondly, after 1936 the organisation of Afrikaner workers on Christian-national lines became one of the three major policy thrusts of the Broederbond. As discussed above, the Bond was itself an exclusively petty-bourgeois organisation with minimal working class membership. All the various Christian-nationalist worker organisations were initiated, inspired and run by Bond members.

As has been discussed at length, following fusion northern 'Afrikaner nationalism' was an almost exclusively petty-bourgeois affair. The extreme weakness of the G/NP in the north, and particularly in the Transvaal, simply reflects the political isolation, disorganisation and weakness of the Afrikaner petty bourgeoisie. The conditions were exacerbated by the class struggles and social developments of the 1930s. The migration to the cities and pro-letarianisation of rural Afrikaners and the rise of industrial unions with a largely Afrikaans-speaking membership, all threatened further to isolate the Afrikaner petty bourgeoisie and 'its' brand of *gesuiwerde* Afrikaner nationalism from other classes. As the official history of perhaps the most important Christian-national trade union grouping makes clear, until this petty bourgeoisie began to organise for itself a working-class base, their *gesuiwerde* Afrikaner nationalism 'stared death in the face' (Naude 1969:13). From roughly 1930 onwards, the Bond began publicly to raise the dangers of class divisions within the Hertzog Party. Particularly after fusion, the Bond ideologues became obsessed with the dangers of class divisions for *volkseenheid* (national unity) – itself in tatters – and the 'denationalisation' of Afrikaans-speaking workers organised into class-conscious unions. In the words of the OFS G/NP leader: 'class consciousness . . . is systematically encouraged by the trade unions . . . they make an appeal to the class conscious section of the people. It is in direct conflict with the principles of the Afrikaners' (HAD 1937: column 5464).

The mobilisation of Afrikaner workers became the *sine qua non* of Nationalist political power. And Afrikaner workers occupied a key role in the Bond strategy aimed at developing Afrikaner capital. The savings of Afrikaner workers were to provide an important source of capital for the Afrikaner economic movement (pp. 155–63 below). It was thus doubly important that they be weaned from the ideological and organisational hold of class groupings.

The individual Christian-nationalist organisations were almost exclusively petty bourgeois in composition and in their concerns. In the struggle for power within the mining industry, both the Afrikanerbond van Mynwerkers (Afrikaner Mineworkers' Union) and its successor, Die Hervormers Organisasie binne die Mynwerkers Unie (Mine Workers Union Reform Organisation), were formed and run by the NRT. The NRT was formed in October 1936 by Drs A. Hertzog, P.J. Meyer, N. Diedrichs and T.E.W. Schumann, together with a manager of the Bond-founded Volkskas bank, F. de Wet, and dominee P.S. du Toit. It was a body designed 'to form right [wing] inclined trade unions and thereafter serve as a liaison body with the Afrikaner nation' (Naude 1969:27). Its board comprised academics, clergymen, bankers, cultural activists and the widows of two prominent Afrikaner Nationalist politicians (one of whom, Mrs 'Jannie' Marais, provided the initial £10,000 finance). It also included the Bond chairman and secretary, J.C. van Rooy and I.M. Lombard. Bond divisions were instructed to give 'the strongest support' to the NRT (Pelzer 1979:150).

From its official history, two factors appear to have weighed heavily in the decision to form the NRT. The first was the effect of proletarianisation on the potential political base of Afrikaner nationalism in the north. As the NRT moving spirit, Albert Hertzog had been particularly struck by the political muscle of European trade union movements. He argued the need to develop a working-class base for Afrikaner nationalism to prevent 'the rapid decline of Afrikanerdom' (Naude 1969:13). The major objective was to break the power of the Labour Party:

> As the so-called guardian of the worker, over a period of years, the Labour Party developed into a powerful factor in South African politics. . . . *This bond between*

the worker and the Labour Party had to be broken – only then would the struggle of Dr Hertzog and his small group acquire any meaning or significance. *This was then their major theme* (Naude 1969:258; my italics).

Not only was northern Afrikaner nationalism without a mass base, it was also in financial straits, largely dependent on southern largess (for example, the formation of Voortrekker Pers by Nasionale Pers in 1937 – see below, pp. 105–6 – and the NRT itself). The funds under trade union control were a major inducement. Albert Hertzog told the 1939 Ekonomiese Volkskongres (People's Economic Congress): 'If we succeed in capturing the trade unions, every year, year after year, a sum of at least £290,000 could be devoted to the reconstruction of our volk rather than its subversion.' This, he reminded delegates, would far exceed the projected *Reddingsdaadfonds* (Rescue Act Funds, hereafter fonds) which, after years of effort, might garner £200,000. Control of trade union funds and subscriptions would 'unleash a financial giant' (Naude 1969:271).

Yet the achievements of the NRT were limited. Though its *hervormers* (reformers) eventually succeeded in gaining control of the Mine Workers' Union in 1948, other unions established by the NRT in opposition to both the GWU and the Building Workers' Industrial Union, failed to gain much support. By 1942, strong discontent was being expressed within the Bond over the 'lack of success' of the NRT's *hervormer* group in the Mine Workers' Union (MWU), and the lack of results on other fronts. By 1944 the Bond-dominated Economic Institute of the FAK withdrew its financial support (Naude 1969:102). Certainly during the war years both the NRT and the *hervormers* seem to have been moribund – though Naude (1969:179–97) claims the group was quietly rebuilding its organisation and looking after the general welfare of miners.

In 1943 a rival organisation was established. In a move which provoked some bitterness within both the Bond and the NRT, Dr P.J. Meyer resigned from the NRT to head the OB's newly formed Arbeidsfront (Labour Front). Meyer argued (1944:83) that the NRT had failed in its self-appointed task. The Front was explicitly designed to attack class divisions: to 'hammer home' to the 'broad masses' that 'ties of blood and volk come first and those [forged] in work or industry are coincidental'. In keeping with the OB's view of itself as a broad *volksbeweging* (national movement) designed to bypass the 'deficiencies' of political parties, the Front was to combat divisions within the volk, 're-uniting' urban and rural Afrikaners (Ossewa Brandwag 1946:79–90). The method of achieving this unity was: 'together with the ideological cultivation of the workers, to win the trust and devotion of the worker by offering him OB support without asking him to leave or weaken his trade union or other organisations' (*Kommandant-Generaal's Report*, Moodie 1975:232).

The OB did not directly organise Afrikaner workers, but sought to wean them away from 'communistic' influence. Its achievements too were limited – though Moodie (1975:232–3) offers interesting tentative evidence that the Arbeidsfront participation revived the Hervormers Organisasie binne die Mynewerkersunie (reform organisation within the MWU; hereafter Hervormers) after the war. Assessment of its influence through membership is impossible as figures are not available – membership figures for the OB generally are notoriously unreliable. Like the OB itself, the Arbeidsfront faded after the war. Like the OB, its leadership was overwhelmingly petty bourgeois.

The other major formal groups were likewise exclusively petty bourgeois in composition and purpose. By definition, the Breë Kerklike Komitee (Broad Ecclesiastical Committee), formed to intervene in the struggle within the GWU, was composed of clergymen anxious to prevent the 'spiritual enslavement' of Afrikaner women workers – though notably unconcerned about their wages. The Komitee received 'financial and moral support' from the Bond (Pelzer 1979:152). Its activities were taken over by the Blankewerkers se Beskermingsbond (White Workers' Protection League – BWBB) in 1945. The BWBB was itself formed as the labour front of the Herenigde Nationalist Party (HNP) in June 1944 and seen by the OB as the Party's direct response to the formation of the OB's Arbeidsfront.[1] The formation of the BWBB was brought to the attention of the Bond's Executive Council by that leading HNP militant, Dr Verwoerd. It too, enjoyed strong Bond financial and moral support (Pelzer 1979:152). The two people who served as its secretary were, respectively, a school headmaster (Jan de Klerk – later Minister of Labour) and 'a special representative of SANLAM', the large Afrikaner insurance company. The remainder of its board consisted of five clergymen and a number of HNP politicians, such as Dr Verwoerd and Ben Schoeman (first Minister of Labour in the HNP cabinet) (*Die Transvaler* 24/5/45). The BWBB was not a workers' organisation. It was open to all Afrikaners willing to help in 'the great struggle to preserve white civilisation'; to 'mobilise the whole volk to drive this [class] cancer from our national life' by weaning workers from 'communist influence'; to 'unite them with the rest of the nation' and 'preserve them for our Christian-national struggle'. As a petty-bourgeois group connected with the Afrikaans economic movement, one of its major aims was to foster support from workers for 'the formation of genuinely South African undertakings'. As the child of the NP, concerned to break the power of the Labour Party, it hypocritically 'pointed out the dangers' of trade unions 'operating in the political field', and of various 'foreign ideologies' of which communism was the 'most dangerous'. Infused with an us/them view of the Afrikaner petty bourgeoisie on the one hand and the workers on the other, it saw its aim as not to seduce workers out of the trade unions but: 'To make workers trade union conscious, and encourage *them* to take an *intelligent* interest in their trade union. Only if *they* do that will *they* understand the real purpose and struggle of the trade union and get rid of *undesirable* leaders' (*Inspan* April 1947; my italics).

In June 1946 the BWBB claimed a membership of 1,058 workers in 72 occupations, and 1,308 'others' – farmers, professional men, housewives, pensioners and those of no stated occupation (*Die Blankewerker* November 1947). Despite regular financial contributions from the HNP – somewhat at odds with its warnings on the dangers of party political connections – the organisation soon ran into financial difficulties and was taken over by the RDB which struggled on 'till it could no longer bear the financial burden' of the BWBB (E. P. du Plessis, 1964: 196). After the 1948 election it, too, quietly sank from view.

The RDB was the fourth major Christian-national organisation to concern itself with Afrikaner workers during this period. Established by the Ekonomiese Instituut of the Federation of Afrikaans Cultural Associations (i.e. the Bond) following the first Ekonomiese Volkskongres, the RDB was a broad organisation designed to mobilise mass support for the emergence of Afrikaner capital after 1939 (pp. 137–43 below). Its major tasks were to make Afrikaans-speakers 'economically conscious' (i.e. to support Afrikaner business undertakings) and to foster *volkseenheid* (unity) in the days of extreme schism during the war. Just as the Bond strove to preserve a semblance of unity behind the scenes within the elite, so too the RDB attempted to transcend the divisions between the HNP and OB and to maintain a broad unity through a wide spectrum of economic and cultural activities. By 1946 its membership stood at 64,771 in 381 branches, though this too fell off rapidly (*Inspan* January 1946).

In both its attempts to transform economic consciousness of Afrikaans-speakers and to forge unity, the Afrikaner worker occupied a key position. His savings and custom were to be an important source of capital for the economic movement. If Afrikaner workers maintained their class perspectives, talk of *volkseenheid* was nonsense. Given their numbers, Afrikaner workers 'form the kernel of our nation. That is why we must see the incorporation of the Afrikaner worker as one of the main objects of the *Reddingsdaadbond*'. The 'incorporation' of Afrikaner workers into the 'organic unity' of the volk meant they were to be 'rescued' from the 'claws of the un-national power of the trade unions' (RDB Chairman, *Die Transvaler* 3/10/52). The RDB thus strove 'to make the Afrikaner worker part and parcel of the life of the volk and to prevent Afrikaner workers developing as a class distinct from other classes in the life of the volk' (RDB nd(a): 27).

The RDB wove a cultural mesh around Afrikaner workers. Like the NRT, however, the RDB realised that support from workers would not be won 'by pretty speeches and large cultural gatherings' (Naude 1969:13). Economic interests had to be looked after. Apart from the many cultural activities, the RDB offered cheap life assurance schemes, set up trade schools and a work placement bureau which found employment for 8,127 of the 18,275 applicants – mainly with Afrikaans undertakings (RDB 1944: 26–30; E.P. du Plessis 1964:196).

Thus the coordinating groups which arose were all petty-bourgeois in form and content. Obsessed with the fear of class division they were driven by the need to capture working-class support for their nationalism. The often vicious disputes between the HNP and the various other nationalist political organisations between 1940 and 1946 (chapter 9) did not detract from this common aim – though they did weaken appeals to Afrikaner workers in the name of *volkseenheid*. These coordinating groups concentrated their attacks on the ideologies of class which still prevailed within the trade union movement.

Central to an understanding of the Christian-national labour movement is the fact that these organisations were formed, and operated, as an essential part of the Bond's economic movement – the attempt to develop an explicitly Afrikaner capital. The leaders of each of these various labour organisations were also the key members of the organised economic movement and quite clearly saw the Christian-national labour movement as but an element – though admittedly a vital one – in that economic movement. This point is examined in detail below (chapter 11, especially pp. 155–62). Here the place assigned to Afrikaner workers within Christian-national ideology is simply summarised.

Within the divinely-ordained organic unity of nations, the innate inequality of their individual members establishes an hierarchical order – with a correct, divinely-allotted place and task in the hierachy for all. Within the ideal Christian-national society, the division of labour reflects the will of God, as does the relationship between social strata, each with rights and duties relative to other strata (the term class is not used – God did not intend societies to be divided into antagonistic classes, but stratified in an ordered ranking). Those who, through natural ability, rise to the higher strata, have correspondingly heavy duties to match their privileges. Entrepreneurs, for example, have a duty to provide 'service' in return for the right to profit – profit being the just reward for the execution of Christian duty. The state exists to mediate the organic unity of the nation, and the relations between the individuals within it, particularly the specific functions of the various social strata.

In this view, black and white workers belonged to different nations, thus governed by very different divine laws. The Christian-national incorporation of 'workers' referred only to those of the Afrikaner 'nation'. Like all other members of the 'nation' workers were assigned a place and function in the social hierarchy, with corresponding rights and duties. Labour and the production of surplus are both a command and worship of God (*Koers* April 1946). The first duty of workers is to work hard in return for the right to a 'fair' wage (*Inspan* December 1948). Over and above their duty to provide 'surplus labour', Afrikaner workers are duty-bound to invest their savings in certain Afrikaans business undertakings (*Koers* April 1941). Afrikaner workers had become 'workshy'. They should be 'disciplined' to strive toward the chief traits required of industrial workers: discipline, efficiency and coordination, diligence and application (*Inspan* January 1941). The workers' relationship with other social strata was also important. Again, through biblical references workers were shown the true function of capital, divinely-bestowed and intended for creative, communal 'service'. The relationship between worker and capitalist is interdependent. As they shared the same 'national' interests, strikes should not be allowed (*Inspan* February 1949).

In this view Afrikaner workers were exploited not as workers, but as Afrikaners. This was because, in South Africa, capitalists were largely 'foreigners'. Not part of the 'Afrikaner nation', they lacked the 'national sympathy' which would prevent exploitation. Were Afrikaners in charge, exploitation would wither away in the cooperative organic unity of the volk. Afrikaners would never exploit fellow Afrikaners who did their duty and worked (Naude 1969: 266–8; *Volkshandel* November 1941; *Inspan* November 1950). The existing trade unions were likewise 'foreign' institutions run by 'foreign/communistic' leaders. Imbued with the 'cancerous' ideology of class, they set workers and capitalists against each other in one continuing struggle (*Die Transvaler* 4/11/44). As the 'kernel' of the Afrikaner nation, workers had thus to be weaned from such 'unnational' trade unions and incorporated into the organic unity of the volk. Only in this way could their true interests – both spiritual and material – be guaranteed.

If the existing ideology of trade unionism was to be attacked, however, it had to be replaced. If the divisions between capital and labour were to be done away with, new 'enemies' had to be found. Here again, the relatively disadvantaged position of Afrikaner workers in the labour process during the period under review presented the key. All their woes could be blamed on two external sources – foreigners' 'imperialism' on the one hand, and blacks, incited by 'communism', on the other. Thus the perception of self and group identification cultivated by Christian-nationalism was that of being part of the volk, beleaguered by foreign, racial and ideological enemies (cf. Stoker, p. 73 above). The presentation of material interests in cultural and racial terms became one of the major ideological themes of the period. Given the already-existing racial division of labour in South Africa, the contradiction of a (white) labour movement and its political party predicated on an ideology of class, yet refusing to organise the (black) majority of the working class, was particularly exploitable. The gains made by white workers over the past fifty years had entrenched the racial division of labour – they had been at the expense of black workers rather than capital. Through an acceptance of race rather than class as the basic social division, white workers could make further 'gains', with minimal costs for capital. This was the message of the aspirant capitalists who ran Christian-national trade unionism.

STRUGGLES FOR TRADE UNION POWER

In the period 1934 to 1947, only one Christian-national trade union of any consequence existed – Spoorbond, on the railways. Christian-nationalists fought for control of unions in the mining, building, iron and steel, clothing and leather industries. Their only real success was in the mines, where the Hervormers finally captured control of the MWU in 1948. The Iron and Steel Trades' Association's withdrawal from the South African TLC in 1947 was prompted less by Christian-nationalism than by policy differences. An alternative building union met with limited success, and those in the clothing and leather industries failed dismally. In these latter three industries the NP government after 1948 tried to achieve what the Christian-national assault could not do, and break the unions through the Suppression of Communism Act. Analysis of the successes and failures of these assaults involves many variables, but in each case, a combination of conditions specific to the labour process within each industry and/or the situation within the existing union, provides the basis for explanation. Grand ideological appeals to the mystic unity of the volk played little role in winning worker support for Christian-nationalism. When AB labour activists restricted their activity to mere ideological appeals, they met with very little success. Only when Christian-national organisers began to fight for the material interests of workers – to organise around the internal contradictions in the labour process and the unions – did they achieve any success.[2] The three industries in which Christian-nationalists concentrated their energies were the railways, mining and clothing. Each is examined briefly.

Spoorbond was formed in 1934 by the founder and first chairman of the Bond, Henning Klopper (later Speaker of the House of Assembly). By 1937 it claimed 16,000 members, and had forced the dissolution of the National Union of Railway and Harbour Servants (NURAHS). Yet its origins too were petty bourgeois. It was initially formed as a salaried staff's association to protest against discrimination by the Administration against Afrikaners in the salaried staff. Refused recognition by the Administration, it then turned its appeal to the mass of Afrikaners employed by the railways, agitating for the replacement of Africans and Coloureds by whites. The railways were the largest single employer of Afrikaners in the urban areas. In 1939, one in eleven of all adult male Afrikaners worked on the railways (Pauw 1946:235). These were almost all newly proletarianised rural migrants, clustered at the lower levels of skill – the railways being the focus of state 'civilised labour' policy to provide employment for 'poor whites' by replacing African labour. In the period 1930 to 1935, this produced a fall in the number of Africans employed on the railways of over 25 per cent (US 1960: G-15). Membership of NURAHS was open to all employees, but the union did little to organise new recruits and only 25 per cent of employees were unionised in 1933. Spoorbond was able both to attack its inactivity and appeal directly to the interests of the newly proletarianised Afrikaans-speaking workers. In 1936 when the eight craft unions opposed Spoorbond's claim to speak for all grades of railway employees, the Administration introduced group representation, confining Spoorbond to the lowest-paid workers. In 1942, the year it was finally recognised by the Administration, it represented 29,000 of the railway's 77,000 white employees (*Inspan* December 1946). Yet it was never able to break the craft unions.

As the trailblazer of Christian-national trade unionism, Spoorbond provided three broad examples to the petty bourgeoisie who were to organise in its wake. Firstly, it showed that the organisation of economic interests rather than mystical ideological appeals was the basis on which Afrikaner workers could be drawn into Christian-national unions. Secondly, it offered a new kind of trade unionism which rejected class divisions and strikes, relying on 'friendly cooperation' and negotiation. Members were encouraged to follow the union's motto 'Conquer through Service' and render loyal service. And thirdly, it showed the potential of Afrikaner workers as a source of capital for the later economic movement, if their savings could be mobilised. A mere three years after it was formed, Spoorbond spawned its own savings bank, Spoorbondkas, with a capital of £170,000 (*Inspan* December 1946). Though later bankrupted, Spoorbondkas initiated the Saambou building society (pp. 195–6 below).

The struggle for power within the MWU was the single most important Christian-national attack on any trade union. Its outlines can only be sketched. Early in 1937, the NRT formed an alternative union to the MWU, Die Afrikanerbond van Mynwerkers. This threat to 'the good understanding with the unions' prompted the Chamber of Mines to reverse its longstanding policy, reiterated only the previous year. In return for a promise of industrial docility, the Chamber concluded a closed shop agreement with the MWU and the eight craft unions also represented on the Mining Unions Joint Committee (Transvaal Chamber of Mines 1937:33–50, 63–9). The Afrikanerbond disbanded, to re-emerge in October 1938 as the Hervormers. After ten years of often bloody struggle – involving assassination, sabotage, suspension of elections, endless court cases, two large strikes against the MWU and three government commissions to investigate corruption within the union – the Hervormers finally won control of the union in 1948. By this stage, the issues transcended Christian-nationalism, and the Hervormers had themselves submerged into the United Mineworkers Committee, which drew widespread support from English-speaking miners with little interest in Christian-national ideology.

Two broad sets of factors account for the choice of the MWU as the NRT's first target. Firstly, the mining industry was clearly strategic in both the economy and the development of a racial division of labour in South Africa. After the railways, the mines were the largest employers of Afrikaans-speakers in 1939 and, as the biggest white union, the MWU was a vital prop in the TLC structure. Secondly, these strategic considerations apart, the nature of mining weighed heavily. It is crucial to note that the class position of white miners was both ambiguous and fluid. As the highest-paid group of white workers, the level of their wages was determined by the productivity of the gang of African workers they supervised. With a direct economic interest in the intensified exploitation of African workers, there was thus little chance that white miners would seek to organise or identify their interests with the African workers over whom they exercised daily supervision and control on behalf of mining capitalists. In the words of the official NRT history, white miners 'are not only workers – they are also bosses' (Naude 1969:19). This status of white miners as supervisors of labour particularly attracted the NRT.[3]

The abandonment of the Gold Standard in 1932 led to a rapid expansion of goldmining output. In a period when white mining employment remained relatively static, the size of the African mine labour force almost doubled. White miners were required to supervise increasing numbers of Africans. During the war, there were repeated protests that white miners were being replaced by African labour (MUJC 19/8/40). In 1941 a strike at the Grootvlei mine was fought on this issue. White mining wages rose relatively slowly during this period. The cash earnings of onsetters and skipmen, for example, rose by just 3.7 per cent between 1937 and 1947. Though this is not a totally representative case – the corresponding increase for machine stopers was 30 per cent (US 1960:G-21) – it points to important changes in the relative position of less skilled white miners *vis-à-vis* both the artisans employed in the mines, and white industrial labour generally. In 1942 a special delegation of MWU members argued before the Mining Unions Joint Committee that their real wages had fallen and that the MWU leadership was doing nothing about it, making 'the mineworkers a fertile field for agitators'. Delegate Cilliers predicted prophetically that, unless something were done, 'the war over Fascism may be won, but at the expense of the influence of the trade unions' (MUJC 16/2/43). By 1946, the once large differentials between white miners and other white industrial workers had closed, the respective minimum wage indices reading 144.4 and 146.8 (US 1960:G-31). Those white miners clustered at the lower levels of skill bore the brunt of this drop, not the artisans whose unions scornfully rejected the case of the MWU special delegation (MUJC 2/3/43); and, given the pattern of proletarianisation, over 90 per cent of the approximately 14,000 white miners who did not qualify for membership of the craft unions in 1937 were Afrikaans-speaking (Pauw 1946: 235).

Under the leadership of first Charles Harris (assassinated by an Hervormer in 1939) and then B.B. Broderick, the MWU was highly corrupt and autocratic, and seen to be in league with the Chamber of Mines. In the 1937 closed shop agreement with the Chamber, the MWU undertook to 'discourage and prevent any actions of their officials and members which may have the effect of causing unrest and undermining discipline' (Transvaal Chamber of Mines 1937: clause 17). The undertaking was zealously implemented. After 1937, the MWU became in effect the Chamber's policeman, its very existence now dependent on the good will of the Gold Producers' Committee (GPC). Elections were rigged, and then suspended for the duration of the war – the MWU being the only union thus affected. The Constitution was kept away from members, minutes were falsified, members who asked questions were beaten up and expelled from the union, losing their jobs under the closed shop agreement. Revealing the perceptions of white miners who supervised large gangs of African workers, witnesses before the 1946 Commission of Enquiry into the MWU complained that the general-secretary (Broderick) 'had no time for members and treated them like kaffirs' (MWUC 1946: para. 260).

In no sense could the MWU be considered an organisation fostering its members' interests. Corruption within the leadership was extensive. The closed shop agreement and suspension of elections gave the executive committee free reign to feed off the hapless membership (MWUC 1946 paras. 60–264). Following overwhelming pressure from members, the MWU finally put in a 30 per cent wage claim in 1944. This was rapidly withdrawn in return for an annual payment to the union of £ 100,000 for five years by the GPC 'for housing and other cooperative schemes' to be agreed upon between the GPC and the MWU. The MWU leadership agreed to submit no further wage demands unless 'existing conditions should change very materially' (Transvaal Chamber of Mines 1944). The farms purchased with this 'grant' were rapidly bankrupted, members receiving virtually no benefit whatsoever (MWUC 1946: para. 11; MWUC 1953: Part II, para. 1A).

The MWU was indeed, as delegate Cilliers said, a fertile field for agitators. Disillusionment with the union was neither the product of 'Afrikaner solidarity' nor confined to Afrikaans-speakers. The membership perceived their economic position worsening as a result of the changes of the war years. Far from fighting for higher wages and improved benefits, the union leadership was seen to be an ally of the Chamber of Mines. The MWU appeared to act not to defend white miners but as a vehicle to aid in their exploitation. By fulfilling some of the functions neglected by the union – pushing for phthisis benefits, workmen's compensation, pension entitlements, widows' pensions etc. – the Hervormers' organisers were able to win much support. Through constant ideological attacks they were able to erode support for ideologies of class and the existing class organisations of the white workers. Both the Labour Party and the TLC correctly attacked the reactionary character of the Hervormers, yet they defended the corrupt, autocratic MWU leadership as the valiant foe of fascism. In the 1943 general elections, the Labour Party had been 'uniformly successful in all its contests' with the NP (Heard 1974:25). By 1948, however, its base amongst the largely Afrikaans-speaking white workers on the Rand was in tatters, and the Party did not even field candidates in the mining constituencies which had been the traditional heartland of its support. Such was the anger with the Labour Party's perceived connivance with the MWU leadership that, had the party contested the mining constituencies in 1948, it would have suffered major defeats. Under its new Hervormer leadership, the MWU withdrew from the TLC in 1949. Its membership was disillusioned with TLC prevarications and its intervention in their 1947 strike against the Broderick MWU leadership. The racist appeals of Christian-nationalism began to find support, particularly amongst white miners, who faced falling living standards, a large influx of African labour, a corrupt union, and hints that the UP government might introduce changes in the racial division of labour. These factors, rather than the innate susceptibility of Afrikaner miners to the appeals of Afrikaner or Christian-nationalism, explain the successful takeover of the MWU. But what of the Christian-national failure to erode the support of the Afrikaans-speaking membership of the GWU?

The situation of the garment workers differed both in respect of their position in the labour process and the responsiveness of their trade union. Unlike white miners, who supervised large gangs of African producers, white employees in the clothing industry were themselves productive workers. Critically important, too, they were women. The employment of white females at low wage rates was one of the prime strategies of the state to maintain the racial division of labour in the face of changes in the labour process in the 1930s. The textile and clothing industries were the areas of the greatest rise in the employment of white women between 1921 and 1936, from 6,742 to 16,837 (falling slightly to 15,544 by 1951). The overwhelming majority of these new industrial workers was Afrikaans-speaking. As significantly, the number of Coloured women employed in the same category rose even more dramatically from 1,545 in 1921 to 3,050 in 1936, rocketing to 16,589 in 1951.[4] As an industrial union in a sector in which the increasing employment of Coloured labour presumably provided Christian-national organisers with much exploitable material, the GWU managed to rebut a fifteen year attack, culminating in the banning of its secretary, E.S. (Solly) Sachs, in 1952. These attacks ranged from constant vituperative condemnations of the 'communist/Jew Sachs' (which regularly resulted in successful libel actions), the establishment of a Christian-national newspaper *Klerewerkersnuus* (bankrupted when Sachs brought a successful libel action), continuing violence against both the members and leaders by the *Bondswag* or Blackshirts (who, in the approving words of the NRT history, 'armed themselves with various weapons and operated as the military wing of the campaign against communism in the trade unions' – Naude 1969: 81–2), and an abortive attempt to form an alternative union, to the interventions of the Breë Kerklike Komitee, concerned with the 'spiritual enslavement of *Boeredogters*' (daughters of Boers – *Inspan* April 1947).

The garment workers were direct producers of surplus value. The contradictions between productive white workers and productive black workers were not of the antagonistic character of those between African miners and their direct supervisors, white miners. Further, unlike the MWU, the GWU was well organised, ably led, democratic and responsive to its members' demands. In the period of Sachs' secretaryship, 1928 to 1952, the average weekly wage of women workers in the industry rose from £1 to £7, the working week was reduced from 50 to 40 hours and paid annual leave increased from 2 to 28 days, largely as a result of union action (Hepple 1954 : 48). Membership of the union was thus seen to improve the workers' material position. Sachs was particularly adept at manipulating Afrikaner cultural symbols to mobilise workers in class terms. Through the redefinition of job categories he was able to prevent potential friction between white and

Coloured workers. Through instant litigation he remained on the offensive against Christian-national attacks. Yet it was not Sachs himself who resisted these attacks, but rather the extensive, continuing support he was able to mobilise from union members. Christian-national trade unionism could offer no material rewards the GWU could not produce – and, as Sachs was able to point out, given its ideology of 'mutual interdependence' between workers and bosses, was likely to offer the highly class-conscious GWU members much less. In the face of the material improvements in living standards produced by the Union, the grand ideological appeals of Christian-nationalism to the *boeredogters* in the GWU fell largely on deaf ears.

With the exception of Spoorbond and the takeover of the MWU, the Christian-national attack on individual trade unions was generally unsuccessful. However, the concerted attacks on individual unions and the wider Christian-nationalist activities from 1936 to 1948 both weakened class ideologies amongst white workers and further undermined the unity of the registered trade union movement. At the 1946 TLC congress, the Iron and Steel Trades' Association argued that, in the face of the Labour Party's impotence, the TLC should seek as strong as possible direct representation in Parliament (Simons & Simons 1969:565). The following year the TLC split on a proposed amendment which would debar African unions. The withdrawal from the TLC was led by the Iron and Steel Trades' Association, which formed the Coordinating Council of South African Trade Unions the following year.

Thus by 1948, the (predominantly white) registered trade union movement was hopelessly divided. Through organising around contradictions within the labour process and the labour movement itself, Christian-national organisers were able to win support from specific strata of white wage earners, and for the first time, to incorporate them in a class alliance which put an Afrikaner nationalist coalition into power in 1948 (chapter 15 below). Yet this is to run ahead. Of all the Broederbond's activities in the 1930s, the economic movement had the greatest significance. It is to this the focus now turns.

7

The beginnings of the economic movement

The historical trajectory of capitalist development in South Africa produced a pattern of ownership of the means of production in which Afrikaans-speaking whites controlled an insignificant proportion of production in all sectors except agriculture (pp. 52–3 above). By 1934, the development of capitalism had transformed Afrikaans-speakers into 'poor whites', proletarians, petty bourgeois or capitalist farmers, but had not produced Afrikaner capitalists in industry or commerce. Only in the Cape had there emerged anything resembling capitalist undertakings controlled by Afrikaans-speakers.

These Cape undertakings formed the core of one wing of the economic movement after 1934 – a wing often at odds with the Bond leadership. An examination of their formation and development is highly revealing on a number of points: the complex and changing interrelationship between the development of Afrikaner business and Afrikaner nationalism; the alliance between a petty bourgeoisie bent on accumulating capital and the farmers who were to be the source of that capital; the key role of certain strategists in the economic movement; and the class character of the 'regionalist' tensions in organised Afrikaner nationalism.

THE GROWTH OF THE ECONOMIC MOVEMENT IN THE CAPE

In 1913, General Hertzog and his followers finally broke with Botha and Smuts on the issue of South Africa's constitutional relationship with Britain. The following year Hertzog formed the Nationalist Party of the OFS. South Africa's declaration of war against Germany, and the military suppression of the consequent armed revolt by many Afrikaans-speakers (the *Rebellie* of 1914–15), provided the real catalyst to the development of a nationalist movement (A.H. Marais 1975). In the Cape, a pro-Hertzog vigilance committee was established, with a lawyer, W.A. (Willie) Hofmeyr, as one of its leaders. Hofmeyr was to become the kingmaker in the Cape NP and dominate its three associated business undertakings. In the words of his biographer, Hofmeyr, first among Afrikaner intellectuals, saw the golden opportunity 'to

96

develop the national consciousness into a business consciousness'.[1] Together with a small group of associated professional men in the Western Cape, he pursued this vision with an iron determination.

In December 1914, this petty bourgeois group around Hofmeyr formed Die Nasionale Pers to publish a pro-Hertzog newspaper, *De Burger* (the Citizen)[2]. The initial £8,000 capital was provided by a few wealthy Stellenbosch wine farmers – beginning a long-standing economic and political alliance. In June 1915, a month before the first issue of *De Burger* appeared, a congress of 100 delegates in the northern Cape town of De Aar resolved to form a Cape Nationalist Party under the chairmanship of Hertzog's leading Cape parliamentary supporter, English-speaking Professor H.E.S. Fremantle. The formation of the Fremantle party had Hertzog's blessing. Yet the professional men around Hofmeyr 'were not prepared to accept this', and fought to exclude the professor. Mobilising support from Western Cape and Boland farmers, they promptly formed their own NP. Hofmeyr refused the proffered leadership, but invited Dr D.F. Malan to leave his pulpit, lead their party and edit *De Burger*. Following three months of rivalry between these two NPs, they eventually merged in September. Malan was elected chairman, Fremantle vice-chairman, and Hofmeyr the chief organising secretary. In the 1915 general elections, held barely a month later, this fledgling Cape NP won 7 of the province's 51 seats.[3] A significant by-product of this 'unity congress', was the formation by *De Burger* of the Cape section of the Helpmekaarsvereniging (Mutual Aid Association) to pay the fines and otherwise assist those imprisoned participants in the *Rebellie*. *De Burger* played a vital role in mobilising contributions for this appeal, which collected almost £$\frac{1}{4}$ million. The *Helpmekaar* movement significantly demonstrated how nationalist sentiment, coordinated through press, party and special institutions, could be an extremely powerful mobiliser both of the revenue of rich farmers – in six weeks, 500 people each donated the then huge personal sum of £100 – and the meagre savings of the petty bourgeoisie and workers. According to the official chronicler of the economic movement: 'All at once *the Afrikaner* realised that, comparatively poor as *he* was, there nevertheless lay locked up in *him* a dispersed capital which could and must help *him* to find *his* economic feet – if the money could be effectively mobilised' (E.P. du Plessis 1964: 48; my italics).

Long before the GNP attempted this, the Helpmekaarsvereniging organised together Afrikaans-speakers from different classes, reinforcing the idea of a classless nation.

> The *Helpmekaar* movement was the first to show what the Afrikaner could do if he stood together, if his strength was mustered. The *Helpmekaar* provided the driving-force for the Cradock congress [on the 'poor white' problem]; the *Helpmekaar* gave rise to the mighty clarion call to the volk to try to conquer the last stronghold, the business world. Then would dawn a new day. And out of the combined influence of the awakened nationalism, the *Helpmekaar* and the Cradock congress, each backed-up and interpreted by *De Burger* and the Nationalist Party, were born those symbols of victory in the Afrikaans business

life of South Africa – Santam and Sanlam – with their fitting and illuminating motto, 'Born out of the *Volk* to serve the *Volk*' (le Roux 1953:125).

The first Afrikaner to realise this potential was W.A. Hofmeyr. As a direct result of his experience as chairman of the Peninsular Helpmekaarsvereniging, he formed, in 1918, the Suid-Afrikaanse Nasionale Trust Maatskappy (the South African National Trust Company – Santam). The £20,000 initial capital was provided by the same Western Cape farmers who financed *De Burger*. Santam was initially intended to effect both short- and long-term assurance. Within a few months the two operations were separated. In June 1918, a wholly-owned subsidiary life assurance company was formed – Sanlam. Two months later, a further division of life and industrial assurance was effected. Though its own paid-up capital stood at a meagre £20,000, Santam splashed out £120,000 to buy the African Homes Trust and Assurance Company, outbidding financial magnate I.W. Schlesinger (E.P. du Plessis 1964: 84–6).

By 1919, the stable of Santam, Sanlam, and the African Homes Trust offered a range of short- and long-term insurance services. Santam's major function as a trust company was to provide short-term credit to agriculture. Sanlam's investments were also predominantly in the field of agricultural credit institutions, where it competed with the Schlesinger group. This almost bankrupted the company in 1922 when the OFS Chamber of Executors, in which 60 per cent of Sanlam's capital was invested, was liquidated. Only a £50,000 unsecured loan from the Standard Bank saved it.

Growth was slow. Competitors used every jingoist device and emotion to confine Sanlam's activities to the petty servicing of agriculture (le Roux 1953: 55). Moreover, as the potential investors and clients, Afrikaner farmers had to be weened from the hoary myth that 'the Afrikaner is no businessman and could accomplish nothing in the business world' (E.P. du Plessis 1964: 55). The group's major weapon in its struggles to attract business was a self-conscious evocation of nationalist sentiment, well revealed in the 1921 Chairman's report.

> Sanlam is an authentic institution of the Afrikaner *volk* in the widest sense of the word. As an Afrikaner, you will naturally give preference to an Afrikaner institution. I would just remind policy holders that we are busy furnishing employment to young Afrikaners, and training them in the assurance field. We hereby intend to provide a great service to South Africa. If we want to become economically self-reliant then we must support our own institutions. To that end, Sanlam offers you the opportunity.[4]

Santam and Sanlam were credit institutions. A major function of such establishments is to draw together various kinds of disposable money scattered in larger and smaller sums over the surface of society. These 'unseen threads of credit' are then a specific mechanism for the centralisation of capital (Marx 1976: 778). Such a centralisation of disposable money, and its transformation into productive-capital was the group's expressed aim. As the

1921 chairman's report shows, this was to be effected primarily through long-term assurance: 'The life-assurance industry is capital-forming by nature. Gradually there comes to be built up a large assured fund standing at millions of pounds. The fund is composed of Afrikaner capital and control of the capital ought to be in the hands of Afrikaners, to be employed in the service of developing our country' (le Roux 1953: 28–9).

Though it is spelt out in detail below (pp. 181–4), it is as well here to consider the implications of this financial strategy in slightly more detail. The Santam/Sanlam group aimed to pool the money resources of all Afrikaans-speakers in a central fund, there to be converted into productive-capital. This money was to come from a number of sources. Through the mobilising agency of Afrikaner nationalism it sought to draw together the revenue of capitalist farmers, the latent money-capital released by the long turnover cycle of agricultural capital, and the small savings of the urban and rural petty bourgeoisie.

The most important source of funds was Afrikaner farmers. The ability of the group to centralise money-capital was determined above all by the accumulation of capital in agriculture, particularly in the Cape. The years 1918 to 1937 saw a concentration of capital in Cape agriculture beyond anything occurring in the other regions.[5] Whilst South African agricultural statistics are notoriously incomplete, this concentration can be shown in a number of ways. During these years the number of white-owned farms in the Cape actually increased (from 31,119 to 38,326). Though data on how these 'farms' were actually being farmed is unavailable, the expansion of production and concentration of capital is strikingly revealed, firstly in the 130 per cent increase in the size of the Cape agricultural labour force during this period (from 131,900 to 203,628), and secondly in a 1,100 per cent increase in the number of tractors employed (from 218 to 2,630). A further agent and index of the concentration of agricultural capital was the rapid development of the agricultural cooperative movement following the Cooperative Association Act of 1922. (The most important cooperative, that of Cape wine growers – the Ko-operatiewe Wynbouers-Vereniging (KWV) – had been established in the same year as Santam/Sanlam.) The cooperatives were instrumental in the concentration of agricultural capital through the processing and marketing of their members' products; the collective – hence cheaper – purchase of seeds, implements, machinery, etc.; and the provision of various services, for example, repairs. By 1937 the Union-wide membership of agricultural cooperatives stood at 75,316, with a total turnover of £15.9m (Department of Agriculture 1961: 3, 11, 13; Finlay 1976: 58).

Yet, despite this concentration of Cape agricultural capital, the accumulation or the expanded reproduction of agricultural capital occurs at a rate much slower than that of industrial capital. There are two reasons for this. Firstly, the turnover cycle of agricultural capital is tied to the natural cycle of the seasons and can be speeded up only within certain very narrow limits. Secondly, the extreme fluctuation of agricultural prices, and the particular susceptibility of this sphere of production to overproduction, renders profitability uncertain, thus adversely affecting the reproduction of such capital. The significance of the prices question in South African agriculture was discussed at length above (pp. 36–7). Suffice it to say that, during the Depression, many agricultural capitals were in fact obliterated by the effects of price fluctuations.

Thus, dependent for the bulk of its funds on Cape agriculture, the growth of Sanlam was slow. By 1928, its assets stood at £ 500,000. It achieved an annual premium income of half a million pounds in 1936 and was providing interest-free loans to holders of all policies over £ 1,000 (E.P. du Plessis 1964 : 222). Other factors hindered Sanlam's growth. Firstly though it enjoyed support from Cape farmers, it had not gained a real foothold in the north. Given the conditions of northern agriculture less latent money-capital was available for centralisation in the north. Secondly, farmers with capital available for placement in credit institutions would not necessarily wish to invest it all in life assurance, where they had to wait long for any return, and faced difficulties in withdrawing funds should it become necessary. Moreover, whilst Sanlam had centralised money in its assured fund, all sorts of statutory limitations hedged in the investments of life assurance companies. A minimum of 40 per cent of all funds had to be placed in state approved securities. Thus, by 1937, the company was confined largely to small-scale credit and had not been able to move into productive investment in industry.

Sanlam's actuary and financial strategist, M.S. Louw, had long planned to move Sanlam out of the narrow world of assurance and agricultural credit. These plans were held up by the Depression. The divisions after fusion delayed them further. But above all Sanlam lacked the resources to mobilise the necessary funds on a national scale. Thus Louw's biographer: 'Even though Sanlam had been in existence for 21 years, its own resources were still limited, so widely dispersed across various areas, so prescribed by statutory and other limitations, that relatively little finance was left over for investment in commerce and industry' (Bezuitenhout 1968 : 74).

In 1937, after three years of intense political struggle, the UP government finally delivered one of the more important of the promised fruits of fusion in the shape of the Marketing Act. This provided for a single-channel marketing system for agricultural commodities, guaranteeing minimum prices on the internal market. Prices were now determined by the producer-dominated Control Boards according to the costs of production (Finlay 1976 : chapters 3–4). The production of agricultural commodities for the internal market was thereby assured a relatively stable profitability. It was now clear that greater potential agricultural profits would be available for centralisation through credit institutions. The major beneficiaries of the Act were Transvaal and OFS farmers, precisely the areas in which Sanlam lacked the resources for their mobilisation. Only in the year of the Marketing Act did Sanlam make its first approaches to the Bond, seeking its assistance to utilise the resources of the FAK to gain access to this potential capital.

The evocation of nationalist sentiment to mobilise and centralise the latent money-capital of agriculture points to perhaps the most significant character-istic of these growing Cape undertakings. They were born out of, as an integral part of, the nationalist movement at the Cape. Santam and Sanlam were as much part of Cape Afrikaner nationalism as the party and its press. W.A. Hofmeyr's position as founder and first organising secretary of the Cape NP; founder, managing director and first chairman of Die Nasionale Pers, which published *Die Burger* as the NP's official organ; and founder and chairman of Santam and Sanlam, simply highlights the solid integration of all these bodies. Moreover, the Cape Party, Die Nasionale Pers and Santam and Sanlam had all been formed, and were fundamentally sustained by an economic and political alliance between Western Cape capitalist farmers and the group of professional men around Hofmeyr. This alliance constituted the foundation on which the political and financial institutions of the Cape nationalist movement were built.

Thus, by fusion in 1934, the slow centralisation of agricultural capital in the very process of its concentration had produced a small group of Cape Afrikaner financial capitalists. Their economic existence was totally de-pendent on the accumulation of capital in Cape agriculture. These men were politically experienced. For almost twenty years they had dominated the machinery of the Cape Party, controlled its press, and, in this role, oversaw the political representation of the interests of Cape agriculture.

The situation in the OFS and the Transvaal was very different. The concentration of agricultural capital was less developed and had not given rise to centralising institutions like Sanlam. The few 'financial' undertakings which did exist, such as the Suid-Afrikaanse Spaar- en Voorskot Bank (South African Savings and Loan Bank, hereafter Sasbank) and the Afrikaner Verbond Begrafnis Ondernemings Beperk (Afrikaner League Burial Undertakings Ltd, hereafter AVBOB), were very small establishments dependent largely on the petty savings of Afrikaner workers. Other existing 'Afrikaner business' consisted of the forms of petty commodity production discussed in chapter 3. The NP had been *gesuiwerd* virtually out of existence. It had little organisation and no press of its own, except for *Die Volksblad* in Bloemfontein. But this was owned by Die Nasionale Pers and toed the Keerom Street line.

Thus the gradual development of the economic movement in the north occurred under different conditions from that in the Cape. When Sanlam's need for access to the profits of northern agriculture drove it into an approach to the Broederbond in 1937, this involved much more than business cooperation. It required above all ideological and political coordination.

THE AFRIKANER BROEDERBOND AND THE ECONOMIC MOVEMENT IN THE NORTH[6]

Following the formation of the FAK as its 'public front' in 1929, the Bond increasingly turned its attention to economic issues. The 1930 congress resolved to strive for 'the economic self-sufficiency of the impoverished section of our volk, and for the training of a commercial community among Afrikaners'. The first of many economic commissions was appointed. Its report recommended action to reform the credit system, the establishment of a central fund – while admitting that it did not know how to achieve this – and further thorough investigation. Nothing came of this, and another commission was appointed in August 1931 to draw up Bond 'economic policy'. Its report was considered at an extra-ordinary 'Economic Bond Congress' in November 1931, where discussion concentrated on the 'stranglehold of foreign capital' over commercial banks, and the need for an Afrikaner-oriented commercial bank (Pelzer 1979: 121–2).

No immediate action was taken but the Bond's concern with banks was not new. Professor L.J. du Plessis first raised the need for an Afrikaner bank in 1924. In December 1928 he was mandated to draw up a report, and a high-powered committee under du Plessis was constituted a few months later. The August 1931 Bond congress decided that a 'people's bank' should be established, but nothing was done till 1933, when a further commission was appointed with the Bond treasurer, J.J. Bosman, as its 'moving spirit'. After an extensive discussion of Bosman's proposals, the bank Volkskas (literally 'people's treasury') was established in Pretoria by sixty *broers* in April 1934. Volkskas was always regarded as the Bond's bank. All vacancies on its board were filled by the Bond Executive Council. Professor L.J. du Plessis was its first chairman, and the remainder of its board comprised Bond chairman J.C. van Rooy, secretary I.M. Lombard, J.J. Bosman, L.J. Erasmus, Dr A. Hertzog and Professor J.P. van der Merwe.

Volkskas began as a cooperative bank with a paid-up capital of £5,000. Although 'not announced at the time' the bank later acknowledged that it had always intended to abandon this cooperative form. Responding to charges that the Board misled the public, it argued that the initial adoption of the cooperative form was necessary 'to gain the cooperation of the Afrikaner masses' (*Volkshandel* June 1947). Volkskas immediately faced great hostility from both the big commercial banks and the existing volk's banks (notably Sasbank). The former refused it clearing facilities, and endeavoured to get Volkskas prosecuted under the Usury Act, whilst the latter bitterly attacked it within the ranks of the volk as a 'capitalist' institution.[7]

But the Bond connection was used to mobilise support for the bank. The first manager, J.J. Bosman, travelled throughout the country with the Bond and FAK secretary, I.M. Lombard, 'to get support for all FAK bodies and Volkskas'. They were accompanied on their journey by another Volkskas director, Dr A. Hertzog, fund-raising for the NRT (Naude 1969:97). The role of the Bond in mobilising rural financial support for both the NRT and Volkskas was thus crucial. Within five years, Volkskas had eighteen branches across the country. Its paid-up share capital rose from £1,500 in 1937 to £37,000 in 1940; its deposits from £10,800 to £519,600; and total assets from

£13,100 to £572,000. In 1941 it was registered as a commercial bank (*Volkshandel* July 1955).

In 1935 the Bond set up yet another economic commission, this time composed of 'businessmen'. Its report argued that the further development of Afrikaner business should be the responsibility of private enterprise – the Bond as such should not involve itself directly in commercial undertakings. Acknowledging the ignorance of both the volk and its self-appointed *krygsraad* (war council) on financial matters, the Bond Executive Council decided in October 1936 that it had to educate both, beginning with the *broers*. Now a 'permanent' economic commission was appointed to draw up specific proposals on the establishment of a central import agency, to win support for Afrikaner business and develop cooperation between existing and future undertakings. These proposals were very different from the programme eventually adopted at the Ekonomiese Volkskongres (Economic Congress of the volk) convened by the Bond in October 1939. Since 1926 at least six different Bond committees and commissions had reported. Apart from the establishment of Volkskas in 1934, a small Pretoria cooperative store – Uniewinkels – in 1935, and another – Sonop – in Bloemfontein in 1937, little had been achieved. On its own, the Bond could go no further. Only when Sanlam proposed cooperation in 1937 did workable schemes emerge.

But the period had seen extended debate within the Bond on economic questions. Moreover, through its various fronts it sought to involve a much wider 'group of Afrikaners' in the debates. Once again *Koers* took the lead. Its first issue warned of the 'golden Chains' of growing economic domination by 'imperialism' (August 1933). Following fusion, the journal continually returned to the theme of the 'economic reorganisation of our national (volks) life' (L.J. du Plessis 1933). The perilous position of 'Afrikanerdom' was blamed on a long series of 'profiteers'. The development of the credit system was held particularly responsible for reducing large numbers of Afrikaners to debt and, through lack of access to large-scale credit, preventing their transformation into entrepreneurs. This led to the regular demand for easy credit 'to suit the national requirements rather than capitalist profit'. A key interventionist role was assigned to the state, which should regulate the market, protect domestic industry and agriculture, ensure the complete segregation of the races, and organise the unemployed into a 'labour army' to fulfil 'national requirements' (*Koers* August to December 1933).

These issues were taken up by Dr Diedrichs in the ANS organ, *Wapenskou*. Here particular stress was laid on the inter-connection between the struggles for language and economic equality. Readers were urged to 'buy Afrikaans' and to insist on using Afrikaans in all economic activities. But this was not enough: 'Consider further how you can contribute to the struggle. Act individually, act together with others, but ACT, ACT, ACT! We must seize this [economic] struggle and win through' (*Wapenskou* February 1936).

Outside the Bond, the venerated NGK pastor J.D. 'Vader' Kestell regularly raised economic issues in his column in *Die Volksblad*, concentrating particularly on the 'poor white' question. In a series of articles in 1932, 1935 and 1937 he pleaded for collective action under the slogan *'Saamwerk, Helpmekaar, Redmekaar'* (cooperation, mutual aid, collective redemption), and urged the creation of another central fund similar to the old *Helpmekaar*. This would finance the return of 'poor whites' to the land.

In a number of other forums, the economic question had been brought to the centre of debate amongst Afrikaner intellectuals. Much of the early discussion focused on the 'poor white' question. The NGK had busied itself with this issue as early as 1886, and had established a number of rural settlement schemes. In 1930 a joint NGK/governmental conference investigated possible areas of cooperation. In the early 1930s the Carnegie Corporation mobilised many Afrikaner intellectuals in a full-scale study on the issue. The five volume report (1932), fully outlined the extent of 'poor whiteism' blaming it on the failure of the (white) rural community to adapt to a 'modern' (i.e. capitalist) economy. Building on the Carnegie Report, the 1933 congress of the Afrikaanse Vrouevereniging (women's union) devoted its entire proceedings to the question. In 1934, the NGK convened a National Congress to discuss the issue. Strongly influenced by the Bond (Pelzer 1979:105), it abandoned the old panacea of resettling 'poor whites' in the rural areas and sought avenues for their urban employment. This was to be secured through a more rigorous application of the 'civilised labour policy' and development of native reserves, together with a relaxation of the apprenticeship system and the 'dilution of other labour safeguards' (E.P. du Plessis 1964:87).

Yet despite the regular discussions of economic questions, the direct achievements of the Bond in the economic field prior to 1939 were negligible. The explanation is simple. While the Bond harnessed the talents of the intellectual cream of the northern petty bourgeoisie, in the blunt words of its official history on economic questions the *broers* were 'stupid' (*dom*) (Pelzer 1979:124). They not only lacked business experience, above all else they lacked capital. Precisely because the Bond was a purely petty-bourgeois organisation; precisely because, unlike their southern counterparts, the northern petty bourgeoisie were politically isolated from capitalist farmers; precisely because Hertzog's Smithfield attacked on the Bond and his regular vituperative condemnation of all things *gesuiwerd* won wide support from northern farmers, the petty bourgeoisie of the Bond were cut off from all sources of capital, and politically too weak to begin to achieve a similar centralisation of agricultural capital as in the Cape group. Furthermore, the Bond was weak in the Cape itself. It had relatively few Cape members and the Keerom Street mafia jealously guarded their political dominance of the Cape and their privileged access to the capital resources of Cape agriculture.

This point is crucial to an understanding of developments after 1937. Only after the enactment of the 1937 Marketing Act, when Sanlam approached the Bond, did the Bond's concern with economic issues begin to be translated into effective action (see following chapter). Both groups needed each other.

Sanlam needed the Bond's control of the levers of cultural legitimacy while the Bond needed Sanlam expertise and capital. But it was always a conflictual relationship. According to a leading Bond ideologue, this was concretised in great tension between W.A. Hofmeyr and the Afrikaanse Nasionale Kultuurraad (an offshoot of the FAK). There were differences of 'political and economic outlook', and fear in the Bond of 'political and economic domination' of the north by the 'established interests' of the Cape (interview, P.J. Meyer). This tension too is central to an understanding of the development of organised Afrikaner nationalism. It is revealed most clearly in two incidents.

Following fusion, the Nasionale Pers daily, *Die Volksblad*, was adopted as the official organ of the OFS G/NP. But the Transvaal party had no newspaper and was confronted by the pro-Hertzog daily, *Die Vaderland*. In September 1935, W.A. Hofmeyr called a meeting in Cape Town to set up a nationalist newspaper for the Transvaal. Most of the initial capital was provided by Pieter Neethling, who had heavily funded the founding of Die Nasionale Pers and Santam. Eventually, the Voortrekker Pers was established to publish *Die Transvaler* as the official organ of the Transvaal G/NP. The Hofmeyr group aimed to tone down Transvaal republicanism through its total control of Voortrekker Pers (Moodie 1975:144). Of the nine directors, Hofmeyr was chairman, and five others – including Dr Malan – were Cape men. The Transvaal G/NP, whose official organ this was to be, had but two representatives, J.G. Strijdom and Mrs M.M. Jansen. The leader of the OFS G/NP, Dr N.J. van der Merwe, completed the board. The editor was appointed by Hofmeyr. Making very clear his intention to use his financial control to retain control of the ideological direction of the paper, over Strijdom's strong objections, Hofmeyr chose a Cape man – the young Professor of Sociology at Stellenbosch University, Dr H.F. Verwoerd.

This choice was perhaps the major political blunder of Hofmeyr's life. Unexpectedly, Verwoerd refused to become the witting tool of Keerom Street. From his very first editorial in 1937, an anti-Semitic tract which aroused a furious rebuke from Hofmeyr, chairman and editor were locked in a personally bitter struggle. Of course Verwoerd could simply have been fired. But such a blatant demonstration of Cape dominance would have led to open rupture with a prickly Strijdom – who now fully supported Verwoerd's line. After two years of constant wrangling, Hofmeyr resigned from the Board and withdrew most of his capital, leaving an investment just large enough to keep a seat on the Board for Dr Malan. In the early 1940s Voortrekker Pers fell into dire financial straits. Pleas were made to Nasionale Pers to re-purchase shares in the company. But in these years of deep ideological division in the Transvaal party Hofmeyr was bent on total control. He offered only 7/6d for a nominal £1 share. Strijdom refused and *Die Transvaler* struggled on (Meiring 1973b).

According to P.J. Meyer, this incident crystallised and reinforced northern fears of economic and political domination by the 'financial powers' which ran the Cape party. Jealous of his tiny preserve, the Transvaal leader, J.G. Strijdom, developed a deep mistrust of the south, which coloured the remainder of his political life with a deep 'provincialism'. There emerged within the Transvaal G/NP and Bond a lasting bitterness against and suspicion of Hofmeyr, Die Nasionale Pers, *Die Burger*, Sanlam and, to a lesser extent, the Cape party.

A second incident further embittered the north/south differences. The NRT was initially funded by a £10,000 donation from Mrs J. Marais – widow of the Stellenbosch farmer who had first financed Nasionale Pers and Santam. Despite strenuous attempts by the Bond and FAK to raise money for the NRT, it became clear that the necessary large sums were available from wealthy Cape farmers. But here the NRT infringed on the exclusive preserve of the Hofmeyr group. In principle, the managers of the economic and political organs of Cape nationalism had little quarrel with the NRT's aims. But, when it began to compete for the same sources of finance, open conflict ensued.

By 1938, the coffers of the NRT were almost empty. Albert Hertzog approached his maternal uncle, the selfsame Pieter Neethling who provided part of the initial capital for Nasionale Pers, Santam and Voortrekker Pers. Neethling agreed to set up a trust fund for the NRT. As Neethling was a founder and director of Santam, his chairman, Hofmeyr, spread rumours that Hertzog was robbing his ageing uncle and threatened immediate dismissal to any of his employees assisting Hertzog. Inevitably Santam won and set up a trust fund of which it was the prime beneficiary. The NRT was simply allowed the use of interest accruing on Santam's trust. This incident reinforced a deep bitterness against Hofmeyr, his 'southern financial power' and its apparent attempts to dominate all aspects of Afrikaner nationalism.[8]

There was thus much mutual suspicion between the members of the Bond in the north on the one hand and the Cape leadership on the other hand. In view of this, during the 1930s the Bond developed into an alternative to southern dominance. Yet, with the increasing emphasis on economic issues within the Bond, and Sanlam's need for expansion out of its narrow base, the two groups needed each other. Cooperation began in earnest in 1937. But given the different interests and class bases of the northern and Cape groups, the emerging economic movement always assumed a contradictory aspect. A sometimes open, sometimes silent conflict between north and south was to characterise both the organised economic movement and the wider nationalist movement in the years after 1937.

8

The Ekonomiese Volkskongres

The first-fruit of the Sanlam–Broederbond cooperation was the Ekonomiese Volkskongres, convened by the FAK in October 1939. This 'congress of the volk' adopted the plans carefully worked out in advance by Sanlam and the Bond. Here was laid down the strategy for the development of the economic movement in the 1940s.

The Sanlam–Broederbond collaboration began in 1937, when the enactment of the Marketing Act promised to make available potentially large sums of latent-capital in agriculture, to be centralised in credit institutions. Realising that Sanlam on its own lacked the resources to mobilise such potential capital its financial strategist, M.S. Louw, now discussed his plans with 'leaders of the FAK', that is, the Bond leadership (Bezuitenhout 1968:63). When Louw made his approach in late 1937, the Bond was itself planning a *volkskongres* on the 'poor white' question. According to his biographer, on hearing this Louw immediately realised that 'the formation of such a finance company would acquire much greater weight if the plan could receive the support of such a representative *volkskongres*, and it would therefore be in the interests of the volk if he made his plan part of the programme of action of the congress' (Bezuitenhout 1968:63). No doubt what was good for Sanlam was good for the volk.

Through the good offices of a leading Cape *broer*, Dr E. Dönges, Louw again approached the Bond, this time through the Nasionale Kultuurraad, headed by P.J. Meyer. His plans were extensively discussed within the Bond, leading to a very different emphasis in the proposed *volkskongres*. By July 1938 it had been decided that the focus of the *kongres* would be on the economic position of the Afrikaner and how to transform it. Louw was appointed to the Bond committee, chaired by L.J. du Plessis, charged with organising the forthcoming *kongres*. Louw himself was especially mandated to draw up detailed proposals for an investment company.

The volk were to be carefully prepared for a *volkskongres*. The Bond was organising the celebrations for the impending centenary of the Great Trek (pp. 76–7 above). It was now decided to make these celebrations 'serve the economic interests of the Afrikaner' (Pelzer 1979:125).

Meanwhile, plans were being devised how best to *create the right climate* for such a *volkskongres*, and to *make the volk receptive* to its ideas and proposals. The right time to inspan the energy of the volk arrived with the celebration of the Centenary of the Great Trek in 1938. The celebrations *would have to be of such a kind* that they would grip the entire volk and shake them into a realisation of the great destitution in which a large section [of the volk] lived (Bezuitenhout 1968:64; my italics).

The *Eeufees* or *Tweede Trek* more than succeeded in preparing Afrikaans-speakers for an economic *volkskongres*. All along the route, the economic plight of urban Afrikaners was a leading theme as significant voices stressed economic issues. Dr Verwoerd reminded the volk that the 300,000 'poor whites' were the descendants of the Voortrekkers, whose message to the living was 'Afrikanerise the cities and assume your rightful place in commerce and industry.' Diedrichs saw the *Eeufees* as divine deliverance from class divisions:

> When the nation heard its Call, it was not united. Its children were scattered and divided, and frequently stood estranged and hostile against each other . . . In two great camps was the nation divided, rendering our volk weak and powerless . . . the tree threatened to split down the middle and wither to its roots. But, the ox-wagon came! It called, and all followed . . . The ox-wagon made us one again, and now it is my task and your task to ensure that what has been achieved shall not wither away, and that which has been united will never again be sundered (Bezuitenhout 1968:54, 56).

The venerated 'Vader' Kestell, pastor to the Boer commandos during the Anglo-Boer war and doyen of the NGK clergy, best captured the spirit and function of the *Eeufees*. In a powerful speech in front of the wagons in Bloemfontein, Kestell encapsulated his writings of the last nine years in an emotional plea for a great 'deed of Salvation' (*reddingsdaad*), by which the volk would rescue itself from poverty. Kestell's theme '*n volk red homself*' ('a volk rescues/redeems itself'),[1] became the slogan of the economic movement. He went on to propose the establishment of a multi-million-pound central fund as the instrument of redemption. All Afrikaners were called upon to contribute every penny possible to this *reddingsdaadfonds* (hereafter fonds). Kestell had been arguing this for years. Now this plea was taken up by the Bond.

Whilst the Bond was 'creating the right climate' for the Volkskongres, Louw pressed ahead with his planning of the finance company. In the midst of the *Eeufees*, he laid his first proposals before the Sanlam directorate. They are worth quoting at some length.

> The question of how to advance the interests of the Afrikaner in the commerce and industry of our country is one which has attracted the growing attention of thinking Afrikaners in the past year or two. As one of the problems which the urbanisation process has brought in its wake, [this question] today takes its place in the developing national consciousness alongside equally great cultural questions . . . Everywhere in the country one comes across the spontaneous

feeling that action must be taken. Here and there Afrikaner businesses have already been established . . . but to remedy the situation, an undertaking on a much larger scale is necessary, some thing which, like Santam and Sanlam, grows out of the volk itself and enjoys nationwide interest and support. Such an undertaking must be able to provide for the great need felt by all the smaller businessmen:CAPITAL. The volk are ready for a large-scale movement of this nature. It now awaits constructive action and the person or institution to take the lead. If the volk has the assurance that such an undertaking will further the real interests of the Afrikaner, that the concern will be conducted on sound business principles, then I am convinced that the necessary capital will be found (Bezuitenhout 1968:64 original emphasis).

Louw proposed the formation of a finance company with a capital of £1m. It would aim firstly to secure the largest possible profits for its shareholders, but, secondly, 'the major aim shall always be to strengthen the position of the Afrikaner in commerce and industry'. Sanlam itself should take the initiative in the establishment of such a finance company:

> I cannot propose a more effective method than this, to employ the mobilised capital of *the* Afrikaner in the furtherance of *his* national interests in the spheres of commerce and industry, and to capture key positions [in the economy]. Such a finance company appears to be the appropriate means through which *the* Afrikaner can realise *his* legitimate struggle to assert *himself* in the economic domain. It will be the starting point of further large scale undertakings, only the first step in a mighty program[2].

Eager for expansion out of the narrow field of insurance, the Sanlam board endorsed these proposals. Sanlam would underwrite the share issue and free one-twelfth of its personnel for the venture, provided the official backing of the forthcoming Volkskongres was secured – Sanlam could not risk such an undertaking without the mobilising resources of the Bond. Louw thus reported favourably to the first meeting of du Plessis' organising committee of twenty-two Bond 'experts'. This committee now readily adopted the Sanlam proposals as the major plank in its programme of resolutions to be put before the *kongres*. A three-man committee of Louw and two other prominent Cape *Broers* – Dr E. Dönges, and Professor C.G.W. Schumann, Dean of the Faculty of Commerce of Stellenbosch University – was appointed to super-vise the detailed planning of the finance company.[3]

This committee was further mandated to proceed with the formation of the proposed company, with the help of 'a well disposed Afrikaans concern'. This was to begin even before the Volkskongres rubber-stamped the plans of Sanlam and the Bond. The committee reported in the first instance to Sanlam, and not to the Bond committee organising the *kongres*. Already control lay with Hofmeyr's group. In a memorandum of 20 April 1939 to the Santam board (which controlled Sanlam), the aims of the proposed finance company were spelled out:

> The company will itself do no business. Its function should be the financing and establishing of Afrikaner commercial and industrial undertakings. Through the

purchasing of shares, or in other ways, it will also obtain control over existing businesses and Afrikanerise them. It will also finance existing Afrikaner undertakings through the discounting of bills etc. A few of the first tasks will be the establishment of an Afrikaner building society and a central purchasing and wholesale establishment. It is planned to recommend to the *Volkskongres* that a large proportion of the *Reddingsdaadfonds* now being collected, will be invested in the shares of the finance company (Bezuitenhout 1968:64–5).

The detailed plans were accepted by the Santam board. When likewise approved by the Bond in May 1939, the three-man committee was mandated to lay these proposals before the *kongres* as its primary plank.

Before examining the proceedings of the Ekonomiese Volkskongres, it is as well to reflect on the import of the primacy given to Louw's proposed finance company. It must be stressed that, despite its hostility to W.A. Hofmeyr, in effect what the Bond was recommending to the volk were Sanlam's plans for expansion. The proposals had been conceived by its actuary and were first cleared by its board. The share issue was underwritten by Sanlam with administration to be undertaken by its specially seconded personnel. For Sanlam, this was the way out of the narrow horizons of insurance. Through the mobilising power of the Bond and its front organisations, the scheme offered Sanlam access to the potential money-capital of a much wider group of farmers, and to the savings of both Afrikaner petty bourgeoisie and workers. Now it would be able to lay claim to these funds by right as the official organ of Afrikanerdom, and so enter entirely new fields of investment hitherto barred to it. On the other hand, Sanlam's proposal transformed the Bond's view of the role of the *kongres*. It opened up much wider possibilities for the northern petty bourgeoisie. What Sanlam had achieved might be open to others as well. But without the expertise and established financial strength of the southern group, movement out of the narrow world of petty trade was unlikely. Thus, despite strong antipathy to and fear of dominance by the financiers of the south, the Bond seized on Sanlam's scheme. Yet the ambivalence and tensions remained.

The proceedings and recommendation of the Volkskongres deeply reflect this ambivalence. On the one hand were the clear-sighted proposals of the Cape trio, making up the main recommendations laid before the *kongres*. Here was advocated a finance company whose shareholders were to be rewarded not with 'pious sentiment', but in the 'jingling coin' of profit. The large-scale capitalist character of this undertaking was unmistakable, and Schumann and Louw, in particular, made no effort to disguise it. On the other hand a great variety of generally utopian cooperative schemes were proposed. These stressed the plight of the 'poor whites' and were geared to 'rescue' them through developing small businesses. All of this was cast in a strong anti-capitalist rhetoric totally absent from the Sanlam proposals. Finally, in the middle, and trying to hold together what were clearly contradictory tendencies through a stress on nationalism and the unity of all Afrikaners, stood the chairman of the organising committee, L.J. du Plessis. Assuming a role with which he was to become increasingly familiar, du Plessis' opening address on the 'Purpose of our Economic Struggle' tried to reconcile both tendencies through a plea for *volkskapitalisme* ('people's capitalism').

> [In the past] we also accepted that the masses who were unable quickly and easily to adapt to capitalism would sink into poor whiteism. Sympathetically we belittled them and distanced ourselves from them, at best philanthropically offering them 'alms' or poor relief from the state. And meanwhile this process of adjustment was destroying our volk by denationalising its economic leaders and proletarianising its producing masses. But, in the awakening of consciousness, the volk has perceived this too, and the new national economic movement sets for itself the goal of reversing this process; no longer to tolerate the destruction of the Afrikaner volk in an attempt to adapt to a foreign capitalist system, *but to mobilise the volk to capture this foreign system and adapt it to our national character* (E.P. du Plessis 1964:104; my italics).

The wide differences between the Sanlam conception on the one hand, and the solidly petty-bourgeois orientation of the northern delegates on the other, are crucial to an understanding both of the economic movement, and of Afrikaner nationalism itself. As these differences were hidden beneath the rhetoric of nationalism, and the acceptance of du Plessis' slogan of *volkskapitalisme*, it is important to draw them out.

Professor C.G.W. Schumann introduced the Sanlam proposals in the first substantive paper of the *kongres*, entitled 'The present position of the Afrikaner in the economic domain'. In sharp contrast to du Plessis' key-note address, and the concerns of many of the delegates with the poverty of the 'poor whites', he bluntly stated that in the past too much attention had been paid to 'this unhealthy section'. Rather than concern itself with 'poor whites', the *kongres* should aim 'to help the Afrikaner become an entrepreneur, an employer and an owner of capital'. This could only be achieved by mobilising the 'capital resources' of the volk. There were two potential sources of such capital. Firstly, Afrikaner consumers controlled an annual buying power of £100m. Secondly, and more importantly, 'The farming community clearly forms the most financially strong [*kapitaalkragtigste*] section of the volk. They should become the source of capital for Afrikaner business in commerce and industry etc.' This would also benefit farmers, as it would provide for the diversification of agricultural capital into other sectors of capital accumulation.[4]

Schumann was immediately followed by Dönges who spoke on 'The Mobilisation of the Capital and Savings-Power of the Afrikaner'. According to Dönges, so many Afrikaans speakers lived in poverty because 'Afrikaner capital power [*kapitaalkrag*] is not being purposively mobilised nor productively employed with the aim of giving the Afrikaner that place in commercial life to which he is legitimately entitled.' Existing Afrikaner financial institutions were designed and developed 'purely to provide for the long term capital requirements of the Afrikaner as an agriculturalist', and were unsuitable for investment in industry and commerce. Any attempt to mobilise 'Afrikaner capital' for investment in such fields faced both the 'psychological preference of the Afrikaner to invest in tangibles, land, houses etc.' and a lack of suitable investment channels.

The proposed finance company would provide the appropriate channel for the investment of such capital. This would ensure 'the Afrikaner his legitimate' place in the economy. Dönges was also very clear on just what that 'legitimate' place was. The aim was to develop a group of Afrikaner capitalists: 'not just to Afrikanerise commerce and industry to a greater extent, also not only to attract more Afrikaners as workers in commerce and industry, *but to increase by ten-fold the number of Afrikaner employers in commerce and industry*'. To ensure the successful functioning of the finance company it should have a management both 'in full agreement with our aims', and 'experienced in investment and [which] has made its mark in the commercial and economic fields'. Only Sanlam fulfilled the requirements (E.P. du Plessis 1964:112–14).

Louw's speech on the 'Application of the financial power (*kapitaalkrag*) of the Afrikaner' showed how this ten-fold increase in the number of Afrikaner capitalists could be achieved by drawing together the capital of farmers and the small savings of Afrikaner workers and petty bourgeoisie in a great alliance – L.J. du Plessis' *volkskapitalisme*:

> The finance company will stand in the forefront of the forthcoming struggle of the Afrikaner to find his legitimate share in the commerce and industry of our country. It will mesh together the farmer, the investor, the consumer and the employee on the one side, and the retailer, wholesaler, manufacturer and credit establishment on the other.

Each section would benefit in this great service to the volk:

> For the investor it will create the opportunity to use his capital in the interests of this Afrikaner concern whilst drawing profit from his investment. The Afrikaner farmer will find Afrikaners to process and distribute his products. Opportunities will be created for the practical training and employment of Afrikaner boys and girls in commercial and industrial undertakings where they can occupy the highest posts.

Yet lest there be any doubts as to the real purpose of the company, Louw bluntly dispelled them. The first aim was profit. Investments would be made with an eye to profitability rather than sentiment or demand: 'If we wish to achieve success, we must utilise the techniques of capitalism as it is applied in the leading industry of our country, the gold mining industry. A finance company must be established which will function in commerce and industry like the so-called "finance houses" of Johannesburg' (E.P. du Plessis 1964:155–17). This alliance of all Afrikaners was thus geared to an aping of 'Hoggenheimer'. Louw's directness must have appalled many.

The proposed share structure of the company clearly revealed the role of Sanlam and its dependence on the Bond to produce mass support for its expansion plans. The company was to have an authorised share capital of

£300,000, consisting of 100,000 (5½ per cent) cumulative preference shares, and 200,000 ordinary shares. The preference shares were to be offered to 'existing Afrikaner establishments'. This was in effect to secure Sanlam's investment. Sanlam and Santam together underwrote the entire share issue. In addition, Sanlam had undertaken to buy a minimum of 50,000 of the preference shares, *provided* the Bond could sufficiently mobilise the volk to purchase a minimum of 100,000 of the ordinary shares. The whole extent of Sanlam's participation depended on the Bond delivering the requisite mass support. A further 25,000 of the preference shares were held in reserve for the fonds (controlled by the Bond), leaving but 25,000 preference shares for other Afrikaner establishments.

In effect the Volkskongres was a pure rubber-stamp for these plans. Indeed the preparatory committee had been mandated to proceed with the establishment of this Sentrale Volksbeleggings (Central Volk's Investment) Company even before the congress, but 'it was however decided not to anticipate the decisions of the congress'. But all had been decided. A board of directors – 'Afrikaners who have already made their mark in commerce and industry' – had already been appointed by the committee. Most were senior Sanlam employees or close associates like Dönges and Schumann. And Sanlam was to provide the management and administration of the new company.

The capitalist character of the proposed company is clear. The Cape trio made little attempt to dress it up in plebeian Voortrekker garb. Concerned with the position of small operators, what L.J. du Plessis referred to as 'the floundering petty bourgeoisie' (E.P. du Plessis 1964:103), other speakers detailed less grandiose schemes. Great emphasis was laid on cooperatives. A number of speakers argued that cooperatives were the appropriate form for *volkskapitalisme*, as they avoided both evils, monopoly and individualism, by drawing all groups into mutual support and cooperation. Existing cooperatives in banking, retailing and agriculture were extensively analysed. The speech of J.H. van Vuuren on cooperative 'People's Banks' offers a revealing insight into one conception of cooperatives:

> So long as nearly 300,000 Afrikaans-speakers live below the breadline; so long as a large percentage of our fellow Afrikaners remain the hewers of wood and the drawers of water in their own country; so long as the Afrikaner is notable by his absence in our business life; and so long as a large section of the agrarian population are forced by circumstances to migrate to the cities in order to make a living, millions of pounds belonging to Afrikaners *lie around unproductively* (E.P. du Plessis 1964:117–18; my italics).

The 'People's Banks' could centralise such loose money and turn it into productive-capital. Others had a different view of cooperatives. Producer and consumer cooperatives were valued because they provided necessary services to their members and did not strive after large profits for their shareholders. This emphasis on cooperatives emerged as the universal panacea of the congress. Great stress, too, was laid on the coordination of the buying power of Afrikaners to develop Afrikaner businesses. Collective action, emphasising the unity of the volk and the great dangers of class divisions, was a theme constantly echoed in all proposals.

The speech of Albert Hertzog of the NRT on 'the organisation of labour' contained the most explicitly anti-capitalist proposals. Over half the volk were workers. They were exploited by the capitalists of the country, most of whom were 'foreigners'. These capitalists exhibited 'the normal psychology of all employers, that is, to extract as much as possible from the workers whilst giving the minimum possible in return'. Moreover, in South Africa this exploitation was intensified by the fact that these foreign capitalists 'lack that human sympathy which comes from national ties because he confronts the Afrikaner worker as a foreigner.' Yet for Hertzog the establishment of Afrikaner-owned industries was only a partial solution: 'We know of many trades and factories in which Afrikaners are the bosses, and where the conditions of the workers are not a jot better than with the foreigners, where workers are just as badly treated and as exploited as with the foreigners.' The only way to protect (Afrikaner) workers and to give them 'their legitimate share in the profits of the country' lay not through socialism, but in fostering their 'economic interests' in trade unions. Like industry, the existing trade union movement was controlled by 'foreigners' in an unholy alliance with 'foreign bosses'. Thus, concluded Hertzog, 'if you want to rescue the Afrikaner volk' it is the workers who must be saved. Urging support for the NRT's struggle to take over the trade unions, he argued that Afrikaner control of trade union funds would 'unleash a financial giant' (E.P. du Plessis 1964:124–5).

The recommendations of the Ekonomiese Volkskongres accepted as its major plank the plans of the Cape three-man committee to mobilise and centralise all unused capital, savings and loose money in central financial institutions where it could be transformed into productive-capital. Resolution II declared the conviction of the *kongres* 'that this is the most effective plan for the application of Afrikaner capital to improve the position of the Afrikaner in the commerce and industry of our country, and calls on the *volk* to support this undertaking, by taking up its capital'.

To this end, the same resolution mandated the FAK to take steps to ensure that:

> Thrift should be cultivated and strengthened in our volk; full support be obtained for existing Afrikaner savings and credit institutions; greater facilities for the exercise of thrift be provided through the establishment of new savings and credit institutions, if, after investigation, these are deemed necessary; new opportunities for the profitable and safe investment of capital be created through the establishment of new commercial and industrial undertakings, or through the expansion of existing establishments; Afrikaners and financially strong [*kapitaalkragtige*] Afrikaner establishments must be encouraged to invest a greater share of their capital in commerce and industrial undertakings' (E.P. du Plessis 1964:125–33).

The first resolution of the *kongres* recognised that a permanent (Afrikaner) proletariat had been created. It urged the state to provide for the training of this proletariat, and further urged that young Afrikaners be trained in business studies. Other resolutions stressed the importance of cooperatives and the necessity to establish a central cooperatives union. Afrikaner consumers should be organised to provide a market for Afrikaner industries. Industry should be established on a cooperative basis, and an Afrikaner Chamber of Commerce and Industry was proposed. The *kongres* stressed the importance of agriculture as the 'backbone' of the economy of the volk. Since the entire financial strategy of the Volkskongres was predicated on profitable agriculture, much emphasis was laid on the need for stable agricultural prices. Finally, to create the widest possible support for the proposed finance company and other 'supplementary proposals', it was decided that 'The time has arrived for the calling into existence of one large, Christian-national volks' organisation, which will propagate and give effect to these measures, and others which may appear necessary' (E.P. du Plessis 1964: 131). The FAK was further mandated to call into existence a new Ekonomiese Instituut (economic institute, hereafter EI) to give effect to all the resolutions and to take any further steps.

The Ekonomiese Volkskongres is one of the great turning points in the development of Afrikaner nationalism. The Bond's official history argues that 'never before . . . was such an important congress held' (Pelzer 1979:126). Here was crystallised a strategy to transform the position of the Afrikaner petty bourgeoisie within South African capitalism. This was elevated to the status of a great national movement under the joint direction of the Bond and Sanlam. The economic struggle of the petty bourgeoisie became the central core of the nationalist movement in the 1940s, and was clearly seen as part and parcel of the overall nationalist political struggle. This was plainly revealed in Verwoerd's speech. Echoing Dönges, he declared the goal of the economic movement to be the achievement of the Afrikaner's 'legitimate' place in commerce and industry – that is, as an employer of labour: 'What weapons can Afrikanerdom use in this great struggle? There is that of state power. If we can take possession of it, public credit could be used, *inter alia*, for the founding of industrial banks, and firmly to establish Afrikaner undertakings, particularly industry' (E.P. du Plessis 1964:121).

The economic strategy was straightforward. First and foremost, utilising the full organisational and ideological resources of the Bond working through the FAK, all 'loose money' was to be drawn out of the pockets of Afrikaans-speakers of all classes and into the coffers of the new finance company. Here it would be transformed into productive-capital in commerce and industry. Through a coordinated centralisation of money-capital, industrial capital would be generated. But this was predicated above all else on a further centralisation of agricultural capital. As has been repeatedly stressed, the capitalist farmers were the major source of capital. They had to be persuaded that the accumulation of their capital should occur in a new form. Instead of always being reinvested in more land, part of the profits guaranteed by the Marketing Act should be invested in the new finance company, to be utilised productively in commerce and industry. But the savings of workers and the petty bourgeoisie were also seen as a source of such money capital. Yet it was not expected that workers would be able to buy shares in the new company. Their small savings should rather be centralised in other kinds of credit institutions.

All this was fine in theory and made a lot of sense. But the difficult part was precisely the mobilisation of such money capital. As Dönges recognised, this involved three sorts of changes. Given the widespread belief that 'the Afrikaner can never be a businessman', it required a major ideological offensive – a 'transformation of economic consciousness' as Dönges put it. As this ideological offensive developed, the transformation of economic consciousness became a redefinition of Afrikaner nationalism itself – of its goals, strategies, alliances, priorities and class character. It became above all a redefinition which stressed the role of the Afrikaner entrepreneur, and in doing so, redefined the relations between classes. Now, more than ever, class consciousness was a mortal danger to the petty bourgeoisie and its developing economic movement. Afrikaner workers had to be made 'part and parcel of the daily life of the *volk*'. Thus, secondly, alongside the gathering ideological offensive in the 1940s, there developed a complex organisational structure to direct and mobilise all classes of the volk for the economic struggle. Again, the Ekonomiese Volkskongres pointed the way through its call for an Afrikaner Chamber of Commerce and Industry, a broad Christian-national organisation to mobilise the masses, and through its appointment of the EI to direct the movement and implement its decisions. Thirdly, and finally, the mobilisation of capital required the establishment of new forms of credit institutions. This was provided for by the new finance company, which finally emerged in 1940 as Federal Volksbelegging (Federal Volks' Investments, hereafter FVB).[5]

In its resolutions on producer and consumer cooperatives, on the coordination of buying power, etc., the Ekonomiese Volkskongres also attempted to develop a strategy which would lead to the development of existing and new smaller undertakings. The volk were also to be mobilised to support these. But already a division appears. The *kongres* was dominated by the Sanlam scheme for a finance company. This emerged as the major recommendation of the *kongres*. The full organisational resources of the Bond (together with those of Sanlam), were put at the service of the new FVB. No other undertaking enjoyed the privilege. The Ekonomiese Volkskongres had mirrored the two views which were to spill over into nationalist politics in the years to come – the straightforward capitalist concerns of Sanlam, and the petty-bourgeois, anti-capitalist rhetoric of the northern delegates.

Part III

Afrikaner nationalism and the development of the economic movement in the 1940s

9

'Hereniging' and 'broedertwis'

If the Ekonomiese Volkskongres marked a great turning point in Afrikaner nationalism, it occurred immediately in the wake of yet another. On 4 September 1939, one month before the opening of the Volkskongres, the South African Parliament voted by a narrow majority of thirteen to declare war on Germany. This step provoked a further realignment in the party political organisation of class forces in South Africa, with far-reaching effects for the development of Afrikaner nationalism.

The years following fusion had been difficult ones for the G/NP. The South African economy had emerged from the Depression into a period of the most sustained growth hitherto experienced. National Income rose from £217m to £395.6m between 1932 and 1939 (US 1960:S-3). All sectors of capitalist production flourished. Between 1932 and 1940 the value of gold exports shot up from £47m to £118m (Houghton 1976:106). Increased foreign exchange earnings from gold exports in effect financed the import of capital goods necessary for the large-scale expansion of manufacturing. During these years manufacturing expanded more rapidly than any other sector – the gross value of its output grew from £67.3m in 1932 to £161.7m in 1939 (US 1960:L-3). Much of this increased industrial production was due to heavy investment in a wide range of industries by 'large overseas concerns' seeking to avoid heavy protective tariffs through the establishment of 'branch industries' in South Africa (BTI 1945:127). Agriculture likewise flourished. The gross value of agricultural and livestock production almost doubled from £37.4m in 1932/3 to £72.9m in 1939/40 (Department of Agriculture 1961:35, 69).

In this climate of relative capitalist prosperity, the governing UP enjoyed widespread support from all sections of the capitalist class. It faced few crises likely to drive northern farmers into the *gesuiwerde* camp. Moreover, the rapid expansion of white (especially Afrikaner) industrial employment (p. 79 above) eased the 'poor white' problem. Attempts by the G/NP to win support from Afrikaner workers met with scant success. The May 1938 general election provides a useful index of the G/NP stagnation, particularly in the Transvaal.

The UP defended the so-called 'fruits of fusion', with particular emphasis

119

on the rapid growth of the economy under its stewardship. The G/NP campaigned for a republic to guarantee the sovereignty and neutrality of South Africa. Moreover, it emphasised racial issues, calling for residential segregation, job reservation to protect white workers, and an end to the 'wholesale buying of land for Natives' under the 1936 Land Act (National Party 1938).

The election results were a severe blow to the G/NP. It won only 27 seats, against 111 for the UP. Although G/NP parliamentary representation increased by seven seats, all but one of these were in the Cape rural areas where the party was already strong. If the G/NP was ever to win power, it would have to build a strong base amongst Transvaal farmers. However, despite an intensive campaign to capture Transvaal rural areas, the G/NP was routed in all constituencies except Waterberg. Even here, J.G. Strijdom's majority was halved. After four years of strenuous activity, the G/NP's attempt to build an alliance between agricultural capital and the petty bourgeoisie seemed stillborn. The UP retained firm control of the rural areas of the Transvaal and lost only one seat to the G/NP in the OFS.[1]

This severe electoral setback reinforced the heavily extra-parliamentary character of northern nationalist politics. Throughout the 1930s, the extreme disorganisation and isolation of the northern petty bourgeoisie, the continuing weakness of the G/NP and its failure to establish itself as the dominant nationalist grouping, all spawned an array of weird and wonderful lunatic fringe Afrikaner political groupings, particularly in the Transvaal. Some, such as the National Republican Unity Front, which formed around the publication *Die Republikein*, split from the party because of the dominance of the relatively moderate Cape group. Others, such as Louis Weichardt's Greyshirts, were openly Nazi. Semi-clandestine, conspiratorial, putschist organisations such as Boerenasie and very many others, sprung up for shorter or longer periods. The northern, and particularly Transvaal, Afrikaner petty bourgeoisie seemed unable to find for itself an appropriate form of political organisation. Only the highly elitist and relatively small Bond appeared to be able to maintain a viable existence.

The Bond was the most important and influential Transvaal Afrikaner nationalist grouping during the 1930s, far eclipsing Strijdom's G/NP, and now carving out a substantial base in all four provinces. Indeed, in the months following the *Eeufees* some leading members of the Bond, especially in Potchefstroom, began to attack the entire system of party politics, calling for a realignment which would in effect dissolve the G/NP. Van Rooy gave strong support to a plan by Professor A.C. Cilliers to form a new 'Afrikaner' party based on 'the ox-wagon sentiment' (Cilliers 1939). Malan, W.A. Hofmeyr and the OFS G/NP leader, N.J. van der Merwe, met with the Cilliers group in February 1939 but resolutely defended the necessary dominance of the party. Yet so insistent was the growing antipathy to political parties in the Bond that the OFS leader of the G/NP, leading Broederbonder and FAK chairman, van der Merwe, felt compelled to publish an article defending party politics (*Koers* August 1939).

The outbreak of the war transformed this situation, by posing anew the issue of political alignments within the state. South African involvement in the Second World War clearly stemmed neither from direct internal accumulation imperatives of any branch of capitalist production nor from any specifically South African conflict with Germany. On the contrary, during the 1930s Germany had developed into an important market for South African agricultural exports, particularly wool. Throughout the decade the Hertzog government sought to expand trade with the Third Reich under the 1934 Trade Agreement (Kienzle 1979). This growing German market enabled farmers to avoid some of the disabilities placed on their exports under the Imperial Preference system. Thus not only did South African farmers have no interest in fighting Britain's 'imperialist' war, but by the declaration of war with Germany an important market was closed to them in the interests of 'imperialism'. With the exception of the jingoistic Natal sugar farmers, the overwhelming majority of South Africa's capitalist farmers were firmly united in opposition to South African involvement in the war. The declaration of war with Germany drove them out of the UP and into broad acceptance of the need for a republic to protect their interests against 'imperialism'.

It would be a mistake, however, to present opposition to the war as if it were limited to farmers. A large majority of Afrikaans-speakers of all classes were outraged by the decision and by the way in which a pro-war Cabinet had been imposed on the country without elections. Most commentators agree that, had an election been held on the war issue in 1939, as Hertzog recommended, the white electorate would have returned a decisive anti-war majority. The declaration of war with Germany thus united, as had nothing before, a majority of Afrikaans-speakers of all classes. Over and above the fact that the economic interests of neither farmers nor white workers nor Afrikaner petty bourgeoisie dictated support for the war, this now became an issue of naked 'imperialist' domination. Afrikaners would again be called upon to pay in blood and money to defend 'our only foreign enemy' against a friendly power. Opposition was wide-ranging, intense and bitterly emotional. Thus the declaration of war did far more than simply detach agricultural capital from the UP. It destroyed for ever the Hertzogist conceptions of cooperation with 'imperialism' which underpinned the UP, and again raised the question of South Africa's constitutional links with Britain as a burning political issue. Virtually overnight Afrikaner republicanism became an extremely potent political force.

Thus, just five years after fusion, the UP split on the war issue. The Governor-General rejected Prime Minister Hertzog's recommendation to dissolve Parliament and hold elections. Smuts was asked to form a government. Led by Hertzog, thirty-seven UP MPs, most representing northern rural constituencies, withdrew from the UP to form the Volksparty.

The Bond leaped at this chance to unite all Afrikaans-speakers against the war. A great public meeting was hastily arranged at the site of the Voortrekker monument, where the climax to the *Eeufees* had been held nine months previously. Before 70,000 Afrikaners, Bond vice-chairman, J.C. van Rooy, presided over an emotional joint appearance of Hertzog and Malan as the spokesmen of an apparently 're-united' volk. By January 1940, the strenuous mediation of the Bond had produced a very shaky party political *hereniging* (re-union) of the followers of Hertzog and Malan into the Herenigde Nasionale or Volksparty (Re-united Nationalist or People's Party, hereafter HNP). With Hertzog as its nominal national leader, the HNP opposed the war on a republican platform.

With the formation of the HNP, agricultural capital and the Afrikaner petty bourgeoisie were again allied in a republican party, one which could now claim to represent all Afrikaners. Yet it was a wary, contradictory alliance. Simply to bring about *hereniging* had been a protracted, difficult process, which was nearly wrecked on a number of occasions. *Hereniging* was strongly opposed by powerful G/NP leaders in the north – most notably Strijdom and Verwoerd in the Transvaal, and Swart in the OFS. They were unwilling to compromise *gesuiwerde* principles with the 'traitor' Hertzog in his belated re-conversion to republicanism (Roberts & Trollip 1947: chapter 1). They also feared that the small northern *gesuiwerde* party would be swamped by the Hertzog *smelter* element. The formation of a single political party could not resolve the important contradictions between the major class forces on which the HNP was based: capitalist agriculture and the petty bourgeoisie. These two groups were differentially affected by, and responded differently to, both the declaration of war and the development of the economy during the war. Newly-won Afrikaner unity soon dissolved in a four-way split, in which the nature of the desired republic and the manner of its achievement were the major issues. Two points are noteworthy here.

Firstly, given their different places in the reproduction of capitalist social relations, the content of the republicanism of northern agriculture on the one hand and that of the petty bourgeoisie on the other differed markedly. For the vast majority of farmers, the re-acceptance of the need for a republic was dictated by their need to protect their interests against 'imperialism'. However, the envisaged republican state was to be little different from the existing one. Pragmatic in conception, it involved no radical restructuring of the state and social relations. This was clearly revealed in the draft Programme of Principles Hertzog drew up for the HNP. For the northern petty bourgeoisie, however, the declaration of war on behalf of British imperialism reinforced the demand for an exclusively Afrikaner ethnic republic within which the relations between social groups would be dramatically restructured.

Secondly, the rapid development of the economy during the war affected these classes differentially. Despite agriculture's wide opposition to this 'imperialist' war, the economic position of farmers soon improved dramatically. In just three years the gross value of all farm products rose by 67 per cent (table 5, p. 187 below). This gradually undermined farmers' vocal opposition to the war, particularly in the Transvaal. A number of MPs returned to the UP, and in the 1943 general elections the UP won back control of fifteen Transvaal rural constituencies from the HNP. Moreover, even for those farmers whose republicanism and opposition to the war remained unshaken, the prosperity of agriculture during these years increasingly limited the lengths to which they would go in their opposition and struggle to achieve a republic. This was to have vitally important effects for the direction and forms of nationalist politics.

If the expansion of capitalist production during the war led to prosperity for farmers, its effects on the Afrikaner petty bourgeoisie were very different and appeared both to reinforce the barriers to social mobility on their part and to threaten their existing social position. The war saw a restructuring of industrial and commercial capital which strengthened the power of monopoly. Not only was 'Hoggenheimer' the prime beneficiary of economic growth during the war, but for the first time since Union in 1910, the wartime Cabinet contained a majority of English-speakers. Its Afrikaans-speaking members, such as Smuts, Hofmeyr and Steyn, were all partisans of close links with Britain. Under the rule of what was seen as a nakedly 'pro-imperialist' government, other far-reaching social changes appeared to threaten the economic, social and political position of the Afrikaans-speaking petty bourgeoisie. The development of wartime industry saw a massive inflow of Africans into semi-skilled positions in a wide range of industries. A militant African trade union movement developed, and, after years of relative inactivity, the African National Congress began to put forward a series of demands for the abolition of all racial discriminatory measures. An extremely militant Congress Youth League urged the need for mass action by Africans to force the state to abandon segregationist policies. From 1941 onwards, a series of public utterances by government leaders and reports of government commissions created the definite impression amongst all elements that the Smuts government was softening its position of racial segregation, and rethinking some of its policies. While there can be no question whatsoever that the UP was moving towards a policy of non-racialism, to the Afrikaner petty bourgeoisie, under increasing social, economic and political pressures in these years, it certainly did appear as if South Africa was on the slippery slope to racial equality.

All these developments seemed to imply the further isolation of the Afrikaner petty bourgeoisie and to present even more formidable barriers to their economic and social advance. Again it was domination of the interest of 'Hoggenheimer' in the state and economy which was deemed responsible for this situation. The only way out appeared to be through a radical restructuring of both state and economy to ensure the domination of 'Afrikaner' interests. The result of these effects of economic development was to drive the Afrikaner petty bourgeoisie into an ever more extreme and exclusivist republicanism. The early 1940s saw intense debate over the form of the forthcoming

123

Afrikaner republic. These were apotheosised in the Draft Republican Constitution, prepared by the Bond and presented to the volk in 1941.

The bitter, sometimes violent struggles between various 'Afrikaner nationalist' groupings in the 1940s present an often bewildering array of issues and disputes. In the existing literature they are largely interpreted simply as ideological and tactical differences, embittered by personal rivalries between various ambitious leaders.[2] In my view the *broedertwis* (division between brothers) of the 1940s and the particular forms it took can only be comprehended through grasping the contradictory effects of wartime development on agricultural capital on the one hand, and on the Afrikaner petty bourgeoisie on the other. But a word of caution is necessary here. It would be completely incorrect to interpret the various splits simply as a division between farmers and petty bourgeoisie. Wartime developments produced a range of responses which divided the petty bourgeoisie itself into conflicting political factions, again mainly in the north. Precisely the extreme isolation and political disorganisation of the northern petty bourgeoisie again threw into question the unresolved issue of the 1930s – the appropriate form of political organisation for this class force.

The first split in the ranks of the 're-united' volk occurred in November 1940. In the short period of *hereniging*, the OFS HNP had been wracked by harsh conflicts between the old *smelter* and *gesuiwerde* elements (Roberts & Trollip 1947: chapter 2). Finally, amidst enduring bitterness, Hertzog resigned from the party and retired from politics when the first congress of the OFS HNP rejected his platform of equal rights for English-speakers in the forthcoming republic. Eleven of his parliamentary followers then formed the Afrikaner Party (AP) under Havenga to carry on the fight for 'Hertzogite principles'. The AP was based predominantly in the OFS. All the ex-United Party OFS MPs joined it, together with four Transvaalers. But it was never able to establish a firm base for itself. As a small protest grouping, tied to the woolly and now discredited creed of 'Hertzogism', it lacked an organisation, a press, a clear programme and dynamic leadership. In the past, it was precisely the broad, inclusive character of 'Hertzogism' which had been able to unite divergent class forces and ideological tendencies. However, the war issue now polarised the alternatives. The centre truly could not hold the divergent tendencies together. The OFS HNP on the other hand now had the branch and organisational structure of the old UP firmly under its control. It received unwavering support from the Bloemfontein daily, *Die Volksblad*, possessed a clear political programme, and in the person of C.R. Swart it had a new and forceful leader – one who had dared to challenge and beat Hertzog himself at the 1940 Party Congress.[3] The re-awakened anti-imperialism of the OFS farmers found expression now through the HNP, and the AP was unable to generate a following.

The unity of the HNP was soon shaken by two more significant challenges. The first occurred in the Transvaal. Before *hereniging* with Hertzog, the Transvaal G/NP was weak, and possessed but one MP, Strijdom himself. It has been stressed that the G/NP was based mainly on the petty bourgeoisie. With *hereniging* the HNP became the spokesman for the majority of Transvaal farmers. Not only had the class basis shifted yet again, but twenty-three ex-UP MPs were added to Strijdom's solitary figure, swamping the *gesuiwerde* element. Strijdom and his closest lieutenant, Dr Verwoerd, had opposed *hereniging* on precisely the grounds that it would weaken *gesuiwerde* policies. The re-union of the two parties immediately witnessed much jockeying within the new Transvaal Party between the former *gesuiwerdes* and the old *smelters*. Much of this centred around the position of Oswald Pirow.

Still a young man in 1940, Pirow had already been a Cabinet Minister for ten years. As Hertzog's closest political confidant after Havenga, in the 1930s he was widely spoken of as a future Prime Minister. After Hertzog's resignation, Pirow refused to join the AP, but formed the Nuwe Orde Studie Kring (New Order Study Circle, hereafter NO). Drawing explicitly on fascist theories, the NO preached the end of 'liberal capitalist democracy'. Under God's guidance, the coming 'New Order' would sweep away democracy and substitute a Christian, white, National-socialist republic, severed from the British Crown and founded on the principle of 'state authority' and national discipline. In this vision, the paraphernalia of effete liberal-capitalism, such as political parties, Parliament, elections, etc., would follow its demise. Significantly, this vision of the coming New Order followed Hertzog in ignoring the ethnic distinctions between Afrikaans- and English-speaking whites (Pirow 1940).

The NO attracted wide support from MPs of the Transvaal HNP, fourteen of whom joined the NO. Thirteen were ex-*smelters* and one an ex-*gesuiwerde*. Only five Transvaal HNP parliamentarians remained outside the NO, with Strijdom again the solitary *gesuiwerde*. Strijdom and Verwoerd had originally strenuously opposed *hereniging* with the *smelters*, arguing that they had betrayed 'genuine Afrikaner ideals' at fusion and would do so again (Roberts & Trollip 1947:61). Hertzog's withdrawal from the HNP, the AP breakaway and now the schismatic manoeuvrings of the Pirowites simply confirmed this assumption. Organised through the NO, the ex-*smelter* threatened to dominate the Transvaal HNP, and the *gesuiwerde* wing felt particularly threatened – seeing the NO as a direct *smelter* challenge to its leadership in the Transvaal. Thus, through the columns of *Die Transvaler* and in the party branches, Strijdom and Verwoerd launched a vigorous campaign to destroy the NO. While the Pirow group had the votes in the caucus, it lacked a press and an organisation. More significantly, the NO suffered from two fundamental political weaknesses. Firstly, the petty-bourgeois ex-*smelter* politicians who rallied to the NO were unable to carry their rural constituents with them. The explicit and convoluted National-socialism of the NO exerted little appeal to the capitalist farmers of the Transvaal. The NO offered farmers little that was not already present in the policies of the HNP, whilst its ideology was inspired by Salazaarite National-socialism rather than Afrikaner culture. Strijdom could attack it as a 'foreign importation' to great

125

effect. Pirow's National-socialism and failure to stress the ethnic divisions between Afrikaner and English were both condemned as 'un-Afrikaans' and contrasted with the allegedly 'ethnic' and 'democratic' Afrikaner republican tradition (*Die Transvaler* 15/3/41).

Thus the NO MPs cut themselves off from their rural base, and were driven into ideological conflict with other petty-bourgeois elements in the HNP, which themselves retained strong rural support. This points to the second weakness of the NO. As an essentially ex-*smelter* ginger group it enjoyed scant support in the solidly *gesuiwerde* Broederbond, itself highly suspicious of Pirow's political ambitions. In its elaboration of a National-socialist ideology for South Africa, the largely *smelter* NO in effect challenged the solidly *gesuiwerde* Bond for the ideological direction of the volk. Had Pirow won rural support, the Bond would have had to come to terms with this competition, but by 1941 the NO represented nothing but a small petty-bourgeois faction. Furthermore, Pirow and his followers had to be extremely careful not to step outside the bounds of HNP policy. Already under attack from Strijdom and Verwoerd, now accused of factionalism, they could not engage in direct ideological struggle within the party. In June 1941, the Union Congress of the HNP banned factions in the party. Two months later the Pirow group was soundly trounced at the Transvaal HNP congress. They finally withdrew from the HNP caucus in January 1942. Already cut off from any solid basis of support, in this anticipation of their prophesied demise of political parties the NO committed political suicide. It refused to contest the 1943 elections, and its members sank into political obscurity.

Within a year of *hereniging* the unity of both the Transvaal and the OFS HNP had been sorely tested, in what amounted to struggles between the former *gesuiwerde* and *smelter* elements. In both cases the Bond had rallied strongly behind the *gesuiwerde* position. More importantly, in both cases the old Hertzogite elements had been unable to retain the rural support they had for so long represented. Hertzogism had been politically destroyed, most of the *smelter* MPs had left the HNP, and farmers rallied to a party dominated by the old *gesuiwerde* leadership. It appeared as if the long struggle to build an alliance between agricultural capital and the petty bourgeoisie in the north was finally bearing fruit, giving the HNP a strong political base in the Transvaal and OFS. The crises over the AP and NO did not affect the Cape HNP, which remained largely unaltered by *hereniging*. The five *smelter* MPs were quietly re-absorbed (though one left for the NO), and formed a small, easily-controlled element in the Cape party.

However, no sooner were these provincial threats contained than the HNP was confronted by a far more significant challenge on a national level from OB. Moreover, the lines of division were no longer *gesuiwerdes* versus *smelters*, but now went to the heart of the *gesuiwerde* wing and split the petty bourgeoisie of the Bond itself.

The OB had been formed by the somewhat eccentric Colonel Laas in February 1939 as a cultural movement to 'safeguard the ox-wagon spirit' and forge *volkseenheid*. This was the period marked by a proliferation of fringe movements (p. 120 above). The OB focused on cultural and communal activities, seeking to draw Afrikaans-speakers of all classes into a broad volks movement. Organised on semi-military lines, and presided over by a *kommandant-generaal*, it paraded its members in uniform, and introduced regular military drilling in its attempts to mobilise the entire volk. Before the war, this openly militarist character of the OB attracted the odds and sods of the fringe political groups into its ranks – there to cultivate further their semi-clandestine, conspiratorial politics. A paramilitary wing of Stormjaers (shock troops) was organised. But the OB was an amorphous 'cultural' grouping without any clear direction, perspective or programme. Under Commandant-general Laas its leadership was inept and divided. Five months after its formation only five members of the original fourteen-man OB Groot Raad (Grand Council) remained in the organisation. Whether the OB would have been able to sustain itself as a mass movement is an open question, but certainly the declaration of war and the intense militarisation of all levels of South African social life acted as a rapid spur to its growth. In the words of one of Moodie's informants: 'The English were signing up all around us, war was in the air. People felt compelled to take *some* action, and the militarily constituted OB seemed a good substitute' (Moodie 1975:193). By August 1940 the OB claimed 200,000 members (*Die Volksblad* 24/8/40) and in February 1941 Malan stated in Parliament that the OB had between 300,000 and 400,000 members.[4]

While the OB lacked coherent direction and remained a mixed bag of elements fed up with party politics, precisely because of its emphasis on mass mobilisation along the lines of *kultuurpolitiek*, it occasionally blundered into the political field. In April 1940, in just that period when much manoeuvring was going on between former *smelters* and *gesuiwerdes* in the HNP over the character and manner of achievement of the forthcoming republic, the Transvaal OB published a draft republican constitution with strong National-socialist overtones. Malan objected strongly to what he saw as encroachment on the terrain of the party. The Bond quickly intervened to patch up differences, and, in the 'Cradock Agreement' of October 1940, the party and the OB undertook not to meddle in the affairs or domain of the other. The HNP would work on the party-political front, whilst the OB would confine itself to the 'non-political field' (*Die Burger* 31/10/40). A month later, the bumbling Colonel Laas was finally eased out of the OB commandant-generalship, and replaced by the Administrator of the OFS, protégé of General Hertzog, and self-confessed Nazi, Dr J.F.J. van Rensburg.

van Rensburg's accession to the OB leadership marks a significant turning point in its development. This mercurial, ambitious politician immediately began moving the organisation away from its emphasis on cultural matters into an increasingly political stance in three ways. Firstly, his frequent speeches emphasised the obsolescence of all political parties (presumably including the HNP) in the 'Revolution of the Twentieth Century'. Secondly, van Rensburg and many in the OB leadership began an aggressive propagation of National-socialism as the answer to the woes of the volk. And thirdly, under van Rensburg's leadership the elite Stormjaer paramilitary corps of the OB initiated an intensive programme of sabotage, aimed at undermining South African participation in the war (Visser 1976). This sabotage campaign led to the internment of many of its leaders, including 'General' B.J. Vorster.

Wartime developments subjected the Afrikaner petty bourgeoisie to increasing social, economic and political pressures, producing an ever more extremist response, which emphasised the complete transformation of the state into an exclusivist Afrikaner republic. The rapid politicisation of the OB under van Rensburg reflected and intensified this ideological development of the petty bourgeoisie, harnessing the gathering discontent with party politics and channelling it for the first time into a mass movement. While the OB laid great emphasis on the unity of the entire volk, the bulk of its support came not from farmers, but from the rural and urban petty bourgeoisie – from teachers, traders, clerks, students, etc. Unlike the HNP, which remained within the narrow confines of parliamentary politics, the OB directly involved the petty bourgeoisie in political action. With its increasing militarisation on the one hand, and its emphasis on National-socialism and mass action on the other, during 1941 the OB rapidly developed into the mass organisation of the petty bourgeoisie. Unlike the equally petty-bourgeois Bond, it organised openly and directly involved the masses in its activities. Particularly in the Transvaal, where the old G/NP had always been weak and the tradition of extra-party, extra-parliamentary nationalism strong, many of the Bond's leading intellectuals began to gravitate towards the OB. P.J. Meyer became its propaganda chief at an early stage. The Potchefstroom academics, too, were greatly attracted towards this mass movement.

Ever since fusion, the ideological leadership of northern nationalism lay with the Bond rather than with the party. In the years of schism between *gesuiwerdes* and *smelters* the Bond had been obsessed with uniting the volk. By 1940, its successes were manifold. Following the Ekonomiese Volkskongres L.J. du Plessis wrote in his regular column in *Koers* (February 1940) that the (Bond-controlled) FAK 'already acts in great measure as the organisational centre of all Afrikaans national (*volks*) movements, with the exception of the political'. Whilst lending full support to the HNP in its campaign against the Hertzogites of the AP and NO, the Bond was striving to correct this lacuna. In October 1940 a fourteen-member Bond 'General Policy Committee', chaired by L.J. du Plessis and including Diedrichs, Meyer and Verwoerd, was appointed to prepare a draft republican constitution (Pelzer 1979:168). It was expected that the draft constitution would provide a focus of unity for all groups. Meyer and du Plessis in particular sought to erect a broad *volksfront* (national front) which would act as one at all levels.

This clearly raised the question of the relationship between the OB and the

HNP. Especially under van Rensburg, the OB saw itself as such a *volksfront*. The party, on the other hand, regarded itself as the supreme body of Afrikaner nationalism. The party leadership was determined that if there was to be such a *volksfront*, it must both be led by the HNP and the party must retain its autonomy. The entire Cape party hierarchy in particular watched these Bond schemes very warily. They were ready for cooperation, as this could only strengthen the party, but there was a grim determination neither to be steamrollered by the Bond intellectuals, nor to fall into any arrangement which would give them effective control.

The same Union Congress of the HNP which attacked the NO by banning factions in the party in June 1941 elected Malan both party leader (after Hertzog's resignation) and *volksleier* (supreme leader of the volk). This congress was carefully coordinated by the Bond to effect the maximum unity. Malan's election as *volksleier* was accepted by the OB, the FAK, the Reddingsdaadbond (see the following chapter) and the Afrikaner churches. du Plessis' Bond General Policy Committee (now renamed the 'Unity Committee') published a 'Declaration on Behalf of the Volks' Organisations' signed by the leaders of all these bodies, emphasising their determination to maintain *volkseenheid*. Appended to the Declaration was the Draft Republican Constitution framed by du Plessis' committees. This was highly authoritarian in character and based on a system of rigid ethnic exclusion which relegated English to a secondary level. The details are not of concern here,[5] but rather its effect on the relationship between the HNP and the OB.

The draft constitution was produced by the Bond, not the party. It was the apotheosis of the ideological debates amongst the petty bourgeoisie within the Bond since 1934. The ideological stream which Malan represented, first within the G/NP and then the HNP, had played little part in these debates, and none at all in the framing of the constitution. It was the exclusive product of the northern Bond intellectuals. Malan had publicly accepted the Declaration on Behalf of the Volksorganisasies, as confirmation of his position as *volksleier* and as approval for the policy of his party. But he rejected any common policy council with the OB as an infringement of party autonomy. He further argued that, while the draft constitution was acceptable as a basis for discussion, the time was not ripe for its publication. As later became clear in *Die Burger's* critique of the draft constitution, the Cape Party leadership had strong reservations about this child of the Bond. In essence the objection ran over the actual path taken by the Bond's ideological redefinition of Afrikaner nationalism – in which the Cape had played almost no part. *Die Burger* appealed to 'a Nationalist principle as old as the Party itself' (i.e. older than the Bond):

> that is, the principle that out of the two sections [English- and Afrikaans-speaking], a united nation must be built which will be bound by a common love of the fatherland and national pride . . . No person in his right senses can hope that unity will ever be attained in a republic if the language and culture of one of the two sections is slighted (*Die Burger* 23/1/42).

These were precisely the principles which had been thrown overboard by the Bond since 1934. It had firmly rejected any notion of equality for English-speakers, arguing for an ethnically Afrikaner republic, and the 'Afrikanerisation' of all sections of life.

But for the moment a *volksfront* had been established with the HNP at its apex. The party hastened to consolidate its position. Pleading that the unity effected at the Bloemfontein congress could only be safeguarded by more effective organisation at the political level, Malan announced a thorough re-organisation of the party in July 1941. Although this was explicitly denied, the new structure was very similar to that of the OB, and was designed to facilitate much more effective organisation and mass mobilisation. Discipline, too, was to be enforced. Asserting the HNP claim to be the sole spokesman of the volk, Malan declared that the party carried the unity, strength and welfare of the volk in its own hands. The lesson of Afrikaner history declared that there had to be 'a single political entity' – the HNP (*Die Vaderland* 1/7/41).

Despite Malan's denials, this move clearly aimed to usurp the OB's claim to be a *volksfront* and deny it both autonomy and any political role. In particular the HNP rejected outright the OB assertion that political life could be divided into party politics (the sphere of HNP) and *volkspolitiek* (the sphere of the OB). As Dr Verwoerd informed an August 1941 meeting of the Bond Executive Council, called to reconcile the party and OB, the HNP had the 'sole right' in the political sphere.[6] In these terms the party's sweeping attacks on the Pirow group and its 'foreign' and 'un-Afrikaans' National-socialism were seen as thinly veiled assaults on the strongly Nazi OB. With its organisational structure usurped, the legitimacy of its strongest ideological tendency under constant attack, and its right to any political role effectively denied, the OB clearly had to respond. In July 1941, without authority, it published 100,000 circulars containing a summary of the Draft Republican Constitution.

The HNP leadership interpreted this as deliberate OB interference in the political field of the party, and another abrogation of the Cradock agreement. In August, Malan accused the OB of sabotaging the party and the unity which had been cemented at the Bloemfontein congress (*Die Burger* 28/8/41). By October 1941 the *volksleier* called on all party members to resign from the OB, and a special HNP campaign against the OB was launched in the Transvaal. In November 1941, Malan drew the attention of the 'Hoggenheimer' government to the 'subversive' nature of the OB, inviting the state to act against it (Visser 1976:69).

Here it is vital to note that the decision to destroy the OB as a political force was not simply Malan's but equally that of Strijdom and Verwoerd. This point is significant because the publication of the Draft Constitution by the OB simply provided an excuse for the official split. The Cape party had rejected the Draft Constitution. On the other hand, writing as editor of the official Transvaal HNP organ, Verwoerd endorsed the Draft without reservation when it was finally published – as indeed, as one of its framers, he was bound to do.

The essence of the struggle between the HNP and the OB lay in what were effectively the different class bases of the two groups, leading to different conceptions of Afrikaner nationalism and the forms of political struggle. As argued above, whilst the OB strove to unite all Afrikaners, under the van Rensburg leadership it did so on a fascist platform which catered almost exclusively for the more extreme elements of the petty bourgeoisie. Or, to put this another way, the OB's political platform and its entire method of political struggle alienated agricultural capital. Its stress on the socialist component of National-socialism was sometimes seen as an attack on property itself. Many feared that the drastic plans of the OB for the total reorganisation of South African society would undermine private initiative. Indeed the HNP attacked the OB as 'communistic', arguing that it could not cater for the interests of farmers (*Die Vaderland* 17/11/44). It is significant to note here that whilst some prominent individual ideologists of the economic movement supported the OB (in particular Meyer and du Plessis), it did not attract support from any of the successful businessmen of the *reddingsdaad* movement. Moreover, by late 1941 the economic position of agriculture was improving dramatically. This growing prosperity for farmers began to dampen their ideological ardour, in the Transvaal in particular, and at the very least placed severe limits on the lengths to which they were prepared to go in their republicanism and political opposition to the Smuts government. As argued above, some elements of the Afrikaner petty bourgeoisie, on the other hand, were driven into ever more extremist forms of opposition to the government by precisely these wartime developments. It was this group that the OB catered for. The violent antipathy of the OB leadership to 'effete' party politics, the military drilling given to its members, its stress on mass struggle to overthrow 'imperialism', and the extensive sabotage programme undertaken by its Stormjaers, all further alienated the great bulk of farmers from the OB, particularly in the Transvaal. It rapidly became clear that the only way in which the OB saw the winning of political power was through armed confrontation with the state, not something which many farmers were prepared to contemplate.

Nor were the petty-bourgeois politicians of the HNP prepared to accept the ideological and militaristic tendencies of the OB, precisely because these clearly threatened to isolate further the petty bourgeoisie and to destroy the possibility of an alliance between petty bourgeoisie and farmers, driving agriculture back into the UP. Whatever the broad areas of agreement on many issues between HNP leaders, such as Strijdom and Verwoerd, with OB ideologues like Meyer and du Plessis, the struggle between the two organisations was really a struggle within the petty bourgeoisie. Whilst the OB in effect stood for the independent organisation of this class, Strijdom and Verwoerd (let alone Malan of the Cape) realised very clearly that the success of both the political and economic struggles of this group rested on the development of an alliance with agricultural capital, particularly in the Transvaal. This was the meaning of *volkseenheid*. With its ever more extreme National-socialism and militarism the OB was effectively undermining that

131

alliance, driving out the farmers. Unless it were smashed, such an Afrikaner nationalist alliance could not be built. Above all else, this meant that the party had to establish its absolute and unchallenged hegemony as the leader of the *volksfront*; the party had to control the unswerving allegiance of all nationalists.

Whilst reorganising the party to provide for greater mass participation and discipline, the HNP leadership set out to destroy the OB and to demand exclusive loyalty. It was a ruthless, vicious and violent fight which divided virtually all nationalist organisations and reopened a deeper *broedertwis* in the bosom of the volk. The two Transvaal HNP republican 'extremists', Strijdom and Verwoerd, were particularly relentless in their pursuit of the OB's destruction. Its National-socialism was roundly condemned as 'un-Afrikaans', and the organisation was labelled 'anti-volk'. These labels stuck precisely because the OB did alienate a key section of the volk, the farmers. OB members were hounded out of all important positions, particularly in the economic movement.[7] Over the next five years, the two organisations combated each other in every field. On occasion, the OB's Stormjaers abducted HNP activists, who were 'ge-bonnetted' by being lashed across the bonnet of a motor car and thrashed with hippo-hide whips. An HNP member of Parliament, Dr F.E. Mentz, was severely beaten up by the Stormjaers. An attempt to mete such treatment out to Dr Verwoerd was thwarted by his legendary single-mindedness when he harangued his attackers into flight.

Itself an exclusively petty-bourgeois organisation, the Bond was deeply divided by this struggle. Some senior *broers* supported the OB – most notably P.J. Meyer, L.J. du Plessis and other Potchefstroom academics. Others, such as Verwoerd and Dönges, were four-square behind the party. Still others, most notably Diedrichs and Albert Hertzog, tried to remain outside the conflict, occasionally initiating attempts to heal the rift. But, as the official Bond history admits, the numerous and occasionally desperate Bond attempts to reconcile party and OB were all wrecked on the implacable opposition of the HNP. Within the Bond Executive Council Verwoerd, Dönges and L.W. Hiemstra – all extreme HNP partisans – denied the OB any right to exist and implicitly threatened an open split in the Bond if the neutral groups sought to meddle in this struggle. As a result of this temporary impotence in nationalist politics, the Bond concentrated during these years 'on the economic, cultural and social terrain' (Pelzer 1979:178, 176–80).

These various divisions were the major preoccupation of Afrikaner nationalist politics from the declaration of war in September 1939 to the general election in July 1943. By the time of this election, 29 of the 67 MPs who had formed the HNP in January 1940 had left, or been expelled from, the party. Almost all of them were ex-*smelters*. During all these struggles, the party had consolidated its dominance over nationalist politics. The 1943 general election finally entrenched this dominance. In this election, the HNP concentrated its main fire not on the governing coalition under Smuts, but against what its manifesto termed 'the wreckers of Afrikanerdom' (*The Friend*

21/6/43). Neither the OB nor the NO fielded candidates. They had turned their backs on elections as an 'effete' form of struggle (though van Rensburg had offered an electoral pact with Malan, Pirow and Havenga). No AP candidate was elected, only two of them polling more than 1,000 votes (Heard 1974: chapter 2). Though it lost 8 seats to the UP, the HNP emerged from the elections with 43 MPs and as the sole nationalist body with any political credibility.

The 1943 election is a significant pointer to the emerging class basis of the HNP. The most striking aspect of its performance, compared with that of the G/NP in 1938, was its increase in rural support in both the Transvaal and OFS. Strijdom's party now held 11 seats in the Transvaal compared to 1 after the 1938 elections. The OFS HNP captured all but 1 of the 14 OFS constituencies (compared with 6 in 1938). Thus a significant part of the rural support for fusion had now shifted to the ever more reactionary republicanism of the HNP. Yet the governing coalition of the United, Labour and Dominion parties still controlled 42 of the 82 rural constituencies throughout the country and virtually all the urban ones. If the HNP was to capture power, it would have to break the UP's rural base, particularly in the Transvaal, and make inroads in the urban areas. In another significant development, the HNP had captured one working-class constituency on the Witwatersrand and registered considerable advances in five others. This represented a small pay-off for the work of the NRT, and another potential source of major advance for the HNP in the next elections.

These years of political division were also the formative years of the economic movement. The attempt to build mass support for the struggle to develop Afrikaner business – an attempt which, in the words of M.S. Louw, involved a 'meshing together' of the interests of farmers, workers and petty bourgeoisie – was carried forward by the Bond in the face of bitter political divisions.

10

The organisational network of the economic movement

In his speech to the Ekonomiese Volkskongres, Dönges identified the two major tasks confronting the economic movement. First was the mobilisation of capital in a central finance house. All the other schemes for cooperatives, the coordination of buying power, etc., were subordinated to this aim. But, as Dönges warned, such a strategy ran up against a major 'psychological'/cultural stumbling block. Afrikaner farmers, workers and petty bourgeoisie all tended to regard urban capitalism, and finance and investment houses in particular, as the personification of 'imperialism', and the epitome of the power of 'Hoggenheimer'. These views were deeply ingrained in contemporary Afrikaner cultural values. If Afrikaner capital were to develop along the chosen path, such views would have to be broken down, and the cultural legitimacy of Afrikaner capital established. The mobilisation and centralisation of Afrikaner capital thus depended, secondly, upon a cultural and ideological offensive to transform what was termed the 'economic consciousness' of the volk. In effect this involved a significant shift in cultural values, and, in the process, a transformation of Afrikaner nationalism itself. This was the second great task confronting the Bond-directed economic movement. It was a condition of the success of the first.

Here, organisation was the key. Economic consciousness would be transformed not simply by intellectuals elaborating new economic ideas, but rather through directly involving Afrikaans-speakers of all classes in various types of new organisation where their daily lives and activities would be structured by such new values. Only through organisation could the ideals and schemes of the Bond intellectuals become embedded in a transformed popular consciousness. In this the Broederbond played the leading role.

A great deal has been written about the 'sinister' role of the Bond in the 1940s. Elaborate conspiracy theories about Bond 'control' of the economic movement have been woven.[1] These fail to grasp the real role of the Bond in the economic struggle. The Bond took almost no part in the day-to-day running both of the 'official' FVB and the myriad other undertakings which sprang up. This was left to management and the laws of capitalist competition. In this sense the Bond did not 'control' what came to be called 'Afrikaner

134

capital'. If any one organisation can be said to have done so, it was Sanlam rather than the Bond.

The crucial role of the Bond lay rather in developing an increasingly complex organisational structure, both to direct the ideological and cultural mobilisation of the volk, and to shake loose and mobilise their savings and capital. What the capitalists did with this capital was not under Bond control – though it was certainly consulted. It was this Bond-directed ideological, cultural and economic mobilisation of the volk for economic ends which shaped and defined Afrikaner culture and the developing nationalist movement during the 1940s, giving clearer purpose to what Dr Meyer has labelled 'its political wing', the HNP (interview, June 1975).

The three years following the Ekonomiese Volkskongres produced the three major organisations of the economic movement. The EI of the FAK was the 'planning council'. The RDB was charged with mass mobilisation, whilst the Afrikaanse Handelsinstituut (Afrikaans Commercial Institute, hereafter AHI) developed as the specific organisation of Afrikaner businessmen. Each of these organisations played crucial, though different, roles in shaping the economic movement. Though the Bond's relationship with each differed, it presided over the birth of all three.

THE EKONOMIESE INSTITUUT OF THE FAK

The Ekonomiese Volkskongres had mandated the FAK to form an EI to implement the decisions of the *kongres* and to control the fonds (fund for the act of rescue). Formed in consultation with the Bond, the EI comprised the FAK executive and economic commission, together with Afrikaner financiers, industrialists, traders, farmers and representatives of Afrikaner labour organisations, universities, technical colleges, welfare organisations and the churches (Pelzer 1979: 127). It saw itself as the 'economic planning council' of the volk (FAK 1955: 112).

Its chairman was L.J. du Plessis, with two very senior *broers*, P.J. Meyer and I.M. Lombard, as its secretary and treasurer respectively. In effect, the EI was a Bond economic committee functioning in public. As such it brought together the cream of the Bond intellectuals and Afrikaner businessmen to determine the direction of the economic movement. Its major function was a theoretical and policy-making one. It laid down the general direction for coordinated organised action. The EI was, moreover, the final arbiter in disputes over policy. Here the full weight of the Bond's authority could be brought to bear.

From the outset, the EI was embroiled in a number of conflicts. These centred on the desired trajectory of the economic movement, and brought into confrontation class forces whose interests dictated differing paths of development. At its very first meeting, the EI tried to prevent the consumer cooperative, Koopkrag, and the wholesale company, Kopersbond, from competing with the FVB campaign to win investment from the volk. The

Voortrekker Motor Club likewise 'infringed on the terrain and mandate allocated to the *Instituut* and RDB by the Volkskongres' and was brought to heel (E.P. du Plessis 1964: 135–40). The EI was immediately flooded with requests from existing and proposed undertakings for 'official' recognition. An OB demand for representation was referred to the RDB, but nothing came of it. However, the demands for recognition created more serious problems, promoting rivalry and resentment between larger and local undertakings. Initial EI policy granted 'official' recognition to nationwide concerns only, whilst local undertakings would apply to the nearest branch of the RBD for recognition. In effect this meant that only the Sanlam and Volkskas groups received official sanction. Much abused by companies unjustifiably claiming official status, this policy was greatly resented by local undertakings, and aroused opposition amongst consumer groups. The EI thus reversed this policy in November 1940, on the grounds that it might lead to 'the even greater exploitation of the Afrikaner community by certain Afrikaner businessmen than by the foreigners of today'. Henceforth only FVB would carry the official recognition and sanction of the EI. The public was again urged to invest exclusively in FVB (*Volkshandel* January 1941).

This only intensified the conflict, however. Many local undertakings resented the blessing given to one large finance company, arguing that it was precisely the small undertakings which should enjoy maximum assistance from the volk. So strong was the resistance to this scheme from local operators in the rural areas that FVB very nearly failed to raise the minimum capital for registration under the Companies Act (see chapter 13). Attempts to placate this opposition, by making a sum of £5,000 available for small loans to small undertakings, had little effect and the attacks of the small undertakings on the 'capitalist' character of FVB continued.

The EI further became embroiled in the dispute between cooperative and non-cooperative trading companies. The former accused the latter of being 'capitalist' in their pursuit of profit, whilst private operators assailed the 'unfair' and 'monopolist' competitive position of the cooperatives (*Volkshandel* December 1940). This struggle gradually entered the conflict between the OB and the HNP, with the OB stoutly advocating cooperatives as the ideal form of undertaking for the volk. Eventually the EI issued an 'official' directive setting out the 'legitimate' fields of operation for both cooperative and non-cooperative undertakings (Ekonomiese Instituut 1946).

Despite Bond attempts to keep the HNP/OB division out of the economic movement, it surfaced in other ways. The removal of the two leading OB stalwarts on the EI, chairman L.J. du Plessis and secretary P.J. Meyer, has been mentioned (Note 7). The struggle between the HNP and the OB stemmed from their different class composition, embodying differing conceptions of the interests of the 'volk'. The issues ranged over the entire character of the Afrikaner nationalist movement, clearly affecting its central component in the 1940s, the economic movement. The OB stood for 'the small man', whilst the 'official' economic movement was built on a broader alliance in which a major element was the capitalists of the south. Similarly, the conflicts within which the EI was embroiled reflected the differing conceptions of whose interests the economic movement should serve. In many cases this took the form of friction between small local concerns and the larger 'national' undertakings favoured by the EI, particularly FVB.

In its attempts to resolve these conflicts the EI constantly stressed the need for unity in the economic struggle. However, as the 'theoretical and planning council' of the economic movement it could do little to bring this about. This was left to the other organisations which emerged, the Reddingsdaadbond and the AHI. The EI (and through it the Bond) presided over the birth of both.

THE REDDINGSDAADBOND AND THE REDDINGSDAADFONDS

The Ekonomiese Volkskongres mandated the EI to establish 'a large, Christian-national, *volk's* organisation' (E.P. du Plessis 1964:130–1). The RDB was formed at the first meeting of the EI. The then Bond chairman, Dr Diedrichs, was appointed RDB *hoofleier* (leader-in-chief). Its officials 'were always AB members' and the Bond 'also used the RDB as a public front' (Pelzer 1979:128). If the EI was the planning council of the economic movement, the RDB would mobilise the masses for the implementation of these decisions. Or, as the RDB journal put it, in the symbols of the Great Trek, if the 'experts' of the EI were the leaders of this economic *Tweede Trek*, the RDB members were its oxwagons (*Inspan* March 1950). As an organisation to mobilise mass support for Afrikaner businesses, the RDB was to concentrate on three broad areas: firstly, that of *bewusmaking*, or a transformation of mass consciousness on economic issues; secondly, the mobilisation of the 'savings power' of the Afrikaner masses, to centralise these savings in Afrikaner financial institutions; and thirdly, the mobilisation of 'Afrikaner buying power' in support of Afrikaner traders and the products of Afrikaans companies (FAK 1955:112).

The success of such mobilisation rested on the inculcation of the idea of unity and common interest amongst all members of the volk. There were two aspects of this stress on unity. Firstly, Afrikaners of all classes were to be drawn into supporting the economic movement. It had to be firmly established that this was not simply a movement in the interests of existing commercial concerns. In the early 1940s the English language press reported opposition to the economic movement from the rural areas on precisely the grounds that 'it has devoted its main energies to the towns, to the rehabilitation not of the poorest section of the community, but of the commercial and trading section'.[2] Much work had to be done to mobilise the support (and capital) of farmers for the economics movement. Moreover, Afrikaner workers displayed an unhealthy 'class hatred' for all employers. The RDB thus saw one of its prime tasks as 'the integration of the Afrikaner worker in the life of the volk as a whole, of which he forms an organic part, and from which we must not allow him to be sundered' (RDB 1941:10–11).

137

The RDB emphasis on unity referred secondly to the split in Afrikaner politics. As a mass, public arm of the Bond, the RDB was concerned to maintain unity in the face of such division. It had played a leading role in the Bond's Unity Committee, chaired by L.J. du Plessis. The RDB *hoofleier*, Dr Diedrichs, was one of the signatories of the Declaration on Behalf of the Volks' Organisations (above, p. 129) – and was attacked at the 1941 RDB congress for thus 'dragging the RDB into party politics'.[3] When the split between the HNP and the OB was final, the first issue of the RDB and FAK organ tried to transcend this by proclaiming itself 'the policy paper for the entire Afrikanerdom' (*Inspan* October 1941). This was clearly a Bond attempt to retain direction of the volk outside the political divisions. The RDB withdrew from the Unity Committee so as not to become embroiled in these divisions.

Throughout the period of this political split, the RDB was the one overt organisation which managed to maintain a tenuous unity between HNP and OB elements. Standing on the fringes, claiming concern purely with 'economic' issues, it did attract support from both groups. The RDB management was a peculiar blend of Potchefstroom academics, who inclined towards the OB, the Cape theoreticians, who were behind the HNP. Diedrichs was the ideal leader. Firmly identified with neither group, enjoying close links with leading individuals in both, his political role since 1935 had always been to emphasise unity. Nevertheless, the RDB did not escape the effects of this struggle, admitting that the split made it extremely difficult to play a unifying role (*Inspan* June 1943). And here, too, du Plessis and Meyer were forced to resign.

The RDB did generate something like a mass character, however. During the war, its membership rose from 45,890 in 282 branches in mid-1940 to 67,131 in 343 branches in March 1942. Throughout the war years, the claimed RDB membership was relatively stable – in December 1945 it stood at 64,771 in 381 branches. The Cape and Transvaal had by far the largest number of members, accounting between them for 75 per cent of the membership in 1942.[4] Yet a number of campaigns to increase the membership to 100,000 failed, and a rapid decline of the RDB set in after 1946. Again, conflicting figures are given in official sources. The RDB reported to the second Ekonomiese Volkskongres in October 1950 that membership had fallen to 32,757 in 267 branches by 1949. Yet the 1952 (and last) RDB congress was informed that the 1949 figures were 52,522 members in 353 branches. Certainly the regular bewailing of the RDB decline by its leaders after the war, and particularly Diedrichs' stinging attack on 'Afrikaner apathy' at the 1949 congress – where he claimed that some new spectacular event was necessary to re-stimulate popular enthusiasm for the economic movement – would lend greater credence to the lower figures (E.P. du Plessis 1964: 195; *The Star* 2/10/52; *Rand Daily Mail* 6/7/49).

The main task of the RDB was the inculcation of the desired 'economic consciousness' amongst the mass of Afrikaners. The RDB's official handbook decreed that the first and foremost duty of each branch was constantly to impress upon the volk:

    (a) that no volk could enjoy either cultural or political independence without a measure of economic independence;

    (b) that today our volk is still trapped in the most acute stage of economic dependence, in that we are still a nation of employees, particularly in industrial and commercial life;

    (c) that a volk which finds itself in such a state of economic dependence cannot be rescued by other nations, *but by itself alone*;

    (d) that a volk can *never* rescue itself through individual action, but only in a collective, *organised* manner (RDB 1944:25, original italics).

The complex ideological development required to achieve the 'psychological adjustment' Dönges wrote about is discussed in the following chapter. The point here is that the mobilisation of the financial power, savings power and buying power of all Afrikaners demanded more than an ideological offensive. Preaching to people is a notoriously inadequate method of changing their behaviour. The RDB clearly recognised that a transformation of 'economic consciousness' also required a transformation of the daily lives of the volk through direct involvement in the *reddingsdaadbeweging* (as the economic movement was known). This was the really vital area of the RDB's operations. Mass consciousness was to be transformed through the direct organisation of all Afrikaners. The Bond leadership strove to develop the RDB into an all-embracing movement which catered for and organised every aspect of the daily lives of all Afrikaans-speakers and, in doing so, transformed their thinking. Afrikaners of all classes would thus be drawn into the economic movement and mobilised for the development of Afrikaner capital.

Certainly its activities were wide-ranging and affected all classes. Particular emphasis was placed on cultural activities. Each RDB branch had a department devoted to the regulation of every minute of the 'free time' of its local constituents. These *vryetydsafdelings* organised traditional dances, plays, concerts, and art contests. They set up travelling libraries, handicraft schools, discussion groups, etc. A cultural mesh was woven around the local Afrikaner community in which all cultural activities were controlled by the RDB, and all were encouraged to take an active part in such activities. At a national level, a film division, Reddingsdaadbond-Amateurrolprent Organi-sasie (RARO), produced films with 'Afrikaner themes' and organised film competitions. The national *vryetydsafdeling* also developed and sold a number of 'national' homegames, such as *Slagveld* (battlefield) – a variation of snakes and ladders, involving Boers and Kaffirs.

These efforts to involve the volk in the economic movement went beyond cultural activities. As an organisation, the RDB simultaneously combined the intense cultural mobilisation of Afrikaans-speakers of all classes with various activities catering directly for their economic interests. Cheap life assurance policies (underwritten by Sanlam) and burial schemes were automatic benefits of RDB membership. These 'particularly attracted the less well-to-do section of our volk' (*Inspan* October 1950). RDB trade schools were established in Port Elizabeth, Johannesburg, Ermelo and other centres. Loans were provided for those who wished to further their studies. Secretarial training schemes were set up in a number of towns, a vocational guidance centre was formed, and an RDB Employment Bureau found work with Afrikaner companies for 8,127 of 18,275 applicants (E.P. du Plessis 1964: 196).

Such mass mobilisation aside, the RDB established an Aandeel Buro to trade in the issued shares of non-listed Afrikaner companies, and to facilitate the transfer of such shares whilst ensuring that they remained in Afrikaner hands. In its early years the RDB provided loans of £100 to £400 to small undertakings. As the official thrust of the economic movement favoured large operations, and as FVB soon decided not to invest in small undertakings, there developed a huge demand for these RDB loans. A total of £13,000 was lent to 74 undertakings. But demand so overran supply that in 1942 the system was scrapped. This money was now used for study loans. Yet small undertakings clamoured for capital, angrily claiming that the national undertakings were monopolising the economic movement. Eventually the RDB established Kleinsake Finansieringsmaatskappy (Small Business Finance Co.) in 1946. However, it ceased operations after a mere three years, as not one of its loans led to successful development. The company was forced to take 'firm and unpopular measures' to recover its loans to small undertakings (*Inspan* December 1949).

The failure of the small loans scheme was in some respects repeated with the fonds. This had been established during the *Eeufees* when 'Vader' Kestell called upon all Afrikaners to contribute to a multi-million pound fund to resettle Afrikaners on the land. The Bond undertook to mobilise the volk for such a fund, but now it was to be an element in the struggle to establish Afrikaners in the urban economy. The Ekonomiese Volkskongres viewed the building up of such 'a mighty central fund' as a major weapon in the struggle to 'save' the volk. While FVB depended for its share subscriptions mainly on the more well-to-do elements, the fonds collected even the pennies of the impoverished. The fonds was placed under the control of the EI. An annual grant of £3,000 was set aside for the NRT, though this was withdrawn after three years because of 'lack of progress' in the trade union struggle. The rest of the money was placed in the hands of three curators – W.A. Hofmeyr, M.S. Louw and Dr A.J. Stals. They would decide how best to invest the fonds, subject to the stipulation that 50 per cent, up to a maximum of £25,000, would be invested in the cumulative preference shares of FVB, with a further 10 per cent in the company's ordinary shares.

In the event, contributions fell far short of Dr Kestell's euphoric multi-million-pound vision. The collection began reasonably well. Diedrichs informed the first RDB congress in July 1941 that £63,000 had already been received. Yet it took two more years before the total reached £100,000. The regional breakdown of this figure is illuminating. The Cape took the lead with £37,000. The Transvaal contribution was £36,000, with the OFS just short of

£20,000. A mere £3,600 came from Natal and the balance from contributors in Kenya, Bechuanaland and the Rhodesias (*Inspan* June 1943). But hereafter the fonds grew slowly. In 1945, with a great fanfare, the RBD launched a totally unsuccessful campaign to persuade the volk to donate a day's wage each year. By March 1946 income had dried to a trickle. Campaigns for the fonds were suspended, with total contributions standing at £149,088. 19.2 (*Inspan* March 1946). The RBD itself was, by now, in severe financial straits, and all money henceforth collected would go straight into its own coffers rather than to the EI for the fonds. Over the next five years, the RDB collected a further £30,000, but this did not resolve the problem. By the second Ekonomiese Volkskongres in October 1950 its financial situation was so severe that the fonds' curators recommended that 20 per cent of its investments be realised and lent to the RDB to finance its continued operation. [5]

Accounting for the spending of the fonds is tricky. The *Financial Mail* claimed in a special supplement on Afrikaner business that the RDB had 'lost' half a million pounds (30/7/65). This is probably an overestimate, yet figures in the three most authoritative sources do not tally (E.P. du Plessis 1964; *Inspan*; Potgieter 1954). The official FAK history of the economic movement claims that the £150,000 was spent as follows (E.P. du Plessis 1964: 193):

(a) Share investments, £58,545. Some of this can be accounted for. A total of £25,000 was invested in FVB preference shares, and a further £11,050 placed in ordinary FVB shares. Volkskas received an investment of £12,000, while a 'substantial' amount was invested in Sasbank (RDB n.d. (b): 11–12).
(b) Study loans, £19,000 – though presumably this was repaid, as the strictest securities were demanded.
(c) Grants and gifts, £42,229.

Amongst the recipients were the RDB, FVB, NRT, the FAK, AHI, the Vereniging van Uitvoerende Beamptes, the Buro vir Ekonomiese Navorsing and various charities. The EI was entitled to 10 per cent of the fonds for administration costs, thereby accounting for a further £15,000. Even if none of the loans were repaid, this still leaves over 10 per cent of the fonds unaccounted for.

At the second Ekonomiese Volkskongres in 1950, the whole economic movement was put under the microscope by the Bond leadership. The RDB received particularly close scrutiny. Co-chairman of the *kongres*, L.J. du Plessis, pronounced the fonds 'a relative failure', declaring that the RDB had not lived up to the high expectations many had had of it (*Inspan* November 1950). By 1950 the RBD was in serious financial difficulties and was losing members rapidly. In 1952 its official journal *Inspan* stopped publication. The RDB had effectively ceased to exist, though it was only officially disbanded in 1957 when its assets were transferred to the EI.

But L.J. du Plessis' assessment of the RDB was not correct. While it may not have fulfilled the expectations of those, like du Plessis, who genuinely believed in the possibility of a *volkskapitalisme*, the RDB played a vital role both in mobilising popular support for the economic movement and in the regeneration of Afrikaner nationalism. Its 'failure' lay in the impossibility of reconciling *volkskapitalisme* with the development of large-scale undertakings. By 1946 it was clear to all that the petty-bourgeois vision of rapid economic advance through the development of small undertakings was a utopian dream. Despite the formation of thousands of new undertakings after the first Ekonomiese Volkskongres (chapters 13 and 14 below) these would now obviously never be a great success. The mobilisation of the buying power of Afrikaners might generate a little business for rural traders, but the tasks of *volksredding* (saving the volk) – defined by the *Volkskongres* as the achievement of the Afrikaners' 'legitimate' place as capitalists – could not be accomplished through such small, locally-based undertakings. Rather, as had always been recognised by the Cape men, and as was implicit in the emphasis given by the EI and RBD to large undertakings, only those undertakings with access to relatively large amounts of capital, and which could invest it productively, would succeed.

Thus, I would argue, by 1946 the Bond leadership of the RDB was largely moving away from the petty-bourgeois vision and coming closer to that always held by the Cape economic theoreticians, Louw and Schumann. The RDB loans to small businessmen, together with the Kleinsake Finansieringsmaatskappy were both admitted failures. Yet the RDB was fundamentally successful in its main task. It had transformed economic consciousness, and adjusted Afrikaner workers and petty bourgeoisie to capitalism. This was recognised very clearly by the larger undertakings. M.S. Louw informed fellow businessmen at the 1944 AHI congress: 'Traders and industrialists do not fully realise what the RDB has meant to them. The RDB is of crucial significance as *it has created the necessary climate of sympathy* for Afrikaner business amongst the Afrikaner public. We are greatly indebted to the RDB' (*Volkshandel* December 1944; my italics).

The RDB had organised thousands of Afrikaners in support of the economics struggle, involving them in a myriad ways. It had partly channelled their savings towards Afrikaner credit institutions; it had been at the forefront of the struggle against the trade unions; it had given training and jobs to many. The particular combination of cultural mobilisation and the catering for direct economic interests which characterised the RDB, directed a clear message to all Afrikaners – only as part of the Afrikaner volk, only in exclusively ethnic and Christian-national organisations, would their economic interests be fostered. Through its many-sided activities the RDB had successfully imparted this message and succeeded in legitimising the struggle to develop Afrikaner business as part of officially-defined culture.

The RDB was significant for a further reason. In this period of intense political *broedertwis*, it was within the RDB – that is, outside the realm of 'politics' – that first was forged the organised mass alliance of class forces which the HNP was finally only able to organise politically in 1947/8. In this sense, then, Diedrichs' bold claim that the RDB was 'the most important [Afrikaner nationalist] organisation of our time' is not the exaggeration it seems at first.

THE AFRIKAANSE HANDELSINSTITUUT

The first meeting of the EI in December 1939 was informed by a Heilbron attorney and businessman, J.G. van der Merwe, of the imminent publication of an Afrikaans commercial journal, *Volkshandel* (volk's commerce). The EI welcomed the move, but rejected van der Merwe's request that the journal become the official organ of the EI. The first issue appeared in March 1940. Edited by the ubiquitous P.J. Meyer (then also EI and RDB secretary), *Volkshandel* described itself as: 'An authoritative journal providing reliable information on economic affairs, and a clear direction to the struggle of the Afrikaner for material prosperity' (*Volkshandel* March 1940). Owned jointly by van der Merwe and Diedrichs, *Volkshandel* was to play a leading role as the organ of Afrikaner business. It set out to be a journal of the Afrikaner entrepreneur, and broadly speaking, provided direction on all key issues to this inexperienced, newly-forming group.

The early years of the economic movement were notable for intense competition and conflict between private undertakings and the cooperatives. As a both a garage owner and managing director of a small cooperative – Saamwerk Handelaars – J.G. van der Merwe was caught right in the middle of this conflict. From the outset, his journal argued the need for coordination between the private and cooperative undertakings. The first issues of *Volkshandel* had frequent editorials on the theme of 'cooperation in the retail trade'. The RDB had produced cooperation between Afrikaner retailers and 'the Afrikaner consumer'; now the EI should facilitate 'the combination of Afrikaner retailers' (*Volkshandel* October 1940).

In March 1941, following discussions with M.S. Louw, *broer* van der Merwe wrote to the EI proposing the appointment of a commission of enquiry to investigate such cooperation, together with the issue of supplies and finance. The suggestion was adopted, and early in 1942 a Bond committee of 'experts' recommended, *inter alia*, that the RDB should set up an AHI.[6] Even before these recommendations were published, the Bond appointed a six man 'RDB' committee, chaired by van der Merwe, charged with forming this *Handelsinstituut*. Organised by the RDB in Bloemfontein in August 1942, the founding congress of the AHI was attended by representatives of 59 Afrikaner companies, together with the EI and RDB. *Volkshandel* was named the official organ of the AHI – although van der Merwe remained its sole owner until 1948 (Diedrichs had sold his shares).

The impulse for the formation of the AHI came from the small northern undertakings. Apart from M.S. Louw's initial consultation with van der Merwe, the Sanlam group was not involved in any of the Bond Committees which presided over its birth. The small traders were prompted in part by the conflict between the private and cooperative undertakings which marred even the AHI's founding congress. When it was agreed to admit cooperatives 'a leading private businessman', J.A. Rautenbach of Kroonstad, walked out of the meeting. Further stimulus to the formation of such an institute was provided by the generally disastrous business climate facing small traders in the war years, particularly the acute shortage of supplies from wholesalers. Moreover, according to a leading light in the agitation for the formation of the AHI, fears of the heavy Cape dominance of the EI, then largely under the theoretical spell of M.S. Louw and C.G.W. Schumann, were of crucial importance in the formation of the AHI (interview, P.J. Meyer).

The AHI constitution was designed to prevent control by any large group. Yet, given both its relative size and level of organisation, Sanlam soon assumed a leading role. Its countrywide network of representatives did much of the initial organisational work for the AHI, and three of the eleven-man AHI management were leading Cape figures (Louw, Schumann, and D.P. de Villiers of FVB). Once again, resentment of this Cape predominance featured prominently in the AHI. The 1944 AHI congress was informed by chairman van der Merwe:

> In the beginning the idea was to create an organisation which could act in the *interests of small dealers*, but, in the past year it has become increasingly apparent that the big undertakings, on their own initiative, have begun to take an interest in the activities and work of the AHI... We must be careful not to permit that certain groups gain control at the expense of others. It is through group control that international capitalism – which the Afrikaner dislikes – exists. This Institute chooses coordination above monopoly (*Volkshandel* September 1944, my italics).

The AHI likewise became embroiled in the growing wartime conflict between agriculture and commerce over the price control mechanisms of the Marketing Act (see chapter 13). This issue was raised sharply at the same AHI congress, when the chairman of the OFS Agricultural Union warned traders; 'In the distribution of farmers' produce, some people had made disproportionately high profits. The organised farming community had no intention of being the hewers of wood, and unless the established commercial interests gave way, the struggle would be waged until one or the other went under.' The result was an agreement with the Agricultural Union in which the AHI sided with the farmers against the Associated Chambers of Commerce (*Volkshandel* September and December 1944).

Despite these various conflicts, the AHI grew increasingly strong. By 1945 it established a system of local business chambers (*sakekamers*) directly affiliated to the national body. Three years later, subsidiary divisions were established within the AHI to coordinate the separate interests of the various sectors of Afrikaner business, that is, an Industrial Chamber, a Financial Chamber, and a Commercial Chamber. With the election of the Nationalist/Afrikaner Party coalition government in 1948, the AHI was given statutory recognition as the representative organisation of Afrikaner commerce and industry.

The AHI was formed with the explicit aim of providing guidance and direction to Afrikaner business undertakings and to facilitate greater contact and cooperation between them.[7] With its formation, established and budding Afrikaner capitalists were brought together in an organisation designed precisely to shape, give expression to, and fight for their common interests. With the formation of the AHI as the class organ of Afrikaner capitalists struggling for their 'legitimate place' in the economy, the EI was gradually eclipsed as the 'planning council' of the economic movement.

Indeed, by December 1946, so far had the EI been displaced that the Bond Executive Council felt obliged to convene a meeting in Cape Town with twenty-nine Bond businessmen to consider 'in a frank but brotherly manner' whether the spirit of the Bond sufficiently permeated Afrikaner business undertakings. Thereafter, a special meeting of Bond businessmen and the Executive Council preceded every Bond congress till 1950 (Pelzer 1979: 129–30). As the organisation of Afrikaner business, the AHI played a unique role. Its journal, *Volkshandel*, provided inexperienced Afrikaner businessmen with a regular flow of advice and information on all matters – from how to keep books to the desirable character of the future economy. In this manner *Volkshandel* did more than represent the interests of Afrikaner business, it actually helped to shape and form them. The Bond-controlled editorial board sought continually to direct and channel these emerging interests. Over time, this was built into an ideology of Afrikaner capital, in terms of which these interests were expressed – an ideology which formed the core component of nationalist ideology (see the following chapter). At all levels, official and commercial, the AHI fought to protect the (sometimes contradictory) interests of its members. Through the AHI, Afrikaner capital came increasingly to be constituted as a class force, organised and coherent, its interests defined by the historical place of Afrikaner business in the process of capital accumulation.

There were clear differences of interest between the members of the AHI – the conflicts between the private and cooperative undertakings, and between the smaller operators in the north and Sanlam, need only be mentioned. But despite the differing conceptions of the desired character of *volkskapitalisme*, in the 1940s at least, all members of the AHI confronted a common foe. Both the petty traders and Sanlam fought against the existing monopolies in their fields, and were united in this effort. It was no contradiction that at this stage all AHI members were anti-monopoly, and that the major thrust of AHI activity was to combat the effects of monopoly wherever possible.

This can be seen at a number of levels. The first major effort of the AHI reflected its origins as the child of rural traders. The wartime system of rationing supplies gave preference to long-established, large wholesalers. Discriminated against because of low turnover and a lack of the right connections, small rural traders, especially newly-established ones, were the last to receive supplies. This had been one of the factors leading to the formation of the AHI, which was charged by the EI with coordinating the buying of stocks for small traders. After failing to persuade Diedrichs' wholesale company, Kopersbond, to supply all Afrikaner traders, the AHI established its own wholesale operation, Voorrade Inkopers en Verspreidings Maatskappy (hereafter VVM), in February 1943. During the war, VVM achieved some small success in supplying Afrikaner traders on a strictly cash basis, and was recognised by the Director-General of Supplies as the AHI's importer. Yet this period also saw a complex restructuring of commercial capital (chapter 14 below). Large chain-stores were moving into the rural areas, displacing small traders, whilst simultaneously setting up their own wholesale operations. VVM could do little more than fight a rearguard action, and was forced into liquidation after the war.

The formation of VVM apart, the AHI repeatedly though unsuccessfully sought governmental protection for small and new undertakings against the retail and wholesale monopolies. It further advocated restriction of trading by state undertakings, and campaigned for the post-war abolition of price controls, resulting in the government's acceptance of an AHI request to raise statutory maximum profit margins on a number of staple items of the rural retail trade (*Volkshandel* April 1947).

In many other ways the AHI sought to represent and shape the interests of its members. At a general level, a permanent committee under C.G.W. Schumann and A.J. Stals was appointed, in 1942, to study potential post-war commercial and industrial conditions. In effect this was a Bond committee whose recommendations would enable the open organisation (the AHI) to formulate 'a commercial policy based on the interests of the small man and not on the financial might of a few monopolies'. Two major issues raised by this committee and consistently fought for by the AHI were, firstly, a revision of the system of company taxation to enable new undertakings to build up capital reserves, and secondly, great stress on the need for the further protection of South African industry. The free trade proposals of the Atlantic Charter were roundly rejected, as the AHI insisted that the massive increase in British industrial production should not be given free access to the post-war South African market (*Volkshandel* January and August 1944).

This concern with foreign capital was deepened by the huge post-war inflow of British and, particularly, American capital into manufacturing industry. Early in 1947 the AHI warned that the economy was 'increasingly being controlled from abroad', and urged the state to limit foreign holdings in any new undertaking to 49 per cent (*Volkshandel* March 1947). A permanent watchdog committee on foreign investment was established. Its report warned that 'no less than 89% of banking, 53% of the gold mine industry, 35% of the insurance sector and 33% of manufacturing industry is controlled by foreign investors' (*Volkshandel* December 1948). While foreign investment was necessary to help develop natural resources, the state should ensure that 'locally controlled financial institutions' controlled both banking and 'strategic industries' (*Volkshandel* March 1948).

In its early years, AHI's ideal view of economic life assigned a central interventionist role to the state. Whilst guaranteeing private ownership in all sectors of the economy, and maintaining conditions for 'an increase in National Income' (i.e. expanded capital accumulation), the state should act forcibly to root out monopoly, protect local interests against foreign capital, limit speculative profits and maintain economic stability. It should achieve this through a permanent economic planning council. Yet the definitive AHI memorandum on 'Private Initiative and Governmental Control' cautioned that over-hasty action would threaten economic stability. Thus, 'the obvious shortcomings of the existing system can nevertheless be immediately tackled whilst work can begin on a carefully considered, well coordinated, long term policy, which positively keeps in view the great goals of genuine national [volks] prosperity, white civilization and the protection of Afrikaner culture' (*Volkshandel* May 1945).

The AHI's representations to the UP government concentrated on these 'obvious shortcomings', while such 'carefully considered long term policy' was being studied in Bond circles. Particularly after the end of the war, the AHI pressed very hard on some of the issues which would later form the basis of such a policy. The question of African workers increasingly emerged as a central concern.

The years 1942 to 1945 were the only period in South African history in which the wage differentials between white and black workers actually closed slightly. This was largely the result of the dramatic growth of a powerful, militant, African trade union movement. Both the rise in African wages and the intensified class struggle seriously frightened the AHI. The pages of *Volkshandel* were increasingly filled with demands for a lowering of African wages. Immediately after the violent suppression of the August 1946 African mineworkers' strike, the AHI congress warned that, unless the cheap labour policy was maintained, the post-war industrial development of the country was in jeopardy (*Volkshandel* September 1946). This concern was heightened when the government introduced an Unemployment Insurance Fund (UIF) which covered black workers. The AHI waged a protracted compaign against the UIF, arguing that the payment of unemployment benefits to African workers effectively raised their wages, subsidised 'idleness', and undermined the 'disciplining' effects of unemployment. By 1948 so strong was opposition to the UIF that some local *sakekamers* refused to pay their statutory subscriptions to the fund (*Volkshandel* December 1947 and May 1948). This was simply the last of a long line of issues in which the AHI came into conflict with the UP government.

Thus, by 1942, the Bond had established the complex organisational structure of the economic movement in the EI, the RDB, and the AHI. These bodies were each designed to organise and mobilise particular elements of the volk in different ways. As the 'theoretical and philosophical guide', the EI formulated the broad strategies. The RDB was particularly charged with the task of mobilising all classes of the volk; of planting the new economic ideology in the minds of all; of directly involving the volk in the economic movement through cultural and other activities; and of persuading all groups that their particular interests could only be realised within the framework of the volk as a whole. The AHI was to educate and guide the businessmen themselves, to shape and form their interests. Out of their organisational network emerged the economic ideology of the *reddingsdaad* movement. To this the discussion now turns.

11

The ideology of Afrikaner capital

The intense ideological debates amongst Bond intellectuals following fusion gradually fashioned a system of social thought labelled 'Christian-nationalism'. Throughout the 1930s most Afrikaans-speakers displayed little interest in these convoluted formulations. If the intellectuals had elaborated a new ideology at the literary level, it had not yet percolated into popular consciousness. By 1948, however, Christian-nationalism was a powerful mobilising ideology with a clear resonance in the daily consciousness of Afrikaans-speakers of all classes. This transformation was wrought not by simple ideological exhortation but through an extensive network of cross-cutting organisations which came to structure the everyday activities of very large numbers of Afrikaans-speakers in terms of Christian-nationalist precepts. In the face of the deep political divisions after 1941, the organisations of the economic movement, and the RDB in particular, were the crucial *via media* through which this transformation of popular consciousness was achieved. This chapter examines the 'new economic consciousness' which emerged from the operations of the EI, the AHI and RDB. It seeks to draw out the general ideology through which these organisations mobilised Afrikaners of all classes – the ideology through which Afrikaner capital developed.

A word of caution is necessary to pre-empt conspiratorial interpretations of this emerging ideology. Most of the minute literature in English dealing with the *reddingsdaad* movement treats it, and the ideology which grew out of it, as a cynical ploy of the 'super-Afrikaners' of the Bond to mislead the volk for their own ends. This is largely due to total reliance on wartime military intelligence reports depicting the Bond as a vast, sinister conspiracy. Its description of the RDB neatly encapsulates this approach:

> The *Reddingsdaadbond*, under the present leadership of Broer Dr N. Diedrichs . . . became the South African equivalent of the *Winterhilfe* organisation of the Nazi system. Like the *Winterhilfe* it professes to help the poor, where it is in actual fact a purely capitalist and highly lucrative concern which unscrupulously exploits the needy and the gullible for the benefit of a select and powerful few. Some of these men figure on every single board of directors of the most powerful of the innumerable economic concerns which are wholly or completely controlled by the AB (Military Intelligence 1944: Section V).

The point is not that the leaders of the economic movement cynically hid their intention to become capitalists from the mass of Afrikaners and manipulated ideology and organisation for their own ends. Within its petty-bourgeois and racist limits, their hatred of what they understood by 'capitalism' was perfectly genuine. Some, like du Plessis and Meyer, and much later, Albert Hertzog, went into the political wilderness for these principles. Yet their strategy of accumulation and the ideology through which the volk were to be mobilised for this accumulation, could have only one result: the emergence of a new group of capitalists from the ranks of such 'anti-capitalists'.

'CAPITALISM' AND THE AFRIKANER VOLK

To overcome the 'psychological' barriers to Afrikaner business which Dönges identified at the Volkskongres required a transformation of economic consciousness. Here, the notion of the volk, of the organic unity of a divinely-created Afrikaner nation, was of vital importance. The ideologues of the economic movement – the very same individuals involved in the ideological debates of the 1930s – ceaselessly argued that the volk as a whole were sunk in economic oppression and moral turpitude. All were dispossessed, all were exploited by 'capitalism', no matter what their class position. Every Afrikaner thus had a direct interest in the success of the economic movement which would for ever end their national exploitation. In this view, 'the Afrikaner' or 'Afrikanerdom' or 'ons' (we/us) as a single, united social group, all in identical straits, shared identical interests. The only requirement for success was unity. In Malan's words urging support for the economic movement:

> [The Afrikaner] acknowledges that he is in need of salvation. He became the prey of political and economic forces which were too powerful for him. Stooped in his poverty and humiliation, pathetically he sought here and there for help. Unorganised, we tried to work out our salvation whilst others organised themselves against us. Thank the Lord we have now discovered the source of our weakness. Because we were unorganised and disunited we became the hewers of wood and the drawers of water in the patrimony of our fathers (*Die Vaderland* 31.8.140).

The inclusive terms 'ons', 'volk', 'Afrikanerdom' all referred to a single group of people subjected to a common political oppression and economic exploitation by 'imperialism'. The very concept of the nation here deplored the impact of 'imperialism' in dividing the volk into classes, dismissing any idea that class divisions are either primary or necessary. The OB spoke for all nationalists when it strove to 'hammer home to the broad masses that ties of blood and volk came first, and those [forged] in work and industry are coincidental' (Ossewa Brandwag 1946: 87). The analysis of the economic position (singular) of 'the Afrikaner' (singular) emphasised the common helotry of all, from the poorest 'poor white' to the chairman of Sanlam. An official tract of the '*Tweede Trek*' series put it succinctly: 'As a question affecting Afrikaners, the problem of pauperisation must be seen in its causes, character and solution as a phenomenon of the pauperisation of the entire volk; so too in its dangers and results' (J.H. Coetzee 1942:37). The title of this incendiary work, *Verarming en Oorheesing* (Pauperisation and Domination) further points to the ideological explanation of the perceived economic backwardness of '*the* Afrikaner'. Hand in hand, 'capitalism' and 'imperialism' had enslaved the entire volk, both politically and economically. I have spelt out the meaning of the term 'imperialism' in this context (p. 34 above). It is necessary to be equally clear on the meaning of this usage of 'capitalism'. The powerful attacks on 'Godless capitalism' did not question the sacred right to private property nor to private profit. The capital relation between the owners and non-owners of the means of production was never called into question. Rather, the foe was monopoly. As Dönges told the first RDB congress: 'The aim of a struggle against the capitalist system does not mean that you are opposed to capital as such. The movement [RDB] is against the system which concentrates capital in a few hands' (RDB 1941:48).

Foreign/English/monopoly capitalism – in a word, 'Hoggenheimer' – together with its political manifestation, 'imperialism', was responsible for all the woes of the Afrikaner. The Afrikaner had blazed the trail of 'civilisation' in South Africa. Yet thanks to imperialist monopoly, the pioneers were now helots in the land of their birth, deprived of their birthright. This presumed national dispossession is nowhere better expressed than in G.A. Watermeyer's poem, *Volkshandel III*:

> *We* bled open the very gates
> through which trade now richly flows,
>
> *We* hacked wide the open plains
> where mine gantries are rooted in reefs;
>
> with Trekkers' woe and three-year grief
> we measured out the plots
>
> where shopping centres now reach the clouds;
> but few of our names stand forth
>
> on signboards, or are embossed
> in heavy gilt upon the doors;
>
> and when the dividends are declared
> in front page columns of 'The Star'
>
> we page on – seeking rooms
> to be rented from our meagre wage.

In failing to attack the capital relation, this form of 'anti-capitalism' was forced into subjective explanations of exploitation and capitalism itself. Here, 'exploitation' equals 'unfair' – it is a moral question. When workers are not paid 'decent' or 'fair' wages, they are 'exploited'. The relationship between capital and labour is thus reduced to one of subjective morality. This fits in neatly with the anti-monopoly position. The greatest such 'exploiters' are the monopolies whose power enables them to use 'unfair' methods. Addressing Parliament on the 'poor white' question, the *gesuiwerde* MP Dr Bremer argued that 'this great reservoir of unskilled labour' was the product of 'capitalism' – 'a system which allows unlimited profits and unlimited exploitation'. He proposed that 'we should look to an entirely new system which will do away with the possibility of continued exploitation. Exploitation by capitalism is not the exploitation by small capital which makes sound profits. It is exploitation by means of a system which, in some cases, makes unjustifiable profits by unfair means' (HAD 23/4/35: columns 4327–8).[1]

Such attacks on 'capitalism' contained a number of recurring themes. Firstly, the pattern of capitalist accumulation in South Africa implanted 'the devouring cancer of class division' in the bosom of the volk (*Inspan* January 1940). Not only had the solidarity of the Boer rural communities been destroyed, but now escalating class conflict (particularly during the war) appeared to threaten the existence of the urban petty bourgeoisie. Secondly, 'capitalism' had impoverished the entire volk, whilst thirdly, through monopoly and thus the resulting 'unfair competition', small producers were rapidly being displaced. To the petty-bourgeois militants of the Bond, the 'unjust' nature of monopoly was the characteristic feature of capitalism in South Africa. Controlled by scheming Hoggenheimers, it cheated the volk of their land, decent wages and their small businesses, driving them into competition for jobs with blacks. Finally, this capitalist exploitation of the volk was controlled by 'foreigners' – the 'fortune hunters' who sent their profits 'home'. This national oppression embodied exploitation not simply between individuals, but of one nation by another. The journal of Afrikaner businessmen summed up 'the Afrikaner's' rejection of capitalism thus:

> Every sober-minded, thinking Afrikaner is fed up to the top of his throat with so called laissez faire – or let-it-be-capitalism, with its soul-destroying materialism and spirit of 'every man for himself and the devil for us all'. We are sick of it because of its legacy of Afrikaner poor whiteism and the condition which makes the Afrikaner a spectator in the business life of his own country (*Volkshandel* September 1941).

To end such problems, the 'anti-capitalism' of developing Afrikaner capital proposed that Afrikaners should take control of their 'legitimate place' in the economy: 'Whereas the foreign section of the population has thus far had the predominant influence in economic life, the Economic Institute of the FAK has taken the position that *it is the right* of Afrikaners to hold the dominating interest' (*Volkshandel* September 1943, my italics). The economic movement aimed 'to help *the* Afrikaner to become also an entrepreneur and owner of capital on a much larger scale than ever before' (Schumann 1940: 1327). Only then would the Afrikaner free himself from foreign domination. But this could only be guaranteed in an Afrikaner republic – free of political chains.

Unlike the existing 'capitalists' in South Africa whose sole motivation was the relentless pursuit of profit, Afrikaner business claimed motivation by 'higher aspirations' (*Volkshandel* May 1942). Elaborating Calvin's notion of 'just price', Afrikaner business presumed to pursue first the goal of service to the entire Afrikaner community. In return it received a 'reasonable' (just) profit. The EI defined the kernel of the economic movement as 'service to the volk with reasonable compensation for the provider of the service' (*Volkshandel* May 1942). This relationship between service and profit was perhaps the most common single theme of the early issues of the economic journals *Volkshandel* and *Inspan*.

Moreover, the economic movement aimed at no simple enrichment of one class. This was to be a *Volkskapitalisme*. It sought to benefit every single member of the volk.

> The mobilisation of Afrikaner capital for the erection of our own commercial and industrial undertakings, as envisaged by FBV, will ensure inter alia: (i) that the large profits yielded by these undertakings will flow back to Afrikanerdom; (ii) the Afrikaner would become both the employer and joint creator of the field of labour for his own fellow members of the volk; and (iii) the conditions under which the Afrikaner employee caried out his work would be determined by his fellow Afrikaner (*Volkshandel* November 1940).

This last clause by definition presumed to exclude 'exploitation'. Whilst the EI realised that some Afrikaans-speaking employers did 'exploit' their volk fellows, this was explained and condemned as 'unAfrikaans' behaviour, and thus a betrayal of the volk (*Volkshandel* January 1942).

In the light of this 'anti-capitalism', a major preoccupation of both individual Afrikaner undertakings and the organised economic movement as a whole was to answer charges that they were capitalists. Not until the second Ekonomiese Volkskongres in October 1950 was 'economic consciousness' so transformed that this description could be acknowledged as correct. The sheer number of attempts to rebut such charges in the early years indicates the severe embarrassment it caused, and the frequency with which it was levelled, particularly by the cooperatives. In the ongoing conflict between cooperative and private undertakings two of the worst insults in the nationalist lexicon were traded. Private dealers accused the cooperatives of engineering a 'mighty *monopoly* which could steamroller the pioneer and self-sufficient Afrikaner trader out of business' (*Volkshandel* December 1940). In return, the business-men of the AHI were labelled capitalists. FVB in particular was attacked by the cooperatives for being motivated by the pursuit of profit rather than service to the volk. The virtual campaign against FVB in the rural areas very nearly smothered it at birth (p. 191 below). M.S. Louw defended his brainchild as follows:

> The question here is whether we are not attaching too much value to the external form of an institution. Do we not know a tree by the fruit it produces?... The *form* therefore does not determine the *purpose*. Even the capitalist form can encompass the cooperative ideal. I advocated the capitalist form for the finance company because it is more flexible and better suited for the purpose we have in mind (*Volkshandel* May 1940).

Attempts to still criticisms of the *reddingsdaad* movement were not effective. In February 1942 a *Volkshandel* editorial stated that 'many Afrikaners are busy undermining our struggle for economic self-reliance by labelling flourishing Afrikaans undertakings as capitalist', warning that the issue was becoming mixed up with 'political differences' – a clear reference to HNP/OB divisions. The RDB picked up the question when the March 1942 issue of *Inspan* proclaimed its struggle to be 'anti-capitalist', lamenting that this was not understood by some Afrikaner anti-capitalists who attacked the RDB. This was followed by two long articles by P.J. Meyer, defending the *reddingsdaad* movement as a struggle against 'capitalism', in its opposition to 'the capitalist tendency' to concentrate economic and hence political power in ever fewer hands; to separate material prosperity from spiritual welfare; and to introduce class antagonisms between labour and capital. On the contrary, 'this false division of society on the grounds of economic ownership must be replaced by an organic, labour-communal, self-reliant, unity-ordination'. The RDB would thus not do away with the profit motive and private initiative, but link them to service in the interests of the entire volk, not just the capitalists (*Inspan* March and April 1942).

Meyer's role is important here, given *Volkshandel*'s admission that the issue now touched on political differences. By 1942, he was the OB's leading ideologist. More than any other individual he stressed the 'socialist' side of its National-socialism.[2] If Meyer adjudged the *reddingsdaad* movement to be anti-capitalist, few Afrikaners would quibble. But that he felt forced to do so, both as editor of *Volkshandel* and in *Inspan*, is indicative of the intensity of these attacks.

Again and again the economic journals returned to this theme. In January 1943, *Volkshandel* warned that unless Afrikaners were very clear as to the meaning of 'anti-capitalism', it could become 'a hollow phrase behind which was concealed the most naked capitalism'. This official organ of Afrikaner business defined the 'true anti-capitalist' undertaking as ensuring:

> (a) that through the service it delivered it fulfilled a want of the volk in the most economical manner without overlapping on other Afrikaner undertakings, but in cooperation with the rest of the entrepreneurial sector;
> (b) that the existence of the undertaking is in the first instance justified by the service it delivers to the volk as a whole, and not only by its profit potential;
> (c) that it provides constructive employment opportunities to fellow members of the volk, incorporating the employees serving in the industry as real participants and self-sufficient volk-fellows provided with a decent livelihood;
> (d) that effective provision be made for training employees, for their care in times of ill-health, old-age, etc., for their healthy relaxation and direct cooperation and incorporation in the managing of the business;
> (e) that following proper provision for the requirements of the undertaking, the surplus be employed in the general service of the volk; THUS, the overriding question is whether the managers of the undertaking display the inclination to genuine service of the volk (*Volkshandel* January 1943).

The end of the war, and the intensification of the struggle to take over the Mineworkers' Union, produced yet another rash of 'capitalist' charges against the economic movement. The response by both *Volkshandel* and

Inspan was notably much less defensive. Answering the question 'are there Afrikaner capitalists?', *Volkshandel* stressed the trend for managers to replace private owners in business. It informed Afrikaner businessmen that as 'the Afrikaner had been in the forefront of this trend, *he* could not be accused of being a capitalist' (*Volkshandel* April 1946). *Inspan*'s different audience led it to take a different line, clinging to the old criterion of service to the volk. And as all Afrikaner undertakings were so serving the volk, there could be no question of their being 'capitalist'. QED. (*Inspan* March 1946.)

FARMERS AND WORKERS IN THE IDEOLOGY

If every Afrikaner were persuaded that the volk was an organic unity, with a common interest; if they were convinced of the 'anti-capitalist' character of the economic movement, and that it would improve the economic position of each individual member of the volk, this still did not go far enough. The strategy of accumulation adopted by the Ekonomiese Volkskongres assigned different roles to the various social groups amongst the volk. Thus, these general aspects of 'economic conscientiation' apart, the organisational network which made up the *reddingsdaad* movement had to drive particular messages home to specific groups of Afrikaans-speakers. Each class was to be mobilised in different ways, each was to be taught to do different things. The EI, RDB and AHI directed their mobilisation efforts to different class forces amongst the Afrikaans-speaking population. Through this differentiated organisational structure, the developing ideology of Afrikaner business was directing different messages at the different classes of the volk. Each was being shown its particular place – its 'calling' in Calvinist terms – within this broad 'national movement', within the organic whole.

Afrikaner farmers had to be persuaded to centralise their capital in *Afrikaner* financial companies: 'In that the farming community is the most financially strong [*kapitaalkragtigste*] section of the Afrikaner volk, it is principally the farmer who can make his capital available for the building up of an independent Afrikaner commercial and industrial sector' (*Volkshandel* November 1940). Essentially two changes were required of farmers here, one relatively easy to effect, the other more difficult. They had firstly to place now, in Afrikaner credit institutions, the latent money-capital which could not yet be accumulated in expanded production. This required no transformation in the pattern of accumulation and investment by farmers, but simply a change in the institutions in which such funds were lodged from non-Afrikaner to Afrikaner. Once persuaded of the financial stability of these institutions, and the competitive character of their services, such a shift was relatively easy to effect.

However, the second change was more problematic as it involved a change in the pattern of accumulation of agricultural capital. In the long turnover cycle of agricultural capital, farmers tended to hoard profits which could not yet be accumulated – that is, profits whose mass was still insufficient to provide a fund for investment in expanded production. Moreover, once such profits could be capitalised, they were generally invested in more land. The prime aim of undertakings like FVB was to persuade Afrikaner farmers to invest such additional capital now, not in land, but to capitalise it in industry and commerce through shares in the finance companies. By doing so, Meyer argued, they would both strengthen the position of the Afrikaner in industry and commerce and improve their own position: 'The tendency of farmers to place their surplus in mortgages, or to buy more land, leads either to higher prices or higher mortgage rates. Farmers would be much better advised to invest their reserves outside the farming sector to ensure an extra income in times of bad crops' (*Volkshandel* November 1940).

This was easier said than done. There was strong rural opposition to the economic movement. In a powerful and widely circulated attack, the leading ideologist of Hertzogism castigated RDB strategy as a 'private scheme' by urban Afrikaners to exploit the rural population. Rejecting the ethnic exclusivism of the economic movement it argued that the most significant social divisions in white society were not Afrikaner/English but between town and countryside (Cilliers 1941). Attempts to get farmers to contribute to the fonds had sometimes met with open opposition,[3] and FVB almost collapsed in the face of general rural apathy. Afrikaner farmers did not rush to hand over their capital as instructed by the economic movement.

To change the pattern of accumulation of agricultural capital thus involved, in effect, a significant shift in cultural values. The Broederbond redefinition of Afrikaner nationalism after 1934 sought to grapple with the conditions of *urban* capitalism. As its official history makes very clear, the Bond's cultural activities strove, *inter alia*, to change the Afrikaner farmers' view of themselves and their place in the volk. This was a major emphasis in the *Eeufees* in particular (Pelzer 1979:147–8). In order 'to retain advantages inherent in farming for the Afrikaner community as a whole', the 'stubborn individualism' of the Boer was to give way to a cooperative attitude. In particular farmers were to be weaned from their suspicion of all things urban. 'Afrikanerdom' was no longer a rural community, but an increasingly urban one, whose major struggles were now directed against 'foreign' control of urban life. Through the RDB in particular, the Boer (farmer) was to be reminded of his new place in, and obligations to, the volk and its struggles (Pelzer 1979: 146–50).

The Bond was aware that something had to be given in return. Throughout the 1930s its influence was used 'to foster the interests of the farming community' (Pelzer 1979:148). This cooperation was taken over by the economic movement. In the long struggle over the operation of the Marketing Act in the 1940s, after some initial hesitation the AHI consistently supported the Agricultural Union against the Associated Chambers of Commerce. A joint committee was established, and in December 1944 *Volkshandel* proudly announced that not only had Afrikaner traders not become embroiled in 'the struggle between the established commercial interests and organised agriculture', but thanks to the decision to support the Agricultural Union, 'both agriculture and Afrikaner commerce have emerged stronger out of this struggle'. But the opportunity for re-emphasising the quid pro quo was not lost: 'The agriculturalist must remember that the development of the commercial and industrial sector creates the market for his products. In view of this, cooperation between agriculture and Afrikaner commerce and industry must flow logically' (*Volkshandel* May 1944).

Periodically the AHI reminded farmers of their duty to the volk, particularly in times of high farming profits. Opening the 1946 AHI congress, chairman J.G. van der Merwe referred to the 'sudden prosperity of the farming community in the areas surrounding the new Free State Gold Fields', and warned that 'they must invest their capital in the right places. Part of their capital must be invested in Afrikaner investment and business undertakings' (*Volkshandel* September 1946).

Afrikaans-speaking workers, too, were vital to the success of the economic movement. Their savings were to provide an important source of finance. Moreover, workers were the real source of wealth in any society. *Volkshandel* explored this question in a series of articles on the desired nature of the future economy. Optimism was expressed over the Afrikaner's economic struggle because 'the abundance of labour-power on which any economic structure is built, is in *his* possession. In this sense *he* is the bearer of industrial life in South Africa.' This remarkably clear recognition that labour-power creates wealth goes on to argue that the wealth accrues not to its owner, but to its user. In South Africa, non-Afrikaners were enriching themselves on the labour-power of Afrikaners:

> The potential riches lying in the abundance of labour-power should belong to *the* Afrikaner, but the real riches from the profitable employment thereof have passed over to a people which are not Afrikaners. If this situation is allowed to continue unhindered, it can only have disastrous consequences for our volk, and its potential riches will become a source of poverty (*Volkshandel* November 1941).

This journal of Afrikaner businessmen thus prescribed that, on the basis of private capital and private initiative, the Afrikaner should 'enjoy the profitable employment of Afrikaner labour-power' – that is, become capitalists exploiting Afrikaner workers. In return, Afrikaner workers would not only be paid 'the necessary wage', but would also be provided with the opportunity to share in 'the cultural achievements of the volk' (*Volkshandel* October 1941).

The provision of wealth in this dual manner apart, Afrikaner workers occupied a key position in the *reddingsdaad* movement in another sense. If the movement was to succeed in its aim of producing a large group of Afrikaner capitalists, it was clearly recognised that the capture of state power was necessary. Verwoerd had made the point at the Ekonomiese Volkskongres (p. 115 above). This could not be emphasised during the war as the

reddingsdaad movement was constantly rebutting charges of political motivation from both the UP and the Hertzogites. However, given that both the
political movements and the economic movement were dominated by many of
the identical individuals – Meyer, du Plessis, Diedrichs, Dönges, Stals,
Verwoerd, W.A. Hofmeyr, etc. – the conclusion is obvious. Reviewing the
reddingsdaad movement in 1975, Dr Meyer told me that 'a sympathetic
political climate was essential for the progress of the economic movement'.

Such political power was but a pipe dream without the support of white
workers, few of whom supported the HNP by 1940. Yet the Labour Party had
virtually collapsed. Dominated by a combination of elitist craft unions and
corrupt leaders, it offered little to Afrikaner workers who occupied the lower
levels of skill in industry. After 1934 the Bond mounted a gathering
campaign to seize control of certain unions under the banner of
'Christian-nationalism' (chapter 6). At an ideological level, such Christian-
national 'trade unionism' involved educating Afrikaner workers in a number
of principles. First and foremost was an outright rejection of class divisions as
'un-national': 'We must combat the devouring cancer of class divisions and
incorporate every [Afrikaner] worker as an inseparable part of the body of the
volk' (*Inspan* January 1949). All the various Christian-national trade union
and umbrella organisations were premised on this basic principle. However,
the NRT, the Blankewerkers se Beskermingsbond (White Workers'
Protection League, hereafter BWBB), and the OB Labour Front were all
hampered by the HNP/OB struggles. The most influential of the Christian-
national bodies which sought to mobilise Afrikaner workers during this
period, and which stood partially outside this conflict, was the RDB.
Particularly during the years of *broedertwis*, the RDB was charged by the
Bond with the task of maintaining the unity of the volk. Any idea of class
division was ruthlessly combated. The RDB chairman claimed that workers
'form the kernel of our nation. That is why we must see the incorporation of
Afrikaner workers as one of the main objects of the Reddingsdaadbond'. This
meant that they were to be rescued from the 'claws of the un-national power of
the trade unions' (*Die Transvaler* 3.10.52). The RDB thus strove 'to make the
Afrikaner worker part and parcel of the life of the volk and to prevent
Afrikaner workers from developing as a class distinct from other classes in the
life of the volk' (RDB n.d.: 27).

According to Dönges, the RDB thus had two tasks. The first was to 'make
right the new South Africa for the Afrikaner worker'. This was to be achieved
not through socialism, but 'by the better employment of Afrikaner capital in
commerce and industry'. While preparing South Africa for the worker, the
most important task of the RDB was 'to prepare the Afrikaner workers for the
new South Africa' (RDB 1943:4). The various ways in which the RDB sought
to incorporate and involve Afrikaner workers were discussed in the previous
chapter. Here I am concerned with the particular ideological view of
Afrikaner workers which emerged. The view of African workers is discussed in
the following chapter.

This conception of Afrikaner workers was firmly rooted in Christian-national Calvinism. The first premise held that labour distinguishes man from beast. Labour is both a command of and the worship of God. Human labour is performed in the 'unshakeable belief' that God also labours: 'Be Man! This is his Divine Calling, fulfilled as co-workers of God, at one with God as the Son is one with His Father. All human labour thus lies in the concern of God. All Labour is to be performed in imitation of God' (Die Calvinistiese Beskouing van die Arbeid, *Koers* October 1946). Within this universal obligation to worship God through labour, the divine taskmaster 'calls' each human being to a specific task, establishing a hierarchy of 'calling' within the divinely-ordained organic unity of the volk. In God's estimation these callings are equal:

> No one's task is too humble, because in the national economy we are all members of one body, in which there is indeed a head and a heart, but also the lesser members without which the body would be crippled. There is nothing wrong with the types of work we do . . . it is all needed to serve the church, the volk and the state (*Koers* October 1946).

Thus the true worship of God lies in the faithful acceptance and execution of the tasks of that divine calling, no matter how humble (or badly paid) in the divine scheme of things: 'We must all do our duty!' (Die Arbeider, *Inspan* January 1949). Moreover, 'Labour places us in a moral/ethical relationship with our fellow workers, and with all those who labour under us. They are one with us in communal labour. For this labour we shall be judged by God' (*Koers* October 1946).

The duty of workers thus established, both 'capitalism' and communism were roundly condemned for emphasising only the product of labour. Both are anti-Christian in removing 'the spiritual and moral from labour as such, and thus brought enslavement'. The resulting heretical division of the volk into antagonistic classes leads to conflict between those who should work jointly in Divine service (*Inspan* January 1949). Thus basing labour on the Holy Word produced two fundamental principles of labour organisation. The first rejected the internationalism of communism in its denial of the primacy of the divinely-ordained basic social unity – the nation. All labour problems should be approached from 'a national standpoint'. Workers formed an organic part of the volk. Their loyalty belonged first to that volk rather than to the man-made unity of class, comprised of different (and some heathen!) nations. Secondly, because labour was given a moral value, this protected the material position of the worker as 'the reliable worker is worth his wage' (Christelik-nasionale Arbeidsorganisasie, *Inspan* July 1944). If the worker was 'worth' the value of his labour-power, the capitalist was also 'worth' his 'reasonable' profit – the unpaid surplus labour extracted from such 'protected' workers.

In return for the 'decent' wage which he was 'worth', the first duty of the worker was to labour hard (Die Arbeider, *Inspan* December 1948). Moreover,

159

Afrikaner workers were also duty bound to provide 'surplus labour' in the service of the volk (*Koers* April 1941). This was surplus labour over and above the surplus unpaid labour extracted by every capitalist. It would seem that the Afrikaner capitalist had a special right to indulge in super exploitation.

But the onerous duties God imposed on Afrikaner workers did not end there. Apart from passive acceptance of the divine hierarchy, apart from the dutiful provision of surplus labour with psalm on lips, they had the further Christian duty to SAVE. The *reddingsdaad* movement was to foster thrift in an extravagant volk. This required 'The cultivation of a positive view and attitude to life which flows from a psychological education process which is simultaneously Christian and national' (*Koers* April 1941). Once they had abandoned riotous living and developed the necessary Christian habits of sobriety and thrift, Afrikaner workers were to hand over their savings to Afrikaner credit institutions where they would be invested in 'safe, profitable shares in Afrikaner undertakings' – the profit accruing not to the worker but to the undertaking using his savings (*Koers* April 1941). Any worker who so stinted himself in the service of God and volk must assuredly earn a place amongst the Calvinist elect.

Alas, we live in an imperfect world. The ideologists of the *reddingsdaad* movement found Afrikaner workers far from the ideal, and guilty of great offence against God. *Volkshandel* regularly urged Afrikaner workers to strive for the ideal traits required of an industrial worker – 'discipline, efficiency and coordination, diligence and application' (January 1941). But, argued this journal of Afrikaner capitalists, Afrikaner workers had lost the habit of obedience and discipline and had become 'work-shy'. Clearly their mortal souls were in peril and in the face of such a threat the Faithful had to act resolutely. Afrikaner workers had to be disciplined. *Volkshandel* thus declared that one of the prime tasks of the RDB was to inculcate discipline in Afrikaner workers, whilst training them for new jobs (December 1942). The theme was constantly repeated by both *Volkshandel* and *Inspan*. Indeed the question of disciplining the volk was a burning issue in Afrikaner nationalist circles during this period. All the political organisations placed great stress on disciplining the volk for the coming republic, which all agreed was to be strongly authoritarian. The 'Declaration on Behalf of Volks' Organisations' (p. 129 above) spoke for all: 'Strongest emphasis must be laid upon the purposive disciplining of the volk. The leaders must be able to expect complete obedience and faith from Afrikanerdom' (*Die Transvaler* 13.6.41).

Besides instructing Afrikaner workers in their own duties, this 'psychological education process' had also to teach them the duties of other social strata, and the proper relations between them. Again the Bible provided the guide. Genesis 1:28–30 enjoined man to be fruitful and multiply. Thus, God clearly sanctioned accumulation, and with it 'a certain egoism' (Die Calvinistiese Beskouing van die Arbeid, *Koers* October 1946). Moreover, as the great scriptural patriarchs such as Jacob, Abraham and Job (!) were 'rich and powerful and lived like potentates', God obviously intended some men to be rich, the better to reflect His Image (*Koers* April 1941). Workers were thus not to be envious of capital. It too was divinely-bestowed and intended for creative, communal service. For the 'Christian-capitalist' the ownership of capital meant 'the opportunity to do much good and help many people': 'Christ loved the wealthy youth who was a capitalist. The Master had no objection to his capital, but to the purposeless, almost fruitless way he used it. Christ would have him use his capital to help the poor. Service was the great stipulation the Master laid down for capital.'

With the capitalist providing service to the volk (in return for a 'reasonable consideration'), the relationship between worker and capitalist was not antagonistic, but harmonious: 'How different would the world be if capital and labour everywhere became allies? If each helped and served the other: if the capitalist strove to provide as many as possible of the good things in life for the worker; and if the worker strove to give the capitalist the best and most abundant labour' (Die Christen-Kapitalis, *Inspan* February 1949).

In a long article on the desired relationship between (white) workers and capital, *Volkshandel* declared that the coming Afrikaner republic:

> demands that capital and labour cooperate in fulfilment of a social duty, i.e. the achievement of the highest possible level of production compatible with the health and happiness of both parties. Joint labour agreements which reconcile the interests of employers and employees and subordinate them to the higher interest of the community and production must be brought about through mutual consultation in the observance of the position of white and non-white in this country, and the relevant state prescriptions. Labour strikes will not be allowed (*Volkshandel* September 1941).

The false prophets of class struggle presented the major obstacle to this perfect world. Whilst Christian-nationalism did not reject trade unions out of hand, the existing trade union movement led workers astray in two ways. Firstly, these were 'foreign' institutions, run by 'foreign' (and mainly Jewish!) leaders in unholy alliance with 'foreign' capitalists, designed to line the pockets of both. But secondly, 'foreign/communist' leaders, imbued with the 'cancerous' ideology of class, set workers and capitalists at each other's throats in a continuing struggle which threatened the entire social fabric.[4] For the theoreticians of Afrikaner capital, the working-class movement posed a threat which had to be contained. Thus C.G.W. Schumann:

> If this [workers'] movement falls into irresponsible hands, it could mean the subversion and destruction of our entire social order. However, if it is coupled with increasing knowledge and insight on the part of its leaders, and if some form of cooperation with the best leaders from other classes is possible, it [the workers' organisation] could lead to peace and progress. It is precisely here, that we Afrikaners, with our sense of law and order, justice and dignity, can play a leading role in building a healthy, prosperous community (*Inspan* August 1949).

But for such cooperation to take place, and especially to forestall that worst of all possible nationalist nightmares, the combined organisation of white and black workers – which was the major thrust of the Communist Party's efforts in these years – it was necessary to 'redefine the rights and duties of workers'. The future HNP Minister of Labour argued that existing trade unions acted as the guardians of the workers, when that was properly the role of the (capitalist) state (Ben Schoeman, *Die Transvaler* 4.7.44). Furthermore, in its 'ceaseless materialism' – the endless pursuit of higher wages and improved working conditions – the godless trade union movement further undermined discipline and imperilled the soul of Afrikaner workers. The self-appointed guardians of this 'soul' interpreted it somewhat broadly. A nationalist MP later wrote of his activities as a BWBB organiser: 'I asked them [Afrikaner workers] what they could possible gain by concentrating only on money and other so-called benefits, when, in the meantime, at a given moment, they are robbed of their whole nationhood, of their white skins and of their Christian religion' (J. du Pisane, *The Star* 6.10.52).

Caught in the middle of the struggle between labour and capital, subjected to constant social, economic and political pressures, and determined to escape this position through its own accumulation, the Bond-organised petty bourgeoisie in the *reddingsdaad* movement sought a restructuring and stabilisation of the social formation, and particularly of the relations between classes. Again in the words of Ben Schoeman: 'The existing labour system must be destroyed and a new one created. The time has arrived that in the interests of employers and employees self-government in industry and collective bargaining should be eliminated from our economic life' (*Die Transvaler* 4.7.44). The state was to play a central role in restructuring the economy. This was fully in keeping with all the various strands of Christian-nationalist ideology. The HNP, the NO and the OB all viewed the forth-coming Christian-national state as authoritarian. In line with these views, *Volkshandel* called for an economic 'Afrikaner-Christian New Order' (February 1941). Early in the war, when a German victory appeared imminent, the issues raised by National-socialism were voraciously discussed. *Volkshandel* devoted a number of issues to the desired nature of the forth-coming volk's economy. Its views on the role of the state in enforcing coope-ration and class harmony between labour and capital have been cited (p. 161). *Laissez-faire* capitalism was rejected. While the *Volksekonomie* would be based on private property and 'the greater entrepreneurial spirit evinced by private capital', capital would be placed under the supervision and control of the state, to ensure its use in the service of the volk. State control would protect both the volk against exploitation by monopolies, and local industry against 'foreign competition and exploitation'. Moreover, the state would erect and finance all basic infrastructural industries. But such a state could only function if 'freed' from 'imperialism'. Only a republic guaranteed this vision (Die Struktuur van Ons Volksekonomie, *Volkshandel* September 1941).

CONCLUSION

The *reddingsdaad* movement of the 1940s grew out of the specific sets of economic, social and political pressures to which the pattern of capital development had subjected the Afrikaans-speaking petty bourgeoisie in South Africa. As such, the *reddingsdaad* movement was predicated on a particular kind of understanding of the ruinous impact of the development of capitalism on '*the* Afrikaner'. The resulting anti-capitalism produced a strategy aimed at overcoming these effects. This conception of, opposition to, and strategy to transform this 'capitalism' was essentially subjective. The particular analyses and descriptions of the impact of 'capitalism' on 'ons' (we/us), on 'the Afrikaner', grew out of the peculiar place of this petty bourgeoisie in the struggles around capitalist development. In effect, they refer to the implications of the various effects of capitalist development for the economic, social and political position of the Afrikaner petty bourgeoisie itself.

Thus, nowhere in the powerful anti-capitalist rhetoric is to be found an attack on the objective condition of existence of capitalism, that is, the capital relation itself. The petty bourgeois *reddingsdaad* movement did not oppose the division of society into owners and non-owners of the means of production. On the contrary, its 'anti-capitalism' stemmed from a subjective reaction against some of the unpleasant effects of capitalist accumulation on the petty bourgeoisie, caught as it always is between labour and capital and subject to intense social, economic and political pressures. The entire strategy of the *reddingsdaad* movement as elaborated at the *volkskongres* aimed to reduce these subjectively unpleasant effects by transforming the petty bourgeoisie from 'spectators in the business life of our own country' (*Volkshandel* September 1941) into the owners of the means of production. All the organisations of the *reddingsdaad* movement fought for the maintenance of the capital relation as the basis of accumulation for Afrikaner business. It produced powerful ideological arguments defending and justifying in biblical terms precisely such a division of society into the owners and non-owners of the means of production.

Moreover, far from opposing the exploitation of the latter class by the former, emerging Afrikaner capital favoured and implemented an intensification of the exploitation of labour by capital. Afrikaner workers were to provide ever more 'surplus labour' to the fellow Afrikaners who employed them. A major thrust of the ideological elaboration of the period was to 'prove' to Afrikaner workers that their intensified exploitation by Afrikaner capitalists was in their own interests as part of the volk.[5] As discussed in the following chapter, in this conception of things African workers were fair game. Beyond the pale (quite literally), outside the organic unity of the volk, an inferior race placed by God in perpetual service as hewers of wood and drawers of water for a more 'civilised' nation, their Christian duty was to observe the 'proper relations' between master and servant.

In a period of escalating class struggles the *reddingsdaad* movement depended on white workers for economic and political support. Thus, hand in hand with the ideological justification of intensified exploitation as being in the interests of white workers as part of the volk went the ideological notion of class harmony within the volk. At the level of production, the ideologists sought the maintenance of the capital relation. At the ideological and political level, they sought not to abolish class contradictions, but rather to harmonise them – in effect to deny the antagonism, just as the ideology denied anything but subjective exploitation. Within their formulations, class antagonisms were neutralised by reducing them to simple differences within an organic whole. Every person had a divinely-allotted place within that organic whole. Individuals were completely equal within it. Thus the meaning of these class differences at a political level was denied (and rigorously combated through the various Christian-national trade union organisations). Yet if the existing class antagonisms within the volk were neutralised, the ideology emphasised antagonism between the volk and other social groups – 'imperialism', African workers (p. 73 above). In effect, then, all this rested on the elaboration and development of the concept of a new historical subject – the Afrikaner volk – whose unity was the *via media* to success and prosperity for all categories within it. Marx's comments on French petty-bourgeois democrats apply equally to the petty-bourgeois Afrikaner nationalists:

> But the democrat, because he represents the petty bourgeoisie, that is, a transition class in which the interests of two classes [bourgeoisie and proletariat] are simultaneously mutually blunted, imagines himself elevated above class antagonisms generally. Though democrats concede that a privileged class confronts them, but they, along with the rest of the nation form *the people*. What they represent is the *people's rights*; what interests them is the *people's interests*. Accordingly when a struggle is impending they do not need to examine the interests and positions of the different classes . . . They have merely to give the signal, and *the people*, with all its inexhaustible resources will fall upon the oppressors (Marx 1968a: 122).

Thus the central themes of the 'anti-capitalist' Christian-national economic ideology of the *reddingsdaad* movement enshrined most of the pre-suppositions of capitalism. This is clearly seen in its concern with private property, private initiative and profit, and its obsession with social stability, class harmony and the control of class action by workers. The point is emphasised by its insistence on disciplining the working class, on surplus labour and detraction of wage demands, and in its view of the fourfold function of the state: firstly, to guarantee 'national' interests against 'foreign' monopolies; secondly, as the proper protector of the worker; thirdly, to hold the balance between all classes and guarantee the appropriate conditions of accumulation for all businessmen, and fourthly, where necessary, to restructure the relations between classes to ensure (capitalist) 'prosperity'.

The elaboration of a specifically 'Afrikaner' economic ideology during the 1940s necessarily stimulated the further development of broad Christian-nationalist ideology. No less an authority than the official FAK and RDB journal described the emergence of Afrikaner business as the most important advance made by Afrikaner nationalism during the decade. The 'struggle of the volk' in the economic field was clearly recognised as the central aspect of its struggles in other spheres (*Inspan* May 1947). Through the economic movement, the abstract intellectual debates of the 1930s were given a concrete economic and social content. Through the organisation of Afrikaans-speakers in the RDB and AHI, and through the Bond's domination of the content and organisation of Afrikaner culture, such concretised Christian-national ideology began to permeate popular consciousness, effecting a real ideological transition.

This further elaboration of Christian-nationalist ideology which the economic movement stimulated was cast firmly in the framework of the symbols and myths of Bond-defined Afrikaner culture. Indeed Malan himself termed the economic struggle the *Tweede Trek* (Second Trek), and a major series of ideological publications appeared under the same title. The economic struggle itself was cast in terms of yet another stage in the heroic struggles of a united volk against the overwhelming weight of 'imperialism' on the one hand and the engulfing tide of African barbarism on the other. This was rooted firmly in the belief in the divine calling of the volk.[6] The ideological elaboration was cast likewise in a rigidly Calvinist framework – it was both Christian and nationalist.

This dual reference to the past, firstly in terms of the symbols and myths of the history of the volk (what Moodie refers to as 'the sacred history' – 1975:ix), and secondly in terms of the strict prescriptions of Kuyperian Calvinism, has led to consistently incomplete interpretations of Afrikaner nationalist ideology. Two variants of idealism have predominated. Both interpret the ideology specifically within its own terms and make no attempt to penetrate and explain its symbolic structure. On the one hand, the Christian-nationalism of the 1940s is viewed as the development of the archaic, reactionary vision of 'the frontier' – the credo of a stern, patriarchal, frontier Calvinism, now transplanted to the cities. On the other hand it is treated as the development of an inherent 'Afrikaner' *Weltanschauung,* in Moodie's phrase, the Afrikaner 'civil region'. Both views stress the continuity of Christian-nationalism with the past. Whilst there clearly are continuities and whilst the symbolic language and cultural validations remain very similar, this misses the most important point. The overriding significance of the development of Christian-nationalism in the 1940s lies not in the continuity, but in the break with the past, precisely concealed by the symbolic structure of the ideology. This was now the ideology of a new class alliance, developed to mediate and transform the new, urban experience of capitalism, and to lead to the formation of an entirely new class of Afrikaner commercial, industrial and financial capitalists. All this was profoundly new, and seen as such by the ideologists in the regular assertion that they were breaking new ground.

When men undertake new ventures, when they seek to transform the world in new ways, they often cling to the familiar images, usages, symbols and known supports of their past in order to do so. By dressing themselves in Trekker garb, by appealing to the God of Piet Retief and Paul Kruger, the militants of the *reddingsdaad* movement were not harking back to that past, but using it to transform their present. Marx's well-known words are relevant here:

> Men make their own history, but they do not make it just as they please; they do not make it under circumstances chosen by themselves, but under circumstances directly encountered, given and transmitted from the past. The tradition of all the dead generations weighs like a nightmare on the brain of the living. And just when they seem engaged in revolutionising themselves and things, in creating something that has never yet existed, precisely in such a period of revolutionary crisis they anxiously conjure up the spirits of the past to their service and borrow from them names, battle cries, and costumes in order to present the new scene of world history in this time-honoured disguise and this borrowed language (Marx 1968a:96).

And if Luther donned the mask of the apostle Paul, and the French Revolution of 1789 to 1814 cloaked itself in a Roman toga, likewise the militants of the Bond and the businessmen of the AHI pulled on the corduroys, felt hats and *veldskoens* of the Voortrekkers and Paul Kruger. They were breaking new ground, entering new areas of struggle, taking up new weapons. As beginners learning a new bourgeois language, they translated it always back into their mother-tongue. And in these familiar traditions and symbols of the past they found: 'the ideals and art forms, the self deceptions that they needed in order to conceal from themselves the bourgeois content of their struggles and to keep their enthusiasm on the high plane of great historical tragedy'. The awakening of the ghosts of Retief, Cilliers, Kruger and Jopie Fourie served the purpose of 'glorifying the new struggles and not of parodying the old, of magnifying the given task in imagination, not of fleeing from its solution in reality' (Marx 1968a:97). Thus the analysis of this ideology must needs concentrate on the content of these struggles and not be misled by the symbolic forms in which they were cast. To penetrate these 'misty creations' of ideology, it is essential to begin with the real relations – the social position and social struggles – which give rise to them.

12

Afrikaner capital and the ideology of apartheid

The ideology of the *reddingsdaad* movement assigned the state a central role in restructuring relations of exploitation to facilitate accumulation by Afrikaner businessmen. The relationship between this movement and apartheid ideology should be seen in these terms. A full analysis of the apartheid phenomenon is beyond the scope of this study. Here I wish simply to indicate its place within the ideology of the economic movement. The significance of 'apartheid' in the coming to power of the HNP in 1948 is discussed in chapter 15.

In its early years, the *reddingsdaad* movement was not directly concerned with racial questions, nor the elaboration of new racial policy. White domination was taken for granted as one of life's certainties, yet an explicit concern with 'racial' issues only came slowly to the fore after the 1943 election. Only after the Second World War did attention become centrally focused on this area, as the political question of the character of future social organisation in South Africa began to be posed (chapter 15 below).

The first official use of the term 'apartheid' within the economic movement was in the May 1943 *Volkshandel* editorial on economic segregation. This attacked UP policies as half-hearted and confused, calling for a thorough investigation into all aspects of racial policy. It demanded a decision either way on equality or full segregation, and strong policies, whichever course was adopted. Declaring its preference for a policy of 'apartheid and guardianship', it acknowledged that these were yet largely empty words and that a consistent, thorough policy remained to be developed.

The *reddingsdaad* movement's concern with the 'racial question' over the following months can be chronologically and thematically separated into two aspects – the so-called 'Indian question' and the so-called 'native question'. The treatment of both illuminates the class concerns of the economic movement.

THE 'INDIAN QUESTION'

So far as the *reddingsdaad* movement focused on 'racial' issues during the war, its prime emphasis was on the 'Indian question'. Here the concern lay with the

167

position of Indian traders as competitors with whites. As small traders, general dealers, etc., the Indian petty (and not so petty) merchant class operated in precisely that area of commerce which the more petty-bourgeois element of the economic movement was attempting to corner for itself – general retail trade. In the 1930s, Jews had been seen as the great threat in this sector, and a strong anti-Semitism developed on the *platteland* and in the cities. Now Indian merchants were the great threat, and a vicious racism developed against 'alien coolies' who had insolently forgotten their 'place'. *Volkshandel* consistently monitored the issue of trading licences to Indians, reporting with dismay in May 1944 that 66,369 such licences were issued between January 1940 and December 1943.

By 1946, small rural traders were being severely hit by the post-war recession and a rapid decline in the rate of profit in the retail trade (chapter 14). The 'Indian question' was elevated into a burning issue. Pressured by its Natal supporters, the Smuts government introduced the 'Pegging Act' restricting Indian traders to certain prescribed areas. *Inspan* devoted its entire May 1946 issue to the 'Indian question'. The editorial reveals the concerns of this racism quite clearly:

> The one time pitiful pedlar has become *a financially strong trader, whilst many hardworking established white businessmen have been squeezed out by the previously despised interloper*. The Indian has captured for himself a position of power – power, inter alia, over his white customer. In place of the bundle on his back, today he owns valuable premises and buildings in the European section of the city or town. His employees are in many cases whites – frequently former competitors; his customers are whites, who, particularly in this time of limited supplies, are dependent upon him for their daily necessities; his neighbours are whites whom he treats with suspicion and enmity, but with whom he also demands equality.

The attempt of the Indian government to censure South Africa at the United Nations over its treatment of Indians further exacerbated this intense racism. Early in 1947, a 'spontaneous' boycott of Indian traders by Afrikaners spread throughout the Transvaal, lauded by *Inspan* as a true example of a volk rescuing itself. The journal argued that the 'negative', anti-Indian side of this movement was necessary to give emphasis to its 'positive' side – 'the self-preservation of whites'. In an illuminating sentence, this was tied to the major thrust of the boycott, that is, to secure 'support for their own business undertakings'. The competitive position of Afrikaner traders thus became an issue of the 'self-preservation of the white race', something only 'an unbalanced idealist' would oppose. In defence of this position, '*the* Indian' was described as

> an unwelcome alien in our portals, not only from a moral and religious point of view – he has enriched himself at the expense of his white clients, he has attempted to squeeze his European competitor out of the business world through illegitimate trading methods – but has, moreover, challenged and defamed the country in which he trades as a guest, in an insolent manner. To this

the volk has reacted instinctively – a fact for which we ought to give thanks, because had the opposite been the case, we must necessarily have reached the conclusion that white South Africa suffers from an unbelievable lack of insight or is devoid of all self-respect and vitality.

The editorial concluded with a clarion call to the volk 'to drive all alien exploiters out of our business life'. 'There are enough deserving Christian undertakings worthy of our support; and where such businesses do not yet exist, it is the duty of every white to do everything in his power to facilitate the establishment of new undertakings. *The continued existence of the white race is at stake* !!' (*Inspan* April 1947).

The link between anti-Indian racism and the competitive position of the Afrikaner trader on the one hand, and the orchestrated anti-Indian feeling the Bond so assiduously cultivated on the other, is well revealed in a short parable entitled 'I Began to Wonder', published in *Volkshandel* immediately prior to the second Ekonomiese Volkskongres. It is worth quoting in full:

It was in a Johannesburg suburb. The day was particularly warm and I felt truly thirsty . . . Ah, actually here was a small but nice, clean shop where one normally bought groceries and could simultaneously quench one's thirst. The woman was friendly. 'Two cold drinks please, madam, this heat really gives a man a thirst.'

Because the shop was quiet I went on, 'I am rather surprised to see how many Afrikaans-speakers have businesses here, madam'. 'Yes', came her reply. 'But we find it heavy going to make a living.' 'I don't understand you', I answered, 'but surely the largest section of this community is Afrikaans-speaking and doubtless supports you very well.' She smiled sympathetically. 'That's what I also thought, sir, and that's why I opened my shop here. I see you don't believe me, but I can assure you that only 10% of my customers are from my own people.'

I thought about it for a while, but still could not believe it. 'But where do the Afrikaners of this area shop then, madam?' was my next, slightly hesitant question.

With her finger she pointed to the shop across the road, with the signboard, 'Ishmail Abdoul'. I thought that this woman was obviously a bit cynical, but then saw in the Asian shop, a well-dressed woman with a young girl next to her, probably her daughter. They stood talking pleasantly with the Asian, the daughter with her elbows propped on the counter while she emptied a bottle of cold drink. . . I felt a blush rising in my cheeks . . . I began to wonder.[1]

These long quotations do not simply demonstrate the evocation of a racist stereotype of an alien, cheeky, cheating 'coolie', who has forgotten his place. Over and above this, and the clear link they reveal between the propagation of such racism and the direct economic interests of Afrikaner traders, these citations point to a significant failure of the *reddingsdaad* movement. The strategists always held that success entailed the mobilisation of three resources of the volk – capital-power, labour-power, and buying-power. Noticeable success was achieved in the first of these aims, yet all attempts to mobilise and coordinate Afrikaner buying-power – to direct Afrikaner custom to uncompetitive Afrikaner traders – were largely unsuccessful. Not even the RDB achieved much in this area. Afrikaner traders faced competition from the monopoly chain stores and from Asian traders. Regular, fierce condemnations were made of both. They were, however, wildly unequal opponents. Endless fulmination against the large commercial monopolies did little to take their customers away. This group was politically powerful. Its leading spokesman, Richard Stuttaford (owner of Stuttaford's Stores) sat in Smuts' Cabinet. Asian traders on the other hand were much more vulnerable – politically, socially and economically.

The 'spontaneous' boycott movement shows this clearly. What *Inspan* termed its 'negative' side, the deliberate incitement of extreme anti-Indian feeling, was organised by Afrikaner traders – the 'advocates of the [boycott] movement in the first instance plead that *their own businesses* should be supported by their race' (*Inspan* April 1947). Having failed to mobilise the buying-power of fellow Afrikaners through intense nationalist organisation and ideological exhortation, having thus failed in their 'positive' attempt to get support from the volk, Afrikaner traders increasingly turned to racist incitement to win the custom of a cost-conscious volk and to undermine their vulnerable competitors. This 'negative' aspect partially achieved what 'positive' nationalism had not. The second Ekonomiese Volkskongres was informed in October 1950 that the small advances registered by Afrikaner commerce were mainly the result of Afrikaner traders in the Transvaal displacing Indian traders (*Volkshandel* September 1950).

So far as the 'Indian question' is concerned, the developing racist perspectives and policies of the nationalist movement clearly grew out of the petty bourgeoisie's concern with their fellow petty-bourgeois competitors. The economic 'threat' of Indian competition was then elevated into a political one. *Inspan* emphasised the 'direct political threat' posed by the economic power of Indian traders. Such traders also exploited Africans, thereby exacerbating racial tensions. Moreover, they set themselves up 'as the chosen leaders of the non-white group in the general movement to resist the whites in their dominant economic and political position – a leadership they have in fact assumed not so much in the interest of other non-whites, as for themselves'. Such Indians were the 'vanguard of the Asiatic world' in Africa, which already 'threatens the existence of the whites and the continued survival of Western Civilisation' (*Inspan* April 1947).

These issues were taken up by the HNP. Its 1944 'Social and Economic Manifesto' pledged that 'non-whites' would be issued with trading licences only in areas where the overwhelming number of consumers was non-white (*Die Kruithoring* 1/3/44). Yet at this stage 'Indians' were not mentioned as such. The 1948 HNP Sauer Commission, on which its election manifesto was based, went much further: 'The Party holds the view that the Indians are an alien, foreign element which can never be assimilated. They can never become natives of this country, and must be treated as an immigrant community.' The major policy thrust would be 'repatriation'. In the interim, Indians would be removed to separate 'group areas' and would not be allowed to live, own property, or trade in white areas (*Die Burger* 29/3/48). This policy was implemented in the 1950 Group Areas Act.

THE 'NATIVE QUESTION'

If the policy of the *reddingsdaad* movement on the 'Indian question' grew directly out of the economic position of Afrikaner traders, the situation with regard to what was termed the 'native question' is more complex. Emerging Afrikaner capitalists in finance, trade and industry were not large-scale employers of African labour, and, ideologically at least, were committed to a policy of exploiting white rather than black workers. The focus of the AHI and RDB on the 'native question' must be seen from a wider perspective. The budding capitalists of the *reddingsdaad* movement were concerned with more than the specific interests of their own operations. The changing conditions of accumulation and reproduction of capital in general were of vital interest to them, and to the success of their struggle. The particular conditions in both industry and agriculture during the 1940s are relevant here.

A significant restructuring of industrial capital in South Africa took place during the war, leading to increasingly capital-intensive operations. While this is discussed in more detail in chapter 15, here it should be noted that the combined effect of the large-scale movement of African workers into semi-skilled operative positions, produced by the increasing mechanisation of production, together with militant struggles by a strong African trade union movement, led to a rapid rise in real wages for African workers in industry. The few existing Afrikaner industrial concerns were small-scale operations (chapter 14). The concentration of industrial capital and rapidly rising labour costs placed them in increasingly uncompetitive positions. The *reddingsdaad* movement as a whole became thus ever more vocal in its demands that the state intervene in this process of rising labour costs to sustain a 'cheap labour policy'. As Professor T.E.W. Schumann informed the July 1943 RDB congress, the question of 'native policy' was the central issue of future industrial policy (*Volkshandel* August 1943).

As racial issues surfaced in *Volkshandel*, they were almost exclusively concerned with the question of wages. By May 1946, the AHI was pressurising the government to allow industries established outside the major industrial centres to pay African workers wages below those fixed by Wage Board determinations. This would restrict the flow of Africans to the cities by providing 'profitable' employment and was thus 'in the interests of the country, of our manufacturing industry, and its employees' (*Volkshandel* May 1946).

This concern is most strikingly revealed in the AHI's protracted campaign against the statutory Unemployment Insurance Fund (UIF), set up under the 1946 Unemployment Insurance Act. Claiming to voice the objections of all Afrikaner employers, especially those in the *platteland*, four objections were raised against the act. Firstly, there was no danger of unemployment in South

Africa except for the 'perennially unemployed'. By providing such benefits, the UIF 'reduced the [size of the] working class'. Secondly, this mollycoddled workers, leading to ill-discipline:

> It has been lost sight of that absolute security [of employment] is the greatest enemy of progress and is fatal to a young country such as South Africa. A certain measure of insecurity brings the best in people to the fore. Comprehensive unemployment insurance therefore places a premium on an aversion to work and damages rather than advances the progress of our country (*Volkshandel* December 1947).

Thirdly, the act applied without differentiation to white and black workers. As the majority of the unemployed were Africans, white workers and white employers were 'subsidising' black unemployment. At the 1948 HNP National Congress a delegate argued that the act 'benefited only the Natives and encouraged them to loaf' (*Volkshandel* May 1948). Finally, it objected that employers in the rural areas were subsidising the urban unemployed. In effect, Afrikaner capitalists objected to the UIF on the grounds that it interfered with the present form of reproduction of the working class and particularly with the reserve army of labour, in such a way as to raise the value of labour power, further undermining cheap labour policies. It provoked strong resistance. The AHI chairman informed the 1948 HNP National Congress that Afrikaner businessmen in his town of Swellendam had refused to pay further subscriptions (*Volkshandel* May 1948). When the HNP came to power a month later, one of its first acts was a drastic revision of the UIF along the lines proposed by the AHI.

However, the key to understanding the particular form in which the 'native question' surfaced in the economic movement, lies in the fact that emerging Afrikaner capital in finance, trade and industry was born out of, tied to, and dependent upon agricultural capital. The centralisation of agricultural capital was, after all, the prime strategy of the *reddingsdaad* movement. The maintenance of healthy conditions of accumulation in agriculture was a *sine qua non* for the successful emergence of Afrikaner financial, industrial and commercial capital. During the war years the overwhelming concern of agricultural capital lay with the acute labour shortage rapid industrialisation fostered in agriculture (chapters 13 and 15 below). The emerging apartheid proposals advocated rigid influx control measures to restrict the flow of labour from the farms to the cities. As such it was concerned to maintain and restructure the conditions of accumulation in agriculture. To this extent, such a policy was in the direct interests of all elements of emerging Afrikaner capital.

Since 1935, the Suid-Afrikaanse Bond vir Rassestudie (South African League for Racial Studies) had busied itself with a study of 'segregation'. By 1943, it was calling for a policy of 'apartheid', and Malan was beginning to use the term in his speeches. Yet beyond a firm desire to 'maintain the purity of the white race' and secure a continued supply of cheap labour to the farms, 'apartheid' remained a vague concept. As *Volkshandel* noted (May 1948), a consistent, thorough policy remained to be elaborated. In September 1944, through its FAK front, the Bond convened another *volkskongres* in Bloemfontein on 'the Racial Policy of the Afrikaner'. Only four papers were delivered to the *kongres* – on the historical principles of 'Afrikaner racial policy'; its religious basis; miscegenation; and missionary policy. The *kongres* acknowledged that no basis for a 'practical policy' of apartheid yet existed, and appointed a commission to determine and propagate policy. Yet the keynote address by Natal HNP leader and future Minister of Native Affairs, E.G. Jansen, made it clear that the issue was one of the 'proper' relations between master and servant in a world in which each knew his place:

> The relationship between *the* Afrikaner and *the* Native arose through their learning to know and understand each other and because *each knew what his duty was towards the other*. The Boer regarded the Native as someone for whom he was responsible and *from whom he would receive the labour expected of him. The Native regarded the Boer not only as his Master*, but also as a friend and helper to whom he could turn for help and advice in times of difficulty. There was mutual trust (*Inspan* October 1944; my Italics).

The rapid industrialisation of South Africa and inflow of African labour to the cities transformed these relations, particularly for farmers:

> At the moment we are concerned with conditions as they exist at present. They are conditions which have developed on a large scale since the Afrikaner was no longer able to work out and apply his own policy in respect of the Native, and *they are conditions which are deteriorating at a rapid tempo*. In the old days there was no influx of Native women to the cities. The men went to work in the diamond fields and in the gold fields, but comparatively few women found their way into the cities. Today there is an influx also of Native women which is quite uncontrolled. Certain industries are busy supplying housing where their Native employees can reside with their families. This will increase the influx even further. Already there are thousands of Natives living in our urban areas who know no tribal ties and have become permanent urban dwellers. Their numbers are growing steadily. The question is: what must be done with this large urban population? The answer is that the Afrikaner's policy of Apartheid must be applied (*Inspan* October 1944).

Though no coherent policy had yet been formulated, the deliberations of this Volkskongres made very clear that the emerging apartheid-idea sought to grapple with the social transformations wrought by capitalist development during the war. The apartheid concept crystallised and condensed the responses of various class forces to their transformations. It reflected the farmers' concern over their declining labour supply and inability to compete for labour against the higher wages paid in industry and commerce. It encompassed the concern of emerging Afrikaner business for a cheap labour policy to ensure their own accumulation. And it pandered to the fears of specific strata of white workers at being displaced in the new industrial division of labour by cheaper African labour.

A series of long, authoritative articles on 'The Racial Question in Our Country' in *Inspan* in 1947 confronted these issues head on. It was argued that the racial question had developed above all into a question of labour. South Africa's economic development 'has been built on, and is dependent upon, the cheap labour-power of the native'. The success of the system of cheap migrant labour rested on the maintenance of 'chronically over-populated and overworked native reserves ... which conditions force large numbers of natives periodically to leave these areas and seek employment in the white areas'. But now, the authors argued, this system was breaking down. The reserves were so overcrowded and landlessness so acute that permanent urbanisation was taking place. Moreover, African workers no longer accepted this system of low-wage migrant labour: 'As a matter of fact, it is well known that the natives are busy organising themselves to improve their position, and through collective action to force their demands on their white employers – as evidenced in last year's mine strike and the agitation for the recognition of native trade unions, to cite but two examples.' The existing system encouraged Africans to think they could eventually win full equality through greater pressure and agitation. They had 'to be brought to the realisation that such equality was totally and utterly unthinkable' (*Inspan* April 1947).

Not only were the old economic relations rapidly disintegrating during this period, but the intensification of industrial and political struggles awoke fears of rapid political change. This was clearly articulated by Dr Jansen: 'Afrikaners compare present conditions with those of some years ago and see how propaganda for equality increases daily and how the communists spread their doctrine unhindered throughout the land. They see how one by one the customs which have stood up against equality are broken down. They are tired of these things.' There was to be no equality in work or politics between master and servant. Unless 'Europeans' retained control of the state, those who work for them – who in the old days knew that their duty was to labour for the Boer – 'will come to govern the country. I do not think the Europeans in our country will be prepared to allow such a possibility' (*Inspan* October 1944).

The emerging apartheid concept held above all that 'the Native' was to be kept in his proper place as a worker. This was fully in keeping with Calvinist prescriptions. Bantu and Boer belonged to different nations. The biblical justifications were numerous. Genesis 11 was clear that ever since the tower of Babel incident God had imposed a separate existence on nations and divided and distributed them over the face of the Earth. Deuteronomy 32:8 provided further proof: 'When the Most High gave the nations their inheritance when he divided the sons of man he fixed their bounds according to the numbers and sons of God.' Acts 17:26 put the matter beyond doubt: 'From one single stock He not only created the whole human race so that they could occupy the entire earth, but He declared how long each nation should flourish and what the boundaries of its territory should be.'[2] God willed the differences between nations, because, according to Malan, 'He has placed before each Volk a unique destiny, a unique calling like that of any other individual' (Moodie

1975: 71). Each nation was fixed in place in the divinely-ordered hierarchy – a comforting notion to members of those nations He willed 'to receive the labour expected' of other nations over whom they were placed as masters. And if heretical notions of equality threatened this divinely-willed exploitation, 'the Afrikaner' would fulfil 'his' destiny by reimposing it.

Even before the details of apartheid policy were elaborated, its broad outlines were clear. It would concern itself firstly with measures to restrict the flow of labour from the rural areas to the town, but above all from white farms to the towns. Secondly, it would exercise the tightest possible control and discipline over the African work force, permitting no form of organisation which challenged the (divinely-willed) existing division of society. Thirdly, measures to maintain low wages and regulate conditions of work so as to permit an intensification of exploitation would be introduced. Fourthly, the jobs and superior positions of white workers within the industrial division of labour would be protected from competition from cheaper African labour. And finally, since any conception of 'racial equality' encompassed all the evils inherent in the changes experienced during the 1940s, racial segregation would be reinforced and extended in all fields.

In a nutshell, then, this emerging emphasis on the 'Native question' concerned itself with the conditions of accumulation for a fledgling capitalist class, tied to the apron-strings of agriculture. Here it is important to be clear what these general notions of 'apartheid' implied and what they did not. Except for a few intellectual visionaries locked in the Afrikaner ivory towers, apartheid, or 'practical apartheid' as *Inspan* and *Volkshandel* took to labelling it, was never intended to imply the total economic segregation of the races. It was designed to secure and control the supply of labour for all capitalists, not to deprive any employer of it. The AHI was very firm on this point. A series of articles in 1947 and 1948 emphasised and re-emphasised that while the AHI fully supported the apartheid policy, 'the policy of the segregation of the native is often advanced without an analysis of all its implications, or a definite scheme. . . Today it is impossible to do without non-white labour' (*Volkshandel* February 1947; also May and June 1947).

Lest the point be misunderstood, the AHI's congratulations to the new HNP government made its position extremely clear. Total segregation might be the ideal, but it was doubtful if it could ever be achieved:

> No, a person must be practical. It must be acknowledged that the non-white worker already constitutes an integral part of our economic structure, that he is now so enmeshed in the spheres of our economic life that for the first fifty/hundred years (if not even longer), total segregation is pure wishful thinking. Any government which disregards this irrefutable fact will soon discover that it is no longer in a position to govern (*Volkshandel* June 1948).

The new government was urged to limit itself to the practical task of improving the system of influx control, developing the native reserves, and segregating the public places and certain residential areas.

175

THE ECONOMIC MOVEMENT AND THE HNP

If the *reddingsdaad* movement formed the real motor of Afrikaner nationalism during the war years, and if its elaboration of an 'Afrikaner' economic ideology crystallised the further development of Christian-nationalism, how did this translate into the programme of the HNP?

In the period between *hereniging* in January 1940 and the May 1943 general elections, the HNP was preoccupied mainly with internal struggles and the conflict with the OB. While certain HNP leaders were deeply involved in the *reddingsdaad* movement – Dönges, for example, played a leading role in the RDB – it certainly did not enjoy the party's central attention. However, once the HNP established its dominance over all other nationalist groups in the 1943 elections, its gaze increasingly shifted to the economic issues raised by the *reddingsdaad* movement. A committee of MPs was appointed to draw up an economic programme in consultation with the 'economic leaders'. Finally published in March 1944, this 'Economic Plan for South Africa' reads like a manifesto of the AHI (*Die Kruithoring* 1/3/44).

The programme described itself as 'the Nationalist Party's method for the achievement of the revolution of the Twentieth Century'. This 'revolution' would avoid the 'three extremes' of Communism, National-socialism and unbridled *laissez-faire* capitalism. Echoing C.G.W. Schumann's call at the first RDB conference for a capitalist system with strong state control (Reddingsdaadbond 1941:34–6), the party opted for the 'sensible path' of a 'controlled economy' based on private property and private enterprise. It would defend the prevailing class structure of South Africa: 'The HNP preserves [*handhaaf*] the various economic groups in their rights and functions as separate members of the same body.'

A Central Economic Council would be set up to oversee the economy. A strong interventionist role was assigned to the state in other areas. State support to agriculture would be increased. Stress here was placed on the better provision of credit, the tightening up of marketing schemes to make them more profitable to farmers, and state control over the labour market to ensure a sufficient supply of labour for agriculture. Monopolies in commerce and industry would be 'combated', and foreign investment brought under firm state regulation. All 'key industries' would be placed under 'state control' (though not necessarily state ownership), and the protection of local industries intensified. The party favoured a system of international free trade and the abolition of all trade preferences. In the commercial sector, apart from the 'combating' of monopoly, the issue of trading licences to 'non-whites' would be limited to non-white areas. In the financial sector, a Central Banking Council representing the state, the Reserve Bank and the commercial banks would formulate general credit policy and control interest rates. All banks operating in South Africa would have to have their headquarters in the country. Their directors would have to be South African citizens.

The proposals with respect to labour rested on the basic principle that 'the position and civilisation of the white race' should be protected. Consequently, 'apartheid' would be introduced in employment 'to prevent the exploitation of one race by another'. The labour problems of agriculture would be placed in a separate category, exempting agriculture from minimum wage legislation. Wage determinations would be based upon 'the different living standards' of white, coloured and African workers. Whilst trade unions would be allowed to operate, they would be controlled by the state to prevent them being misused for anti-state or anti-volk purposes, or *for disturbing the proper and necessary balance between the various sectional interests in our economic life'*. The appointment of trade union officials would likewise fall under state control. The programme concluded with a list of general welfare measures to ensure social security for all white workers.

All this followed very closely on the prescriptions and policies of the *reddingsdaad* movement for the future *'volksekonomie'* outlined in the previous chapter. Yet this programme is further notable for its failure to elaborate on the apartheid idea. Beyond calling for the 'preservation of the white race and civilisation' behind certain 'essential social barriers', and asserting general segregationist principles in employment and residential areas, nothing specific is made of 'apartheid'. A further glaring omission is the lack of any reference to a system of influx control, again beyond the general commitment to 'state control over labour affairs, to ensure the necessary supply of farm labour'.

By 1944, the HNP was only at the earliest stages of a programmatic elaboration of apartheid. The 'apartheid-idea' was still little more than a loose set of principles, the most important of which was the need to secure the labour supply of agriculture in the face of the massive movement of labour from the rural to the industrial areas. A mere two weeks after the publication of the HNP economic programme, the leader of the party's study group on racial affairs – M.C.de Wet Nel – informed Parliament, when opposing a motion to abolish the pass system as a hindrance to industrialisation, that: *'We must go into* the question of labour conditions. These conditions are chaotic, as has been proved repeatedly. Just take the Free State or the Transvaal. One simply cannot get a Native to work there. The farmers are at their wits' end.' His solution to this agricultural labour crisis lay not in abolishing the Pass Laws but in the establishment of a system for the licensing and rationing of labour, 'whereby different undertakings such as mining, industry and agriculture etc. would be assured of their necessary and legitimate share of labour'. In doing so 'tribal ties' in the native reserves should be maintained as the influence of the cities undermined the 'national characteristics' of African workers (HAD vol. 48, column 3098).

The later development of apartheid ideology largely followed the ideas here laid down by de Wet Nel. As he made clear, apartheid sought primarily to secure a stable labour supply for agriculture. It attempted to reinforce the 'ethnicisation' of African culture as a major means of retaining strong control over a fragmented workforce. Moreover, apartheid ideology also began to focus on measures to protect the employment of white workers in industry, to ensure their political support for the HNP. As argued in the previous chapter, this likewise involved an 'ethnicisation' – a drawing of Afrikaner workers into the cultural bosom of the volk through a full frontal assault on conceptions of class solidarity. Thus, the 'racial question' was raised in the *reddingsdaad* movement, firmly within the conception of the need to restructure economic and social relations to ensure rapid accumulation on the part of Afrikaner business. The following chapters explore that process of accumulation.

Part IV

The accumulation of Afrikaner capital in the 1940s

13

Agricultural and finance capital

In 1949, the AHI undertook a comparative survey of Afrikaner business in the years 1938/9 and 1948/9. Published on the eve of the second Ekonomiese Volkskongres, the AHI survey is an incomparable source of information on the development of Afrikaner business. Table 2 summarises the growth in each sector (p.182).

These figures indicate impressive growth. The number of undertakings increase by 350 per cent. Total turnover rose by over 500 per cent from £61m to £322.7m. In absolute terms, all sectors except mining witnessed a rapid extension of Afrikaner enterprise. The *reddingsdaad* movement aimed to place 'the Afrikaner' in 'his legitimate place' in industry and commerce, which the EI defined as the 'dominant position'. However, despite the doubling of the percentage share of Afrikaner undertakings in total turnover after ten years of concerted effort, Afrikaner-controlled enterprises accounted for only one-tenth of the total business life of South Africa.

The relative successes and failures of the economic movement during this period are best shown by an examination of the effects in each sector of the overall strategy developed at the Ekonomiese Volkskongres. This accumulation strategy was predicated predominantly on the centralisation of money-capital in financial institutions. All loose Afrikaner money was to be drawn together and transformed into productive-capital in a number of ways. The revenue of all classes was to be tapped – from the petty savings of Afrikaner workers to the large personal income of Afrikaner farmers and other capitalists. Afrikaners of all classes were prodded to save in various Afrikaner credit institutions. However, the primary source of such money-capital lay in the centralisation of agricultural capital. Here it is necessary to develop the theoretical explanation of such centralisation at greater length.

In the second volume of *Capital*, Marx demonstrates that a characteristic feature of the circulation process of capital is the formation of hoards of potential or latent money-capital. Such money-capital is latent, rather than active capital because the capitalist is as yet unable to reconvert such stored up capital-value from its money form back into its productive form. As such, this latent money-capital cannot yet be used to expand the scale of production:

Table 2. *The growth of Afrikaner business per sector, 1938/9–1948/9ᵃ*

	Number of undertakings		Number of employees 1948/9[b]			Turnover		Afrikaner share of total turnover per sector	
	1938/9	1948/9	White	Non-white	Total	1938/9 (£m.)	(1948/9 (£m.)	1938/9 %	1948/9 %
Commerce[c]	2,428	9,585	37,500	36,180	73,680	28.0	203.7	8	25
Manufacturing[d]	1,239	3,385	14,450	26,480	40,930	6.0	43.6	3	6
Finance[e]	40	68	3,340	285	3,625	27.0	74.4	5	6
Mining	3	9	215	2,600	2,185	1.0	1.0	1	1
TOTAL	3,710	13,047	55,505	66,545	121,050	61.0	322.7	5	11

Notes: (*a*) The survey was conducted in 1949 and turnover for 1938/9 was requested. Where this was not given it was estimated on average turnover per employee.
(*b*) Data on the number of employees 1938/9 not available.
(*c*) Includes trade in agricultural commodities, distribution trade, and service establishments.
(*d*) Includes those undertakings with less than 3 employees, normally excluded from census returns.
(*e*) Indicates funds under control rather than turnover.

Source: Volkshandel September 1950.

Since the proportions in which the production process can be expanded are not arbitrary but are prescribed by technical factors, the surplus-value realised, even if it is destined for centralisation, can often only grow to the volume at which it can actually function as additional capital, or enter the circuit of capital value in process, by repeating a number of circuits. (Until then, therefore, it must be stored up.) The surplus-value thus builds up into a hoard, and in this form it constitutes latent money-capital. Latent, because as long as it persists in the money form, it cannot function as capital. Thus the formation of a hoard appears here as a moment that is comprised within the process of capitalist accumulation, accompanies it, but is at the same time essentially different from it. For the reproduction process is not itself expanded by the formation of latent money-capital. On the contrary latent money-capital is formed here because the capitalist producer cannot directly expand the scale of his production (Marx 1978:158).

This necessary process of the formation of hoards withdraws money from circulation, but does not create additional wealth. In the hands of an individual capitalist a hoard functions as passive rather than active capital, and though a necessary element in the circulation of that particular capital, does not itself re-enter the circuit of that individual capital. Through the credit system, however, the hoarded latent money-capital of one capitalist is temporarily placed in the hands of other capitalists. Here it can be transformed into active, or productive capital in enterprises other than the one in which it was generated. In being so transferred between capitalists, latent money-capital can lead to an expansion of production precisely because it loses its latent from and becomes active capital.

It is a feature peculiar to the agricultural branch of capitalist production that the hoards so formed are large relative to advanced capital, and remain in latent form for relatively long periods. In contrast to industrial capital, the turnover cycle of agricultural capital is tied to the natural cycle of the seasons and can only be speeded up within certain narrow limits. Given this long turnover time and the high investment required to expand production, the active capital of agriculture tends to be expanded slowly relative to the branches of capitalist production. As a result of the relatively long periods required to build up an accumulation fund in agriculture, this branch of capitalist production tends to build up large hoards of latent money-capital.

The *reddingsdaad* movement sought to lay hold of these hoards of latent money-capital generated in agriculture in two ways. Firstly, by persuading farmers temporarily to place these hoards in Afrikaner credit institutions; but by simply transferring hoarded funds to Afrikaner credit institutions, agricultural capital would not be required to change its pattern of accumulation. However, the second way in which the *reddingsdaad* movement sought to lay hold of the latent money-capital generated in agriculture did require a change in the pattern of accumulation. It was the widespread practice of Afrikaner farmers finally to reinvest hoarded accumulation funds in expanded agricultural production through the purchase of more land. The *reddingsdaad* movement sought to transform this pattern by persuading farmers to invest their accumulation funds in industry and commerce (p. 156 above). In other words, latent money-capital generated in agriculture was to be permanently detached from the parent stock of agricultural capital, and, through being centralised in such financial institutions as FVB, would be advanced as new money-capital in other branches of capitalist production. Through this process of the centralisation and segmentation of latent money-capital generated in agriculture, a new class of Afrikaner financial industrial and commercial capitalists would be brought into existence. In return for this volk's service. Farmers would receive interest on the capital they advanced for this purpose. In order to assess the progress of this centralisation and segmentation of agricultural capital, it is firstly necessary to review the growth of agricultural capital during this period.

AGRICULTURE

The decade 1939 to 1949 saw significant developments in South African agriculture. The 1937 Marketing Act established a single-channel, fixed-price Marketing System. Producer-dominated Control Boards set the prices of various agricultural commodities, and were the sole buyers of the commodities concerned. Trading and commercial bodies would then purchase the product from the various control Boards. In effect, the state intervened to ensure the conversion of commodity-capital back into money-capital. In this way, the realisation of the surplus value embodied in such commodities was assured. The prices fixed by the Control Boards were based on production costs, calculated on those of the less efficient producers. As enacted in 1937, the Marketing Act then guaranteed a stable profitability to all farmers, and surplus profits to more efficient producers.[1]

Together with the massive expansion of demand for agricultural commodities during the war, the now guaranteed profitability led to a rapid concentration of agricultural capital. Ever larger tracts of land were brought into production. Land under irrigation increased by 26 per cent. Whereas land prices remained fairly stable from 1912 to 1940, from 1940 they started to rise rapidly. This increase in the volume of employed means of production likewise saw a 47 per cent growth in the size of the African labour force working on white farms (Department of Agriculture 1961:9, 11). This was a period of rapid mechanisation of agriculture. The number of tractors in use increased eight-fold between 1937 to 1950. The Department of Agriculture (1961:13–17) recorded similarly large rises in the use of 32 other types of agricultural machines, and a corresponding decrease in the employment of simple implements. This period also saw a notable increase in other forms of fixed capital investment in agriculture (Wilson 1971:151). The combined gross value of agricultural and livestock production rose from £72.9m to £213.2m between 1939 and 1949. If divided by the total number of white farms, this gives a very crude index of average annual product per farm, rising from £678 in 1939 to £1,366 in 1946, reaching £1,607 in 1948.[2]

Table 3. *Membership and turnover of agricultural cooperatives, 1936–1949*

Year	Total membership	Total annual turnover	Average annual turnover per member
		£ m	£
1936	70,119	14.4	205.3
1941	109,152	30.4	278.5
1946	160,994	52.4	327.1
1949	200,027	111.2	354.4

Source: Compiled from data in 'Die rol van die Kooperatiewe Beweging in die Ekonomiese Vooruitgang van die Afrikaner', *Inspan* November 1950.

Three factors stand out for consideration during this period: the rapid growth of cooperatives; the changing price structure of agricultural commodities; and the growing labour shortages on white farms. The 1937 Marketing Act explicitly favoured cooperatives in the appointment of agents for the receiving, collecting, processing and marketing of produce under the aegis of the various Control Boards set up by the Act. By 1940/1, cooperatives in the maize, wheat and tobacco industries were handling 66 per cent, 85 per cent and 100 per cent of the respective crops (Finlay 1976:58). With the circulation of agricultural commodities increasingly channelled through cooperatives, this period saw a very rapid growth in the cooperative movement (see Table 3). The membership figures in Table 3 are slightly misleading, however. The cooperatives played such a vital role in the reproduction cycle of agricultural capital that many farmers belonged to more than one. By 1950, 95,000 white farmers, or over 90 per cent of the total, belonged to one or more cooperative (*Inspan* November 1950).

Through the cooperative purchase of farm implements and machinery, the provision of technical services and credit facilities, and the processing and marketing of agricultural produce, the cooperative movement facilitated the concentration of agricultural capital. Cooperatives moreover played an important role in the centralisation of agricultural capital. The capital reserves of agricultural cooperatives grew from £2.2 m in 1936 to £12.2 m in 1949.[3] These funds were deposited predominantly in Afrikaner credit institutions. By thus assisting the centralisation of agricultural capital, the reserve funds of the cooperative movement directly contributed to the development of Afrikaner financial institutions. In facilitating the concentration, and hence more rapid accumulation of agricultural capital, the cooperatives indirectly made greater sums of latent money-capital and revenue available for investment in such credit institutions.

The concentration of capital in agriculture during this period involved, secondly, significant changes in the price structure. The demand for agricul-

Table 4. *Price index of select agricultural and livestock products (1936 = 100)*

Year	Wool (per lb)	Beef (per 100 lb)	Mutton (per lb)	Butter (per lb)	Maize (per 200 lb)	Wheat (200 lb)	Sugar cane (per ton)	Tobacco payment (per lb)	Good wine (per leaguer)
1939	84	132	130	130	119	125	101	160	91
1940	119	131	114	133	118	131	103	188	91
1941	102	138	120	135	144	137	105	205	109
1942	104	170	144	162	147	163	120	253	114
1943	129	197	184	181	200	179	119	284	132
1944	131	226	198	191	213	215	115	321	130
1945	132	220	204	221	233	215	125	355	139
1946	122	233	220	249	253	234	141	366	146
1947	169	225	232	257	300	242	168	424	202
1948	266	237	248	286	283	245	167	466	202
1949	342	243	258	302	293	257	186	452	202

Source: Department of Agriculture 1961: table 6, p. 11.

Table 5.   *Gross value of farm products 1939/40–1948/9*

Year	Gross value of agricultural products (£1,000)	Gross value of livestock products (£1,000)	Total gross value of farm products (£1,000)
1939/40	38,363	34,526	72,889
1940/41	42,503	36,063	78,566
1941/42	46,857	44,517	91,374
1942/43	61,667	58,495	117,152
1943/44	60,798	59,172	119,970
1944/45	64,714	58,579	123,293
1945/46	68,779	61,799	130,558
1946/47	84,230	69,283	153,513
1947/48	104,116	82,446	186,562
1948/49	93,409	92,522	185,931

Source: Department of Agriculture 1961: Table 35, p. 51. Table 70, p. 69.

tural commodities increased sharply during the war. Despite large increases in the volume of production, shortages of such commodities were common. In a bid to stimulate production, agricultural prices were raised by various Control Boards. These increases were further exaggerated by soaring world prices. Table 4 shows the rise in agricultural prices during this period (p. 186).

These were years of prosperity for farmers. The British government guaranteed to purchase everything South African agriculture could produce, and there were no unsaleable agricultural surpluses during the war. The terms of trade between agricultural and non-agricultural commodities shifted in favour of the former. Table 5 indicates the rapid rise in the value of agricultural and livestock production during this period. However, despite these rapid price increases, the pricing mechanisms of the Marketing Act were increasingly used to limit accumulation in agriculture. The various Control Boards were originally envisaged as producer-controlled bodies under government supervision. Through these Boards, farmers would be able to realise an average profit by setting statutory prices for agricultural commodities. During the war, however, the combination of sometimes acute domestic shortages and rocketing world prices led to a change in function for these Boards. Increasingly the Control Boards became the vital instruments of rationing by the government. Under the direction of the Food-Controller, their price-fixing powers came to be used to hold down agricultural prices, and to prevent them rising as rapidly as world prices.[4]

As the war progressed, the question of the operation of the Control Boards led to fierce conflict within the capitalist class over the very existence of the Marketing Act. By 1944, the powerful Associated Chambers of Commerce (Assocom) recommended a repeal of the Act and drastic inroads on the statutory privileges – particularly in taxation – enjoyed by agricultural cooperatives. Following the end of the war, the issue of the Control Boards resolved itself into a struggle between those who advocated their use as the controlling instruments of a 'cheap food' policy on the one hand, and organised agriculture, which fought for producer control and higher food prices, on the other. In the period of aggravated food shortages immediately after the war, the Control Boards were in fact used to hold down agricultural prices, and there were strong pressures from commerce and industry to extend this policy.

While the political significance of this struggle is examined in chapter 15, one conclusion should be drawn here. By the end of the war, the growing inroads on price increases again shifted the terms of trade between agricultural and non-agricultural commodities against the former. The position of capitalist agriculture had improved beyond recognition. Yet, had South African agricultural prices been allowed to follow those of the world market, agricultural profits would have been even higher and accumulation more rapid. Farmers were acutely aware of this. The use of the Control Boards to hold down prices was clearly perceived as a limitation on accumulation. This presented a definite barrier to the further mechanisation of agriculture, necessary if South African producers were to remain competitive on world markets. This issue directly affected the emerging capitalists of the *reddingsdaad* movement. A barrier to accumulation in agriculture was a barrier to their own accumulation and, as the formal alliance between the Agricultural Union and the AHI after 1944 shows, was resisted by both (chapter 15 below).

The third significant feature of the concentration of agricultural capital during these years was the large increase in its labour force. The number of African males employed in agriculture rose from 403,491 in 1937, to 567,569 in 1946, reaching 636,794 in 1950 (Department of Agriculture 1961 : 11). This large increase in agricultural labour was but part of a wider series of transformations wrought in the South African economy during this period. Its most notable feature was the rapid expansion of industrial production, witnessing an even greater influx of African labour into industry. An additional 232,000 African workers entered industrial employment between 1940 and 1950 (US 1960: G4-7, G-13, G-15). The great bulk of this new influx of industrial labour came from white farms. In other words, labour was leaving the farms for higher wages in the urban industries (Morris 1977). Yet the effect of this drain of labour off white farms was spread unevenly. It was felt most severely in those areas where the labour tenancy system persisted. Attempts to implement the 1936 Land Act were not effective and led to intense rural resistance by Africans. Worst affected were OFS and Transvaal farmers. As de Wet Nel had told Parliament in 1944, 'one simply cannot get a Native to work there' (p. 177 above). A breakdown of African farm labour in the various provinces reveals this very clearly (see Table 6).

The size of the African male labour force on Cape farms more than doubled between 1937 and 1946, rising from 76,681 to 162,027, and reaching 173,770

Table 6. *African farm labour, 1937–1950*

Union

Year	Male	Female	Total	Percentage change
1937	403,491	184,276	587,767	–
1946	567,869	139,164	706,933	+ 20.3
1950	636,794	230,566	867,359	+ 22.7

Cape

Year	Male	Female	Total	Percentage change
1937	76,681	25,561	102,242	–
1946	162,027	36,608	198,635	+ 94.3
1950	173.770	66.353	238.123	+ 19.9

Natal

Year	Male	Female	Total	Percentage change
1937	88,321	31,887	120,208	–
1946	118,523	21,579	140,102	+ 16.5
1950	132,663	29,316	161,979	+ 15.6

Transvaal

Year	Male	Female	Total	Percentage Change
1937	149,661	76,129	225,790	–
1946	190,051	40,945	230,996	+ 2.3
1950	222,838	70,993	293,831	+ 27.2

OFS

Year	Male	Female	Total	Percentage change
1937	88,828	50,709	139,537	–
1946	96,968	40,032	137,000	– 1.8
1950	107,523	64,903	172,426	+ 25.9

Source: Department of Agriculture 1961: Table 6, p. 11.

by 1950. Moreover, Cape farmers also employed Coloured labour, the numbers rising from 61,667 in 1937 to 80,692 in 1952. Compared with the Cape, Transvaal and OFS farmers were short of labour. The size of the African male labour force in the Transvaal increased by little more than 25 per cent between 1937 and 1946. Moreover, as Jansen complained to the 1944 Volkskongres on racial policy, this period saw a significant movement of African women from white farms to the cities (p. 173 above). In the Transvaal the number of women workers on white farms almost halved. Taking male and female labour together, the size of the African farm labour force increased by a minuscule 2.3 per cent in the Transvaal between 1937 and 1946, and actually declined by 1.8 per cent in the OFS (Table 6).

The war saw a rapid concentration and accumulation of agricultural capital and general prosperity for capitalist farmers. However, these processes had proceeded under contradictory pressures. Prevailing conditions at both the levels of production and circulation increasingly began to impose limits on and barriers to the further accumulation and concentration of agricultural capital. In doing so, they held back the restructuring, through mechanisation, of agricultural capital. By 1946, particularly in the OFS and the Transvaal, the single most important factor in accumulation – that is, an increasing supply of exploitable labour – was being eroded by the flow of labour from the farms to the cities. Farmers now began to organise to change the conditions under which labour was secured in agriculture. They fought for strong state intervention to control the influx of labour to the cities and a revision of the application of the Marketing Act to generate higher agricultural prices.

The political implications of retarded accumulation, particularly in Transvaal and OFS agriculture, are discussed in chapter 15. However, the general point made with respect to the struggle over the marketing boards bears repeating. The strategy of growth of Afrikaner business pursued by the *reddingsdaad* movement was predicated on the accumulation of capital in agriculture, and its centralisation in financial institutions. The wartime concentration of agricultural capital certainly assisted this process. But precisely the conditions which retarded the further concentration of capital in agriculture likewise limited its centralisation in such financial institutions and therefore operated to hold back their development. By 1945 the *reddingsdaad* movement was complaining that capital from the 'volk' was drying up, thus inhibiting investment in commerce and industry (p. 141 above). The struggles of organised agricultural on both the labour and marketing issues, therefore, enjoyed the strong support of budding Afrikaner capitalists, leading to formal cooperation between the AHI and the South African Agricultural Union (SAAU).

FINANCE

The rapid wartime expansion of the South African economy vastly increased the amount of money in circulation – the index rose from a base of 100 in 1938 to 204 in 1942, 424 in 1946 and 516 in 1948 (*Inspan* November 1950). The *reddingsdaad* movement aimed to fasten on money in circulation and convert it into productive capital. In the four years following the 1939 Ekonomiese Volkskongress, the RDB calculated that as a 'conservative estimate' Afrikaners had made £2 m available for investment in Afrikaner undertakings (Reddingsdaadbond 1943:1).

The Volkskongres intended this capital to be placed in finance institutions. The following analysis of Afrikaner finance firstly investigates the development of specific companies. It attempts to show which groups controlled these companies, and seeks to locate each within the spectrum of Afrikaner nationalist politics. It then turns secondly to an overview of Afrikaner finance in 1950. As FVB was designed as the official investment company of the volk, it is appropriate to begin here.

Federale Volksbeleggings

The establishment of FVB proved far more difficult than anticipated. On the one hand there was strong rural opposition to what was labelled a 'capitalist' undertaking. In an attempt to win support for FVB, M.S. Louw was forced into a public rebuttal of this charge (p. 153 above). The FAK secretary, P.J. Meyer, had to traipse 'from town to town' cajoling and pleading with the volk to support 'their' investment company. On the other hand, FVB encountered strong opposition from other Afrikaner businessmen trying to interest farmers in investing in local undertakings. A 'whispering campaign created much suspicion against FVB'. Louw himself was attacked in the press. The EI finally 'officially' instructed all other Afrikaner companies to reduce their share-sale campaigns in an attempt to gain greater investment for FVB (Bezuitenhout 1968:78). Yet even this did not help. So serious was the lack of support that FVB very nearly did not meet the statutory minimum of 10 per cent paid-up ordinary shares by the prescribed date for registration under the Companies Act. Only 910 of the required 20,000 minimum shares were paid-up. The project was saved by a last-minute appeal to a Cape doctor who borrowed £20,000 from Volkskas and invested it all in FVB (E.P. du Plessis 1964:194). Only in October 1940, a full year after the Volkskongres, was FVB finally authorised to begin business.

The company was established with an authorised share capital of £300,000, divided into 200,000 ordinary shares and 100,000 5$\frac{1}{2}$ per cent cumulative preference shares. The Articles of Association empowered the directors to refuse the transfer of shares. This was explicitly intended to keep control in the 'right hands'. M.S. Louw told the first Annual General Meeting in October 1941 that it was envisaged that 'the public' would be slow to invest in the ordinary shares of an untried company (in the event, even slower than anticipated). In that case the 'considerable' funds required for FVB to operate as an investment company could only be obtained from existing Afrikaner credit institutions and charities. The preference shares were intended for them.

From the outset, then, established Afrikaner capital was to control FVB.

The very first preference shares were taken out by the Cape Helpmeka-arsvereniging (whose chairman was W.A. Hofmeyr of Sanlam). The fonds subscribed another 25,000. Santam underwrote 50,000 preference shares and Sasbank, the small OFS savings bank, underwrote 5,000. But control was vested predominantly in Sanlam, which had been mandated by the Volkskongres to form FVB. The statutory foundation meeting was held in Sanlam's boardroom. Santam acted as FVB secretary until the end of June 1941. Hofmeyr's deputy at Sanlam and Nasionale Pers, C.R. Louw, was appointed FVB chairman and the first Board of Directors was dominated either by Sanlam or Cape NP men. The first three senior officials of FVB, C.H. Brink (secretary), W.B. Coetzer (commercial advisor), and Dr P.E. Rousseau (industrial advisor) were recruited by Sanlam.

In the early years, capital trickled only slowly into FVB. The first share issue was only fully subscribed five years after the Ekonomiese Volkskongres. In late 1944 a new share issue brought the authorised capital up to £600,000, increasing to £1m in 1946.

The statutory (i.e. inaugural) meeting of FVB laid down a ten-point investment policy. This proclaimed that while FVB was a 'volk's' institution, it was also a business undertaking, geared to paying dividends to its shareholders. In the first instance it sought to establish Afrikaner undertakings in commerce and industry through investing in shares of appropriate undertakings. This could not be done on a small, local scale. The company would not, therefore, finance small or local undertakings, except those with a proven capacity to expand. Where FVB was going to invest in new, untried operations, it would demand full control. In the case of established, flourishing businesses, control would not be a condition of support, as FVB wanted to encourage rather than suppress private initiative 'by steering it in the right direction' (*Volkshandel* January 1942). In practice, as was later confirmed by the chairman, the directors had early decided that FVB would not concern itself with small businesses but would concentrate only on 'financially strong undertakings' (*Volkshandel* January 1948).

As a temporary measure to provide an interim return, the first £50,000 of FVB capital was placed in $3\frac{1}{2}$ per cent government bonds. By January 1941 FVB had made loans to two companies (one of which, Voorbrand Tabak, later evolved into the Rembrandt corporation) and bought shares in a furniture store, a furniture factory and a wood and building materials wholesaler. Yet these were precisely the small, local operations FVB wanted to avoid.

By November 1942, FVB had direct interests in twelve companies. Its largest investments were concentrated in the fishing, wood and steel industries. A pattern was now emerging. Small investments would be made in a number of profitable industries while the major resources of the company were concentrated in clearly defined fields. In its early years FVB investment was primarily centred in the highly profitable fishing and canning field. In an industry dominated by the giant Irving and Johnson Company, it built up

Laaiplek Visserye and the Marine Production Corporation into powerful concerns. In 1946, a new subsidiary, Federale Nywerhede (Federal Industries) was established to bring together FVB's numerous fishing interests. This extremely profitable field provided the backbone to FVB in the 1940s and the base for its rapid expansion in the 1950s.

A second major area of FVB investment was related to agriculture. Wartime restrictions more than halved the imports of agricultural implements, and only a 100 per cent increase in local production satisfied agriculture's needs. Here FVB cashed in early by taking control of the small South African Farm Implements Manufacturers (Pty) Ltd. (hereafter Safim), and building it into a major supplier of agricultural implements and equipment. These were the years of the rapid mechanisation of agriculture, in which Safim played an important role. In the next decades, Safim developed links with Canadian capital, and FVB obtained a 50 per cent share in Massey-Ferguson (South Africa), which dominated the market for agricultural machinery.

FVB's catering for farmers' requirements was further extended in financing the establishment of Agricura Laboratoria, manufacturing veterinary products, and Cape Lime products was built up through FVB finance. These companies also provided a toehold in the chemical industry. During the 1940s FVB was given representation on the board of the state-owned chemical producer, Klipfontein Organic Products, and took over this company in the 1950s, moving into chemicals on a much larger scale.

The fourth major field of FVB investment during the 1940s lay in coalmining. By 1950 the group had a strong base in the industry through its control of the two mining companies, Klipfontein Koolmyne and Klippoortjie Koolmyne. Significantly, the latter was the first South African coalmining operation to be fully mechanised. These coalmines provided the basis for a large-scale expansion of FVB's mining interests in the 1950s, culminating in the take-over of one of the seven major mining houses – the General Mining and Finance Corporation – in 1963 (p. 250).

Thus, together with a small toehold in the engineering sector, fishing, farm implements and machinery, chemicals and coalmining were the major areas of FVB industrial interests. Over and above its extension of 'Afrikaner ownership' into these sectors of industry, FVB, fifthly, also made selective, small-scale investments in a number of flourishing Afrikaner commercial concerns. The larger Afrikaner-owned trading companies – such as Sonop, Uniewinkels, Brink Broers, Robertson Handelsvereniging, and W. Woods – were all recipients of FVB share capital. The AHI wholesale company VVM, was partly financed by FVB. The small OFS savings bank Sasbank, together with its associated clothing company, Veka Ltd., also received FVB support, as did the powerful Nasionale Pers.

In 1944, FVB set up the subsidiary Federale Beleggings (Federal Investments) as a 'pure' investment company, to hold shares and provide financial advice, while the parent company concentrated on the necessary investigatory work prior to investment in new undertakings. A division of labour emerged in what was now the Federale Group. Federale Nywerhede coordinated specific related industrial interests, Federale Beleggings acted as a holding company and management and investment advisor, while FVB itself managed the group as a whole, decided where investments would be made, provided finance, etc. A lucrative side of the latter's activities lay in underwriting new share issues of Afrikaner companies. This enabled FVB to collect a tidy underwriters' premium at low risk. This purely financial side of the group's activities would be further extended in the 1950s, when it moved into discounting and commercial banking through its Federale Bank and Trust Bank subsidiaries.

The early pledge that shareholders would be paid 'in jingling coin rather than pious sentiment' was fulfilled. By 1946, early losses had been turned into a healthy 6 per cent dividend on ordinary shares. In one sense then, the centralisation of money in FVB had achieved what the *volkskongres* intended. It had given 'the Afrikaner' (i.e. Sanlam) a toehold in industry. Given the restructuring of commercial capital during the war (see following chapter) its achievements in the field of commerce were distinctly more limited. Moreover, precisely because the company deliberately avoided small local undertakings, its impressive growth did not really advance the position of the small traders, that is, the petty bourgeoisie itself. FVB was developing into a powerful financial concern increasingly remote from the interests of such a petty bourgeoisie.

The Sanlam group

Sanlam was one of the major moving forces behind the Ekonomiese Volkskongres, and M.S. Louw had virtually singlehandedly developed the strategy 'officially' adopted by the *reddingsdaad* movement. The nationalist agitation of the early war years, and the mobilisation of the savings-power of the volk through the various organs of the *reddingsdaad* movement massively strengthened Sanlam's financial position. It took the company fully eighteen years (1918 to 1936) to develop an annual premium income of £$\frac{1}{2}$m. This was doubled in a mere five years, and doubled again by 1945. By 1942 Sanlam's assets stood at £5 m. Table 7 indicates the company's growth between 1937 and 1949.

M.S. Louw always argued that the life assurance form of credit institution led to the rapid centralisation of money, whence it could be productively invested. As the chairman of the second largest life assurance group in South Africa later put it, life assurance contracts 'essentially involve gathering the savings of individuals, turning these into capital, and putting the capital into productive use' (van der Horst 1980:1). With its swiftly rising premium income, just how rapid this centralisation of money capital in Sanlam was is shown by the quadrupling of its life assured fund between 1940 and 1949. Moreover these figures cover only Sanlam itself and exclude its African Homes Trust life subsidiary. Thus large amounts of centralised latent money-capital were potentially available for productive investment by Sanlam.

Table 7. *Growth of Sanlam 1937–1949*

Year	Annual premium income (nearest £1,000)	Life assured fund at the year end (nearest £1,000)	Contingency reserve fund at year end (nearest £1,000)	Bonus declared (£)
1937	619	2,470	20	2.0.0%
1940	872	3,970	50	1.10.0%
1943	1,355	6,276	100	1.10.0%
1946	2,247	10,184	300	2.0.0%
1949	3,451	16,706	400	2.2.0%

Source: Sanlan's report to second Ekonomiese Volkskongres, *Inspan* October 1950.
Note: The bonus rate was lowered during the war as 'a safety measure', and undivided profits were used to strengthen the company's financial position.

Limitations remained, however, which severely hedged in the company's capacity to invest these funds productively. Firstly, life assurance companies were under a statutory obligation to place 40 per cent of investable assets in gilt-edged securities. Secondly, all insurance companies tended to spread investments widely to ensure maximum security for maximum return. In a comparison of different types of credit institutions, Louw estimated that less than 10 per cent of the investable funds of insurance companies were productively invested as risk capital.[5] New Afrikaner undertakings provided neither maximum security nor maximum return. Direct investment by Sanlam in Afrikaner industrial and commercial undertakings was thus limited, as its board followed an extremely conservative policy. Its preferred method of investment was indirect, that is, through other financial institutions, preferably with a guaranteed return. Sanlam investment in FVB preference shares is a good example of this policy. In effect, FVB was controlled by Sanlam, and acted as its investment company.

During the 1940s, however, Sanlam developed two new important financial institutions which tapped new sources of money capital, took it into new areas of operation, and finally resolved the problem of the limitations of the insurance form. These were the Saambou ('build together') building society, and a new investment company, Bonuskor.

In June 1942, Spoorbondkas – the savings bank formed by the Christian-national trade union Spoorbond – invested £5,000 to start the first Afrikaner building society, Unie-Bouvereniging. At the instance of the large United Building Society, this new company was forced to change its name in March 1943 to the Saambou (Permanente) Bouvereniging. Spoorbondkas soon fell into financial difficulties and was forced to withdraw its capital after a few months. On condition that the head office of the building society was moved from Johannesburg to Pretoria, Volkskas immediately invested £20,000 in Saambou. Still little progress was made, and the directors then approached Sanlam and FVB. Sanlam finally agreed to finance the undertaking with FVB assistance, on condition that the head office was moved again, this time to Cape Town, where direct supervision could be exercised. W.A. Hofmeyr and his protégé, W.B. Coetzer of FVB, became directors of Saambou, with M.S. Louw an alternate director. Henceforth, Saambou was effectively controlled by Sanlam.

Under Sanlam control, Saambou could utilise the former's national network to extend itself beyond its base more rapidly than would otherwise have been the case. It now made steady progress. The first dividend of $2\frac{1}{2}$ per cent was declared in 1946. Paid-up share capital rose from £10,490 to £530,237 between 1943 and 1950, with a corresponding increase in fixed deposits and capital from £2,352 to £1,132,109. By 1950, Saambou's total assets stood at £1,700,461 (*Inspan* October 1950).

Despite this fairly rapid growth, Saambou was not a source of large amounts of capital available for productive investment. The funds of building societies are built by pooling the savings of 'the man in the street' – that is, workers and petty bourgeoisie. They draw together parts of the revenue of these classes and transform such revenue into loan capital, rather than risk capital. Whilst such undertakings do provide an important source of money-capital, a building society could not alone perform the centralising function which the Ekonomiese Volkskongress saw as the basis of its strategy of accumulation.

By 1946, Sanlam had itself grown rapidly. Moreover, both FVB and Saambou fell under its control, each drawing capital from different sources. Yet Sanlam was still seriously short of risk capital for investment in new fields. The potential sources of such capital for FVB were limited largely to the more well-to-do elements of the volk. Despite the intensive efforts of the RDB, the official historian of the economic movement has conceded that 'in the case of FVB it was generally not the masses of the volk who invested – the necessary investment consciousness was still absent' (E.P. du Plessis 1964:156).

The speeches of M.S. Louw endlessly reiterated that far greater amounts of risk capital for investment in new, untried undertakings were essential for the success of the *reddingsdaad* movement. At the 1945 AHI congress, he bluntly attacked the existing Afrikaner credit institutions for their 'shortsighted investment policies' which limited investments largely to secure loans. Unless such 'worthless' policies were abandoned, Louw warned that the post-war development of South Africa's mines and industries would remain in 'foreign hands'. The *reddingsdaad* movement had to find the necessary risk capital (*Volkshandel* May 1961, special supplement).

But by 1945 donations to the fonds had dried to a trickle. As the failed campaign to win a contribution of a day's wage per annum showed, intensive nationalist agitation was unable to shake much money from the pockets of the volk. Moreover, the now retarded capital accumulation in agriculture was holding back its centralisation in financial institutions. Louw's solution was to free for more productive use the £120m of 'Afrikaner savings' controlled by the insurance companies. 'The solution I propose is none other than the withdrawal of capital out of the normal credit institutions, and their transfer to finance corporations which, in their turn, will utilise this capital productively for the formation and development of our mining and manufacturing industries' (*Volkshandel* May 1961, special supplement).

The mode of this 'withdrawal' and 'transfer' of capital conceived by Louw was both ingenious and historically unique. In effect it boiled down to using the existing capital centralised in Sanlam in such a way as to avoid the statutory and other limitations placed on the productive investments of insurance companies. Even though the 5,000 shares in Sanlam had been owned exclusively by Santam since 1918, the life assurance side of Sanlam was run on a 'mutual' basis. In other words, profits on the life assurance operation were paid out to policy holders through an annual 'bonus' – standing at £2.0.0 per cent in 1946. In common with other life companies, Sanlam offered two basic types of policies – those 'with profits' and those 'without profits'. Premiums on the former were higher, but the 'with-profits' policy holders shared in profits through the annual bonus. By 1949, Sanlam's annual bonus of £2.2.0 per cent was the highest in South Africa. In 1945, Sanlam declared a profit of £435,000. Of this amount, £25,000 went into its reserve fund, and £410,000 was shared out through the £2.0.0 per cent bonus amongst the ordinary policy holders, increasing the total sum assured by £480,000. It was these bonuses which Louw hoped to transform into productive capital. If only half of Sanlam's policy holders followed the scheme, this would free £250,000 for productive investment.

A new company, Bonus Beleggings Korporasie (Bonus Investments Corporation, commonly known as Bonuskor) was established for the purpose. Holders of 'with profits' policies of over £500 would be given the option either to continue receiving their share of profits in the form of additional assurance (known as a reversionary bonus) or be paid the equivalent in cash. The latter would have the further option of converting this cash into a 'contributing share' in Bonuskor. Such 'contributing shares' to the value of £25 would then be converted into one ordinary share in the company, and dividends would be paid in proportion to the amount of each ordinary share which had been paid-up (*Volkshandel* February 1946).

This ingenious scheme offered policy holders a chance to become shareholders of an investment corporation for the price of their assurance premiums. Sanlam proudly claimed that Bonuskor 'enabled the small man also to share in industrial development' (*Volkshandel* January 1946). It did not call upon investors to find new funds for investment, but tapped a new source of capital. In the first instance, revenue of policy holders was to be converted into money-capital, and, through Bonuskor, again transformed into productive capital. This entirely new form of centralising revenue provided a form of 'automatic accretion of capital' (FAK 1954:115). It offered a way round the statutory limitations on the investment of Sanlam's funds, thus 'easing Sanlam's investment problem and enabling it to realise a higher average rate of return on its investments' (E.P. du Plessis 1964:159). Bonuskor was a Sanlam

Table 8. *Growth of Bonuskor, 1947–1960*

Year	Issued share capital (£1,000)	Reserves (£1,000)	Nego- tiated loans (£1,000)	Share invest- ments (£1,000)	Loans granted (£1,000)	Total assets (£1,000)	Net profit (£1,000)	Percen- tage divident declared
1947	389.0	322.1	175.2	392.9	166.6	595.4	33.9	5
1949	713.1	14.8	130.7	664.5	239.4	926.8	44.7	5
1951	1,007.4	28.1	144.2	855.1	287.25	1,249.2	62.3	5
1953	1,437.3	67.4	769.6	1,972.4	616.2	2,433.0	93.8	$5\frac{1}{2}$
1955	2,106.3	105.4	710.5	2,195.1	651.9	3,051.4	132.4	6
1957	3,117.1	166.3	1,124.6	2,952.5	1,322.3	4,589.5	190.2	6
1958	3,568.6	192.5	1,517.7	3,542.8	1,569.8	5,498.9	260.6	$6\frac{1}{4}$
1959	4,275.0	248.5	1,947.2	4,327.3	2,024.8	6,732.4	283.0	$6\frac{1}{4}$
1960	4,532.0	253.2	2,868.0	5,371.0	2,654.6	8,201.4	339.0	$6\frac{1}{2}$

Source: *Volkshandel* May 1961, special supplement.

subsidiary. The Cape Insurance company directly invested £100,000 in the £2m authorised share capital of Bonuskor and retained control through its own insurance policies. W.A. Hofmeyr became the Bonuskor chairman, with Louw as its managing director. The only other director was W.F.J. Steenkamp.

Bonuskor began business in March 1946 with a nominal authorised capital of £2m. At a time when other Afrikaner companies experienced great difficulty in raising capital, over quarter of a million pounds was subscribed in nine months. Table 8 shows its rapid growth.

Bonuskor was formed to provide risk capital for industrial investment. In its early years, very few Afrikaner industrial undertakings existed, and the company was forced to invest in new undertakings not yet yielding a dividend. Its first investments closely followed those of FVB – that is, in the engineering, fishing and coalmining sectors. However, non-divided yielding investments were reduced through a lesser emphasis on new undertakings, and investment in small companies was soon effectively eliminated. A further change in its investment pattern occurred at the end of the 1940s. As the industrial share index fell from 100 in 1948 to 56 by 1953, Bonuskor reduced investments in industry as such, to concentrate on mining, in cooperation with FVB. In July 1953, these two Sanlam-controlled companies merged their mining interests to form Federale Mynbou (Federal Mining), which eventually took over the General Mining and Finance Corporation in 1963 (p. 250 below). The changing pattern of Bonuskor investments is summarised in Table 9.

Thus, by the end of the 1940s a Sanlam 'group' of companies had emerged, comprising Sanlam and its various subsidiaries, together with FVB, Saambou and Bonuskor. Collectively they made up a powerful financial empire, each centralising money from a different source. The growth of the Sanlam group

Table 9. *Breakdown of Bonuskor share investments*
1947–1957

| Year | Percentage of total investments per sector | | | | |
	Industry	Mining	Commerce	Finance	Total
1947	60.0	3.5	7.6	28.9	100
1949	53.3	2.9	20.3	23.5	100
1951	57.1	3.7	20.6	18.6	100
1953	48.9	14.3	14.9	21.9	100
1955	46.9	19.1	13.4	20.6	100
1957	37.7	23.7	20.3	18.3	100

Source: *Volkshandel* May 1958.

was *the* success story of the *reddingsdaad* movement. But its very success increased fears of southern 'domination' amongst both northern operations and the petty bourgeoisie, intensifying the regionalism of Afrikaner nationalism.

Volkskas

The only northern undertaking which came anywhere near matching Sanlam's power was the Bond-controlled bank, Volkskas. Two very important developments in the bank's growth occurred in the 1940s. Firstly, in July 1940 it was registered as a commercial bank. This had always been the intention of the Board, though it was 'not announced' when Volkskas was formed as a loan bank in 1934 (*Volkshandel* June 1947). Its first years as a commercial bank were marked by severe difficulties. The Big Three established commercial banks – Barclays, Standard Bank and the Netherlands Bank – would neither admit Volkskas to the Bankers Organisation, nor, for some time, accept its cheques. Given Volkskas' cooperative structure, the big banks further threatened to bring a complaint under the Usury Act. These particular difficulties were partially overcome through nationalist agitation. Eventually, so many Afrikaners transferred their accounts to Volkskas, the other banks were forced to recognise it. But trouble also came from an unexpected source. Existing Afrikaner 'volk's' banks – such as Sasbank – also refused to recognise Volkskas as it 'acted too unorthodoxly and ambitiously'. A number of reconciliation attempts failed, and the grim epithet of 'capitalist' was regularly hurled at Volkskas (*Volkshandel* June 1947). The rapid growth of Volkskas after 1940 took it beyond the bounds of the Co-operative Act, and a prosecution became a real possibility.

Thus, after four years as the country's sole cooperative commercial bank, the directors announced the second major change in Volkskas' constitution. It had 'outgrown' the cooperative form. In order to compete effectively, it would have to abandon its cooperative basis. This move provoked a fierce response both within and outside the Bond. To many, the cooperative form was the sole guarantee that the bank would not develop into an Afrikaner 'Hoggenheimer'. Cries of treachery were long and bitter. Volkskas' chairman, L.J. du Plessis, issued a very weak statement arguing that the change was not a defeat for the cooperative movement or ideal, but simply meant that Volkskas no longer found this form suitable (*Volkshandel* February 1944). Any effect of his statement was thoroughly undermined when du Plessis resigned from the Board on the day a Volkskas Annual General Meeting approved the changeover (*Volkshandel* November 1944). As late as 1947 the directors were still defending themselves against charges of having misled the volk: 'We had to begin as a cooperative bank because we had to get the cooperation of the Afrikaner masses who individually did not then represent much economic power' (*Volkshandel* June 1947). But if anyone missed the point it was re-emphasised the following year when the two largest Afrikaner retail operations – Uniewinkels and Sonop – both under Bond influence, likewise abandoned the cooperative form.

Despite these various difficulties, as the only Afrikaner bank established on a national scale, Volkskas attracted wide support during the years of the *reddingsdaad* movement. Its growth during the period from 1935 to 1950 is indicated in Table 10. With a thirty-fold growth of total assets, to reach £16,538,900 in just ten years, Volkskas had clearly emerged as a major financial power. Its main strength lay in the north, and it was regarded as an alternative to, and more nationalistically 'pure' than, the Sanlam group. It remained very firmly under Bond control. When du Plessis resigned as chairman he was replaced by staunch *broeder* Dr A.J. Stals, and when the latter was appointed to the Cabinet in 1948, the venerable *broeder* J.H. Greijbe took over as chairman.

However, despite its great financial strength, during this period Volkskas' activities were almost entirely limited to banking. Unlike Sanlam it did not yet enjoy a wide network of financial and industrial interests. While its role in centralising capital was vital, this archly conservative bank was not itself in the business of directly investing in industry. That would occur during the 1950s.

Both Sanlam and Volkskas had been set up before the 1939 Volkskongres. Though relatively small operations, they were nevertheless both firmly established by this date. The organised *reddingsdaad* movement was in fact initiated as a result of a wary cooperation of the driving forces behind each of the two companies – on the one hand the young financiers around W.A. Hofmeyr, led by M.S. Louw, and on the other hand the theoreticians and Bond activists who sat on the Board of Volkskas. The most notable feature of the purely economic side of the *reddingsdaad* movement was the extremely rapid growth of these two groups. Sanlam and Volkskas were without any question the prime beneficiaries of the centralisation of capital aimed at by the economic movement. The 1940s thus gave rise to two powerful Afrikaner financial groups, each based in one of the two most important centres, the Cape and the Transvaal, and each directly linked to a different faction within the nationalist movement – Sanlam to the Cape NP and Volkskas to the

Table 10. *Growth of Volkskas, 1935–1950*

Year ending	Paid-up capital (£1,000)	Total deposits (£1,000)	Loans and discount (£1,000)	Fixed deposits and investment certificates (£1,000)	Savings accounts (£1,000)	Total assets (£1,000)	Number of branches
1935	1.5	10.8	9.9	9.0	1.8	13.1	2
1936	2.7	38.6	36.9	27.7	10.9	44.5	3
1937	8.2	109.8	99.5	87.8	22.0	176.2	6
1938	12.8	215.0	177.5	170.8	44.2	309.0	8
1939	20.0	356.7	294.7	278.1	73.4	399.0	14
1940	37.0	519.6	346.0	374.0	138.9	572.9	18
1941	67.2	1,012.7	660.5	434.2	253.1	1,100.0	21
1942	127.2	1,868.9	1,222.6	725.4	340.8	2,051.3	26
1943	246.0	3,752.9	1,817.3	1,301.6	595.6	4,045.7	31
1944	365.5	6,293.5	3,126.0	1,682.5	1,006.7	6,764.0	34
1945	572.6	7,444.8	4,039.3	2,096.7	1,304.7	8,415.7	50
1946	786.4	9,572.9	5,580.1	2,513.3	1,766.9	10,872.9	51
1947	1,142.9	11,255.8	7,388.4	3,106.5	1,913.1	13,085.5	52
1948	1,240.7	13,234.9	8,262.7	3,436.8	2,058.8	14,986.3	59
1949	1,385.3	14,445.1	9,416.9	3,642.1	2,212.7	16,538.9	70
1950	1,447.7	16,539.9	10,762.9	4,054.6	2,272.7	18,858.6	76

Source: Annual Report 1955.

Bond, which dominated northern Afrikaner nationalism. As the 1940s unfolded, the gathering 'provincialism' within the nationalist movement tended to polarise around these two finance companies.

Rembrandt

The *reddingsdaad* movement gave rise to a third major financial group – the Rembrandt corporation. Unlike Sanlam and Volkskas, Rembrandt is much more difficult to classify, either in terms of its affiliations within nationalist politics or of its operations. In both cases it began as one thing, and seemed to be transformed in the process of growth.

Today the Rembrandt group is a colossal tobacco multinational. Its origins go back to 1940 when the Voorbrand Tobacco Company was formed by Stals, Diedrichs and a 23-year-old graduate of Pretoria University, Anton Rupert. Stals was a leading HNP politician and ever since the 1934 Volkskongres on the 'poor white' problem had been a prominent figure in the economic movement. A staunch Broederbonder, and director of Volkskas, together with M.S. Louw and W.A. Hofmeyr, he was one of the curators of the fonds. Diedrichs stood at the very helm of the economic movement as RDB *Hoofleier*

201

and EI vice-chairman (and Bond chairman from 1938 to 1942). Rupert, the real moving force behind the venture, was a virtually unknown member of the RDB secretariat. True, in 1939 he had been the firebrand editor of the ANS newspaper, *Wapenskou*. As such his ideological orientation was virtually identical to the fascism of Meyer – and in the struggles of the 1940s, *Wapenskou* became a major OB mouthpiece.

With Stals as chairman and Rupert as manager, Voorbrand was one of the small companies to be given a loan from the fonds. Further financial support also came from FVB. The company had been formed to manufacture cigarettes. During the war however, supplies and machinery for cigarette manufacture were allocated only to existing producers. Voorbrand had to restrict itself to the manufacture of pipe tobacco. This was not an overly profitable field, and early in 1943 the company faced a major crisis when FVB gave notice of its intention to sell its Voorbrand shares.

Rupert devised a solution which was initially strongly opposed by his fellow directors. He proposed the formation of a new holding company to buy out FVB's interest. For a while he was forced to act singlehandedly, but then enlisted the financial and moral support of D.W.R. (Dirk) Hertzog. As Albert Hertzog's cousin, Dirk Hertzog shared Rupert's (then) ideological fervour.[6] In March 1943 Rupert and Hertzog formed Tegniese en Industriele Beleggings Bpk. (Technical and Industrial Investments Ltd., hereafter TIB), with a nominal capital of £5,000 and a paid-up capital of £10. Rupert eventually persuaded his Voorbrand co-directors to place their shares under TIB, but in return he had to pay back every penny he had earned at Voorbrand.

In December 1943 TIB bought out a liquor trading company, Forrer Broers. The profits from the extremely lucrative liquor trade were to provide much of the capital on which the Rembrandt empire was built. From its base in Forrers, TIB took over Distillers corporation (SA) Ltd., which marketed a number of Cape wines and a popular brandy. Thus these Bond men of the north became enmeshed in the interests of the Cape wine farmers, a major base of the Cape NP. Distillers had a wide chain of trading outlets, and the growth of TIB was rapid. Within three years the TIB group controlled assets of £1m. Despite the fears of Diedrichs and Stals, it paid out a 5 per cent dividend in 1944, which was raised to 6 per cent the following and subsequent years. Whilst its major base remained in the liquor trade, by 1948 TIB and its affiliate *Tweede* (second) TIB, had large interests in tobacco, wool, coffee and tea, and coalmining concerns.

So profitable were these investments in the liquor trade that in June 1947 Rupert established the Rembrandt Tobacco Company, with an authorised share capital of £200,000. Production of cigarettes began the very month the HNP came to power in May 1948. The composition of Rembrandt's board again reveals the Bond connection. With Stals now in the Cabinet, Diedrichs became chairman. Aside from Rupert, Stals, and Hertzog – all Bond stalwarts – Bond interests in the new undertaking were watched over by its secretary, I.M. Lombard.

From the outset, Rembrandt cigarettes sold extremely well. Within two years, annual turnover stood at £2m. Over and above its links with northern tobacco farmers, the Bond, and Cape wine farmers, the Rembrandt company was notable for a number of things. Firstly, it pursued an extremely aggressive marketing campaign which stressed quality, under the company's slogan: 'Every cigarette MUST be a Masterpiece'. Given the generally poor quality of the products of Afrikaner manufacturers, this helped to dispel the prejudice. Secondly, an emphasis on 'scientific management' likewise distinguished Rupert's company. He summarised the principles underlying such management as follows: respect for labour; industrial participation; and market leadership through research. Though hardly revolutionary principles in 'scientific management', in the late 1940s these were indeed startling innovations for an Afrikaner company. Rupert's great significance in the economic movement was that he was the first Afrikaner industrialist fully to grasp the changing conditions of capitalism of his time, and to adjust management techniques to the latest American principles. He moved much faster than those in the *reddingsdaad* movement who took longer to shed the vestiges of the petty bourgeois consciousness. As early as 1950, Rupert argued the need for a 'Bantu Investment Corporation' to finance the establishment of industries in the reserves – heresy at a time when these were supposed only to export labour. In the same year he proposed *détente* with what he saw would soon be an independent Black Africa, and an accommodation with an African petty bourgeoisie inside South Africa (*Inspan* December 1950). Thus, despite his solid Bond base and the heavy financial support Rembrandt gave to the NP, Rupert himself began to move beyond the Afrikaner nationalist pale in the 1950s. By 1960 Dr Verwoerd publicly ostracised him in the ranks of the faithful, and this company, initiated by the Bond, was regularly grouped together with Sanlam under the rubric of 'southern finance power'.

But the Bond connection was vitally important to the early development of Rembrandt. The company made great play of itself as an Afrikaans undertaking at the forefront of the struggle to place Afrikaners in controlling positions in industry and to attack the evils of monopoly. It contributed heavily to the HNP and ostentatiously sponsored a wide range of Afrikaans cultural groups and projects, all of which were incorporated in its advertising campaigns. To reinforce its Afrikaner image, at precisely the point when Rupert himself was elaborating increasingly heretical notions, none other than Dr P.J. Meyer was hired to head the company's publicity department in 1951. The nationalist stress is neatly encapsulated in one of Rembrandt's advertisements in the second Ekonomiese Volkskongres issue of *Inspan* (October 1950): 'Was it pure coincidence that the first Afrikaner cigarette factory came into being in Paarl where the First Afrikaner Language Movement began 75 years ago? Because every volk needs its *own* of those things which made a difference – its own language, its own culture, its own factories, its own success.'

This link between the manipulation of cultural symbols and nationalism on the one hand, and the rapid growth of the company on the other, is best shown in its labour policies, behind the slogan 'respect for labour'. Rembrandt's factory was the most mechanised of all South African cigarette producers. Its operations were much more capital intensive than those of its competitors. Thus, firstly, it had invested heavily in the productivity of labour. Its advertisements made much play of its 'progressive' employment practices. 'Rembrandt follows a deliberate policy of providing employment to white girls. One hundred and twenty girls are already in service, and with our constant expansion there are openings for many more. Air-conditioning units have been installed in the factory to make their working conditions more attractive and comfortable restrooms ensure healthy relaxation between working hours' (*Inspan* October 1950). Such material went down very well with the volk. A man could give himself cancer with Rembrandt, smug in the knowledge that it came from the highest quality cigarette, produced by an Afrikaner company, untouched by black hands, and that he was providing employment for *boeredogters* (daughters of the Boer volk).

This pretty picture hid the reality let slip in an earlier Rembrandt statement to shareholders:

> Rembrandt follows a policy of providing employment to white girls, and has *hereby succeeded in reducing labour costs to below the world average.* In contrast with Rembrandt's achievement, the Board of Trade and Industry has recently revealed that the tobacco manufacturing industry in South Africa is making increasing use of *non-white* labour and that *labour productivity has dropped in the last ten years* (*Volkshandel* May 1950; my italics).

The employment of *boeredogters* was indeed an attractive proposition. Their labour was extremely cheap, and Rembrandt's sophisticated production line simultaneously ensured a higher level of productivity with reduced labour costs. Rembrandt's workers were both more productive and lower paid than those of its competitors. The employment of *boeredogters*, moreover, virtually guaranteed a docile labour force as the full panoply of nationalist opinion could be mobilised against any attempts to organise Afrikaner women into trade unions. And finally, the employment of *boeredogters* enabled Rembrandt to portray itself as the benevolent employer and protector of the volk. 'Scientific management' and 'respect for labour' were indeed profitable principles.

The main impact of the *reddingsdaad* movement was felt in the two largest provinces, the Cape and the Transvaal. In the OFS, far from the major markets, industrial centres and ports, the emphasis fell mainly on local undertakings. The OFS was the home of Sasbank, formed by the Afrikaans teachers' union in 1922 with a capital of £300. Compared with Sanlam, Volkskas and Rembrandt, Sasbank was a small undertaking with a few branches scattered across the country, providing small loans. By 1950 its capital stood at £300,000 and its twenty-branch operation controlled a fund of £2m. The major significance of Sasbank is that it was used to finance the

Johannesburg garment factory, Veka, which later changed its name to Volkshemde. The OFS was also the home of the burial society AVBOB, which likewise had branches throughout the country. AVBOB centralised the small premiums of burial insurance, and operated a loan fund out of this. Yet it played an insignificant role in the financing of Afrikaner industry.

One other important OFS finance company was formed in 1943. This was the Afrikaanse Sake-Ondernemings Korporasie (the Afrikaans Business Undertakings Corporation, hereafter Asokor), with L.J. du Plessis as its chairman. Asokor was formed to finance the processing and storage of agricultural products. It drew investment directly from agricultural capital, and played a significant role in the concentration of such capital. By 1949, it controlled eight companies, dealing in meat marketing, property, agricultural journals, hides and skins, cold storage, bonemeal, and salt and meat packing. Its paid-up capital stood at £558,300, and its turnover exceeded £4 million (*Inspan* September 1950). While Asokor grew to be a relatively powerful company, unlike Sanlam, Volkskas and Rembrandt it did not become a major centre of political interests within nationalist politics.

CONCLUSION

In 1938/39 there had been in existence a total of 40 Afrikaner credit institutions, controlling funds to the value of £27m. Ten years later, an AHI survey indicated that the number of Afrikaner credit undertakings had risen to 68, whilst funds under their control had grown, to £74.4m. A breakdown of the various types of credit institution is indicated in Table 11(a).

Table 11(b) breaks these data down further to show the relative shares of (i) those companies founded before 1939, (ii) those founded from 1939 to 1945 and (iii) those founded after 1946. This table indicates that 83 per cent of the total funds of all Afrikaner finance companies in 1948/9 were controlled by undertakings formed before 1939. Sanlam and Volkskas accounted for the lion's share of this. Those undertakings set up in the prime years of the *reddingsdaad* movement, 1939 to 1945, controlled 13 per cent of total funds – that is, FVB, TIB, Saambou and Asokor. Those founded after 1946 controlled but 4 per cent, of which Bonuskor accounted for almost all.

In 1939, the collection of small Afrikaner financial undertakings had controlled funds to the value of £27m. This represented but 5 per cent of the total funds controlled by private financial institutions in South Africa. By 1949 the total funds controlled by Afrikaner financial institutions had more than doubled to £64.7m. M.S. Louw was indeed correct when he declared to the second Ekonomiese Volkskongres that the greatest achievement of 'the Afrikaner' as an entrepreneur in the 1940s was as the 'founder and controller of credit institutions' (*Inspan* November 1950). However, this impressive increase in total funds under control of Afrikaner companies represented a growth in the share of total funds controlled by financial institutions from 5 per cent to only 6.16 per cent (Table 12, p. 207).

Table 11(a). *Breakdown of Afrikaner credit institutions, 1948/9*

Type	Number	White	Non-white	Total	Administered funds (£m.)
		Number of employees			
Insurance	10	1,820	90	1,910	21.8
Banks	4	1,120	120	1,240	21.6
Boards of Executors	24	250	40	290	23.0
Finance and investment	20	80	20	100	5.5
Miscellaneous	10	70	15	85	3.5
TOTAL	68	3,340	285	3,625	74.4

Source: AHI Survey of Afrikaner Business 1938/9–1948/9 (hereafter, AHI Survey), (*Volkshandel* September 1950).

Table 11(b) *Breakdown of existing Afrikaner credit institutions in 1948/9 according to year of formation*

Period of formation	Number of institutions	White	Non-white	Total	Total funds administered £m
		Number of employees			
pre–1939	40	3,034	267	3,301	61.6
1939–45	20	281	18	299	9.6
1946–49	8	25	–	25	3.6
TOTAL in 1948/9	68	3,340	285	3,625	74.4

Source: AHI Survey (*Volkshandel* September 1950).

Thus, relative to the growth of the financial sector as a whole, the progress noted by Louw is less striking. Afrikaner companies had done little more than keep up. To emphasise the point, Louw made a further calculation. Of the £1,050m controlled by all the various financial institutions in South Africa, 'Afrikaners' had contributed £300m, or 29 per cent of the total. Yet Afrikaner financial institutions administered but £64.74m, or just over 6 per cent of total funds. In other words, only slightly more than 20 per cent of potential 'Afrikaner' capital had been placed in Afrikaner financial institutions (*Inspan* November 1950). This was a measure of both the relative success and failure of the *reddingsdaad* movement in mobilising the capital of the volk.

Louw's keynote address to the second Ekonomiese Volkskongres of October 1950 thus outlined a policy for the 1950s. The answer still lay in the centralisation of capital in financial institutions. But the experience of the 1940s had taught one crucial lesson: 'Almost without exception our new

Table 12.   *Share of Afrikaner companies in total funds controlled by various types of financial institution*

Type of institution	Total funds controlled (£m)	Funds controlled by Afrikaner companies (£m)	Percentage of total controlled by Afrikaner companies
(a) *Deposit receiving*			
(1) Commercial banks	355.0	17.75	5%
(2) Volk's banks	2.0	2.0	100%
(3) Other			
⎰ includes trust companies and ⎱			
⎱ saving banks ⎰	50.0	15.0	30%
(4) Building societies	243.0	2.43	1%
Sub-total for (a)	650.0	37.18	5.7%
(b) *Non-deposit receiving*	—	—	—
(5) Merchant banks	4.0	—	—
(6) Investment and finance			
companies	200.0	6.0	3%
(7) Insurance companies	196.0	21.56	11%
Sub-total for (b)	400.0	27.56	6.9%
GRAND TOTAL (a) + (b)	1,050.0	64.74	6.16%

Source: *Inspan* November 1950.

institutions can evolve only under the protection of an old, strong company, or with the support of the most influential organisation.' From this he drew a three-point programme. Firstly, the volk had to support and strengthen the existing Afrikaner credit institutions. Secondly, new institutions should be established where necessary, but only under the protection of existing ones. Thirdly, because only non-deposit-receiving institutions provided the requisite risk capital to increase Afrikaner penetration of industry and commerce, the overwhelming emphasis should be placed on the development of these particular kinds of financial institutions, but, above all, on insurance companies (*Volkshandel* November 1950). And if the cynical should remark that, as the managing director of Sanlam and Bonuskor and founder of FVB, Louw was in fact arguing that the Volkskongres should support his own established, non-deposit receiving credit institutions, this was the only way for the volk to save '*itself*'. What was good for Sanlam was good for the volk.

The *reddingsdaad* movement had been initiated through the collective endeavour of Sanlam and the Bond, with the latter extremely wary of the relative financial power of the former. Despite the impressive growth of such companies as Volkskas, Rembrandt and Asokor, Sanlam had been the prime beneficiary of the mobilisation of the volk to centralise money-capital in financial institutions. By the time of the second Ekonomiese Volkskongres, it had grown from a small life assurance company to a powerful financial group strongly represented in four of the seven sub-categories of financial institutions identified in Table 12. As such it dominated Afrikaner business.

This dominance is fairly easy to explain. In the Cape, the Sanlam group was able to draw on the rising profits of Cape farmers, whose base of accumulation expanded rapidly during these years. Moreover, unlike the operations of the north, which were primarily local undertakings, all five of the major companies in the orbit of Sanlam (Sanlam itself, Santam, FVB, Saambou and Bonuskor) were nationally-based operations. Each was centralising the loose money in society in different ways, drawing on a different source of capital. Santam was the major beneficiary of trusts and short-term assurance. It provided credit to agriculture in the form of interest-bearing capital. Sanlam itself had been established as the life assurance company of the 'nationally-minded' volk, and drew on the revenue of all groups, together with the latent money-capital of agriculture for its funds. FVB was the officially-sanctioned investment company into which the volk were constantly urged to place their investment capital. In effect its funds came from the latent money-capital of agriculture. Saambou drew particularly on the small savings of Afrikaner workers and petty bourgeoisie. Finally Bonuskor ingeniously expedited the process of hoarding in assurance and converted such idle money into productive capital, thereby escaping the various forms of restrictions on the investments of such a hoard. Thus in all sectors of the economic life of the volk, and in all regions, one or other member of the Sanlam group stood ready to gather together loose cash, small savings, revenue, and latent money-capital. It lacked only a bank. No other Afrikaner company came near to achieving such an extensive network. Volkskas was the only other undertaking operating on a national basis, and its role in the centralisation of money-capital was limited to the operations of a medium-size commercial bank. Thus the Sanlam group not only cornered the local market of the Cape, but was the major beneficiary of the centralising policies of the *reddingsdaad* movement at a national level. Money which might have gone into small local undertakings went to Sanlam. The growing hostility to 'Southern Financial-Power' (*Suidelike Geldmag*) from the northern petty bourgeoisie was a product of precisely this.

This Sanlam dominance was further enshrined at the second Ekonomiese Volkskongres when Louw, the man whom *Volkshandel* termed 'the father of our business life and financier of the Afrikaner volk' (September 1950), donned his well-known hat as the theoretician and strategist of the *reddingsdaad* movement and told the volk in so many words that it should devote itself to the further consolidation of the Sanlam group. The 1950s were to see a growing reaction within the NP from small traders, urban petty bourgeoisie, farmers and politicians of the north against this southern financial power they had helped consolidate.

208

14

Manufacturing and commercial capital

Through the centralisation of money-capital in financial institutions the *reddingsdaad* movement aimed to increase tenfold the number of Afrikaner industrial and commercial capitalists. Some of the advances into industry and commerce by investment companies were discussed above. This chapter sketches an overview of Afrikaner penetration into manufacturing and commerce.

MANUFACTURING

In purely statistical terms, Afrikaner manufacturing grew rapidly during the 1940s. The total number of Afrikaner-controlled manufacturing concerns almost trebled (from 1,239 to 3,385), whilst their turnover increased from £6m to £43m. The share of Afrikaner-owned manufacturing establishments in the total turnover of the manufacturing sector doubled from 3 per cent to 6 per cent (Table 2, p. 182 above). Table 13 breaks down the types of Afrikaner manufacturing undertaking operating in 1948/9. A clearer picture of the growth of Afrikaner manufacturing emerges by breaking down the total number of such establishments operating in 1948/9 according to their year of formation (Table 14).

Two-thirds of Afrikaner manufacturing establishments operating in 1948/9 were set up after the 1939 Ekonomiese Volkskongres, and more than half of these only began operations after the end of the war. Whilst establishments founded before the Volkskongres accounted for 36 per cent of the total number of Afrikaner manufacturing undertakings, and 56 per cent of their turnover, the most rapid growth occurred in types of undertaking established mainly after 1939, that is, fishing and fish products, fruit-processing, tobacco-processing, beverages, furniture, clothing and engineering.

This statistical evidence of apparently dramatic growth obscures the two most notable features of Afrikaner-controlled manufacturing concerns during this period – firstly, the petty character of most undertakings, and, secondly, the very close links with agriculture. Of the types of establishment listed in Table 13, categories 9 to 12 and 19 comprised almost half of the total

Table 13. *Afrikaner manufacturing establishments, 1948/9*

Type	Number	Number of employees				Turnover	
		White	Non-white	Total	Average per establishment	Total (£1,000)	Average per establishment (£1,000)
(1) Stone, cement and reclamation works	30	230	970	1,200	30	400	13.3
(2) Stone masons	40	140	1,740	1,880	47	400	10.3
(3) Building	980	4,020	9,020	13,040	13	10,700	10.9
(4) Printing works	105	440	790	1,230	11	1,300	12.4
(5) Furniture	70	660	500	1,160	16	1,000	14.3
(6) Printers	80	1,630	390	2,020	25	2,700	33.8
(7) Engineering and welding works	120	810	1,000	1,810	15	2,350	19.6
(8) Garment factories	25	430	140	570	22	950	38.0
(9) Tailoring	300	610	160	770	3	650	2.2
(10) Garage/repair shops	580	1,200	900	2,100	4	850	1.5
(11) Blacksmith and shoemaker	330	600	670	1,270	4	450	1.4
(12) Cobblers	270	440	610	1,050	4	470	1.7
(13) Preserved and dried fruit	15	490	3,760	4,250	283	2,900	193.3
(14) Meat and preserved meat	5	200	640	840	168	1,900	380.0
(15) Butter, cheese, ice-cream	25	530	730	1,260	50	1,700	68.0
(16) Milling	220	890	2,400	3,290	15	8,700	39.5
(17) Beverages	20	260	680	940	47	3,200	160.0
(18) Miscellaneous food products	50	430	950	1,380	28	2,100	42.0
(19) Miscellaneous	120	440	430	870	7	900	7.5
(20) TOTAL	3,385	14,450	26,480	40,930	12	43,620	12.9

Source: AHI Survey, *Volkshandel* September 1950.

Table 14. *Breakdown of Afrikaner manufacturing establishments operating in 1948/9, according to year of formation*

Year of formation	Number of under-takings	Number of employees			Turnover (£m.)
		White	Non-white	Total	
(a) Pre–1939	1,239	7,061	12,564	19,716	24.3
(b) 1939–1945	971	4,311	9,188	13,508	12.8
(c) 1946–1949	1,175	3,078	4,628	7,706	6.5
TOTAL	3,385	14,450	26,480	40,930	43.6

Source: Calculated from data in AHI Survey, *Volkshandel* September 1950.

number of undertakings. Yet each employed on average seven or fewer employees. Collectively, the 1,600 such establishments accounted for just over 7 per cent of the total turnover of Afrikaner manufacturing. The enterprises in these five categories were manufacturing establishments in the true sense of the word – that is, commodities were produced by independent artisans employing a few assistants. The average annual turnover of all Afrikaner manufacturing establishments in 1948/9 amounted to a derisory £12,900, and these establishments employed on average a mere twelve persons each. Afrikaner-controlled manufacturing enterprises made up 25 per cent of the total number of manufacturing undertakings in South Africa, yet accounted for but 6 per cent of total product.

The extremely underdeveloped and petty character of most Afrikaner manufacturing undertakings is starkly shown in the forms of ownership of these concerns (Table 15). A number of salient points emerge from this table. The first is the numerical preponderance of one-man enterprises. These made up over 80 per cent of all Afrikaner manufacturing concerns, employed just over half their labour force, and averaged an annual turnover of £5,500. While no figures are available, the capitalisation of such single-owner undertakings must have been very low. Public companies on the other hand accounted for less than 3 per cent of the total number of Afrikaner manufacturing establishments, and employed 12 per cent of its labour force. Their average annual turnover was £110,000. But perhaps the most striking feature is the average size of cooperative turnover. Cooperatives comprised less than 1.5 per cent of all Afrikaner-controlled manufacturing establishments. Yet they employed 15 per cent of the labour force and accounted for nearly 28 per cent of the total turnover of Afrikaner manufacturing concerns, averaging almost £250,000 per undertaking. These cooperatives were exclusively engaged in the processing of agricultural produce.

The link between Afrikaner manufacturing and agriculture can be shown in a number of other ways. Almost 80 per cent of all Afrikaner-controlled manufacturing concerns were located not in the centres of industrial

Table 15. *Forms of ownership of Afrikaner manufacturing concerns, 1948/9*

| Form of ownership | Number of enterprises | Number of employees | | | Turnover | |
		White	Non-white	Total	Total £m	As a percentage of total
One-man enterprises	2,872	7,869	13,086	20,955	15,828	36.3
Partnership	263	1,067	2,032	3,099	2,589	5.9
Private companies	167	1,739	3,675	5,414	4,312	9.9
Public companies	79	2,393	2,851	5,244	8,837	20.3
Cooperatives	50	1,382	4,836	6,218	12,064	27.6
TOTAL	3,385	14,450	26,480	40,930	43,620	100.0

Source: Calculated from AHI survey, *Volkshandel* September 1950.

production, but in the rural areas. Such rural undertakings accounted for 80 per cent of the total turnover of Afrikaner manufacturing (*Volkshandel* September 1950). Moreover, the 335 undertakings listed in categories 13 to 18 of Table 13 were all processing agricultural produce. These establishments accounted for 47 per cent of the total turnover of all Afrikaner manufacturing. Finally, much of the capital of the few public companies had been garnered through the centralisation of latent money-capital in agriculture. Such public companies accounted for 20 per cent of the turnover of Afrikaner manufacturing. Thus, considered from every point of view, Afrikaner 'manufacturing' was inextricably linked with the turnover cycle of agricultural capital.

The years under review saw a spurt of industrialisation in South Africa which significantly shifted the emphasis of production. Even before the war, the industrial group consisting of metal products, machinery and transport equipment by-passed food and beverages to emerge as the largest single group in the manufacturing sector. By 1950, it accounted for 30.3 per cent of total manufacturing output. Moreover, the growth of industrial production during the war occurred on an increasingly capital-intensive basis. As a crude index of the rising mechanisation of industrial production, the capital to labour ratio of total private manufacturing rose from £981 per worker in 1939 to £1,156 in 1946, reaching £1,327 per worker in 1950 (US 1960: G–8). These changes were particularly evident in the engineering sector. The still minor engineering investments of FVB apart, Afrikaner manufacturers were totally absent from the engineering, metal products, machinery and transport equipment group of industries, which had shown the most rapid growth during the war. Contrary to the general tendency of industrial investment, food and beverages accounted for 47 per cent of total Afrikaner manufacturing output. Moreover, it is safe to conclude that, with the sole exceptions of Marine Products' processing plant and Rembrandt's cigarette factory, even the very few Afrikaner manufacturing enterprises which transcended the bounds of petty commodity production operated with a technical and organic composition of capital lower than the average in each branch of industry.[1] Their competitive position was thus extremely weak.

The most significant Afrikaner inroads into manufacturing were in two limited areas: the processing of agricultural produce almost exclusively under cooperatives, and selective share investments of the various finance companies under Sanlam's control. Again, these were made possible through the centralisation of latent money-capital generated in agriculture. In no sense did an independent 'Afrikaner' industrial capital emerge in the first decade of the *reddingsdaad* movement. The major expressed goal of the Ekonomiese Volkskongres, to elevate 'the Afrikaner' to 'this legitimate [i.e. dominant] place' in the industrial sector, was far from fulfilment.

With the rapid inflow of foreign capital into manufacturing after the war, the transition from competitive to monopoly conditions in South African industry was well under way. As this process accelerated in the 1950s and 1960s, the petty-commodity undertakings comprising the bulk of Afrikaner-owned manufacturing concerns would be largely wiped out. The relatively under-capitalised establishments, which made up the bulk of the remainder, would lead a precarious, uncompetitive existence. With very few exceptions, the real Afrikaner advances in industry would occur through the investments of the finance companies, again with the Sanlam group in the vanguard.

COMMERCE

The growth of Afrikaner commercial concerns during the 1940s was dramatic. The number of Afrikaner-owned commercial establishments increased four-fold (Table 2, p. 182 above). Their total turnover rose by 700 per cent, as their share of the total market jumped from 8 per cent in 1938/9 to 25 per cent in 1948/9. By 1949 Afrikaners held a greater share of total turnover in commerce than in any other sector except agriculture. Table 16 breaks down Afrikaner commercial establishments according to year of formation, and Table 17 lists the fields in which Afrikaner traders operated.

Of all Afrikaner-owned commercial concerns operating in 1949, 75 per cent had been established since the Ekonomiese Volkskongres, although these only accounted for 41 per cent of the turnover of all Afrikaner-owned commercial concerns. While these statistics offer prima facie evidence of striking progress, considered solely on their own such totals and percentages convey but part of the picture and conceal the limits to the growth of Afrikaner commerce. Afrikaner commerce exhibited many of the features remarked upon in the examination of Afrikaner-controlled manufacturing above. The first is the overwhelmingly petty character of these concerns. Of the types of establishment listed in Table 17, categories 1 to 24 made up 96.6 per cent of the total. Together they accounted for but 53 per cent of the total turnover of Afrikaner commercial undertakings, turning over a paltry average of £1,700 per

213

Table 16. *Breakdown of Afrikaner commercial establishments operating in 1948/9 according to year of formation*

Year of formation	Number of undertakings	Number of employees			Turnover (£m.)
		White	Non-white	Total	
(a) Pre-1939	2,428	14,468	17,781	32,255	121.5
(b) 1939–1945	3,078	10,606	8,877	19,483	43.9
(c) 1946–1949	4,079	12,426	9,516	21,942	38.3
TOTAL	9,585	37,500	36,180	73.680	203.7

Source: AHI survey, *Volkshandel* September 1950.

employee per annum. Categories 25 to 28 on the other hand comprised but 3.4 per cent of all such concerns. Yet they accounted for 47 per cent of their total turnover and averaged an annual turnover per employee of £7,350.

Of all Afrikaner-owned commercial concerns, 87 per cent were either one-man enterprises or partnerships. Together they controlled but 44.2 per cent of the turnover of Afrikaner commerce, averaging an annual turnover per employee of only £1,790. Private and public companies, together with cooperatives, on the other hand, accounted for 13 per cent of Afrikaner commercial concerns, but 55.8 per cent of their turnover, averaging an annual turnover per employee of £4,856 (Table 18).

The most striking feature of Tables 17 and 18 is one also noted with respect to Afrikaner manufacturing, that is, the disproportionate share of the relatively few cooperatives. Utilising the more detailed figures given in Table 17, it is seen that cooperatives made up less than 3 per cent of all Afrikaner commercial establishments, but employed 16 per cent of their labour force and accounted for two-fifths of its total turnover.

The Ekonomiese Volkskongres had sought to coordinate Afrikaner consumer buying power to increase Afrikaner control of commercial life. Viewed simply in terms of the rise in the share of Afrikaner traders in total commercial turnover from 8 per cent to 25 per cent between 1938/9 and 1948/9, the *reddingsdaad* movement appears to have been relatively successful in this field. Yet, analysed in terms of actual developments within commerce, it failed miserably, as was acknowledged at the second Ekonomiese Volkskongres. By 1948, the AHI's wholesale company had gone bankrupt, together with the only other Afrikaner-owned wholesale undertaking, Kopersbond. The consumer cooperatives of which so much had been expected were dreary failures. The only real advance was a large increase in local, petty undertakings. Almost 80 per cent of Afrikaner commercial concerns operating in 1948/9 were located in the rural areas (*Volkshandel* September 1950). Only two Afrikaner-owned commercial undertakings operated on anything other than a local scale – the Bond-founded and controlled Uniewinkels, and

Table 17. *Afrikaner trading and service establishments, 1948/9*

(i)	(ii)	(iii)	(iv)	(v)	(vi)	(vii)	(viii)	(ix)	(x)
Type	Total	As a percentage of grand total	White	Non-white	Total	Average number per establishment	Total (£1,000)	Average per establishment (£1,000)	As percentage of grand total
		Numbers	Number of employees				Turnover		
(A) *Retail (private)*									
(1) General dealers	3,330	34.7	11,300	8,020	19,320	5.9	45,100	13.5	22.1
(2) Fruit and vegetable	260	2.7	530	500	1,030	4.0	1,100	4.2	0.5
(3) Agricultural implements	140	1.5	400	260	660	4.7	1,100	7.8	0.5
(4) Building materials	20	0.2	140	140	280	14.0	600	30.0	0.3
(5) Outfitters	310	3.2	1,050	300	1,350	4.4	2,800	9.0	1.4
(6) Furniture dealers	160	1.7	670	500	1,170	7.3	3,600	22.5	1.8
(7) Liquor dealers	60	0.6	150	169	319	5.3	550	9.1	0.3
(8) Butchers	780	8.1	2,250	2,900	5,150	6.6	9,900	10.2	4.8
(9) Nurseries	30	0.3	130	370	500	16.6	200	6.6	0.1
(10) Garages	1,070	11.2	5,540	4,650	10,190	9.5	22,100	20.6	10.8
(11) Shoeshops	15	0.2	70	30	100	6.6	200	10.2	0.1
(12) Pharmacies	110	1.1	380	200	580	5.3	1,100	10.0	0.5
(13) Dairies	300	3.1	750	2,200	2,950	9.8	2,700	9.0	1.9
(14) Booksellers	60	0.6	540	180	720	12.0	1,500	25.0	0.7
(15) Groceries and miscellaneous	265	2.8	1,100	871	1,971	7.4	4,250	16.0	2.0
SUB-TOTAL	6,910	72.0	25,000	21,290	46,290	6.7	96,800	14.0	47.5

Table 17. (Cont.)

(i) Type	Numbers		Number of employees				Turnover		
	Total	As a percentage of grand total	White	Non-white	Total	Average number per establishment	Total (£1,000)	Average per establishment (£1,000)	As percentage of grand total
	(ii)	(iii)	(iv)	(v)	(vi)	(vii)	(viii)	(ix)	(x)
(B) Service establishments									
(16) Cafes and tea rooms	620	6.5	2,020	1,660	3,370	5.9	3,800	6.1	1.9
(17) Hotels	110	1.1	520	1,210	1,730	15.7	2,200	20.0	1.1
(18) Transport contractors	450	4.7	1,120	2,660	3,780	8.4	1,500	3.3	0.7
(19) Photographers	50	0.5	110	30	140	2.8	100	2.0	0.05
(20) Taxis	670	7.0	1,540	260	1,800	2.7	1,000	1.5	0.5
(21) Estate agents	170	1.8	510	130	640	3.7	1,100	6.5	0.5
(22) Auctioneers	90	0.9	920	480	1,400	15.6	1,000	9.9	0.5
(23) Undertakers	150	1.6	400	300	700	4.7	700	4.6	0.4
(24) Miscellaneous	40	0.4	310	310	620	15.5	500	12.5	0.2
SUB-TOTAL	2,350	25.0	745	7,030	14,480	6.1	11,900	5.1	5.8
(C) Private wholesalers									
(25) TOTAL	50	0.5	480	620	1,100	22.1	13,900	278.0	6.8
(D) Co-operatives									
(26) Agricultural products	100	1.1	2,360	6,060	8,420	76.5	64,900	590.0	31.9
(27) Agricultural supplies	60	0.6	890	510	1,400	23.3	10,000	166.6	4.9
(28) Consumer cooperatives	105	1.0	1,320	670	1,990	18.9	6,200	59.0	3.0
SUB-TOTAL	275	2.7	4,570	7,240	11,810	42.9	81,100	294.9	39.8
GRAND TOTAL	9,585	100.0	37,500	36,180	73,680	7.6	203,700	21.3	100.0

Source: AHI survey, *Volkshandel* September 1950.

Table 18. *Forms of ownership of Afrikaner commercial establishments, 1948/9*

Forms of ownership	Number of enterprises	Number of employees			Turnover	
		White	Non-white	Total	Total (£m.)	As a percentage of total
One-man enterprises	7,143	21,768	19,295	41,063	64,831	31.8
Partnership	1,191	4,989	4,215	9,204	25,157	12.4
Private companies	671	3,872	3,685	7,557	18,346	9.0
Public companies	300	2.301	1,745	4,046	19,278	9.5
Cooperatives	280	4,570	7,240	11,810	76,088	37.3
TOTAL	9,585	37,500	36,180	73,680	203,700	100.0

Source: AHI survey, *Volkshandel* September 1950.

the OFS-based Sonop company. During the war, both relinquished their initial cooperative form, to emerge as public companies. Yet they failed to develop into general chain stores and remained dependent on an almost exclusively Afrikaner clientele. The managing director of Uniewinkels brutally summed up the development of Afrikaner commerce in the 1940s when he reported to the second Ekonomiese Volkskongres that the small successes registered were mainly the result of Afrikaner traders displacing Indian traders in the Transvaal (*Volkshandel* September 1950). Here at least the racist campaigns discussed in chapter 12 had great effect.

There are a number of reasons for this poor progress. Wartime restrictions on the allocation of supplies favoured existing dealers. Throughout this period Afrikaner traders faced severe problems of acquiring stock with which to trade. The formation of VVM (p. 146 above) only slightly eased this situation. But, most importantly, the rapid restructuring of commercial capital in the 1940s placed small, rural traders at a distinct competitive disadvantage. Large chain-store operations, such as the OK Bazaars, were beginning to tighten their hold on the retail trade. The 1952 Census of Distribution and Service Industries showed that chain-store operations were the prime area of growth in commerce – their turnover rose by 56 per cent between 1946 and 1951, compared with 35 per cent for general trading (Potgieter 1954:102). At the end of the war, these chain-store groups began expanding out of the cities to establish stores in rural towns. Small, rural traders were unable to compete. The threat posed to the small rural trader was further exacerbated by the rapidly falling rate of profit in retailing. The Census of Distribution and Service Industries estimated that net profit in the retail trade fell from 10.0 per cent of turnover in 1946/7 to 7.8 per cent in 1952. Turnover per employee declined by 3 per cent and the rate of annual turnover had dropped from 6 to 5 (*Volkshandel* January 1955). This reinforced the trend to monopoly in the form of chain-stores, further weakening the position of the small trader.

Despite the fourfold increase in Afrikaner commercial undertakings in the 1940s, the majority of such establishments remained small, local undertakings. Throughout the 1940s changing conditions in the retail trade undermined the basis of their profitable operation. By the second Ekonomiese Volkskongres in October 1950, the vast majority of Afrikaner traders were in an increasingly precarious position, greatly threatened by encroaching monopolies. In the following years the local *sakekamers* in which these local undertakings were organised, constantly reiterated two themes – persistent attacks on Indian traders, and demands for strong state action against commercial monopolies. The 1950 Group Areas Act forbade Indian traders to do business in what were classified as 'white areas', so accelerating the process whereby Afrikaner traders replaced their Indian competitors. But the large chain-stores and their spreading network of supermarkets presented an immovable barrier. A Monopolies Bill was enacted in 1954; northern Nationalist MPs deplored its lack of teeth. During the 1950s the hold of the large retail groups on rural trade grew ever stronger, and the pressures on small dealers intensified.

The effects of this limited progress in the commercial field and the increasing pressures placed on rural traders by penetration of monopolies were again felt predominantly in the northern provinces. A fairly large class of small Afrikaner traders had emerged, but under conditions which increasingly frustrated them. It seemed as if the *reddingsdaad* movement could, or would, do little to assist. The RDB had stopped loans to small undertakings. Kleinsake Finansierings which was set up to finance such local undertakings, had gone bankrupt. FVB and Bonuskor both refused to countenance assistance to small operations. The second Ekonomiese Volkskongres officially decreed that a strategy of accumulation based on small undertakings was doomed. Led by the managing director of Sanlam and Bonuskor, all the major theoreticians declared that now the volk would have to reserve its assistance exclusively for well-established, large institutions, and in particular those which centralised capital for investment. This points particularly to the Sanlam group. In the commercial field, no such large-scale Afrikaner undertakings existed. The second Ekonomiese Volkskongres made it very clear that no capital would be forthcoming to help develop existing small undertakings. Large-scale Afrikaner commercial undertakings could now only be established on the initiative of, and under the supervision and control of, the investment companies dominated by Sanlam. To many rural traders it seemed as if their interests had been sacrificed on the altar of those of Sanlam.

Small rural traders were the driving force behind the formation of the AHI. A mere two years after its founding, fears were expressed about the domination by 'large groups' (p. 144 above). With the rapid growth of the Sanlam group in the 1950s, the intensely anti-monopoly petty bourgeois elements in the north grew increasingly restive about domination by this financial giant. (The Rembrandt group was frequently included in the constant mutterings against 'southern finance power'.) The differences between the two groups boiled down to different interpretations of the interests of the 'volk'. Each argued that in some special way it personified the economic struggles of 'the Afrikaner'. Sanlam could claim the official sponsorship of the *reddingsdaad* movement and point to its successful penetration of industry and finance. To this, the small northern traders retorted that it was the small group of financial capitalists rather than the volk as a whole which had benefited from the growth of Sanlam, and, moreover, resources needed to develop small undertakings had been diverted away from them. To the small traders, the success of the economic struggle was not to be measured in the growth of a few financial giants, but in the advancement of 'the small man' (*Volkshandel* October 1964). This was increasingly blocked, and the larger companies were doing nothing about it. With the growing differentiation of urban Afrikaners, and particularly with the emergence of two distinct classes out of the economic movement – a small group of financial capitalists and a large, restive, petty bourgeoisie – strong differences over the meaning of the economic movement and what constituted the interests of 'the volk' grew more acute. This was to find its reflection in the nationalist politics of the 1950s and 1960s.

CONCLUSION

The organised economic movement of the 1940s both registered successes and ran up against severe barriers to further growth. The number of Afrikaner-controlled businesses in South Africa had increased almost fourfold, and their turnover had risen by over fivefold. The share of these undertakings in the turnover of all sectors of South African business (except agriculture) more than doubled, from 5 per cent of the total in 1938/9 to 11 per cent in 1948/9 (Table 2, p. 182 above). In all sectors of the economy, except mining, there had been striking advances.

The *reddingsdaad* movement sought to mobilise three 'powers' of the volk: savings-power, labour-power, and buying-power. The first involved the centralisation of all forms of loose money in financial institutions. This was the area of the greatest success of the *reddingsdaad* movement, giving rise to a small number of relatively powerful finance companies with growing interests in industry. By the second Ekonomiese Volkskongres in 1950, a small class of Afrikaner financial capitalists had emerged, based mainly in the Cape. In the narrow world of Afrikaner business, they exercised enormous power, often giving rise to hostility and resentment from the smaller operators. However, in the years immediately following the Second World War, the retardation of capital accumulation in agriculture began to hold back the growth of Afrikaner finance. After 1948, these problems were resolved by the NP government in two ways. Firstly, its labour and pricing policies again ensured favourable conditions for accumulation in all sectors, and particularly agriculture, and so directly benefited the finance companies. Secondly the funds and account of government bodies and local authorities began to be transferred to Afrikaner institutions, providing an enormous influx of new capital.

With respect to the mobilisation of Afrikaner labour-power, the achievements of the *reddingsdaad* movement must again be seen from two perspectives. By 1948/9 Afrikaner manufacturing undertakings employed 14,450 white workers, or but 9 per cent of the total employed in private manufacturing. White workers comprised a slightly, but not dramatically, higher percentage of the workforce in Afrikaner-owned manufacturing establishments than in all private manufacturing – 35 per cent as opposed to 29 per cent (US 1960: G-10, G-11). The real success of the *reddingsdaad* movement in mobilising Afrikaner labour-power lay, secondly, in the ideological and political incorporation of the bulk of Afrikaner workers into a nationalist class alliance. The operations of the various Christian-national labour bodies, and above all, the wide-ranging social, cultural and ideological activities of the RDB, had finally weaned many Afrikaner workers from class ideologies. The specific material interests of white workers were now cast exclusively in racist and ethnic form, and so, finally, the political power of the independent political organisations of white workers was destroyed.

Finally, the buying-power of Afrikaans-speakers had been harnessed to some extent, so that by 1948/9 Afrikaner traders accounted for 25 per cent of total turnover in the commercial sector. But these quantitative gains were not matched by qualitative ones. It was at the expense of other (Indian) petty traders that an Afrikaner petty trading class was created, under conditions which led to rising expectations on the one hand, and left it ever more frustrated in a steadily worsening competitive position on the other.

The relative achievement of the *reddingsdaad* movement can be measured in other ways. Its major aim was to place Afrikaners in 'their legitimate place' in the economy. Apart from creating a class of industrial and commercial capitalists, this clearly involved the integration of Afrikaans-speakers into all levels of the urban occupational structure. By 1936, 48 per cent of Afrikaners lived in the urban areas. This rose to 60 per cent in 1946, reaching 69 per cent in 1951 (US 1960: A-18). Relative to other whites, Afrikaners still occupied less favourable positions within the urban economy. However, there had been striking improvements in a number of areas (Table 19). The 294 per cent increase in the number of factory operatives indicates how the extremely rapid growth of industrial employment during the war years finally put an end to the 'poor white' problem. As the 350 per cent increase in the number of Afrikaner fitters shows, Afrikaans-speakers were now moving into skilled positions in industry which, prior to the war, the craft unions had largely closed to them. The very rapid increase in the number of Afrikaners in the entrepreneurial, managerial, professional and trading categories certainly reflects the development of the economic movement during this period. Similarly, the growth in

Table 19. *Relative position of Afrikaner to 'other-white' males in certain urban occupations, 1939–1948*

Occupational category	Afrikaners as a percentage of white males in each category		Percentage increase in those classified in each category	
	1939	1948	Afrikaners	Other whites
(i)	(ii)	(iii)	(iv)	(v)
(1) Directors, manufacturers, etc.	3	5	295	98
(2) Professional	9	15	117	21
(3) Managerial	8	15	208	8
(4) Traders	4	10	212	44
(5) Clerical	19	32	154	29
(6) Teachers	49	61	68	5
(7) Civil servants	43	54	41	− 10
(8) Fitters	8	21	350	52
(9) Carpenters	31	46	88	− 2
(10) Factory operatives	50	63	294	134
(11) Mine workers	69	79	16	− 29
(12) Unskilled workers	82	86	7	− 23

Source: *Volkshandel* November 1950.

the number of Afrikaner clerks and teachers highlights a new social mobility, absent before the 1940s.

Considered in its very broadest terms as a response to the development of capitalism in South Africa, the economic movement was itself a vital moment in effecting the transition from a rural to an urban economy for the vast majority of Afrikaners. One of its greatest achievements was the reconciliation of most Afrikaners to the new demands of urban capitalism. Farmers had been taught new investment patterns, workers had been disciplined for capitalist exploitation, the petty bourgeoisie were trained in commercial skills. Out of the real but limited successes of the *reddingsdaad* movement in the 1940s emerged two major class forces. On the one hand was a growing band of self-confident, innovating, financial capitalists. Standing at the helm of the economic movement and grouped predominantly, though not exclusively, around Sanlam in the Cape, they regarded themselves as the best arbiters of what was good for the volk in the economic movement. On the other hand, largely in the northern provinces, had developed a large, politically aggressive, trading petty bourgeoisie. Increasingly pressured by encroaching monopoly, this petty bourgeoisie grew ever more mistrustful of the directions which the financial capitalists were taking, and competed with them for the ideological direction of the Afrikaner volk.

Part V

Afrikaner nationalism triumphant

15

The coming to power of the Herenigde Nationalist Party

The tenth South African general elections were held on 26 May 1948. Led by ageing Prime Minister Smuts, the UP, together with its Labour Party and Dominion Party allies, went into the elections with a comfortable parliamentary majority of over fifty. It confronted an electoral alliance between the HNP and the AP. The general prediction held that the UP government would be returned to power, perhaps with a reduced majority. Certainly the nationalist coalition expected to pick up several seats, but was pinning its hopes on the elections after 1948 (B. Schoeman, *The Star* 28/5/48). The election results were a rude shock to all such expectations. The nationalist coalition won a tenuous five-seat parliamentary majority on a minority of all votes cast. At the age of seventy-four, Dr D.F. Malan became the country's fourth Prime Minister since Union.

It is of course easy to scoff at Malan's jubilant claim that this upset was evident proof of God's role as the independent variable in South African history and the protector of His chosen volk (*Rand Daily Mail* 2/6/48). Tyriakian's assessment (1960:691), that the 'political slogan' of apartheid won the elections, represents a more widely held view. Yet the literature on Afrikaner nationalism has not been able to explain 1948 without running in explanatory circles as closed as that of Malan's. For Moodie (1975: chapter 12), this was the triumph of *volkseenheid* and the civil religion of Afrikanerdom. Afrikaner 'ethnicity' and developments purely internal to Afrikaner nationalism are advanced to explain the nationalist victory. Stultz (1974: chapter 8) argues that 'traditional' ethnic political alignments, last manifest in 1929, had now been restored – as if nothing had changed in South Africa or Afrikaner nationalism in the intervening years. Much of the literature echoes these themes. Nor, I would argue, can the electoral victory of the HNP be explained as caprice on the part of that wilful, unpredictable creature which bobs and weaves its way through bourgeois psephology – the floating voter (Heard 1974: chapter 3). The changes registered in the 1948 election were not those of the minds of a few thousand perennially uncommitted voters, but rather the balance of forces in the state and the party political representation and organisation of specific class forces. These led to a reorganisation of the capitalist state.

The results reveal a decisive shift in patterns of electoral support from two groups. Firstly, Transvaal farmers deserted the UP *en masse*. Whereas in 1943 the UP captured 15 of 23 Transvaal rural constitutuencies, in 1948 it was wiped out in these rural areas, where the nationalist coalition won all seats. Secondly, there were large-scale defections from the Labour and United Parties by specific strata of white labour, particularly miners and workers in the state-owned steel industry in Pretoria. For the first time ever, the HNP captured 8 constituencies in the mining and industrial centres of the Witwatersrand, and a further 5 working-class and lower-middle-class areas of Pretoria.

Thus, by 1948, the HNP had organised and mobilised a new alliance of class forces, finally building a base amongst Transvaal farmers and Afrikaner workers. The party had sought to organise such an alliance ever since fusion in 1934. Its success by 1948 in the face of so many previous failures cannot be explained simply by internal developments in Afrikaner nationalist organisation and ideology. Nor does it lie in the sudden appeal of the apartheid slogan. Ever since 1934, the HNP had advocated rigid segregationist policies. It still remains to be explained why these should attract support, particularly from Transvaal farmers, where they had not done so previously. Thus, an explanation of 1948 must situate the internal development of Afrikaner nationalist organisation and ideology within a conjunctural analysis of the pattern of capitalist accumulation and class struggle in the 1940s – an analysis which examines the balance of forces, and the specific places, interests, struggles and forms of organisation and ideology of these class forces in this accumulation process.

CAPITAL ACCUMULATION AND CLASS STRUGGLE IN THE 1940s

The South African economy grew very rapidly during the years under review. Gross National Income rose from £395.6m in 1939 to £666.8m in 1946, reaching £850.5m by 1948. Profound changes in the structure of capitalist production occurred at a number of levels. An almost total dependence on mineral and agricultural exports rapidly gave way to relatively high levels of industrialisation. The contribution of private manufacturing to National Income first surpassed that of agriculture in 1930 and outstripped mining in 1943 to account for almost a quarter of National Income by 1950 (US 1960: S-3). A substantial and strategic state-owned industrial sector developed, concentrated in the steel, chemical and infrastructure industries.

Industrial production was restructured on the basis of increasing mechanisation and a tendency towards larger production units. The emphasis of industrial production moved away from wage goods towards engineering, metal products and transport equipment. The steadily rising technical and organic composition of industrial capital during this period (p. 212 above) led to a rapid transformation of the division of labour within manufacturing as the artisan/unskilled hierarchy was displaced by semi-skilled operatives working machines. The result was a relative reduction of labour costs as growing numbers of African workers were drawn into semi-skilled operative positions at wage rates considerably lower than those paid to skilled white labour. This process of 'rationalisation' and mechanisation of industry on the basis of low-paid African labour was actively encouraged by the state (AIRC 1941: paras. 160–91, BTI 1945:42–6).

The expanded accumulation of industrial capital was made possible by the large-scale influx of African labour from the countryside to the cities. Between 1940 and 1946, a further 134,000 Africans entered industrial employment. The ratio of African workers employed in private manufacturing to those engaged in the mines rose from 87:316 in 1932, 187:348 in 1939 to 321:328 in 1946. This flow of labour to the cities was the result of profound transformations wrought by the rapid dissolution of pre-capitalist relations of production in the rural areas. A number of aspects of this process should be noted here.

The development of first mining, then agricultural, and later industrial capitalism in South Africa prior to 1940 took place on the basis of a cheap, migratory labour force. The ideology of South African capitalism held that migrant workers all had access to land in the reserves, on which they could produce most of their subsistence needs. Wages could therefore be pegged at very low levels. This system of cheap migratory labour was thus premised on the maintenance of limited access to land by migrant workers. Yet this was breaking down as early as the 1920s. By the end of the war, for migrant workers 'Reserve production [was] but a myth' (WMNWC 1944: paras. 201–3). As numerous government commissions and reports noted, the overcrowded, eroded and worked-out land in the so-called Native Reserves no longer provided the basis for the reproduction of a migratory male labour force. Landlessness was acute. Even for those with land, so small were the holdings and so meagre their yield that, by the 1940s, most families were totally dependent for subsistence on the constant sale of labour power by male and, increasingly, female workers.[1] Ever more families were driven off the land into the cities. The Fagan Commission noted a dramatic increase in the number of African women in the cities, accounting for one-third of the urban African population by 1947, and concluded that the urbanisation of the African population had assumed a permanent and irreversible aspect (NLC 1948: paras. 18–28). As a growing industrial reserve army gathered in the cities, sprawling slums and shanty towns grew up around the industrial centres of the Witwatersrand.

During this period, the growing concentration of agricultural capital intensified struggles over the rural land tenure system. As yet unable to destroy the last vestiges of African retention of land in the 'white' areas afforded by the labour-tenant system, capitalist farmers in the Transvaal and OFS sought to intensify the exploitation of their tenants in various ways, particularly by increasing the period of labour-service. The 1936 Native Trust and Land Act empowered farmers in 'proclaimed' areas to transform squatters into labour-tenants and to extend the mandatory period of labour service from 90 to 180 days a year. African household heads were authorised to bind their dependants to labour in any part of the country, and were held responsible for breach of contract by any family member. The penal sanctions of the Master and Servants Act were extended to include whippings for African minors in breach of labour contract.

Rural African producers fiercely resisted this intensification of exploitation. The first attempt to enforce chapter IV of the 1936 Act by 'proclaiming' the Lydenburg district led to a peasant uprising. So strong was this resistance that the responsible minister refused further applications to implement the Act on the grounds that: 'I want to live a few more years, not be shot before my time. Lydenburg was the only place where it was applied and we know what happened there' (Morris 1977:12). However, the major form of rural resistance to extended periods of labour-tenancy was simple desertion. In particular, a steadily increasing number of young men of labour-tenant families escaped their farm labour obligations by moving to sell their labour-power in the cities. By the 1940s, white farms provided the single largest source of labour flowing into the industrial centres.[2]

These rural struggles apart, the restructuring of industrial production likewise occurred through a process of escalating urban conflict. An independent and militant African trade union movement mushroomed during the war. By 1945, over 40 per cent of Africans employed in commerce and private industry were unionised (O'Meara 1975b:153). These unions fought for minimum wages, statutory recognition under the Industrial Conciliation Act, and an end to the system of migratory labour. The strike weapon was much employed. A total of 145,522 African workers struck, in the period from 1940 to 1948, for a total of 409,299 man-days, a marked increase over the previous ten-year-period (1930/9) when the corresponding figures stood at 29,251 strikers and 71,078 man-days (US 1960:G-18). Though War Measure 145 outlawed strikes by African workers in 1942, at least sixty such illegal strikes were reported, between 1942 and 1944 (*Race Relations News* January 1945). Despite the 'firm instructions' given to the Department of Labour to prosecute African strikers 'wherever possible', the Department's 1945 Report complained that 'Natives seem to be ignoring War Measure 145' (Department of Labour 1945:19). The increasing organisation and militant action of African labour effected a 50 per cent rise in average real earnings of African industrial workers during the war – the only period in South African history in which the earnings gap between white and black workers actually closed slightly (Steenkamp 1962:96). In 1947 the Director of Native Labour in Johannesburg reported that: 'During the last two years Native Trade Union activity has increased. There are also signs that the dissemination of subversive propaganda has gained ground amongst the Native population and open defiance of constituted law and order has been manifested at various times' (DNA 1948:19). The organised struggles of African workers in trade unions climaxed in a massive strike of over 70,000 mineworkers in August 1946, brutally suppressed by the police.

Heightened industrial struggles apart, the rapid growth of the African proletariat produced intense urban struggles over a range of issues. The acute housing shortage gave rise to a strong squatters' movement, occasionally coming into open conflict with the state (Stadler 1979). Periodic outbursts of unrest over pass laws, liquor raids, transport fares and food shortages were common. The path of capitalist development in South Africa generated fierce conflict not only over wages, but over all facets of urban and rural life. This structurally-induced conflict centred on the system of cheap labour, bringing into question the structure of the system of exploitation. The conflicts came to a head in the period from 1942 to 1946 when the problem of political control over Africans became acute.

The militant struggles of the African proletariat stimulated a steady growth of political opposition by the African petty bourgeoisie during the war. At the level of formal organisation, the African National Congress began to revive, now on a programme of 'full citizenship rights'. Its influential Youth League evolved a militant 'Africanist' ideology which fundamentally questioned the liberalism of the ANC mainstream, advocating mass non-violent struggle to overthrow white supremacy. Under the challenge of a new, younger generation of African leaders, the ideological dominance of white liberals over African political organisation began to be replaced by increasing independent, militant mass action. In 1944 the ANC and the Communist Party organised a campaign against the pass laws which won wide support. The violent suppression of the 1946 African mineworkers' strike catalysed this gathering development of African political opposition. This state action, and particularly the role of leading white liberal (and deputy Prime Minister) J.H. Hofmeyr, in suppressing the strike, further detached the African middle-class political leadership from the ideological hold and influence of white liberals who pleaded for moderation. Even the archly conservative Natives Representative Council – set up under the 1936 'Hertzog Acts' – angrily suspended sittings of its 'toy telephone' in vehement protest at Hofmeyr's refusal to discuss the strike. In the aftermath of the strike, the patient expression of grievances in dignified and constitutional councils began to give way to mass action and passive resistance.

These rising class struggles led to a progressive paralysis of state policy after the war. Faced with a growing challenge from the oppressed classes and the steady withering away of ideological hegemony over the African population, the UP government was able neither to defuse strident African demands for change and restore stability through reform nor to re-impose ideological control. Its own ranks were riven with deep divisions. The wartime restructuring of South African capitalism and the intensified class struggles through which it occurred, produced growing conflict within the capitalist class itself, not only on the question of African political rights, but also on fundamental questions of economic policy. The result was an escalating political crisis in the state.

Wartime industrial development led the state to pay particular attention to the planned rationalisation of production in all sectors of the economy. State policy towards the changing but specific conditions of accumulation within each branch of capitalist production became a source of conflict within the capitalist class. In essence, these divisions centred on the location of and policy towards the now urbanised reserve army of labour.

The expanded accumulation of industrial capital rested on the higher rates of exploitation and mechanisation facilitated by the large-scale movement of African labour to the cities. The maintenance of a large, permanent, urban labour reserve was deemed by industrialists to be a necessary condition of industrial growth. The Federated Chambers of Industry thus advocated the relaxation of existing influx control measures and pass laws, designed to restrict the movement of Africans to the urban centres. The 1942 Smit Committee recommended that the government begin moving towards the abolition of the pass system (IC 1942: paras. 305–6). Such a step would clearly maintain favourable conditions of accumulation for industrial capital.

In the face of rising industrial struggles, organised industry moreover pressurised the government to grant full, statutory recognition of African trade unions as a necessary step to smooth the reorganisation of production and to curb working-class militancy. For, argued the Transvaal Chambers of Industry, 'whatever progress has been made in the efficiency of our labour in this country . . . has been the greater where management had a unified and organised body of workers to deal with. And if Natives are to enter industry in ever increasing numbers, it is clear that their being organised and disciplined in proper unions is an indispensable pre-requisite to their development as stable and productive workers' (Lewis 1976:23).

For the monopoly mining industry on the other hand, the disintegration of pre-capitalist production relations in and increasing impoverishment of the reserves, undermined the cheap migratory labour system on which the accumulation of mining capital rested. After exhaustive investigation, the 1943 Lansdown Commission concluded that for the vast majority of migrant workers, who comprised 98 per cent of the mine labour force, 'Reserve production [is] but a myth', concluding that the Chamber of Mines had an obligation to pay workers a 'living wage'. Throughout this period the mines lost labour to industry and by 1943 were operating with only 84 per cent of their labour requirements (WMNWC 1944: paras. 200–20, 65). These were years of acute struggle between African workers organised in the African MWU and the Chamber of Mines, culminating in the bloody suppression of the 1946 African mineworkers' strike. The Chamber vigorously resisted any move from a migratory to a stabilised labour force, arguing that such a 'disastrous' policy would force the closure of most mines.[3] Moreover, the industry totally opposed granting trade union rights to 'tribal natives' who would fall 'easy prey to alien interests – often acting from political motives'. African workers were 'not yet sufficiently advanced for trade unionism, nor do they themselves want it' (Transvaal Chamber of Mines 1946a).

The contradictory conditions under which the accumulation of capital in agriculture proceeded in the 1940s were discussed at length in chapter 13. Suffice it here to say, by way of summary, that both the labour-tenancy system which prevailed throughout much of the Transvaal, OFS and Natal, together with the state princing policy, gave rise to conditions which retarded the potentially even more rapid accumulation of capital, and held back the restructuring of agricultural production through large-scale mechanisation. Throughout the 1940s, organised agriculture fought this retardation of accumulation through concentration on three broad issues – the implementation of chapter IV of the 1936 Natives Land and Trust Act, designed to force the transformation of labour-tenancy into wage labour; the retention of African labour in the rural areas; and the implementation of the 1937 Marketing Act in a way which would ensure higher prices for agricultural produce.

All attempts to have chapter IV of the 1936 Act enforced were unsuccessful. The government argued that it was not prepared to risk a repetition of the peasant uprisings accompanying the Lydenburg implementation. Likewise, attempts to retain labour in the rural areas met with little encouragement from the Smuts regime. During these years there were constant complaints of a shortage of farm labour, particularly in the Transvaal (p. 190 above). In 1944 the South African Agricultural Union (hereafter SAAU) proposed that the African population be divided into two groups – agricultural labourers and industrial workers, with no mobility permitted between the two categories (Morris 1977:14).

Yet this ran counter to the whole thrust of state policy. The influential Agricultural and Industrial Requirements Commission in fact recommended an extensive restructuring of capitalist agriculture to divert labour from white farms to industry and reduce the existing number of individual farmers. State subsidies and the pricing mechanism of the Marketing Act should be employed in such a way as to produce fewer but more efficient farmers (AIRC 1941: paras. 90–8). In line with this thinking, the Department of Native Affairs refused either to implement chapter IV of the 1936 Act or to intervene to limit the flow of African labour to the cities. Instead, it proposed that farmers retain their labour by paying higher wages and improving working conditions subject to state inspection. (Morris 1977:12). The application of the pass laws in the main urban centres was eased in 1943. Though it was tightened up again in 1946, the UP government was simply not implementing much existing influx control legislation.

Transvaal and OFS farmers were unable to compete with the higher wages paid to African workers in industry. For them, the pass laws and influx control measures were basic mechanisms essential to retain African labour in the rural areas. Any relaxation of these measures, or attack on them, directly threatened the maintenance of an agricultural labour force, and undermined the existing conditions of accumulation in agriculture. Furthermore, the recognition of African trade unions advocated by organised industry, together with various social welfare measures actually extended to African workers in the mid-1940s, were deemed an acknowledgement of, and consolidation of, the permanent urbanisation of African workers. As such, all proposals to extend the urban rights of Africans were rigorously combated by agricultural interests.

During the 1940s the Marketing Act was implemented in such a way as to hold down the price of foodstuffs (p. 187 above). Attempts by organised agriculture to revise the application of the Act were resisted by other capitalist interests. The mining industry had always opposed the Act on the grounds that it drove up the cost of feeding its labour force and was subsidised out of heavy mining taxes. In 1944, following a series of scandals over the pricing of certain agricultural products, the powerful Assocom demanded the repeal of the Marketing Act on the grounds that it led to 'artificially' high prices, and 'diverted labour and capital away from industry' (Johannesburg Chamber of Commerce 1949a, 1949b). By 1946, the Federated Chambers of Industry (FCI) which initially supported the Act, had joined agriculture's opponents in calling for its drastic revision, as it led to 'dear food' and enabled the regulatory boards to encroach on industry's 'legitimate field' by processing agricultural produce (Finlay 1976:75–6).

Thus, during these years, the contradictions and struggles between the exploited and exploiting classes assumed particular and differing forms in the various branches of capitalist production. The expanded reproduction of capital required differing forms of state intervention to secure and restructure the conditions of accumulation. As the 1940s progressed, the differing forms of state policy demanded by various capitals came into increasing contradiction with each other, opening deep divisions within the capitalist class. On the specific issues of the stabilisation of labour, pass laws and influx control, social security for African workers, the recognition of African trade unions, housing, political rights for the African petty bourgeoisie, pricing policy, taxation, etc., there were ongoing political struggles within the capitalist class itself.

In this context, the party political organisation and representation of class forces grew extremely fluid. The ruling UP was no longer able to organise together the increasingly contradictory demands of the various capitals and act as the political representative of the entire capitalist class. It grew ever more divided, ever politically weaker. The result was an extended political crisis which effectively paralysed the government, and so further aggravated the conditions retarding accumulation in agriculture. The contradictions engendered by capitalist accumulation thus gave rise to a gradual re-alignment in the party political organisation of class forces. Of particular significance here is the political disorganisation of both the capitalist farmers of the Transvaal and specific strata of white labour, and their reorganisation by the HNP into an Afrikaner nationalist class alliance.

THE PARTY POLITICAL ORGANISATION OF AGRICULTURE

The UP was formed in 1934 around an alliance of class forces in which Transvaal and OFS farmers were a vital component. With the 1939 declaration of war against Germany, the great majority of farmers withdrew their support from the UP to rally behind the 'anti-imperialism' of the HNP. However, the myriad divisions which splintered the HNP after 1940 severely weakened its support from agricultural capitalists in the north. The various Afrikaner nationalist political groupings in the periods 1940 to 1943 concentrated their energy on these internal struggles. These conflicts were most acute in the Transvaal. The Transvaal HNP regarded itself as the natural *boereparty* (farmers' party). Yet in this context of *broedertwis* and intense ideological struggle, it was in no condition effectively to organise and represent the interests of farmers and clearly stood no chance of coming to power. Indeed, in the 1943 elections the main thrust of the *Herenigde* campaign was directed not at the growing labour crisis for northern farmers, but was reserved for an attack on the AP, NO and OB as 'the wreckers of Afrikanerdom'.

Despite the growing shortage of farm labour and early opposition of most farmers to the war, by 1943 their material position had improved dramatically (p. 187 above). Again, particularly in the Transvaal, the anti-war republican campaign of the HNP was losing support. This rising prosperity for farmers coupled with the effective political paralysis of the HNP explains the large-scale electoral support from Transvaal farmers for the United Party in 1943, when it captured 15 of the 23 Transvaal constituencies. In the OFS, where the *broedertwis* was less intense, the UP regained but one constituency from the HNP – and that in an urban area.

This 1943 UP triumph can be misinterpreted, however. While the UP won the votes of the majority of Transvaal farmers, it did not again become the party which organised and mobilised agricultural capital. The HNP, on the other hand, was able to do so by 1948. Part of the explanation lies in the class character of the UP and the particular ways in which it acted as the political representative of specific class forces. Here the question of ideology is central.

Prior to fusion in 1934, the interests of the majority of the emerging capitalist farmers in the Transvaal had been politically organised in the SAP of Botha and Smuts. While the SAP came under the increasing domination of the faction representing mining interests, it could and did lay ideological claim to being an Afrikaner party. After fusion, the overwhelming majority of capitalist farmers in the northern provinces were organised by the UP. Again, despite the fact that another faction of the UP represented the interests of the monopoly mining industry, in the period from 1934 to 1939 farmers in the UP could be organised ideologically as Afrikaners under the broad banner of 'Hertzogism'. The destruction of Hertzogism in 1940, followed by the deepening splits in the HNP, left particularly the capitalist farmers of the Transvaal politically and ideologically disorganised. In no sense could the post-1940 UP lay ideological claim to being an Afrikaner party.[4]

During the war, the UP was 'united' by the ideology of the absolute primacy of production for the war effort. Increasingly this was interpreted as the primacy of industrial production. As a party seeking to maintain bourgeois consensus, the UP was itself one of the arenas in which the political struggles between the various capitalist interests were fought out. In the context of the wide divisions within the capitalist class, particularly over the labour question, and the aggravation after 1943 of the conditions retarding the accumulation of capital in agriculture, the UP was unable to organise Transvaal farmers. The results of the ten by-elections held after 1943 throw light on the misleadingly massive vote for the UP in 1943. The HNP contested six of these by-elections, capturing three seats from the UP, severely reducing its majority in two others and increasing its own majority in another.

In this context, agricultural interests began to organise themselves outside the party-political structure. Beginning in 1944 the SAAU launched a concerted campaign to mobilise all capitalist farmers around the labour and pricing questions. Farmers were urged to 'close ranks and join their agricultural associations'. At the 1945 congress of the SAAU, its president argued that farmers should 'set aside all political and other differences and organise a strong united front'. This was achieved by September 1946 when all agricultural cooperatives had joined the SAAU (Morris 1977: 21–2).

The crucial element holding together Smuts' UP government was the war itself. Indeed this had been the sole rationale for its formation and provided its ideological cement. All branches of capitalist production prospered during the war. While the war lasted (and while the HNP could be tarred with a pro-German brush as 'Malanazis'), the UP could at least rely on the votes of most capitalists. However, with the end of the war the very motive force of the Smuts government collapsed. The UP was now just a pro-Smuts group, shorn of both its Hertzogite and wartime ideological legitimacy. The economic slackening which set in at the end of the war intensified the contradictions and conflicts within the capitalist class. On all issues the UP government fell between at least three stools. On the central question of the urbanisation of African labour, if the government vigorously implemented influx control legislation as demanded by agriculture, industry and commerce would protest, arguing for the stabilisation of the industrial workforce – again opposed by the powerful mining industry. If it recognised African trade unions as demanded by industry, mineowners and farmers would see this as a threat to their cheap labour policies. On pricing policy and the Marketing Act, organised commerce, mining and industry were ranged against organised agriculture. And the UP was deeply split over how to respond to growing demands for political rights from the increasingly well-organised and militant national organisation of Africans and Indians.

Thus the UP government was unable simultaneously to represent all interests and maintain a coherent policy. Yet, faced with the new problems of developing monopoly capitalism, and exhausted by the rigours of wartime office and deep factionalism within the party, the ageing and unimaginative UP leadership plodded on in the same old way. The party had first been formed to bring together all capitalist interests, and the Smuts leadership still saw this as its primary task. Rather than bold initiative and aggressive policies, all the UP could offer was compromise. It fudged all the key issues of the day as it tried to be all things to all men. Far from uniting the capitalist class, its policies satisfied nobody, least of all the farmers. In the face of the militant African position and growing economic problems, the government appeared weak and vacillating.

This steady weakening of the UP produced a significant shift in the institutional forms in which the political struggles within the capitalist class were fought out. In the years 1945 to 1948, the various class organisations of capital – the Chamber of Mines, FCI, Assocom, SAAU and AHI – all engaged themselves in an unprecedented flurry of public campaigning and conflict, particularly on the key issues of labour and pricing policies, taxation and the granting of some form of political rights to Africans. The governing party itself was increasingly by-passed, seemed increasingly redundant.[5]

It would be a simple but lengthy task to demonstrate how the UP vacillation on all issues, and in particular its inability to organise Transvaal agricultural interests, enabled the HNP to mobilise a new alliance of class forces under the banner of Afrikaner nationalism. I shall concentrate rather on the question which encompassed almost all political issues and provided the HNP with its major platform – that is, the proletarianisation of the African population and what was euphemistically termed 'native policy'.

The UP and HNP alternative solutions to the problems posed by the massive proletarianisation of African producers were contained in the Fagan and Sauer Reports respectively.[6] There was much common ground between them. Both agreed that the 'kernel of the native question... has shifted to the cities' (*Inspan* September 1948; NLC 1948: 51). Both agreed on the need to regulate the movement of Africans to maintain racial separation, and recommended a system of centralised control of such movement. Both advocated a national labour bureaux system, the replacement of the numerous existing passes with a single document and the development of the Native reserves to maintain the families of migratory labourers. Their major difference lay in policy towards the site and size of the reserve army of labour for industry – that is, whether the growing relative surplus population should be permanently located in the cities, or retained on a controlled basis in the rural areas. The forms of labour control and, by implication, which capitals were to be its major beneficiaries, were the points at issue.

From a detailed investigation of conditions in the reserves, the Fagan Commission argued as its basic premise that due to the disintegration of production in the reserves, the urbanisation of the African population was an irreversible process. Permanent urban settlement for Africans employed in industry was declared 'a natural and inevitable' phenomenon. Referring specifically to agriculture's labour problems, the migration of labour from white farms to the cities was likewise deemed 'inevitable'. Such migration had exceeded '*convenient* limits'. Whilst influx of urban labour was 'greater than the requirements of all the towns taken together', it emphasised that 'in estimating labour requirements, one has to remember that where there is great industrial activity, *it is also necessary that there should be a substantial reserve*' (NLC 1948: paras. 17–18; my italics). Here the report plainly gives priority to the maintenance of the urban industrial reserve army, reflecting the demands of industry and commerce. Its recommendations on the development of the reserves, labour bureaux and a simplified pass system did seek to accommodate farmers' demands. Yet, on the most important issue, the Commission rejected a system of influx control which would retain in the rural areas, and thus available for agricultural labour, those unemployed in industry. Local authorities should no larger be empowered to expel unemployed Africans from the urban areas. Under the existing system, local authorities 'put obstacles in the way of permanent settlement' in the urban areas of the 'millions' of Africans 'who no longer have a home in the Reserve areas' by only admitting the worker himself and barring his family. Now, urged the Commission, families should be allowed to settle permanently in the urban areas – this is what is referred to as the 'stabilisation of labour'. Attempting to reconcile this with the mining demand for the maintenance of the migrant labour system, the commission argued that migratory labour would 'continue for generations' whether encouraged or discouraged by the state, concluding in italics that: 'the policy should be one of facilitating the stabilisation of labour; but on the other hand migratory labour cannot be prohibited by law nor terminated by administrative action. There can be no compulsion either way' (NLC 1948: 18). This outright rejection of influx control and insistence that the industrial reserve army should be permanently reproduced in the urban areas by allowing families to settle in the cities, was diametrically opposed to the policies advocated by organised agriculture. The HNP's Sauer Commission took a very different line.

From the first hesitant beginnings of the 1944 Volkskongres on the 'racial question', the development of the apartheid concept was centrally concerned with the question of labour for agriculture (chapter 12 above). The Nationalist rejection of the Fagan Report focused squarely on the question of site of and means of control over the industrial reserve army. In sharp contrast to the Fagan Commission's recommendation to ease influx control measures and establish a permanent urban industrial labour reserve, the Sauer Commission unequivocally stated that:

236

Natives in the urban areas should be regarded as migratory citizens not entitled to political and social rights equal to those of whites. The process of de-tribalisation [read proletarianisation – D.O.'M.] should be arrested. The entire migration of Natives into and from the cities should be *controlled by the state* which will enlist the cooperation of municipal bodies. Migration into and from the Reserves shall likewise be strictly controlled. *Surplus* [i.e. unemployed] *Natives in the urban areas should be returned to their original habitat in the country areas* [i.e. white farms] or the Reserves. Natives from the country areas shall be admitted to the urban areas or towns *only as temporary employees obliged to return to their homes after the expiry to their employment* (*Die Burger* 29/3/48; my italics).

With unemployed black labour to be expelled from the towns and the rest admitted strictly on a temporary basis, the reserve army of labour would be re-located in the rural areas. Here the common misinterpretation that the HNP sought to expel already-employed labour from the towns must be dispelled. At no stage did it advocate removing labour employed in industry and re-locating it elsewhere. Apartheid was designed to secure labour for all capitals, not to deprive any employer of it.

A national system of labour regulation and labour control will be established with a central labour bureau and an effective network throughout the country to allow supply and demand to operate as flexibly as possible and to eliminate the large-scale wastage of labour. A proper survey of the labour force and labour requirements will have to be made *in order effectively to divert labour* into the various channels of agricultural, industrial, mining and urban employment (*Die Burger* 29/3/48; my italics).

Such 'apartheid' was not yet a detailed policy. The HNP election manifesto asked the white electorate to decide on the 'apartheid principle', promising later elaboration of the 'scheme' (*Die Transvaler* 21/4/48). Nevertheless, to farmers confronted with drastic labour shortages and hardly comforted by the Fagan Commission's rejection of influx control, this programme offered resolute action in line with all the demands of the SAAU. Moreover, the HNP social and economic programme promised agriculture 'the special concern and protection of the state'. Apart from 'ensuring an adequate supply of agricultural labour', this involved the 'active promotion of sound and profitable marketing of agricultural products' (*Die Kruithoring* 1/3/44).

Again, this was in sharp contrast with government policy to hold down food prices. In 1947, the price of maize – the staple crop of most Transvaal farmers – was fixed at levels well below that recommended by the Control Boards. This finally eroded any possibility that the UP would win the votes of Transvaal farmers. The HNP on the other hand had fought hard for the demands of the SAAU on both the labour and marketing question. With the *broedertwis* of the early 1940s firmly behind it, in 1948 the HNP not surprisingly won a secure base among the farmers of the Transvaal whom it had wooed for so long. It now controlled 56 of the 66 rural constituencies outside Natal, and its AP partner won a further 5. The nationalist alliance had penetrated even the rural areas of jingoist Natal, where the AP won 2 seats and the HNP another, leaving the UP in control of but 3 rural constituencies in Natal, and 8 in the country as a whole (Heard 1974: 39). The HNP had now finally emerged as the party which organised agricultural interests on a national basis.

THE ORGANISATION OF WHITE LABOUR

The changing industrial division of labour during the war, and particularly the large-scale employment of cheap African labour in semi-skilled operative positions, posed the problem of the allocation of places in production to white labour. Most pressingly, it raised the question of the future employment of highly-paid skilled white workers, whose skills were being rendered redundant through mechanisation. The state envisaged a reduction in industry's 'high cost structure through increased mechanisation so as to derive the full benefit of comparatively low-paid non-European labour' (BTI 1945: 46). However, none of these proposals sought the abolition of colour bars and racial division of labour within industry. On the contrary, a number of state interventions were made to secure the position of white labour. In general, state policy aimed at reassigning white labour upwards, particularly into supervisory positions in the new industrial division of labour. State schemes for the retraining of white labour were introduced, and wartime legislation offered placement in favourable positions to ex-servicemen at the cessation of hostilities.[7]

Despite its rhetoric of protecting white workers, the UP government preferred to achieve this reallocation of work roles in industry through negotiation between employers and white workers rather than by legislation. In this process, those workers organised into strong unions, and particularly the craft unions, were in a more favourable position. Workers occupying the lower strata of places assigned to whites in industrial and state employment – many of whom were unorganised and most of whom were Afrikaners – were usually considered last in this process. For them, the prospects of retraining and reassignment in higher positions 'were in practice much less certain than in the vision presented in commission reports. Indeed according to Nationalist sources there were by 1947 as many as 18,000 frustrated would-be trainees unable to obtain access to any training programme' (Davies 1977: 277).

Thus, despite such schemes to protect white workers, particularly these lower (predominantly Afrikaans-speaking) strata began to feel potentially threatened by the large-scale movement of Africans into operative positions. This was a constant theme of white labour's struggles during the war. A rash of strikes in 1946 and 1947 against the employment of African labour in semi-skilled and skilled positions indicates the degree to which white workers felt threatened.

Table 20.   *Index of real weekly wage rates of adult male white employees, 1939–1945 (1938 = Base 1,000)*

Year	Gold mining	Engineering	General manufacturing	Combined index
1939	1,000	1,001	1,005	1,003
1940	981	991	996	995
1941	982	982	1,005	984
1942	981	993	1,013	974
1943	959	1,073	1,010	997
1944	1,000	1,050	1,049	1,009
1945	1,016	1,024	1,060	1,009

Source: ILC 951: Table 36.

Other aspects of the position of white labour are significant here. For much of this period, the real wages of white workers actually fell, only rising slightly towards the end of the war. Again the brunt was borne by the lower strata of white workers, particularly those in the mining industry (Table 20).

In sharp contrast to the relatively stagnant earnings of white labour, the index of average real earnings of Africans employed in private manufacturing rose from a base of 1,000 in 1938/9 to reach 1,533 in 1945/6 (Steenkamp 1962: 96).

A number of incursions into the rights of white labour were made in the name of the war effort. Workers in certain categories were prevented from changing jobs. The Controller of Industrial Manpower could stipulate a compulsory minimum working week (54 hours in engineering), move workers from one job to another, or compel the working of overtime without overtime pay. Apprenticeship regulations were relaxed to allow semi-skilled operatives to fill jobs previously reserved for 'craftsmen' (Davies 1977: 259–60).

In this context, the pattern of class struggles in the 1940s subjected the economic and political organisations of white labour to increasing crisis. The South African Labour Party (SALP) entered the wartime coalition government. Its leader, Walter Madeley, became Minister of Labour. Throughout the war the HNP denounced the SALP for betraying workers by 'sitting. . . amongst the capitalists and imperialists', and condemned its leaders as 'political acrobats' supporting measures they had formerly opposed (Davies 1977: 262). Though the party withdrew from the government after the war, it remained in a close alliance with the UP on the basis of the latter's 'social security' programme. As this programme virtually collapsed between 1946 and 1948, the Labour Party could offer no alternative, and finally split in 1946. As a small parliamentary rump, the independent existence of the Labour Party was increasingly questioned. At the 1946 congress of the TLC, the Iron and Steel Trades' Association argued that, in the face of the Labour Party's impotence, the TLC should seek direct representation in Parliament.

The white trade union movement was likewise beset by a wide range of problems. The Bond-led attack on, and struggle for power within the MWU and other white unions was discussed in chapter 6. Throughout the 1930s and 1940s the Labour Party had correctly attacked the various Christian-national trade union bodies as reactionary. But in doing so, it had defended the thoroughly corrupt and authoritarian MWU leadership as the valiant foes of fascism. One of the few Afrikaans-speakers in the SALP leadership, the MP for Krugersdrop, M.J. van der Berg, was a lone voice arguing that Labour Party resistance to the Hervormers should simultaneously fight to restore democracy within the MWU. By 1947, thoroughly frustrated at the failure of his ten-year campaign against white labour bureaucracy, van der Berg crossed the floor to the HNP. In the 1948 elections, the Labour Party did not even field candidates in many of the mining constituencies which had traditionally been the heartland of its support.

The rising struggles of African workers further divided the white labour movement. Whilst the TLC was officially committed to full trade union rights for African workers, many of its affiliated unions opposed this policy. Following the narrow defeat of a motion to exclude African workers from the TLC in 1947, five Pretoria-based unions withdrew to form the Coordinating Council of South African Trade Unions – joined by the MWU when the Hervormers finally won control in 1948.[8]

The pattern of class struggle from 1940 to 1948 placed particular strata of white workers under increasing pressure. In this context, the bureaucratic labour movement, formally allied with the governing capitalist party, began to disintegrate. Davies' summary is an apt one:

> Social democracy in the post-war years was, in short, in multiple crisis: a crisis brought about by its manifest failure to represent the economic interests of important strata of its constituent base, and a crisis of credibility and indecision brought about by its inherent inability, given its bureaucratic character, class determination of its base and nature of its alliances, to take any clear cut position on the struggles of the African working class (1977: 283).

This crisis of the organised white labour movement was also a crisis of social democratic ideology. Ever since 1936 various Christian-national trade union organisations had waged a relentless ideological struggle against the labour movement and all ideologies of class. Given the trajectory of the historical process of the formation of the South African working class, skilled positions were overwhelmingly filled by English-speakers. More recently proletarianised Afrikaner workers clustered at the lower levels of skill in the places assigned to white workers in production (p. 82 above). The pressures generated by capitalist accumulation fell most heavily on precisely such (largely Afrikaans-speaking) lower strata during the 1940s. Moreover, the (predominantly English-speaking) craft unions not only failed to organise more recently proletarianised Afrikaner workers, but, particularly during the 1930s, they actively fought to exclude Afrikaners from certain job categories, regarding them as a potential source of undercutting. This attitude persisted into the 1940s. Both the Labour Party and TLC remained dominated by the craft unions and were insensitive to the problems of such (predominantly Afrikaner) lower strata of white workers.

The Christian-national labour movement could thus argue that the particular pressures experienced by such workers were the product of deliberate discrimination against them as Afrikaners. In the face of the corruption of the MWU and the whole bureaucratic structure of the TLC and Labour Party, Christian-national organisers depicted the trade union movement as an alliance of 'foreign' capitalists and trade union leaders, both living off the sweat of Afrikaner workers. The collaboration between the United and Labour Parties during the period, coupled with the movement of Africans into operative positions in industry, was presented as a deliberate plot by the 'imperialist' state, aided and abetted by 'foreign' ['Communistic'] 'Jewish' trade union leaders, to replace white (and particularly Afrikaner) workers with cheap African labour. The competition for jobs which always arises between workers under capitalism, was depicted as a threat to the survival of the white race, and of Afrikaans-speakers in particular. The Christian-national ideologists argued that the material interests of Afrikaner workers could only be secured in the organic unity of the volk.

This last point is crucial. As early as 1936 the Bond set out to win the political support of workers for Afrikaner nationalism and break the Labour Party. Yet this was not achieved merely by appeals to the organic unity of the volk. Nor was it a simple assertion of an inherent attraction of Afrikaner nationalism for all Afrikaans-speakers. Rather, through skilful organisation and a particular emphasis on the material interests of Afrikaner workers, the Christian-national labour movement came to offer an alternative to the ineffectual and crisis-ridden trade unions and Labour Party. The Hervormers built a secure base by fulfilling many of the trade union functions neglected by the MWU – fighting for phthisis benefits, pension entitlements, workmen's compensation, widows' pensions, etc. Indeed, Hertzog had argued at the Ekonomiese Volkskongres that only by promoting the 'economic interests' of Afrikaner workers through trade unions would *reddingsdaadbeweging* win their support (Naude 1969: 271).

The HNP programme paid careful attention to the material interests of Afrikaner workers – trumpeting the arrival of a 'new economic order'. The position of white workers in industry would be promoted and protected through apartheid in employment. The provision of opportunities for the retraining of all white workers was especially emphasised. The party undertook to curtail the power of monopolies, placing banks under 'effective state control' and giving the state 'a controlling interest' in mining and other strategic industries. Here a system of profit-sharing would be introduced. Its programme further called for a wide-ranging social welfare programme for whites going far beyond the measly (and disintegrating) 'social security' programme of the UP Government (*Die Kruithoring* 1/3/44, National Party

1948). The Labour Party and its UP ally by contrast merely offered to continue this social security policy, together with 'The maintenance of white civilisation in the Union. . . [and] the establishment and maintenance of a reasonable standard of living for the country's wage earners with due regard to the different levels of civilisation of the races in the Union' (*The Star* 31/4/48).

It is thus not surprising that the HNP won the votes of specific strata of white workers. But this extension of its electoral base should not be misinterpreted. Despite the effective disintegration of the Labour Party, the HNP did not develop into the party of white labour. It failed to win the support of both artisans and workers in those industrial unions with a history of militant struggle. Throughout the 1950s the regular formation of a series of fringe parties all expressed white labour discontent with the NP.[9]

CONCLUSION

The war marked a period of rapid change in the structure of production and social relations in South Africa. In particular, the final disintegration of pre-capitalist relations of production in the rural areas undermined the basis for the reproduction of a cheap, migratory labour force on which capitalist production had rested since the 1870s. This gave rise to fierce social struggles centred in particular on the question of the reproduction of the urban proletariat and labour policy generally. The contradictions and class struggle generated in the process of rapid capital accumulation in these years led to a complex and growing political and ideological crisis in the state at the end of the war.

At its centre was firstly, the increasing collapse of political control and ideological hegemony over the various classes in the oppressed African population, and the growing challenge thus posed to the existing system of social relations. These heightened class struggles, then, secondly, exposed deep divisions and intense conflict within the capitalist class itself, both on specific issues and over the general long-term direction of state economic and social policy. Taken together, these two aspects of the crisis produced a general vacillation in the state. Its inability to effect decisive reforms one way or the other meant that it was unable to secure the required conditions of accumulation for the capitalist class as a whole. In effect this vacillation began to retard the accumulation of capital in all sectors. Such vacillation thus gave rise, thirdly, to a crisis in the existing party political system, and a collapse of the hitherto prevailing 'South Africanist' ideological consensus. The ruling UP was no longer able to hold together the increasingly contradictory demands of all capitalist interests. It not only lost the support of Transvaal farmers, but fell into a political ineffectuality from which it never recovered. The party of white labour likewise disintegrated. After the end of the war in particular the political conflicts within the capitalist class were increasingly fought outside the party political structure.

In this context the HNP was finally able to organise a new Afrikaner nationalist alliance based on Transvaal, Cape and OFS farmers, specific categories of white labour, the Afrikaner petty bourgeoisie and the emerging capitalists of the *reddingsdaad* movement. Each of the constituent groups of the nationalist alliance regarded itself as adversely affected in differing ways by the trajectory of capitalist accumulation during the 1940s, and in particular the emergence of a large (and increasingly well organised) African working class. The HNP mobilised each group on the basis that they were discriminated against as Afrikaners, a condition which would end only when all Afrikaners were united in a single political movement. This Afrikaner nationalist class alliance was built on a programme pledged to the restructuring of conditions of accumulation of capital in such a way as to defend and advance the material interests of each of these class forces on the basis of the intensified exploitation of African workers. But 'apartheid' should not be seen as an undifferentiated phenomenon. It meant different things to the different groups now constituting 'Afrikanerdom'. The ways in which apartheid directly catered for the demands of farmers and specific strata of white workers was discussed at length above. Chapter 12 examined the relationship between apartheid and the interests of the petty bourgeoisie and emerging capitalists of the economic movement. It remains to be shown how these different specific interests were ideologically drawn together and presented as one. This ideological condensation is well revealed in the nationalist rallying cry that the cities were being 'inundated with natives'.

The great bogey of the *oorstrooming* (inundation/overrunning) of the cities by native hordes neatly encapsulated the differing interests of all constituents of the nationalist alliance and drew them together in a common programme.[10] For farmers, *oorstrooming* meant the loss of labour to the cities. To white workers it evoked fear of competition from a source of cheap labour. *Oorstrooming* particularly threatened the petty bourgeoisie and the capitalists of the economic movement, dependent on rapid accumulation in agriculture for their own economic advance, desperate to maintain the low-wage structure of the migratory labour system, and fearful of the rising tide of mass struggle against all forms of segregation. *Oorstrooming* implied higher wages for African industrial workers, the recognition of African trade unions, the continuation of the hated UIF for African workers, and, above all, demands for equality. All these issues, but particularly the demand for even limited progress towards racial equality, directly threatened the existing social places of each of these disparate class forces. The varying specific interests evoked by the emphasis on *oorstrooming* enabled them to be organised into a resolute united front against any form of racial equality and crystallised in the apartheid programme.

The varying demands and interests of these class forces were further harnessed by, and condensed in, the HNP's anti-monopoly stance. The development of monopoly capitalism adversely (if differentially) affected each of these groups. Even Sanlam was but a small fish in a sea dominated by the sharks of the financial monopolies. In 1948 all these groups could still be mobilised on an anti-monopoly platform. The HNP advocated the expropriation of the great Land Companies, 'state control' of the banks and retail monopolies, and a 'controlling interest' by the state in gold mining and other strategic industries. Whilst the overt 'anti-imperialism' and republicanism of the early 1940s was now decidedly muted, the HNP attacked the Imperial Preference system, emphasising its own 'national' character and determination to pursue South Africa's national interests.

A qualification is necessary here to prevent any misunderstanding. A class alliance such as that finally organised by the HNP in 1948 is not built simply by dangling well-baited political programmes and manifestos in front of disgruntled or politically-disorganised groups. Whilst particular class forces may be available for mobilisation, this does not magically occur on the printing and distribution of a set of demands which supposedly cater for its interests. The cementing of such a class alliance is essentially a question of organisation and ideology. It is a major thesis of this study that, under the often contradictory direction of the Bond and Sanlam, the economic movement was the essential element in achieving both the organisation of disparate class forces and the ideological development which enabled such a class alliance to crystallise under the political organisation of the HNP in 1948.

In the face of deep political divisions ever since 1939, the various component bodies of the economic movement worked to mobilise Afrikaner farmers, petty bourgeoisie and workers in one single movement for *volksredding* (national salvation). A complex organisational network developed to organise each of the various class forces. Here the role of the Reddingsdaadbond was crucial (and more important than most Afrikaner nationalist leaders realised at the time). In the period of *broedertwis* the RDB organised Afrikaans-speakers of all classes into one mass movement. It evolved programmes covering every aspect of the daily lives of all Afrikaners-speakers and involved them in collective, coordinated action. The overriding theme of the RDB, and indeed the entire *reddingsdaad* movement, was unity. All classes of the volk were dependent upon each other, went the RDB line. None could achieve much alone. United they could transform the economic and political structure of South Africa to benefit all Afrikaans-speakers.

This organisation and mobilisation of all class forces through the *reddingsdaad* movement required further ideological elaboration. The rarefied and abstract ideological debates amongst the intellectual elite of the Bond were developed and translated into an easily assimilated Christian-nationalist ideology through the various organisations and journals of the *reddingsdaad* movement. As this ideology was developed for mass consumption in the 1940s, its central emphasis on the unity of the volk elaborated a complex but interdependent set of relationships between the various 'strata' (i.e. classes) within the volk. Its predominant message held that the material interests of these various classes could only be secured through *volkseenheid* (unity) at all levels of social intercourse.

Thus, whilst the various political organisations fought for hegemony in the nationalist movement, the Bond-dominated economic movement of Afrikaner aspirant capitalists moulded the organisations and the ideology which laid the basis for a class alliance under the banner of Afrikaner nationalism. The basis of this class alliance was laid down, and its organisation first developed by the Bond, *outside* the political organisations, outside the HNP.

Here it is important to clarify the relationship between the Bond and the HNP, especially as conventional wisdom sees the latter simply as the malleable tool of a sinister behooded band of Bond conspirators. During the years of *broedertwis*, while prominent Bond leaders were identified with either the HNP or OB, the Bond itself carefully avoided taking sides. After the failure of its numerous attempts to reconcile the two organisations the Bond directed its main activities towards maintaining as broad as possible a unity outside the political organisations (Pelzer 1979: 177–8). The RDB, churches, cultural and other organisations were all used to this end. Though the economic struggle was the field in which it was possible to draw together the widest variety of groups, the Bond was also strikingly successful in coordinating general dissatisfaction with the UP's new 'dual medium' education policy. Arguing that this policy represented yet another attack on 'Afrikaner identity', the Bond mounted a virulent campaign for 'mother-tongue' and 'Christian-national' education. Again, in the years of *broedertwis*, its education campaign was a significant factor bringing together Afrikaans-speakers of different classes, and forging a sense of Afrikaner identity. Indeed some members of the government saw this education campaign as a dire threat to the UP's 'South Africanist' ideology.[11]

Yet the Bond was no political party. Despite its success in laying the basis of a class alliance in and through the economic movement, it was unable to organise these disparate interests politically. Indeed, perhaps the most important aspect of the HNP/OB struggle had been over the question of the appropriate and most relevant form of political organisation of the volk. This issue was finally brought into the open precisely by the efforts of the Bond in 1941 to establish a coordinating council of *volksorganisasies* in which the HNP would be but one member. Furthermore, during the 1940s, the HNP was dominated by the Cape party, whilst the Bond was most firmly established in the north, being relatively weak in the Cape Province. In no sense, then, can the party be considered simply as the party-political wing of the Bond.

However, once the HNP emerged victorious from the intra-nationalist conflicts of the early 1940s, it began the task of the political organisation of a class alliance, building on what had been achieved by the *reddingsdaad* movement. After 1943 it turned its attention four-square to the varying demands of the different class forces it sought to organise. The party was extensively re-organised to revitalise its local bases and tighten discipline. Now began the elaboration of apartheid policy and HNP attempts to organise white labour and develop a social and economic programme which could cater for and bring together these various class forces. Taking its cue always from the economic movement, the HNP undertook this organisation of an alliance of various forces in a highly self-conscious manner. In the words of its economic and social programme: 'Because the HNP is national in the broadest sense of the word, it acts on behalf of every section and every component part of the volk, and has a clear and decisive policy concerning every question which confronts the volk' (*Die Kruithoring* 1/3/44).

The end of the war saw a change in the relationship between the various Afrikaner nationalist political organisations. The OB's anti-parlia-mentarianism was clearly politically dead. van Rensburg reached an agreement with Havenga which permitted OB members – excommunicated by the HNP – to resurface in 'effete' party politics in the ranks of the AP. This simultaneously revived the virtually defunct AP. No longer an anachronistic survival of discredited 'Hertzogism', it now represented the significant sector of the Afrikaner petty bourgeoisie which had supported the OB. This opened the way to cooperation with the HNP. In 1947 Malan and Havenga concluded an electoral pact which allocated the AP one safe HNP seat and designated nine other UP-held constituencies in which the AP would be the nationalist standard-bearer (eight of which it won in 1948). By this alliance, the HNP was assured of the support of the vast majority of the OB, though the sniping between them continued.[12]

The increasingly confident HNP leadership seized upon the UP weaknesses, accusing the government of 'cooperation with the communists', of following a 'weak and vacillating' native policy, adopting a 'weak and neglectful' stance in trading and other external relations, and maintaining a 'totally inadequate' internal administration. Precisely this vacillation and ambivalence enabled the HNP to label the UP as simultaneously the tool of such apparently contradictory groups as the Chamber of Mines, the liberals and the Communist Party (*Die Transvaler* 21/4/48).

Thus, by 1948, the HNP succeeded in mobilising and organising a wide variety of class interests in an alliance, enabling it to capture a slim parliamentary majority of five seats on a minority vote. As mirrored in the election results, the composition of this alliance now shifted the balance between the provincial nationalist parties. The Transvaal party in particular was transformed. No longer a largely petty bourgeois organisation, it was now based solidly on capitalist farmers and drew wide support from Afrikaner workers. It contained 32 of the HNP's 70 MPs, 6 more than the Cape party. In the following years, nationalist politics were to be marked by a sharp struggle for dominance between the Cape and Transvaal parties, in which the latter was to triumph.

One final point needs stressing. The HNP came to power as a result of a protracted and complex political crisis in which the fierce class struggles of the period rendered the state unable to secure the requisite conditions of accumulation for all capitals. The HNP victory marked a decisive shift in the balance of forces in the South African state. Though often depicted as 'anti-capitalist', paradoxically it was precisely this new ruling party – dominated by the aspirant capitalists of the *reddingsdaad* movement – which was able to secure the conditions of rapid accumulation for all capitals where the 'traditional' capitalist party, the UP, had failed. Apartheid was much more than a policy to advance the interests of NP supporters. More fundamentally, it in effect secured the interests of the entire capitalist class, enabling all capitalists to intensify the exploitation of African workers and so raise the general rate of profit.

This was achieved primarily through savage repression of working-class organisations, which enabled the state to restructure key aspects of the relations of exploitation. The intensely repressive character of the apartheid state has been documented in texts too numerous to cite, and is well known. By the early 1960s, draconian security legislation seemed to have broken the back of mass resistance and created the conditions of stability which led to a sustained economic boom from 1963 to 1972, and a rate of return on invested capital which was the highest in the world. Thus, far from representing the triumph of the pre-capitalist frontier which undermined capitalism, as the conventional wisdom has it, the apartheid policies of the NP were a product of the particular character of capitalist development in South Africa and acted as a spur to rapid capital accumulation in a given historical phase of South African capitalism. They created the political conditions for expansion so that, in the period 1948 to 1970, of all the capitalist economies only that of Japan expanded more rapidly than apartheid South Africa.

16

Conclusion: From 'volkseenheid' to Total Strategy

This study has examined the development of Afrikaner nationalism in the crucial period from 1934 to 1948. In opposition to the idealist perspectives of both nationalist and liberal historiographies, it has here been argued that, as Afrikaner nationalism developed in the years under review, it was fundamentally shaped by the imperatives and contradictions of, and struggles around, the accumulation of capital. The policies developed and pursued by the nationalist movement can only be explained through an understanding of these imperatives, contradictions and class struggles. Thus Afrikaner nationalism has here been analysed as one of the forms through which people became conscious of these contradictions, and organised themselves to fight them.

From this perspective, the previously neglected economic movement emerges as the core of Afrikaner nationalism in the 1940s. Here was first organised the alliance of classes that the NP finally mobilised politically in 1948. Here the crucial transformation of nationalist ideology first began to take root in popular consciousness. Here the conflict between growing Afrikaner capital and the Afrikaner petty bourgeoisie first emerged.

The election of the HNP government in 1948 marked a turning point in the development of Afrikaner nationalism. It was followed two years later by another turning point of almost equal significance. In October 1950, the FAK, EI, RDB, and AHI jointly convened a second Ekonomiese Volkskongres to take stock and 'set the course for the future'. It differed from the first *kongres* in many ways. In 1939, Sanlam, Volkskas and a few local undertakings apart, there were few Afrikaner businesses in South Africa. The first Volkskongres sought to develop a strategy to correct this situation. As a mark of its success eleven years later, businessmen had now displaced the petty bourgeoisie as the delegates of the volk – 'The people who have gathered here today are mainly from commerce and industry' (*Inspan* November 1950).

The proceedings of the *kongres* mirrored its now openly capitalist nature. Professor L.J. du Plessis' opening address summed up the past decade and set the course for the years ahead.[1] Acknowledging that there had been mistakes and failure – amongst them the fonds – nevertheless, the *reddingswerk* (rescue

248

work) had been completed as 'the poor white problem no longer exists and Afrikanerdom is now established in the most important strategic points in urban commerce'. du Plessis also laid bare the real character of this *reddingswerk*: 'The major goal has been achieved. *Afrikaans capital has been consolidated*, and both cooperative and other forms of Afrikaans undertakings have been built thereupon in agriculture, commerce and industry'. Now a 'significant shift in emphasis' had occurred: 'The *reddings* idea has gradually given way to the idea of development and consolidation, and the cooperative method has likewise been transformed into a more powerful mobilisation of capital' (*Inspan* November 1950).

These themes were echoed by all speakers. Gone were the petty-bourgeois visions of 'rescuing' the volk through small undertakings; discarded and discredited was the former universal panacea of cooperatives; no longer was the organised economic movement in the business of setting up new undertakings in untried fields. The volk were officially declared to have been 'rescued'. Now, as established businessmen whose capital has been consolidated, the delegates to this 'volk's' congress saw the future task as that of building up and developing (their own) existing undertakings. The volk were exhorted to provide ever more capital to the established capitalist undertakings. In the speech of M.S. Louw cited above (p. 207), this was virtually an injunction to invest exclusively in Sanlam. The popular character of the economic movement was now discarded. Having fulfilled its task of making the volk economically conscious, the Reddingsdaadbond was allowed to fade away in the following years.

The great significance of the second Ekonomiese Volkskongres lay in its 'official' legitimation of the profound shifts in the economic movement. In the 1940s, all Afrikaner undertakings had indignantly rejected any charge that they were 'capitalist'. After the second Ekonomiese Volkskongres it could be admitted that Afrikaner undertakings were indeed capitalist, and dedicated first and foremost to the pursuit of profit.[2] Only after the second Volkskongres could the consolidation of Afrikaner business undertakings be openly discussed without having to cower before accusations of emulating 'Hoggenheimer'. L.J. du Plessis was right. The *reddingsdaad* movement had achieved its primary goal in the consolidation of Afrikaner capital. A small but powerful group of Afrikaner capitalists had emerged from the struggles of the 1940s. The second Ekonomiese Volkskongres was their coming-out party.

The NP government after 1948 secured the political conditions for rapid accumulation by all capital. More particularly, it also created the conditions for an even more rapid growth of Afrikaner capital. This was seen on almost all fronts. Strenuous measures were taken to improve the conditions of accumulation in agriculture. The Marketing Act was again administered in a manner which ensured high, stable prices for farmers. In the first years of nationalist rule, this policy was assisted by rocketing world prices of raw material during the Korean War. Taking 1947/8 prices as a base of 100, by 1953/4 the index of producers' prices for farm products had risen to 146 (US

1960: H-29). With the implementation and extension of influx control measures, a tightening up of pass laws and the gradual introduction of labour bureaux, the labour crisis in agriculture eased. Under NP rule, the Afrikaner finance houses flourished. A number of government and NP-controlled local authority accounts were switched to Afrikaner financial institutions. The total deposits in the Volkskas Bank, for example, doubled between 1948 and 1952, and after ten years of nationalist rule stood at 125.7 m – or 4.75 times the 1948 figure (Annual Report 1973:2). In other fields, a number of important government contracts were awarded to Afrikaner companies – such as that won by Federale Mynbou to provide coal to the state steel company. At a more general level, Afrikaner businessmen were appointed to vital positions on numerous state economic boards, and to senior management positions in state industries. According to the present chairman of Sanlam, the state-owned Industrial Development Corporation was used by the NP government 'to strengthen Afrikaner participation in the industrial progress of the country... (and) as a bulwark against the Anglo-American Corporation'. The government 'fostered the establishment of state-owned corporations as Afrikanerdom's answer to the somewhat overwhelming non-Afrikaner interests in mining and industry' (Wassenaar 1977: 123).

This is no place for an analysis of the growth of Afrikaner business in the 1950s and 1960s, nor its relationship with the state. However, one crucial aspect of this process should be noted. The original accumulation strategy of the *reddingsdaad* movement rested on the centralisation and segmentation of agricultural capital, enabling finance companies to invest in commerce and industry. The consolidation of financial capital in this manner had been satisfactorily achieved by 1950. The most significant feature of the development of Afrikaner undertakings during the rest of the decade was the fact that some of the larger companies, but particularly the Cape-based Sanlam and Rembrandt groups, had so extended their base of accumulation in industry (and, to a lesser extent, mining) that they were now in effect independent of agricultural capital. While Sanlam in particular still drew a large part of its premium income from farmers, the economic performance of the group was no longer dependent on conditions of accumulation in agriculture. By 1962, apart from the earnings of its various subsidiary investment companies such as the Federale group, Bonuskor, etc., Sanlam itself had an annual income from investments of over £5m (Annual Report 1972). With the massive flight of foreign capital out of South Africa during the early 1960s, the Sanlam group invested heavily (and cheaply) in industrial undertakings, further consolidating its independent base of accumulation. By 1963, a key subsidiary, Federale Mynbou, had enlisted the cooperation and assistance of the Anglo-American Corporation to enable this child of the *reddingsdaad* movement to take control of a major mining finance house – the General Mining and Finance Corporation. From this base, Federale's mining interests are now second only to Anglo-American, while the Sanlam group as a whole is probably the second largest conglomerate in South Africa after Anglo-American.

Such open collaboration with 'Hoggenheimer' aroused fierce controversy.[3] This weaning of Afrikaner financial capital from its dependence on accumulation in agriculture, and its increasing cooperation after Sharpeville with non-Afrikaner finance capital, led to important shifts and struggles in nationalist politics. During the 1950s, and particularly the 1960s, the Nationalist Party[4] and all other Afrikaner nationalist organisations experienced growing struggles between the various class forces in the nationalist alliance. Initially this took the form of regionalism. Attacks on the *geldmag* (financial power) of the Cape – on Sanlam and Rembrandt – gathered force in the 1950s. By the time of Sharpeville, these divisions were explicit. Throughout the early 1960s, under the Premiership of Verwoerd, the Cape party, its organ *Die Burger*, and the Sanlam interests were virtually an official opposition within the NP. With the assassination of Verwoerd in September 1966, this conflict burst into open struggles between the so-called *verligtes* (the enlightened) and the *verkramptes* (the reactionaries). In 1969 the leading *verkramptes* were expelled from the NP and, later, the Bond. Led by Albert Hertzog, they formed the *Herstigte* (reconstituted) Nationalist Party, based on the 'pure Afrikaner principles' of the old *gesuiwerde* party.

The *verkrampte/verligte* split was essentially a struggle between those who fought to preserve the alliance of 1948, dominated by the interests of farmers and the petty bourgeoisie, and those who sought to adapt the ideology and policies of Afrikaner nationalism to the changing social composition of the volk. The *verligte* phenomenon was a response to the emergence of a class of aggressive, self-confident Afrikaner capitalists whose interests now went beyond those of the narrow class alliance out of which they had emerged. By the late 1960s, the *verligte* element was no longer confined to the Cape, but was a powerful force in the Transvaal, as businessmen began to pursue policies independent of the interests to which they were previously tied.

The *verkramptes* attempted to use the traditional organisation of the Afrikaner petty bourgeoisie, the Bond, against what they labelled the 'finance power of the South'. A strong move was mounted to portray the factional struggle as a simple conflict between the Bond as the guardian and soul of traditional Afrikaner values on one hand, and the *nouveau riche* 'money capitalists' of the south on the other hand (*Veg* November 1968.) One effect of these struggles, however, was severely to curtail the independence of the Bond, as Vorster finally succeeded in forcing its leadership, under P.J. Meyer, to support the dominant faction in the NP.

Vorster's own position in the party, and consequent style of leadership, were important here. For various reasons (O'Meara 1980: 20–3), in the NP itself he adopted a Bonapartist stance above the factions, and employed as his major power base not one of the provincial parties, but the security apparatuses of the state, especially the Bureau of State Security (BOSS). Similarly, within the Cabinet, in sharp contrast to Verwoerd's authoritarian control, Vorster's premiership was characterised by a 'chairman of the board' approach. In consequence, individual ministries were transformed into

251

powerful political fiefdoms by individual ministers. The factionalist struggle within the NP was increasingly fought within, but more particularly between, various government ministries. As certain ministries were identified with given 'lines' within the party, these interdepartmental tussles were openly discussed in the press. Thus the powerful rivalry between the Department of Foreign Affairs as a seat of *verligtes*, and the Department of Information under the conservative Connie Mulder was well known. Less public, though ultimately extremely important, was the growing conflict between the military and security apparatuses. Through the Department of Defence (presided over by the leader of the Cape NP, P.W. Botha) the military began to play an increasingly open role in South African politics, arguing for militarily defensible policies. The 'reforms' desired by the military leadership in many ways coincided with those argued for by Sanlam, and the military was known to be increasingly restive at the paralysis which NP factionalism foisted on the government. The Security forces on the other hand were reputed to see South Africa's political problems largely in terms of conspiracies by agitators and downplayed any need for reform.[5]

Whilst the economy was booming and relative political stability was maintained, Vorster was able to maintain his Bonapartist role within both party and government with some success. But this became increasingly difficult to sustain with the rapid escalation of economic and political crisis in the mid-1970s. *Verligtes* began to push for far-reaching policy reforms, notably the easing of restrictions on the flow and use of labour, and state control of the economy. This vigorously re-opened the factionalist struggles in the NP. After the Angola débâcle, Vorster's own political position became increasingly identified with the right wing of the NP, now led by the new Transvaal leader and Minister of Information, Dr Connie Mulder. In the face of *verligte* demands, the right insisted upon the maintenance of tight influx control measures, restriction of the employment of skilled African labour, no recognition for African trade unions, and continued state control of the infrastructural sectors of the economy.

Thus by late 1977, in the disastrous political aftermath of the defeat in Angola, the Soweto uprisings, the murder of Steve Biko and the panic banning of eighteen African organisations, now confronted with increasingly organised and militant working-class and mass resistance to apartheid – a resistance now taking an openly anti-capitalist form – under severe international pressure to introduce at least cosmetic changes, and faced with a massive outflow of foreign capital, huge unemployment and the worst recession in South African history, both the nationalist government and party were decisively split over precisely the political questions posed by these multiple crises. On the burning issues of economic and political policy, behind the façade of hardline control, the government was virtually rudderless. Torn in many different directions, it spoke with many different voices.

This political paralysis of the Vorster government finally catalysed significant shifts in the alignment of forces both in the NP and the state. An effective political alliance between the military and the most powerful sections of the capitalist class began to take place. In 1977, through the Minister of Defence, P.W. Botha, the military proclaimed its programme of a 'total strategy' to meet the crises confronting the state. Its fundamental aim, according to the official military journal, was 'a guarantee for the system of free enterprise' (*Paratus* July 1979). This could only be achieved on the basis of a 'comprehensive plan to utilise all the means available to the state according to an integrated pattern' (Moss 1980). But such 'coordinated action in all fields' was not to be understood as a simple defence of a static *status* quo. Political and economic 'reforms' were essential to the defence of the state. In the words of the then Chief of Staff (and present Defence Minister): 'The lesson is clear. The South African Defence Force is ready to beat off any attack. . . but we must take into account the aspirations of our different population groups. We must gain and keep their trust' (*Rand Daily Mail* 13/6/79).

In effect, the emerging Total Strategy Doctrine argued that blacks had to be given a stake in the capitalist system. They would have to begin receiving the 'benefits' of that system, through an improvement in their 'quality of life', hopefully thereby engendering a commitment to the defence of South African capitalism against 'the Marxist threat'. But the doctrine was very clear that such improvements were possible only through the closest cooperation between the state and 'the private sector'. Thus, the Total Strategy Doctrine began to create the basis for an explicit alliance between the military and monopoly interests.

At precisely this stage of now direct military intervention in political struggles in the state, leading businessmen also became directly and stridently involved in a vigorous campaign for 'reform'. The Sanlam chairman published an unprecedented and swingeing attack on economic policy, characterising it as 'A Freeway to Communism'.[6] The influential *Financial Mail* argued that organised and coordinated 'Business Power' could save South Africa (i.e. capitalism) from its multiple crisis. A coalition of the biggest undertakings established the Urban Foundation. Moreover, important shifts took place in the traditional political alignments of the capitalist class. The UP finally expired and the liberal Progressive-Federal Party emerged as the largest opposition grouping.

The political impasse was broken by the protracted 'Muldergate' circus in 1978 to 1979. This finally removed Vorster from power, broke the leader of the Transvaal NP, Dr Connie Mulder, and led to the election of the Cape leader and Minister of Defence, P.W. Botha, as NP national leader and Prime Minister. The detailed politics and significance of Muldergate I have analysed elsewhere (O'Meara 1980). Here it should be noted that the defeat of Mulder marked a significant shift in the balance of forces organised by the NP *qua* party under the banner of Afrikaner nationalism. By now Afrikaner business had effectively established itself as the dominant force in this alliance. Through Botha, it announced its intention to abandon some of the hallowed policies of this alliance, policies which were the basis of support for the alliance from white workers and certain strata of the petty bourgeoisie. But it cannot be emphasised too strongly that Muldergate was no simple struggle internal to Afrikaner nationalism. Afrikaner capital was able to establish its political dominance within the NP over the other forces in the nationalist alliance only because of broader political support outside the NP from other bourgeois organisations and institutions, and the army itself. On its own, the reformist wing of the NP would not have been able to defeat the conservatives[7] and achieve a strong discreditation of the right wing. To do so, it was forced to rely on, and indeed play a relatively minor role in, a broader campaign by various bourgeois political groups (particularly the press) against the right wing of the NP. The defeat of Mulder marked both a decisive shift in the balance of forces within the Nationalist Party and government, and a now open alliance against the NP right on the part of almost all organisations of the capitalist class. It was the confirmation of a transformation of both the ideology and class basis of Afrikaner nationalism.

The old *reddingsdaad* movement fostered the development of Afrikaner capital through a tight unity of the volk, moulded through the symbols and myths of the Trekker past. The entire economic movement had been cast in terms of a *Tweede Trek* to conquer the commanding heights of the economy. By the mid 1960s, this *Tweede Trek* had achieved its primary aim, to forge a class of Afrikaner financial, industrial and commercial capitalists. With the emergence of this class, pursuing its own interest, Afrikaner nationalist ideology began to be transformed. Now these twentieth-century Trekkers had fully learned to express themselves in the language of the stock exchange and boardroom. The time came by the late 1960s when the Ruperts, the Diedrichs, the Louws and the Wassenaars (let alone the generation which followed) had so imbibed the spirit of this new bourgeois language that they could freely express themselves only in it, and stumbled and stuttered when forced to mouth the prayers and incantations of old. By the 1970s, the Trekker mythology of the *reddingsdaad* movement had largely been discarded by Afrikaner businessmen. As Wassenaar's blunt attack on government economic policy implied (1977), both the policies and symbols of that past were now a drag on the pursuit of profit.[8] 'Hoggenheimer' was no longer the oppressor of the Afrikaner volk, but a trusted and valued partner in the joint quest for profit (and the attack on the right-wing of the NP).[9]

By the 1970s, the wheel had turned full circle. The 'anti-capitalists' of the 1940s *reddingsdaad* movement had become the Afrikaner 'Hoggenheimers' of today. Under P.W. Botha, the NP government has gone out of its way to project itself and its 'total strategy' as representing a broad alliance of all sections of the capitalist class. As NP national leader, Botha has attempted to reorganise both the NP and the state apparatuses so as to weaken right-wing attacks on the Total Strategy. He has sought to keep important government portfolios in the hands of his own supporters and so redefine the relationship between the party and government that NP congresses would no longer have the right to question government policy.

More significantly, the Total Strategy programme has produced important changes in the form of the South African state. Government and state bureaucracy have been sweepingly reorganised to concentrate power in the Prime Minister's office. A system of appointed 'Cabinet Committees', responsible only to the Prime Minister, has virtually replaced the Cabinet system of government – transforming the relationship between the legislature and executive within the state. Through this system, senior military officers and a number of leading (non-nationalist) businessmen have been introduced directly into key roles in government. Thus if Botha's election confirmed a shift in the balance of class forces within the NP, this bourgeois domination of the party has been consolidated by directly drawing into government wider elements of the capitalist class. Likewise, in this climate of 'total war' against 'the Marxist threat', the reorganisation of government and state bureaucracy has now given the military a vitally important institutionalised role in the daily governing of the country (O'Meara 1980: 37–40).

As a response to the simultaneous recession and intensifying mass struggles of the 1970s, 'Total Strategy' is based on the institutionalisation of a new alignment of political forces in the state. In its attempt to secure the political and economic conditions for renewed capitalist prosperity and stability, the South African capitalist class as a whole has connived at a notable central-isation of power in the hands of one individual, and, without undergoing the process of a formal *coup d'état*, the thorough militarisation of politics generally. In the process, supposedly monolithic 'Afrikanerdom' has been sundered into bitterly squabbling factions. In effect, the nationalist class alliance of 1948 has virtually collapsed. Within the now sharply divided NP itself, led by the new Transvaal leader, Dr Andries Treurnicht, the right wing has fought very hard against Botha's hesitant reformism. To some extent this has led to an impasse in the policy of small reforms, with which leading capitalists are growing increasingly impatient.[10] Moreover, traditionally nationalist strata among white workers (particularly in the MWU) and large elements of the petty bourgeoisie are increasingly turning their backs on the NP. In the April 1981 elections, extreme right-wing parties won 33 per cent of the 'Afrikaner vote', and a leading NP paper argued that not only was Afrikaner political unity a thing of the past, but that in effect, the NP should not try to resurrect it (*Rapport* 3/5/81).

Volkseenheid (Afrikaner unity) had been the central motif of the economic movement in the 1940s. *Volkseenheid* was then the *sine qua non* of the development of Afrikaner capital. In its pursuit, the economic movement had built an alliance of class forces in the 1940s which put the NP in power in 1948. By the 1980s, however, *volkseenheid* had become an obstacle both to the accumulation of capital by Afrikaner 'Hoggenheimers' and to the policies of the dominant faction in the NP itself. It was sacrificed on the altar of 'Total Strategy' and the unity of the capitalist class.

The organisational and ideological forms of class struggle in South Africa after 1948 are not the subject of this study. Here I have done little more than sketch the outline of the transformation of one of these forms. An analysis of concrete class struggles and development of the state in the post-1948 period is one of the great lacunae in the recent South African literature. Any attempt to correct it would have to come to terms with this transformation of Afrikaner nationalism in the process of, and class struggles around, the accumulation of capital.

Notes

Introduction

1 Since 1948, the term 'apartheid' has been officially superseded by an array of euphemisms – 'separate development', 'separate freedoms', 'multinational development', 'pluralist democracy', etc. However, despite claims that 'apartheid as you know it is dying', the NP's commitment to the basic props of apartheid – white monopolisation of land, political power and citizenship, and the barricading of Africans, stripped of their citizenship, into overpopulated Bantustans until their labour is required by some white capitalist – remains unshaken.

2 The classic statement of this position is Horwitz (1967). Legassick (1974) analyses the emergence of this view.

3 In this election, the NP share of the total vote cast fell from 68 per cent in 1977 to 57 per cent. Noting that 38 per cent of Afrikaners were now 'estranged' from the NP, a leading Nationalist newspaper declared that Afrikaner 'unity in politics no longer exists', and argued that this should be accepted by the NP (*Rapport* 3/5/81).

4 It is common to most writing in Afrikaans. For a useful summary see van Jaarsveld (1964).

5 Legassick (1971) criticises and traces the development of this conception in South African historiography.

6 Adam and Giliomee (1979), for example, use *inter alia* the following terms largely interchangeably: Afrikaner nationalism, Afrikanerdom, the NP, the Afrikaner tribe, the government, the state, white power.

7 The 'Theoretical and Methodological Appendix' to Moodie (1975), is an important exception which provides a useful basis from which to begin a critique of such idealism.

8 The 'fit' of the Japanese variant is extremely problematic. One Marxist historian alleges that Poulantzas has distorted German fascism (Caplan 1977).

9 The following paragraph owes much to Sayer (1975).

10 It is in fact liberal analysts who have gone furthest along the 'ideology as flight from reality' road. See e.g. Thompson (1962), quoted on p. 4.

11 Of the works which do discuss the economic movement, Patterson (1957), Vatcher (1965) and Bunting (1969) are cast in conspiracy theories, Welsh (1974) is a recitation of structures, and Moodie (1974 and 1975) is trapped by his idealist problematic. The Afrikaans literature does contain an 'official' history of the economic movement (E.P. du Plessis 1964), but as yet, no work exists which situates the development of the economic movement squarely within the development of the broader nationalist movement.

Chapter 1 The Depression and the class basis of the Nationalist Party

1 Throughout this study the term imperialism is used in two distinct senses. The first is the Leninist conception of a specific epoch in the development of capitalism on a world scale – i.e.

257

monopoly capitalism. In this sense, then, imperialism is capitalism. This is the meaning indicated in the above sentence. The second sense in which the term is used is that given to it in Afrikaner nationalist ideology. This meaning is discussed on p. 34. To differentiate between these two connotations, the latter appears throughout in inverted commas.

2 van Heerden (1975). A significant factor in Cape farming support for the NP was attempts by the SAP government to force Cape wool farmers to sell their entire clip at fixed prices to the British government for the duration of the First World War. This aroused the fierce opposition of wool farmers who saw their economic interests being sacrificed on the altar of the needs of 'imperialism'.

3 The proletarianisation of white farmers in the northern provinces was a complex process requiring much further research. Apart from periodic depression, droughts, livestock diseases, etc., amongst the other important causes were: the devastating effects of the British scorched earth policy in the Anglo-Boer war; the repeated complex subdivision of farms under Roman Dutch Law inheritance stipulations (one particular heir was entitled to a 296, 387,000/4, 705, 511, 234, 760 share of a 5,347 acre farm); and competition from imported US maize. For a suggestive short sketch, see Salomon (1964).

4 In 1906 Smuts had proposed to the head of the largest mining house an alliance with Het Volk on the grounds that 'their interests (were) in many ways identical ... as large property owners' (Marks & Trapido 1979:73).

5 de Kiewiet (1972: chapters VII–X). In a seminal paper, Kaplan (1977) elaborated de Kiewiet's basic point into the thesis that this reflects the hegemony of national capital (agriculture plus industry) over foreign capital (mainly mining) in the power bloc. This argument is developed for a longer periodisation of the state in Davies, Kaplan, Morris & O'Meara (1976).

6 This is even more clear in the formally correct translation of the Afrikaans Nasionale Party as 'National Party'. See Note on Translation (p. xv).

7 This was particularly the case of the leaders of the two big provincial parties, the Cape and Transvaal. Natal is not considered in this study at all as it provided minuscule support for the NP, and but one of its MPs, the ineffectual Natal NP leader, E. G. Jansen.

8 The Cape party had in fact been formed by this group, which had fought off a purely farmer-based 'NP', formed with Hertzog's blessing (see chapter 7).

9 The deep loathing of the Transvaal leader, Roos, for his Cape counterpart, Dr Malan, caused endless dissension within the Cabinet between 1924 and 1929. On the occasion of the bitter conflicts around the 1927 Flag Act, the 'Lion of the North' brought the Cabinet to the verge of an open split because of his dislike of *Die Doktor* (Meiring 1973a).

10 Hertzog outlined these principles in a major speech to his Smithfield constituents, reviewing his entire political career (*Rand Daily Mail* 8/11/35).

11 Throughout this study, the use of the term 'imperialism' in inverted commas indicates this ideological concept rather than the Leninist conception (see note 1 above). Hoggenheimer was the Semitic-featured caricature of *Die Burger*'s cartoons, the racist symbol for monopoly capital in all its forms. The term was also used interchangeably with 'Imperialism', but, because of its extreme anti-Semitic connotations, had a deeper impact. It is a corruption of the name of the 'Hochenheimer' estate of arch-imperialist mining magnate Sir Percy Fitzpatrick. The character first appeared as 'Hoggenheimer of Park Lane' in a 1902 musical comedy 'The Girl from Kays'.

12 Unless the context indicates otherwise, the term 'agriculture' here refers to the activities of white farmers, and is used as shorthand for 'agricultural and livestock commodity production'.

Chapter 2 The disintegration of the Nationalist Party, 1927–1934.

1 Hertzog's use of the terms 'Dutch-speaking' and 'Afrikaans-speaking' can be confusing to the modern ear. For him, 'Afrikaners' referred to both (white) Afrikaans- and English-speaking

South Africans whose first and only loyalty was to South Africa rather than Britain. By 'Dutch-speaking' he referred to those whose home language was Afrikaans, i.e. those who are today commonly labelled 'Afrikaners'. On the significance of these definitions see chapter 5.

2 Roos campaigned for the purchase of all maize surplus by the state; an extension period for all debt payments (an issue dear to his own debtor heart); a state bank and state lottery; and the replacement of all 'non-white' bus and truck drivers by whites (*Die Burger* 26/1/33). On Grobler's long-standing promise to Roos, see van den Heever (1946:236). *Die Burger* of 29/12/32 names the MPs supporting Roos.

3 See *Die Burger* 28/1/33, and correspondence between Smuts and John Martin, President of the Chamber of Mines in van der Poel (1973:256).

4 Roos wanted the Premiership for himself, together with a post for Smuts, and posts for four other Sappe, four Nationalists and one Labourite.

5 *Die Burger* 28/1/33. Throughout these negotiations, this NP paper was remarkably well-informed on proceedings with the SAP caucus. See also J.C. Smuts Jnr (1952:325) and Pirow (1957:160).

6 It may well be asked why no popular movement emerged to challenge the structure of state power during this crisis. Though a full answer lies beyond the scope of this study, it would have to concentrate on the collapse of effective political leadership within the various popular movements. Contradictions between the class forces supporting both the ICU and the African National Congress, led to the complete disintegration of the former, and a leadership struggle in the latter which left the ANC in the control of an abjectly reformist leadership under Pixley ka Seme. And at precisely this time, the Communist Party was undergoing a series of extreme sectarian purges resulting from the Comintern 'Third Period'. These destroyed the leadership of an emerging militant African trade union movement. See Simons and Simons (1969).

7 As early as March 1932 Hertzog was writing in his diary that the NP would lose the next election (van den Heever 1946:239). On his speech to the caucus, see diary entry 31/1/33 in D.W. Krüger (1960:81).

8 The complex issue of the Excess Profits Tax is unravelled by Kaplan (1976). Here I rely heavily on his arguments.

9 See e.g. Robinson's speech in the House (*Die Burger* 31/1/34). Smuts was very clear on his point; see Hancock (1968:253–4). It is most explicit in the *Cape Times* editorial welcoming fusion, 22/6/34.

10 *Die Burger* 9/8/34. The word '*gesuiwerde*' was never actually officially included in the party's name. It was commonly known by this tag, however. I have retained the word firstly to emphasise the different class basis of the G/NP, and secondly to distinguish it from the various other titles under which the party paraded after 1940.

Chapter 3 The Gesuiwerde Nationalist Party and the class basis of Afrikaner nationalism

1 'Capitalism' here refers not to the private ownership of the means of production, commodity production and private profit, but rather to 'Hoggenheimer' and monopoly capitalism. See chapter 11 below.

2 Scholtz (1975:117). At about the time Hertzog was calling for 'cooperation'. in 1930 (p. 40 above), the Chamber of Mines engaged in a major ideological offensive to 'prove' to Hertzog's followers that it was no longer a body of 'foreign fortune hunters' but a 'responsible' and nationally-oriented industry, functioning for the general good of all South Africans. See its articles in the massive and very important publication of the Hertzog NP (Nasionale Party 1931:197–223). It is highly significant that the NP accepted these articles for publication. It would certainly not have done so five years previously.

Chapter 4 The Afrikaner Broederbond

1 Lombard was in fact Bond chief secretary from 1924 to his retirement on pension in 1952. Greijbe was chairman from 1925 to 1928.
2 Louis J. du Plessis (1951). This L.J. du Plessis was not the ubiquitous Potchefstroom professor.
3 Professor J.C. van Rooy, cited by General Hertzog in his famous Smithfield attack on the Bond, printed in the *Rand Daily Mail*.
4 Moodie 1975:146–8. The Afrikaans verb *handhaaf*, from which the Handhawersbond took its name, has no direct English equivalent. It connotes simultaneously 'to promote', 'to assert', 'to defend', all in a vigorous way. Moodie has coined the clumsy and not totally accurate translation of Handhawersbond as 'Union of Militant Defenders'.
5 Indeed, the wartime director of Military Intelligence claimed that Diedrichs had been recruited as a Nazi agent and trained as such at 'the Anti-Komintern School' (Military Intelligence 1944: section V). Bunting (1969) weaves this claim into an elaborate, and I think false, conspiracy theory of Nazi control over Afrikaner nationalism through the Bond, and the later openly National-socialist Ossewa Brandwag. Juta (1966) claims to have combed all Nazi archives and found no evidence of a Nazi link with the Bond.

Chapter 5 The Afrikaner Broederbond and the development of Christian-nationalist ideology

1 Moodie (1975: chapter 4). This chapter draws heavily on Moodie's analysis.
2 Thus Hexham (1974) quibbles with other idealist explanations, arguing that the *Gereformeerdes* were the only true Calvinists and that therefore, going back to S.J. du Toit in the 1870s, they must be seen as the real source of Afrikaner nationalism. De Klerk (1975) likewise traces everything back to Calvinism, arguing, however, that Christian-nationalism is a perversion of 'the true Calvin'.
3 Booysens (1969 : 239) cites a letter from P.K. Albertyn to D.F. Malan complaining about the 'frightfully English' influence of the daughter of the great NGK evangelist, Andrew Murray. While her thirty years as an educationalist had produced 'blessed Christian work' she had done 'an appalling amount to anglicise the staff and children'.
4 Statement signed by the chairman and secretary, *Die Transvaler* 14/12/44.
5 The Draft Constitution was severely criticised by the Cape NP organ, *Die Burger* 23/1/42. See p. 129.
6 The *smelters* who followed Hertzog into the UP also claimed to be the legitimate representatives of Afrikaner nationalism, with General Hertzog as its heroic figure. In a famous speech in November 1935 Hertzog launched a powerful attack on the Bond. Accusing it of anti-English racialism, he asserted (incorrectly) that the Bond and G/NP were one and the same 'cultural gang', simply operating at different levels (*Rand Daily Mail* 8/11/35). A number of Bond members resigned and others were purged as a result of this speech, which earned Hertzog the Bond's final implacable enmity. Since Hertzog's official rehabilitation some nationalist historians have claimed that he later withdrew these allegations against the Bond (Scholtz in *Die Transvaler* 23/10/72).
7 Here Stoker intuitively acknowledged the distinction between literary and popular aspects of ideology arguing that 'pure leadership in principles and the propagation of principles' was necessary because ' . . . only a small section of our volk was deliberately and purposively Calvinist, whereas a large section of our volk in all its organisations and outside was only intuitively and inadvertently Calvinist'.
8 Bond circular dated 16/1/34, quoted by Hertzog, *Rand Daily Mail* 8/11/35. The nationalist historian G.D. Scholtz has argued that had van Rooy anticipated the impact of this 'maladroit' statement, he would have reconsidered every word (*Die Transvaler* 23/10/72).
9 Moodie cites the diary of the future secretary of the Ossewa Brandwag to this effect (1975 : 180).

Chapter 6 The Afrikaner Broederbond and Christian-national trade unionism

1 Interview, Dr P.J. Meyer, June 1975.
2 This was very clearly realised by the one man who could claim some success in the capture of the MWU. See A. Hertzog, cited in Naude (1969: 263).
3 Davies (1977) argues in fact that this predominantly supervisory character of white miners – i.e. as the policemen of capital – objectively placed these 'white wage earners' in a class separate to productive workers – i.e. as members of 'the new petty bourgeoisie'.
4 These figures are slightly misleading, however. Many Coloured workers were employed in the Cape. During the 1930s an important struggle had occurred between the Transvaal and the Cape GWU, which had nothing to do with Christian-nationalism.

Chapter 7 The beginnings of the economic movement

1 N.J. le Roux (1953:177). The Hofmeyr family were the Kennedys of Cape Afrikaner nationalism. W. A. Hofmeyr's father was a prominent member of the NGK synod. One uncle was J.H. Hofmeyr – the revered 'Onze Jan', leader of the Afrikaner Bond. Another uncle was Professor of Theology at Stellenbosch University; Jannie Hofmeyr, child prodigy and later Smuts' deputy, was a first cousin. Willie's brother George became Secretary for National Education.
2 The paper initially appeared in Dutch. Only when Afrikaans replaced Dutch as an official language in 1925 did the paper's name change to *Die Burger*.
3 Professor Fremantle lost his Uitenhage seat and withdrew from party politics. On Hofmeyr *et al.*'s opposition to the Fremantle party, see le Roux (1953:91). There is a detailed discussion of these events in van Heerden (1975). See also the official history of the Cape NP (van Rooyen 1956).
4 le Roux (1953:28–9). This speech was written by M. S. Louw, who was the financial strategist of both Sanlam and the economic movement for almost fifty years. On his ubiquitous role, see the authorised biography by Bezuitenhout (1968).
5 Here it is important to distinguish between the concentration and the centralisation of capital. The former refers to the increasing concentration of social means of production in individual capitalist undertakings. It thus implies the simultaneous accumulation of capital. The latter process differs from the first in that it only 'presumes a change in the distribution of already available and already functioning capital'. It is thus also distinct from accumulation, although centralisation may speed up the accumulation of capital: Marx (1976: 1975–8). The distinction between latent money-capital and productive-capital is discussed on pp. 181–3. See also Marx (1978: chapter 2).
6 Much of the meagre literature dealing with the Bond and the economic movement is characterised by partial research and a particular over-reliance on the tendentious, and often incorrect, wartime Military Intelligence reports. While an enormous amount of information was available to the careful researcher, some finer points of detail remained obscure. The publication of Pelzer's official Bond history provides reliable information on a number of issues, but is notable for a number of glaring omissions. In particular, no mention is made of the crucial role of M.S. Louw and the three-man Cape committee which developed the major strategy of the 1939 Ekonomiese Volkskongres (see following chapter).
7 Ironically, when a Sanlam-controlled group formed the Trust Bank in the 1950s, Volkskas now baulked at granting clearing facilities to this new Afrikaner bank.
8 The mudslinging over the affair continued for thirty years. Neethling died of a stroke in 1939 while attending a Santam board meeting to resolve the dispute. In a book published in 1969, Naude all but blames the long-dead Hofmeyr for Neethling's death (109–14).

Chapter 8 The Ekonomiese Volkskongres

1 The Afrikaans is stronger, firstly because the volk is referred to by the personal pronoun 'himself' rather than the 'itself' of the correct translation. Secondly, the Afrikaans word *red* carries a dual meaning. It not only means rescue, or save, but also connotes salvation or redemption in the Christian sense. This dual connotation was contained in Kestell's plea for a *reddingsdaad* – in saving itself from poverty, the volk would simultaneously redeem itself.

2 Memo from M.S. Louw to Sanlam board, 2/9/38. Reproduced Bezuitenhout (1968: 64–5).

3 Though Louw was certainly a Bond member by 1939, doubt remains as to when he joined. The partial list of members contained in Serfontein's reliable – if conspiratorial – book (1979), gives Louw's membership number as 764. If compared with the annual membership breakdown in Pelzer, this would have Louw joining the Bond in 1931/2, making him one of the first Cape *Broers*. Though I may be wrong on this, for various reasons I suspect that Louw was only invited to join the Bond after he first presented his proposals in 1937.

4 Again, the usual translation of *kapitaalkragtig* as 'financially strong', conveys a weaker meaning than the Afrikaans. A literal translation would be 'strong in capital'. Henceforth I have retained the Afrikaans term in brackets to indicate this.

5 The Registrar of Companies refused to approve the original name, Sentrale Volksbeleggings.

Chapter 9 'Hereniging' and 'Broedertwis'

1 In a later by-election the G/NP did capture one further Transvaal rural constituency when the Rev. C.W.M. du Toit was returned in Marico. However, he was soon to defect to Pirow's NO group (p. 125).

2 Davenport (1977: 234 – 8) explains these splits almost purely in terms of personalities. Simson (1980: 168) sees only tactical differences between likeminded fascists. Hepple (1954: 17) argues that there were no differences.

3 The former leader of the Free State G/NP, Dr N.J. van der Merwe, died suddenly in August 1940.

4 HAD 1940–1: column 2195. OB Membership figures are notoriously unreliable. In an interview with two American diplomats in 1944, the OB leader, J.F.J. van Rensburg, claimed that the organisation was 'now at the top of its strength' with 100,000 members (Visser 1976: 158–9).

5 The draft was eventually published 'for discussion' in January 1942 (*Die Burger* 23/1/42).

6 Bond Executive Council minutes, cited Serfontein (1979: 60). This book is based on Bond documents handed to Serfontein – including an early draft of the official Bond history. Though marred by a personalised and overly conspiratorial emphasis, the accuracy of its details is confirmed by the official Bond history (Pelzer 1979).

7 In moves never publicly explained, L.J. du Plessis was forced to resign his chairmanship of the FAK EI. P.J. Meyer likewise lost his secretaryship of both the EI and the Reddingsdaadbond, and his editorship of *Volkshandel*. A leading OB and Bond ideologue told me that the pressures of the period were 'psychologically exhausting' and drove him 'up against the wall'.

Chapter 10 The organisational network of the economic movement

1 Especially Patterson (1957), Vatcher (1965) and Bunting (1969), all of whom rely almost exclusively on the often misleading wartime Military Intelligence Reports.

2 *Rand Daily Mail* 17/7/41. The Magaliesburg Cooperative Tobacco Society initially refused to contribute to the RDB on these grounds (*The Star* 15/3/40).

3 *The Star* 4/7/41. However, the congress carried a motion introduced by L.J. du Plessis and P.J. Meyer expressing 'appreciation for the brilliant manner in which the *Hoofleier*, Dr Diedrichs,

interpreted the nature of the RDB when he recently signed an agreement for a unity policy on its behalf'.
4 E.P. du Plessis 1964: 195; *Inspan* April 1942 and January 1946. There are discrepancies in the various official claims of the size of RDB membership. Diedrichs told its first congress in July 1941 that there were 70,000 members in 350 branches, whereas *Inspan* claims only 305 branches for the same period. I came across no other claim which put membership as high as 70,000 at any stage in RDB history. Again, du Plessis' figure of 282 branches by mid-1940 is higher than the 265 *Inspan* claimed for the same period (*Inspan* April 1942).
5 *Inspan* October 1950. At just this juncture, when the RDB could no longer attract donations, the Bond launched its own reserve fund – the Christian de Wet-*fonds*. This collected £21,812 in its first year (Pelzer 1979).
6 Members of this Bond committee were Diedrichs, Meyer, van der Merwe, W. Bürhman (of Volkskas) and J. de Lange. Other recommendations called for more intensive mobilisation of Afrikaner capital; for the RDB to redouble its efforts to train Afrikaner workers and make the volk economically conscious; and the establishment of a single wholesale operation to coordinate supplies to Afrikaner traders (*Volkshandel* April 1942 and May 1942).
7 *Volkshandel* May 1942. The 12 listed subsidiary aims all refer to the kinds of information and guidance to be given to fledgling concerns, e.g. in the fields of credit, bookkeeping, advertising, etc.

Chapter 11 The ideology of Afrikaner capital

1 I am grateful to Rob Davies for drawing my attention to this important speech.
2 Meyer later elaborated a powerful plea for 'Afrikaner socialism' (Meyer 1944). This remarkable history of white trade unionism in South Africa was favourably reviewed by the Communist Party newspaper, *The Guardian*, and condemned by the HNP as proof of 'communistic tendencies' in the OB (*Die Vaderland* 17/11/44).
3 See chapter 10, note 2.
4 These two points are neatly summed up in Albert Hertzog's speech to the *volkskongres*, reproduced in Naude (1969); and by the BWBB leader and future Minister of Labour, Ben Schoeman (*Die Transvaler* 4/7/44).
5 The anti-communist crusader and EI member, Dr G.E.N. Ross, for example, paid Afrikaner workers at his Veka clothing factory wages below the minimum under an Industrial Council Agreement. The company – managed by Albert Wessels – was forced to raise these wages by the Industrial Council. Moreover, despite Ross' attacks on 'Jewish money', when VEKA got into financial difficulties he had few scruples in accepting financial assistance from a Jewish firm, Brown Geisler.
6 See, e.g., and RDB's 'Profession of Faith of the Afrikaner' (*Inspan* June 1943).

Chapter 12 Afrikaner capital and the ideology of apartheid

1 *Volkshandel* September 1950. This parable is rich in the themes of such racism. The juxtaposition of the struggling, upright Afrikaner woman running her shop and the implied loose behaviour of the two women in the Indian shop, further introduces a strong implicit sexual component common to much racist incitement.
2 Paper by Professor J.D. du Toit to the 1944 Rassevraagstuk Volkskongres, *Inspan* October 1940. The author was not only professor of theology at Potchefstroom University; as 'Totius' he was also the Poet Laureate of Afrikaner nationalism.

Chapter 13 Agricultural and finance capital

1 I have not examined the question of the forms of differential ground rent in this regard as it would require precise data, extremely difficult to find in the notoriously unreliable agricultural statistics.

2 Department of Agriculture (1961: 51 and 69). This indicates only very broad tendencies. In reality the average annual output per farm was higher as not all 'farms' were in production.

3 *Inspan* November 1950. The distinction between the *centralisation* and *concentration* of capital is crucial here. See note 5 to chapter 7.

4 Finlay (1976: 58). This and the following paragraph draw heavily on this work.

5 *Inspan* November 1950. An investment profile of the life office industry in 1950 shows the following breakdown: public sector securities 46 per cent; other fixed interest 44 per cent; shares 6 per cent; property 4 per cent (van der Horst 1980: 10).

6 He was later one of the very few Afrikaner businessmen to advocate a policy of 'total apartheid'. The article in which he did so was perhaps the most vituperative racist outburst I encountered during my research: 'Die Naturel in die Unie – Wie dra Wie?' *Volkshandel* May 1947.

Chapter 14 Manufacturing and commercial capital

1 The technical composition of capital refers to the ratio of the mass of employed means of production to the mass of employed labour-power. The organic composition of capital refers to the ratio of capital invested in means of production (constant capital in Marx's terms) on the one hand, to capital invested in labour power (variable capital) on the other.

Chapter 15 The coming to power of the Herenigde Nationalist Party

1 In recognition of this, the 1946 census classified as 'dependants' all African women in the reserves – except those who explicitly labelled themselves 'peasants'. The percentage of economically active Africans classified in the census as peasants fell from 51 per cent in 1936 to 17 per cent in 1946 and 8 per cent in 1951 (US 1960: A-33). Evidence of the decline in reserve production can be found in NEC (1932), WMNWC (1944) and NLC (1948).

2 Morris (1976). The rural land struggles during this period are an area requiring much further research. See Hirson (1976).

3 Transvaal Chamber of Mines (1947a: 46), where the pious argument is advanced that 'Any change from the migratory labour system to stabilised urban communities would have a catastrophic effect on the Natives themselves... (who) would be the first to oppose it.' Presumably the Gold Producers' Committee had not even read the demands of the African MWU before the 1946 strikes, which called in effect for an end to the migratory labour system.

4 There is a further aspect to the difference between the UP of the 1930s and that of the 1940s, and the inability of the latter to represent farming interests in terms of our explicitly Afrikaner ideology. By the 1940s, a younger generation of capitalist farmers had displaced those who had followed Botha and Smuts in the days of the SAP. Hancock (1968: 506) records the 78-year-old Smuts' pathetic response to the rural obliteration of the UP in 1948 and his own defeat in the Standerton constituency: 'My old comrades [of the Anglo-Boer War] have turned against me.' A friend replied, 'Oom Jannie, how could they have turned against you? They are all dead.' The new generation of Transvaal farmers had lost touch with the idea of Smuts as an Afrikaner leader.

5 In a remarkably prescient letter to the Minister of the Interior (J.H. Hofmeyr), the Director of Military Intelligence, Professor E.G. Malherbe, dissected these problems at length, and

predicted virtually step by step the course of post-war political developments (*Hofmeyr Papers*).

6 For the Fagan Report see NLC (1948). The full title of the Sauer Report was *Verslag van die Kleurvraagstuk-Kommissie van die Herenigde Nasionale Party*. An abbreviated version was published in *Die Burger* on 29 and 30 March 1948. A poor and often misleading translation is to be found in D.W. Krüger (1960).

7 This and following paragraphs draw heavily on Davies (1977).

8 They ran it no less corruptly than the 'Broderick-clique'. The *Hervormer* general-secretary of the MWU, Daan Ellis, was convicted of corruption in a private prosecution brought by a member of his union, and sentenced to eighteen months' hard labour. This sentence was later quashed on a technically, and Ellis remained at his post till his death in 1963.

9 The 'Splinter and Minor Parties' file in the library of the Johannesburg *Sunday Times* lists the formation of 31 'parties' between 1948 and the break-away from the NP in 1969. Seventeen of these were formed to foster the interests of white labour which 'were ignored in the NP'.

10 For a detailed analysis of *oorstrooming* see the authoritative and almost booklength series of articles on 'the Native Question' and evaluation of the Fagan Report, *Inspan* April to May 1947, and October 1948 to January 1949. Written by two leading Stellenbosch academics and published with explicit editorial endorsement in this official FAK organ, these articles can be considered the official position of the Bond.

11 See the collection of intelligence reports in the Hofmeyr papers, file Ce. The mother-tongue education campaign was not fully supported by leading Bond members. An intelligence report to the Controller of Censorship on the Bond's Nasionale Instituut vir Opvoeding en Onderwys (dd. 29/11/44 – *Hofmeyr Papers*) cites the complaint of one Bond member that 'there has been positively treasonous action by a small elite group [in the Bond]. Take the question of mother-tongue schools. Our standpoint is very clear – and still in Bloemfontein you find that the leader of the OB [van Rensburg], the editor of *Die Volksblad* [Dr van Rhyn], the manager of *Die Volksblad*, the Director of Education [S.H. Pellisier] (to name but a few) send their children to Grey [a leading English school] although there are two Afrikaans schools. Is this not the worst sort of hypocrisy?'

12 Two future Prime Ministers were defeated in the 1948 elections because of this residual conflict. Dr Verwoerd lost Alberton when he refused OB support, and OB 'General' B.J. Vorster went down by four votes in Brakpan because of HNP opposition to his standing as the AP candidate. Vorster then contested the election as an independent.

Chapter 16 Conclusion: from 'volkseenheid' to Total Strategy

1 Du Plessis had now been re-admitted to the fold after his wartime removal from the EI and RDB leadership because of his support for the OB. Yet bitterness obviously remained as he closed with an ostentatious tribute to OB leader van Rensburg, and fellow purge victim and OB leader, P.J. Meyer.

2 In a speech to the Johannesburg *sakekamer* on the 'Role and task of the entrepreneur in the capitalist economy', the former *hoofleier* of the RDB insisted that the profit motive must be given its 'rightful' recognition: 'When an entrepreneur enters a particular industry, he does not do so purely with the aim of public service, but also, and *most importantly*, to make a profit' (Diedrichs, *Volkshandel* January 1963). Compare this with the RDB's view of the relationship between profit and service in the 1940s (pp. 152–3).

3 Verwoerd disapproved of the deal, and Federale Mynbou donated £5,000 to the NP in an attempt to stifle the intense criticism. The extreme right-wing *South African Observer* of March 1965 carries a useful review of the controversy. Here 'A Concerned Afrikaner' predicted quite correctly that 'the next step will be to build up and portray the men of *Mynbou* as being the real leaders of the Afrikaners and as representing forces of "moderation" and

"progress". Other Afrikaans financial leaders will be encouraged to follow suit, and each time a new Oppenheimer – Afrikaans deal is closed, there will be less and less criticism, to the point of disappearing altogether.'

4 The HNP absorbed the AP in 1951 and the Herenigde was dropped from its name.

5 The 'adventurist' emphasis in BOSS led to a profound miscalculation in Angola in 1975/6, and BOSS was taken completely by surprise by the Soweto uprising of 1976. These two significant failures severely weakened its position within factionalist struggles.

6 Wassenaar (1977). This remarkable (and best-selling) book attacked precisely those policies which, in the 1950s, had facilitated Sanlam's rapid growth. These were now presumably outmoded – for Sanlam. What was good for Sanlam was good for the volk.

7 The terms *verligte* and *verkrampte* have now been replaced by 'reformist' and 'conservative'.

8 After representations from the AHI, and in the interests of 'productivity', the NP government scrapped the previously sacred van Riebieck and Kruger Days as public holidays in 1974.

9 At the height of the Muldergate crisis, the once violently anti-Hoggenheimer organ of the Transvaal NP marked the seventieth birthday of the arch-Hoggenheimer – Harry Oppenheimer – with an editorial wishing long life to this 'great asset' of South Africa. In what was clearly also intended as a comment on Afrikaner magnates, *Die Transvaler* opined that Oppenheimer 'reflects the spirit of a new generation which, with a self-confidence derived from a high degree of expertise turns the country's economic assets to better use than ever before in our history. The fact that *we* now possess this know-how makes *us* the most successful state in Africa, and it is something that cannot be bought at any price. It is an asset that can only be built up arduously through the years' (28/10/78). In the 1940s Oppenheimer was not of 'us'.

10 See the Statement by Oppenheimer in the Anglo-American annual report, quoted in *Rand Daily Mail* 16/7/81.

Bibliography

Official publications and papers

AIRC 1941. *Third (Interim) Report of the Agricultural and Industrial Requirements Commission* (UG 40/1941). Pretoria, Government Printer.

BTI 1945. *Board of Trade and Industries: Investigation into Manufacturing Industries in the Union of South Africa (First Interim Report No. 282).* Pretoria, by authority.

CESO 1965. *Report of the Commission of Enquiry into Secret Organisations* (RP 20/1965). Pretoria, Government Printer.

CTVE 1948. *Report of the Commission on Technical and Vocational Education* (UG 65/1948). Pretoria, Government Printer.

Department of Agriculture 1961. *Handbook of Agricultural Statistics 1904–1950.* Pretoria, by authority.

Department of Labour. *Annual Reports 1933–1951.* Pretoria, Government Printer.

DNA 1948. *Report of the Department of Native Affairs for the Years 1945–7* (UG 14/1948). Pretoria, Government Printer.

GWUC 1950. *Report of the Garment Workers' Union Commission of Enquiry 1948/9* (UG 16/1950). Pretoria, Government Printer.

HAD. *House of Assembly Debates* (select volumes).

Hofmeyr Papers. University of the Witwatersrand Archives. File A. 1.

IC 1942. *Report of the Interdepartmental Committee on the Social, Health and Economic Conditions of the Urban Natives.* Pretoria, by authority.

ILC 1935. *Report of the Industrial Legislation Commission* (UG 37/1935). Pretoria, Government Printer.

ILC 1951. *Report of the Industrial Legislation Commission* (UG 62/1951). Pretoria, by authority.

Military Intelligence n.d. Die Afrikaner Broederbond (from internal evidence, 1943). *Hofmeyr Papers*, University of the Witwatersrand.

Military Intelligence 1944. The Afrikaner Broederbond: 29/3/1944. *Hofmeyr Papers*, University of the Witwatersrand.

MUJC. Minutes of the Mining Unions Joint Committee. South African Mining Unions' Papers, Institute of Commonwealth Studies, London.

MWUC 1946. *Report of the Mine Workers' Union Commission of Enquiry* (UG 36/1946). Pretoria, Government Printer.

1953. *Report of the Mineworkers' Union Commission of Enquiry.* Pretoria, by authority.

NEC 1932. *Report of the Natives Economic Commission* (UG 22/1932). Pretoria, Government Printer.

NLC 1948. *Report of the Native Laws Commission of Enquiry 1946–8* (UG 28/1948). Pretoria, Government Printer.

Bibliography

US 1960. *Union Statistics for 50 Years.* Pretoria, by authority.

WMNWC 1944. *Report of the Witwatersrand Mine Native Wages Commission* (UG 21/1944). Pretoria, Government Printer.

Books, articles, dissertations, pamphlets and papers

Adam H. & Giliomee H. 1979. *Ethnic Power Mobilised: Can South Africa Change?* New Haven, Yale University Press.

Althusser L. 1971. *Lenin and 'Philosophy' and other Essays.* London, New Left Books.

Atmore A. & Westlake N. 1972. A liberal dilemma. *Race,* 14, 2.

Bekommerd (pseud). 1935. *Christus die Deur. Die Twee Rigtings van die Calvinisme.* Cape Town, HAUM.

Bernstein H. & Depelchin J. 1978: The object of African history: a materialist perspective. Part I. *History in Africa,* 5.

Bezuitenhout W.J. 1968. *Dr. Tinie Louw: 'n Kykie in die Ekonomiese Geskiedenis van die Afrikaner.* Johannesburg, Afrikaanse-Pers Boekhandel.

Bleloch W. 1901. *For a New South Africa.* London, Heinemann.

Booysens B. 1969. *Die Lewe van D.F. Malan: Die Eerste Veertig Jaar.* Cape Town, Tafelberg.

Bozzoli B. 1975. The Roots of Hegemony: Ideologies, Interests and the Legitimation of South African Capitalism. D. Phil. dissertation, Sussex University.

Brand S.S. & Tomlison F.R. 1966. Die plek van die Landbou in die Suid-Afrikaanse Volkshuishouding. *South African Journal of Economics,* 34.

Breytenbach J.H. 1949. *Die Betekenis van die Tweede Vryheidsoorlog.* Johannesburg, FAK.

Bundy C. 1972. The emergence and decline of a South African peasantry. *African Affairs,* 71, 285.

Bunting B. 1969. *The Rise of the South African Reich.* Harmondsworth, Penguin Books.

Caplan, J. 1977. Theories of fascism: Nicos Poulantzas as historian. *History Workshop,* 3.

Carnegie Corporation Commission 1932. *Report of the Commission on the Poor White Problem in South Africa,* 5 vols. Stellenbosch, Pro-Ecclesia.

Cilliers A.C. 1939. *Quo Vadis.* Stellenbosch, Pro-Ecclesia.

1941. *Hertzogisme in die Handel.* Stellenbosch.

Coetzee D.J.J. 1975. Mislukte herenigingspogings tussen die Suid-Afrikaanse Party en die Nasionale Party. In *Die Nasionale Party: Deel I,* eds. O. Geyer & A.H. Marais. Pretoria, Academica.

Coetzee J.H. 1942. *Verarming en Oorheesing.* Bloemfontein, Nasionale Pers.

Crafford F.S. 1943. *Jan Smuts: A Biography.* New York, Doubleday & Doran.

Cronje G. 1945. *'n Tuiste vir die Nageslag.* Cape Town, Publicité.

Davenport T.R.H. 1966. *The Afrikaner Bond.* Cape Town, Oxford University Press.

1977. *South Africa: A Modern History.* London, Macmillan.

Davies R. 1975. The Wage Board in the political economy of South Africa. Mimeo, Sussex University.

1977. Capital, the State and White Wage Earners. D. Phil. dissertation, Sussex University.

Davies R., Kaplan D., Morris M. & O'Meara D. 1976. Class struggle and a periodisation of the state in South Africa. *Review of African Political Economy,* 7.

de Kiewiet C.W. 1972. *A History of South Africa: Social and Economic.* London, Oxford University Press.

de Klerk W.A. 1975. *Puritans in Africa: The Story of Afrikanerdom.* London, Rex Collings.

de St Jorre J. 1977. *A House Divided: South Africa's Uncertain Future.* New York, Carnegie Endowment for International Peace.

de Villiers R. 1971. Afrikaner nationalism. In *The Oxford History of South Africa,* vol. II, eds. M. Wilson & L. Thompson. Oxford, Clarendon Press.

Diedrichs N. 1936. *Nasionalisme as Lewensbeskouing.* Bloemfontein, Nasionale Pers.

268

Bibliography

Drummond I.M. 1972. *British Economic Policy under the Empire, 1919–1939*. London, Allen & Unwin.

du Plessis E.P. 1964. *'n Volk Staan Op: Die Ekonomiese Volkskongres en Daarna*. Cape Town, Human en Rousseau. This is the official FAK history of the economic movement.

du Plessis L.J. 1933. Ekonomiese reorganisasie van ons volkslewe. *Koers*, 2, 1.

1941. *Die Moderne Staat*. Stellenbosch, Pro-Ecclesia.

du Plessis L.J., Hugo H.T. & Labuschagne F.J. n.d. *Ons Volksideaal*. Bloemfontein, Nasionale Pers.

du Plessis, Louis J. 1951. *Letters of a Farmer*. Johannesburg.

Ekonomiese Instituut (van die FAK) 1946. *Die Kooperatiewe en die Nie-Kooperatiewe Ondernemingsvorms*. Johannesburg, RDB.

Federasie van Afrikaanse Kultuurvereniginge 1955. *Referate Gelewe by Geleentheid van die Silwerjubileumkongres van die FAK*. Johannesburg, FAK.

Finlay W. 1976. South Africa: Capitalist Agriculture and the State. B.Soc.Sci. dissertation, University of Cape Town.

Garson N.G. 1966. Het Volk. The Botha – Smuts party in the Transvaal 1904–1911. *The Historical Journal*, 9, 1.

1974. Race relations and class conflict as factors in South African twentieth century history. Mimeo, University of the Witwatersrand.

Giliomee H. 1975. The development of the Afrikaner's self-concept. In *Looking at the Afrikaner Today*, ed. H. van der Merwe. Cape Town, Tafelberg.

Gramsci A. 1971. *Selections from the Prison Notebooks*. London, Lawrence & Wishart.

Hancock W.K. 1968. *Smuts: The Fields of Force 1919–1950*. Cambridge, University Press.

Heard K.A. 1974. *General Elections in South Africa 1943–1970*. London, Oxford University Press.

Hepple A. 1954. *Trade Unions in Travail: The Story of the Broederbond-Nationalist Plan to Control South African Trade Unions*. Johannesburg, Unity Publishers.

Hexham I.R. 1974. Dutch Calvinism and the development of Afrikaner nationalism. In *Collected Papers*, vol. I, Centre for Southern African Studies, University of York.

Hirson B. 1976. Rural revolt in South Africa 1937–1951. Mimeo, Institute of Commonwealth Studies, University of London.

Horwitz R. 1967. *The Political Economy of South Africa*. London, Weidenfeld & Nicolson.

Houghton D.H. 1971. Economic development 1865–1966. In *Oxford History of South Africa*, vol. II, eds. M. Wilson & L. Thompson. Oxford, Clarendon Press.

1976. *The South African Economy*. Cape Town, Oxford University Press.

Johannesburg Chamber of Commerce 1949a. *The Present Economic Position of the Union: A Diagnosis, some Comments and Suggestions*. Johannesburg.

1949b. *The South African Economic and Future Policy*. Johannesburg.

Juta C.J. 1966. Aspects of Afrikaner Nationalism 1900–1964. D. Phil. dissertation, University of Natal (Pietermaritzburg).

Kantor B.S. & Kenny H.F. 1976. The poverty of neo-Marxism: the case of South Africa. *Journal of Southern African Studies*, 3, 1.

Kaplan D.E. 1976. An analysis of the South African state in the 'fusion period'. *The Societies of Southern Africa in the 19th & 20th Centuries*, vol. 7. Institute of Commonwealth Studies, University of London.

1977. The state and economic development in South Africa. In *Perspectives on South Africa – a Collection of Working Papers*, ed. T. Adler. Johannesburg, African Studies Institute.

Keegan T. 1978. Peasants, capitalists and farm labour: class formation in the Orange River Colony 1902–1910. *The Societies of Southern Africa in the 19th & 20th Centuries*, vol. 9. Institute of Commonwealth Studies, University of London.

Kestell J.D. 1939. *My Nasie in Nood*. Bloemfontein, Nasionale Pers.

Kienzle W., 1979. German – South African Trade in the Nazi Era. *African Affairs*, 78, 310,

269

Bibliography

Koers in die Krisis. Vol. 1, 1935; vol. 2, 1940; vol. 3, 1941. Stellenbosch, Federasie van Calvinistiese Studentevereniginge in Suid-Africa.

Krüger D.W. (ed.) 1960. *South African Parties and Policies 1910–1960.* Cape Town, Human en Rousseau.

Kruger J.J. (ed.) 1939. *Fees by die Waens.* Bloemfontein, Nasionale Pers.

Kuper L. 1974. *Race, Class and Power.* London, Duckworth.

Laclau E. 1977. *Politics and Ideology in Marxist Theory.* London, New Left Books.

Lambley P. 1980. *The Psychology of Apartheid.* London, Secker & Warburg.

Legassick M. 1971. The frontier tradition in South African historiography. In *The Societies of Southern Africa in the 19th & 20th Centuries.* Institute of Commonwealth Studies, London University.

1974. Legislation, ideology and economy in post-1948 South Africa. *Journal of Southern African Studies,* 1, 1.

le Roux N.J. 1953. *W.A. Hofmeyr: Sy Werk en Waarde.* Cape Town, Nasionale Boekhandel.

Lewis D. 1976. The South African state and African trade unions, 1947–1953. Mimeo.

Malan, M.P.A. 1964. *Die Nasionale Party van Suid-Afrika: Sy stryd en Prestasies 1914–1964.* Nasionale Party.

Marais A.H. 1975. Die oorlogsbesluit, die Rebellie en die Nasionale Party. In *Die Nasionale Party: Deel I,* eds. O. Geyer & A.H. Marais. Pretoria, Academica.

Marais G. 1958. The value of the Ottawa agreement between the Union of South Africa and the United Kingdom reconsidered. *Finance & Trade Review,* 3, 3.

Marks S. & Trapido S. 1979. Lord Milner and the South African State. *History Workshop,* issue 8.

Marquard L. 1960. *People and Politics of South Africa.* Cape Town, Oxford University Press.

Marx K. 1968a. The Eighteenth Brumaire of Louis Bonaparte. In *K. Marx and F. Engels Selected Works.* Moscow, Progress Publishers.

1968b. Preface to a Contribution to the Critique of Political Economy. In *Marx and Engels Selected Works.* London, Lawrence & Wishart.

1968c. *The German Ideology.* Moscow, Progress Publishers.

1976. *Capital.* Vol. 1 London, Penguin/New Left Books.

1978. *Capital.* Vol. 2. London, Penguin/New Left Books.

1971. *Capital.* Vol. 3. Moscow, Progress Publishers.

Meiring P. 1973a. *Tien Politieke Leiers.* Johannesburg, Tafelberg.

1973b. *Ons Eerste Ses Premiers.* Johannesburg, Tafelberg.

Meyer P.J. 1941. Grondslae van die Afrikaanse republikeinse staatsvorming. In *Ons Republiek,* ed. A. Coetzee. Bloemfontein, Nasionale Pers.

1944. *Die Stryd van die Afrikaner Werker.* Stellenbosch, Pro-Ecclesia.

Moodie T.D. 1974. The Afrikaner struggle for an effective voice in the South African economy prior to 1948. *South African Labour Bulletin,* 1, 7.

1975 and 1980. *The Rise of Afrikanerdom: Power, Apartheid and the Afrikaner Civil Religion.* Berkeley, University of California Press. Paperback edition, with supplementary Introduction, 1980.

1977. The rise of Afrikanerdom as an immanent critique of Marxist theory of social class. In *Working Papers in Southern African Studies,* ed. P.L. Bonner. Johannesburg, African Studies Institute.

1981. Class struggle in the development of agrarian capitalism in South Africa. Mimeo, Hobart and William Smith Colleges.

Morris M. 1976. The development of capitalism in South African agriculture. *Economy & Society,* 5, 3.

1977. Apartheid, agriculture and the state. SALDRU Working Paper No. 8. University of Cape Town.

Moss G. 1980. Total Strategy. *Work in Progress*, 11.

Murray M. 1979. The development of capitalism in South African agriculture: the class struggle and the capitalist state during the 'phase of transition' (*c.* 1890–1920). Mimeo.

Nasionale Party 1931. *Die Nasionale Boek. 'n Geskiedenis van die Onstaan en groei van die Nasionale Party van Suid-Afrika.* Johannesburg, Nasionale Boek Maatskappy.

National Party 1938. *Election Manifesto of the National Party.* Cape Town.

1948. *The Road to a New South Africa.* Cape Town, Nasionale Pers.

Naude L. (pseud.) 1969. *Dr. A. Hertzog, Die Nasionale Party en die Mynwerker.* Pretoria, Nasionale Raad van Trustees. This is the official history of the NRT.

Nicholls G.H. 1961. *South Africa in my Time.* London, Allen & Unwin.

Oelofse J.C. 1964. *Die Nederduitsch Hervormde Kerk en die Afrikaner Broederbond.* Krugersdorp, NHK Pers.

O'Meara D. 1975a. White trade unionism, political power and Afrikaner nationalism. *South African Labour Bulletin*, 1, 10.

1975b. The 1946. African mineworkers' strike and the political economy of South Africa. *Journal of Commonwealth and Comparative Politics*, 13, 2.

1977. The Afrikaner Broederbond 1927–1948: Class vanguard of Afrikaner nationalism. *Journal of Southern African Studies*, 3, 2.

1978. Analysing Afrikaner nationalism: The Christian – national assault on white trade unionism in South Africa 1934–1948. *African Affairs*, 77, 306.

1980.'Muldergate', the politics of Afrikaner nationalism and the crisis of the capitalist state in South Africa. Paper to Political Science Department, University of Dar es Salaam.

Ossewa Brandwag 1946. *Lets Oor die Ossewa Brandwag.* Johannesburg.

1948. *Ossewa Brandwag Jaarboek, 1947–8.* Johannesburg.

Patterson S. 1957. *The Last Trek.* London, Routledge & Kegan Paul.

Pauw S. 1946. *Die Beroepsarbeid van die Afrikaner in die Stad.* Stellenbosch, Pro-Ecclesia.

Pelzer A.N. 1979. *Die Afrikaner Broederbond: Eerste 50 Jaar.* Cape Town, Tafelberg. This is the official history of the Broederbond.

Pirow O. 1940. *Nuwe Orde vir Suid-Afrika.* Pretoria, Christelike Republikeinse Suid-Afrikaanse Nasionale Sosialistiese Studiekring.

1957. *James Barry Munnik Hertzog.* Cape Town, Howard Timmins.

Potgieter L.J. 1954. *Die Ekonomie van die Afrikaner en sy Aandeel in die Sakelewe.* M.Comm. dissertation, Potchefstroom University.

Poulantzas N. 1974. *Fascism and Dictatorship.* London, New Left Books.

Reddingsdaadbond n.d.(a) *Ons Reddingsdaadbond.* Johannesburg, RDB.

n.d.(b) *Ons Reddingsdaadfonds.* Johannesburg, Voortrekker Pers.

n.d.(c). *Die Reddingsdaadbond.* Cape Town, Nasionale Pers.

1941. *Reddingsdaadbond en Volksopbou.* Johannesburg, RDB.

1943. *Die Toekomsrol van die RDB in ons Ekonomiese Lewe.* Johannesburg, RDB.

1944. *Die RDB Handleiding vir Takbesture en-Organiseerdes.* Johannesburg, Voortrekker Pers.

Rich P. 1977. The agrarian counter-revolution in the Transvaal and the origins of segregation 1902–1913. In *Working Papers in Southern African Studies*, ed. P. Bonner. Johannesburg, African Studies Institute.

Roberts M. & Trollip A.E.G. 1947. *The South African Opposition 1939–1945.* Cape Town, Longmans.

Sadie, J.L. 1958. Die *Afrikaner in die Landsekonomie.* Cape Town, SAUK.

1975. Die ekonomiese faktor in die Afrikaanse gemeenskap. In *Identiteit en Verandering*, ed. H.W. van der Merwe. Cape Town, Tafelberg.

Salomon L. 1964. The economic background to Afrikaner nationalism. In *Boston University Papers in African History*, vol. I, ed. J. Butler. Boston.

Sayer D. 1975. Method and dogma in Historical Materialism. *Sociological Review*, 23, 4.

Bibliography

Schoeman B.M. 1973. *Van Malan tot Verwoerd.* Cape Town, Human en Rousseau.
1974. *Vorster se 1000 Dae.* Cape Town, Human en Rousseau.
Scholtz G.D. 1942. *Dr Nicolaas Johannes van der Merwe 1888–1941.* Johannesburg, Voortreakker Pers.
1967. *Die Ontwikkeling van die Politieke Denke van die Afrikaner.* Vol. 1. Johannesburg, Voortrekker Pers.
1975. *Hertzog en Smuts en die Britse Ryk.* Cape Town, Tafelberg.
Schumann C.G.W. 1940. *Die Ekonomiese Posisie van die Afrikaner.* Cape Town, Nasionale Pers.
Serfontein J.H.P. 1979. *Brotherhood of Power.* London, Rex Collings.
Simons H.J. & Simons R.E. 1969. *Class and Colour in South Africa 1850–1950.* Harmondsworth, Penguin Books.
Simson H. 1980. *The Social Origins of Afrikaner Fascism and its Apartheid Policy.* Stockholm, Almqvist & Wikselt International.
Slovo J. 1976. South Africa: no middle road. In *Southern Africa: The New Politics of Revolution,* ed. B. Davidson, J. Slovo & A.R. Wilkinson. Harmondsworth, Penguin Books.
Smuts J.C. 1900. *A Century of Wrong.* London. Review of Reviewers. For political reasons this book appeared under the name of (President) F.W. Reitz. Smuts was, however, the author.
Smuts J.C. Jnr. 1952. *Jan Christian Smuts.* London, Cassell & Co.
South African Communist Party. n.d. [1962]. *The Road to South African Freedom.* London, Ellis Bowles.
South African Institute of Race Relations. 1979. *Survey of Race Relations in South Africa 1978.* Johannesburg.
Stadler A.W. 1979. Birds in the cornfield. In *Labour, Township and Protest.* Johannesburg, Raven Press.
Steenkamp W.F.J. 1962. Bantu wages. *South African Journal of Economics,* 30, 2.
Stoker H.G. 1941. *Stryd om die Ordes.* Potchefstroom, Calvyn Jubileum Bookfonds.
Stultz N.M. 1974. *Afrikaner Politics in South Africa.* Berkeley, University of California Press.
Thompson L.M. 1962. Afrikaner nationalist historiography and the policy of Apartheid. *Journal of African History,* 3, 1.
1969. The forgotten factor in South African history. In *African Societies in Southern Africa,* ed. L. Thompson. London. Heinemann.
Transvaal Chamber of Mines. *Annual Reports* (1932–1951).
1945. *Goldmining Taxation: The Case for the Goldmining Industry.* Johannesburg, PRD Series No. 1.
1946a. *Tribal Natives and Trade Unionism: The Policy of the Rand Gold Mining Industry.* Johannesburg.
1946b. *Proceedings of a Special Meeting . . . October 1946.* Johannesburg.
1947a. *Native Laws Commission of Enquiry: Statements of Evidence Submitted by the Gold Producers' Committee.* Johannesburg.
1947b. *The Native Workers on the Witwatersrand Gold Mines.* Johannesburg, PRD Series No. 7.
Trapido S. 1975. Aspects in the Transition from Slavery to Serfdom. *The Societies of Southern Africa in the 19th and 20th Centuries,* vol. 6. Institute of Commonwealth Studies, University of London.
1978. Landlord and tenant in a colonial economy: the Transvaal 1880–1910. *Journal of Southern African Studies,* 5, 1.
Tyriakian E.A. 1960. Apartheid and politics in South Africa. *Journal of Politics,* 22, 4.
van den Heever C.M. 1946. *General J.B.M. Hertzog.* Johannesburg, Afrikaanse Pers. A slightly longer Afrikaans edition was published in 1944.
van der Berghe P. 1967. *South Africa, A Study in Conflict.* Berkeley, University of California Press.

van der Horst J.G. 1980. The role of life assurance companies in the economy. Address to *Financial Mail* annual international conference, Johannesburg.

van der Poel J. (ed.) 1973. *The Smuts Papers*, vol. 5. Cambridge, University Press.

van Heerden F.J. 1975. Die geboorte van die Nasionale Party (1913–1915). In *Die Nasionale Party: Deel I*. Pretoria, Academica.

van Jaarsveld F.A. 1964. *The Afrikaner's Interpretation of South African History*. Cape Town, Simondium Publishers.

van Rooyen J.J. 1956. *Die Nasionale Party: Sy Opkoms en Oorwinning – Kaapland se Aandeel*. Cape Town, Hoofraad van die Kaaplandse Nasionale Party.

Vatcher V. 1965. *White Laager. The Rise of Afrikaner Nationalism*. London, Pall Mall Press.

Visser G.C. 1976. *O.B. Traitors or Patriots?* Johannesburg, Macmillan.

Wassenaar A.D. 1977. *Assault on Private Enterprise*. Cape Town, Tafelberg.

Welsh D. 1974. The political economy of Afrikaner nationalism. *In South Africa: Economic Growth and Political Change*, ed. A. Leftwich. New York, St Martin's Press.

Wilkins I. & Strydom H. 1978. *The Super Afrikaners: Inside the Afrikaner Broederbond*. Johannesburg, Jonathan Ball.

Wilson F. 1971. Farming 1866–1966. In *The Oxford History of South Africa*, vol. II, eds. M. Wilson and L.M. Thompson. Oxford, Clarendon Press.

Wolpe H. 1971. Class, race and the occupational structure. *The Societies of Southern Africa in the 19th and 20th Centuries*, vol. 2. London Institute of commonwealth Studies, University of London.

Newspapers and Journals

Cape Times

Die Blankewerker Journal of the Blanke Werkers se Beskermingsbond.

Die Burger Organ of the Cape Nationalist Party.

Die Kruithoring Organ of the Federal Council of the HNP.

Die O.B. Organ of the Ossewa Brandwag.

Die Transvaler Organ of the Transvaal Nationalist Party.

Die Vaderland Hertzogite daily.

Die Volksblad Organ of the Orange Free State Nationalist Party.

Financial Mail

Forward

Freedom/Vryheid Organ of the Central Committee of the Communist Party.

Inkululeko Organ of the Communist Party.

Inspan Organ of the FAK and RDB.

Koers Potchefstroom theological/political journal.

Natal Mercury

Race Relations News Journal of the South African Institute of Race Relations.

Rand Daily Mail

Rapport

South African Observer

Sunday Times

The Star

Veg a shortlived *verkrampte* journal.

Volkshandel Journal of the AHI.

Wapenskou Organ of the ANS.

Index

Index

Index

Index

Lightning Source UK Ltd.
Milton Keynes UK
UKOW02f1315160914

238653UK00001B/147/P